Taking On the *YANKEES*

HENRY D. FETTER

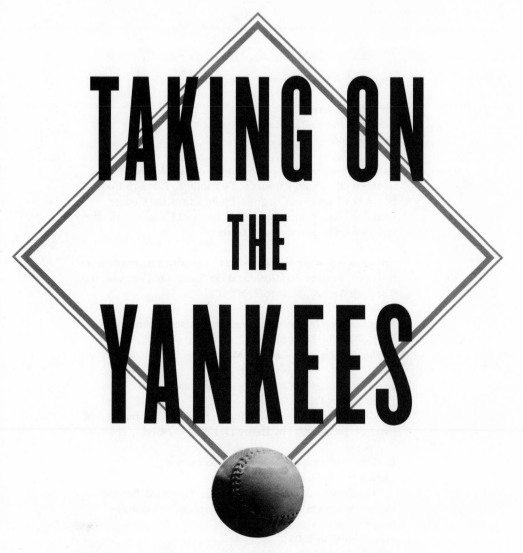

TAKING ON THE YANKEES

Winning and Losing in the
Business of Baseball, 1903–2003

W. W. NORTON & COMPANY

NEW YORK • LONDON

For information about permission to reproduce selections from
this book, write to Permissions, W. W. Norton & Company, Inc.,
500 Fifth Avenue, New York, NY 10110

Manufacturing by the Maple-Vail Book Manufacturing Group
Book design by Dana Sloan
Production manager: Amanda Morrison

Library of Congress Cataloging-in-Publication Data
Fetter, Henry D.
  Taking on the Yankees : winning and losing in the business of
baseball, 1903–2003 / by Henry D. Fetter.—1st ed.
      p. cm.
Includes bibliographical references and index.
  ISBN 0-393-05719-4 (hardcover)
  1. New York Yankees (Baseball team)—History. 2. Baseball—
Economic aspects—United States—History. 3. Baseball—
United States—History. I. Title.
  GV875.N4F48 2003
  796.357'64'097471—dc21

                                                        2003007814

W. W. Norton & Company, Inc.
500 Fifth Avenue, New York, N.Y. 10110
www.wwnorton.com

W. W. Norton & Company Ltd.
Castle House, 75/76 Wells Street, London W1T 3QT

1 2 3 4 5 6 7 8 9 0

To the Memory of My Parents
Simon and Jeannette Fetter

CONTENTS

ACKNOWLEDGMENTS

WORK ON this book began more than two decades ago and had as many interruptions as beginnings, but one. In that time, I accumulated many debts, and only a stringently selective expression of thanks can be offered here.

My cousins Bob and Carol Gruber offered hospitality and support well beyond the call of family, and Bob also offered an abundant store of baseball memory, knowledge, and enthusiasm. My aunt and uncle Ida and Norman Fetter were similarly helpful, especially as this project got underway. Graduate school classmates Paul Howell and the late Bill McNeil kindly read early drafts and encouraged me to persevere. Tom Doniger graciously agreed to a restructuring of our law partnership, which made it possible to bring this oft-deferred venture to a conclusion. Burton Craige introduced me to Fenway Park during our college days and helped rekindle an enduring interest in the sport. Marti Jackson and Marsha Suter transformed hundreds of erratically typewritten pages into a document that made the continuation of this work feasible. John M. Hillman reviewed my statistical methods with an expert eye.

Abigail and Stephan Thernstrom have honored me with their friendship and provided a crucial push toward publication. My agents Glen Hartley and Lynn Chu took in hand a long-stalled project and, quite simply, made this book happen. I am grateful to Bob Weil, Jason

Baskin, and their colleagues at W. W. Norton for believing in my work, editing it with care, and expertly preparing it for publication. Kathleen Brandes's meticulous copyediting significantly improved the final product.

Given the circumstances under which I conducted my research, I have necessarily been dependent on libraries and collections that are open to the public without fear, favor, or institutional affiliation, including the New York Public Library, the Charles E. Young Research Library of the University of California at Los Angeles, the New York State Library in Albany, the East Meadow (New York) Public Library, the Los Angeles County Law Library, the Library of Congress, the Los Angeles Public Library, and the Municipal Archives of the City of New York, as well as the Harvard University Libraries. In that regard, special mention must be made of my reliance on the extraordinary holdings of the Paul Ziffren Sports Resource Center of the Amateur Athletic Foundation of Los Angeles in the final stages of my work. I welcome the opportunity to thank the librarians and staffs of these institutions for their assistance. I would also be remiss if I did not acknowledge my frequent recourse to a number of indispensable reference tools for the writing of any history of baseball: *The Baseball Encyclopedia: The Complete and Definitive Record of Major League Baseball* (New York: Macmillan Publishing Company, Ninth Edition, 1993); James Charlton, ed., *The Baseball Chronology: The Complete History of the Most Important Events in the Game of Baseball* (New York: Macmillan Publishing Company, 1991); Joseph L. Reichler, *The Baseball Trade Register* (New York: Collier Books, 1984); Richard M. Cohen, David S. Neft, and Roland T. Johnson, with text by Jordan A. Deutsch, *The World Series* (New York: The Dial Press, 1976); and the BaseballLibrary.com Website.

My brothers Steven and Robert have shared the love of baseball that inspired this project in the first place. My wife, Lois, accommodated herself to an entirely novel field of interest with much more than good grace, and she has been a source of unfailing comfort and counsel. It is no coincidence that the completion of this work followed closely upon our marriage.

My greatest debt is to my late parents, Simon and Jeannette Fetter, who made my education possible and selflessly supported all my undertakings. It was my father who took the very young Brooklyn Dodger fan that I then was to Ebbets Field during the team's only World Championship season, while making sure that my first glove was a Willie Mays model, as befitted his own allegiance to the New York Giants. With regret that I did not finish it during their lifetime, I dedicate this book to their memory.

Taking On the YANKEES

PROLOGUE

BASEBALL was in crisis. A leading sports newspaper decried "the harm that is being done the game by the players who deal double and the magnates who provoke and condone such conduct," and warned that "it is time that ballplayers woke up to the fact that they are drifting dangerously near some reefs that are likely to prove dangerous. . . .The plebeians who sit up in the bleachers and who, after all, are the loyal supporters of the game, are beginning to wonder if most of their idols have not been shattered."[1] Long-established clubs were being eliminated through unilateral contraction, others were abruptly shifted from one city to another. Legal battles over player contracts kept lawyers and judges busy in courtrooms across the country. Unionized players squared off against team owners and mulled formal affiliation with a national labor federation.[2] The players, a baseball official claimed, "have driven the owners to the last ditch because of their exorbitant salary demands."[3] Pundits forecast that, if such turmoil and conflict continued, "it would probably lay professional base ball on the shelf for years."[4] The future of baseball as a viable enterprise was at stake.

This picture of a trouble-ridden sport is readily recognizable to any reader of today's newspapers, but the year was 1903, not 2003. The subject of this book is the history of the baseball business over the course of that century. Its central theme is the rise and enduring success, without equal in the world of professional sports, of the New York Yankees. Beginning with their first World Series appearance in 1921, the Yankees won thirty-nine American League pennants and twenty-six World Championships through the 2002 season. They have appeared in at least one World Series in every decade since the 1920s and won the Series at least once in every full decade but one (the 1980s). The New Yorkers won three consecutive World Series titles from 1998 to 2000, four from 1936 to 1939, and five from 1949 to 1953. No team in baseball has come close to matching this record. It has not been a bad run for what was (until 1953, when the Boston Braves moved to Milwaukee) big-league baseball's most junior franchise.

The epic saga of the Yankees and their great stars has been told and retold over the years. "I couldna done it without my players," Yankee manager Casey Stengel once said, and the Yankees did, indeed, have the players that made that incomparable record possible. Ruth, Gehrig, DiMaggio, Mantle, Jackson, Clemens, Jeter—not to mention Ruffing, Dickey, Henrich, Berra, Ford, Mattingly, and Williams—formed an unbroken skein of talent armed not just with the skill to win but also with the conviction that they *would* win.

That familiar story will not be repeated here. This book instead examines the business, as well as the sport, of baseball as reflected in the ongoing success of the Yankees and the failures of their opponents. The dramatis personae is found in the sport's executive offices—from Charles and Horace Stoneham of the New York Giants, Harry Frazee of the Boston Red Sox, Connie Mack of the Philadelphia Athletics, Branch Rickey of the St. Louis Cardinals, and Walter O'Malley of the Brooklyn Dodgers to Jacob Ruppert, Mike Burke, and George Steinbrenner of the New York Yankees themselves.

The focus will be on three of the Yankees' prime competitors, the New York Giants, the St. Louis Cardinals, and the Brooklyn

Dodgers, and the ways in which their inability to take on the Yankees illuminate the contrasting strengths of the perennial champions. The business battle between the Yankees and their rivals will be explored in three dimensions. Performance on the field will be only the starting point for a look—from the vantage point of the front office—at the ways in which the business and team management skills of the Yankees, and the shortcomings of their competitors, shaped outcomes on and off the field. In that contest, money has always played a part, but it has been ownership innovation, style, and strategy that have proven decisive in determining the winners and losers in that struggle.

This continuing contest for baseball supremacy will, in turn, be placed in the context of the sport's continuous struggle to respond to a succession of social, economic, and legal challenges thrown up by an ever-changing society. Nothing came easily, or quickly, for the "national pastime" of a nation in flux. Even Sunday baseball—the chance to attract customers on the most lucrative day in the era of the six-day workweek—necessitated a long fight against traditional "blue laws" and would not be fully won until the 1930s. The rise of radio and then television would transform the sport's business model, beginning in the 1940s and accelerating thereafter. The all-white sport's color line would not be broken until 1947. The sport's vintage 1903, and increasingly atavistic, map would not be aligned with that of an increasingly suburban and West-Coast–oriented nation until the 1950s. The shift in bargaining power from management to labor, with the demise of the "reserve clause," would not occur until the 1970s. In each case, baseball's response was awkward, unpremeditated, and uncoordinated, with profound consequences for the balance of baseball power, and the ability of the Yankees to establish, maintain, and, when necessary, regain, their winning ways.

◇

BY THE TIME the American League's bedraggled Baltimore club limped into New York after the 1902 season (stripped of its manager, John McGraw, and most of its stars in a wholesale midseason defection to the National League's New York Giants), more than a quarter of a century had passed since baseball's National League had come into being. By then, baseball's "senior circuit," the National League, already had twenty-five years of history behind it. Founded in the nation's centennial year, just seven years after the first professional baseball game had been played, the National League has enjoyed a longer continuous existence than any other sports institution, and few other national institutions of any kind, can claim. The origins of the National League extend back into a world far removed from us in time, space, custom, and character—a world that was already distant from that in which the "junior circuit," the American League, emerged on the baseball scene. Warren Giles, the National League's president in the 1950s, once noted that his league "was formed at a time when Ulysses S. Grant was President of the United States, George A. Custer was about to be massacred by Sioux Indians in the Battle of the Little Big Horn, there were no telephones, automobiles or airplanes, and the entire land contained fewer than fifty million persons."[5] Giles could have added that on February 2, 1876, when the National League was organized, the American flag had only thirty-seven stars, the Civil War had ended only eleven years earlier, and large portions of the South were still under federal military occupation. Yet the pace of change during the last quarter of the nineteenth century was so rapid that, by the turn of the twentieth century, these events already belonged to an irretrievably vanished past.

The National League had weathered a number of crises since its formation, and had withstood competition from putative rivals, the American Association and the Player's League, but the emergence of the American League proved to be one challenge that it could not rebuff. In 1900, the twelve-team National League had downsized, jettisoning four franchises (in Cleveland, Washington, Baltimore, and Louisville). A new American League, quickly organized to fill the resulting gap in the baseball map, began play as a rival major league in 1901 with teams in recently abandoned Cleveland, Washington, and Baltimore, as well as in Chicago, Detroit, Philadelphia, Boston, and Milwaukee (which was shifted to St. Louis the next season). As the battle between the fledgling American League and the entrenched National League escalated, attendance plummeted in National League cities in which the upstart circuit had planted its own competing franchises. During the 1902 season, the new league prepared to invade the National's prized New York territory, and player salaries spiraled ever upward as the rival leagues competed for talent.

In early January 1903, a small group of baseball executives from the warring circuits assembled in Cincinnati, Ohio, to try to save a sport that was on the brink of self-destruction. After two days of negotiations, representatives of the two leagues agreed to recognize each other's major-league status; they committed to the "Cincinnati Peace Compact" on January 10, 1903.[6] The key terms of that agreement have shaped the business structure of the sport ever since and were remarkably enduring. In the allocation of territories, the National League paid the penalty of being first, having stretched westward along the Ohio Valley axis—Pittsburgh to Cincinnati to St. Louis—of an older America, while the American League seized the Great Lakes perimeter of the rapidly industrializing America of the new century—Cleveland to Detroit to Chicago—as its pathway into the heartland. The resulting lineup (Brooklyn, Cincinnati, and Pittsburgh in the National League; Detroit, Cleveland, and Washington in the American; New York, Boston, Chicago, Philadelphia, and St. Louis represented in both) would last without any change for fifty years.

The one-sided owner–player relationship secured by the peace agreement would prove even more resilient. In the last days of the "war," American League President Ban Johnson had pledged that his circuit "will live up to all its high salaried contracts with ball players until they have expired," but that "a reserve rule, however, has been made absolutely necessary,"[7] and such proved to be the case once peace was restored. The clubs' collective agreement to respect each other's contracts, including an exclusive right to "reserve" the future services of its players, would survive a succession of economic, legal, and political challenges and prevent the development of a free market in players for almost three quarters of a century.

Most long-lasting of all has been the two-league structure of major-league baseball. For the past century, National League and American League teams have waged their battles on the playing field—first to capture their league's pennant and then to compete in the "series of championship games between all of the clubs in both leagues" authorized by the peace compact and held every fall since then, with the exceptions of 1904 and 1994. The professional football, basketball, and hockey leagues that exist today are the result of mergers and consolidations among rival leagues within the past thirty-five years, but the institutional framework of big-league baseball, established in January 1903, would remain intact amid such upheavals. And within that long-lived structure, the Yankees have managed to hold onto a uniquely dominant position.

Overcoming its belated and inauspicious appearance in the ranks of major-league baseball, New York's American League team emerged as the sport's preeminent franchise in the early 1920s. The team's unpromising origins hardly presaged such an accomplishment. For most of its first two decades, that franchise—known first as the Highlanders and then the Yankees—languished in mediocrity, compiling the third-worst cumulative record in their own league[8] and posing no challenge on the field or at the gate to the imperiously dominant

National League Giants, a subservient relationship only underscored by the fact that the American Leaguers were the Giants' Polo Grounds tenants after 1913.

That soon changed. After 1921, the Yankees went on to win twenty-nine of the next forty-five American League pennants and shattered any semblance of competitive balance in the American League. No American League team proved able to mount a sustained challenge to their dominance over the next four decades and beyond. The White Sox, broken by the Black Sox scandal, fell off the competitive chart after 1920, reemerging as pennant-race contenders only in the late 1950s. The Indians similarly foundered through the 1920s, 1930s, and early 1940s, reviving only after World War II. Boston, the American League's (and baseball's) pre–World War I powerhouse, fell farther, and faster, in the wake of the sale of Babe Ruth to the Yankees after the 1919 season, and the ensuing wholesale transfer of Red Sox talent to New York.

By the early 1930s, the Bosox depended on the charity of the league for survival. Even after Tom Yawkey's purchase bailed out the team after 1933, the Red Sox were only able to mount a short-lived, and unsuccessful, challenge to the perennial champs for a brief few years in the late 1940s, before sinking once again into mediocrity. Replacing them on the league's life-support system would be Connie Mack's Philadelphia A's, who limped out of the great Depression with no assets on the field and mounting debts to the league on its books. The 1930s saw the rise of the Tigers, but they too fell by the wayside as the Bronx Bombers regrouped after the war and again swept away all before them. Of Washington and St. Louis, it was said, "first in war, first in peace, and last in the American League," and "first in shoes, first in booze, and last in the American League," respectively.

A composite "average" season league standing for the years between 1921 and 1960, when the American League fielded eight teams—before expansion increased the number of teams to the current fourteen—reveals the extent of the Yankees' dominance, with the New Yorkers leading the next-best team by twelve games and holding a twenty-plus-game edge over five of their rivals (see Table 0.1 in the appendix).

Not surprisingly, the Yankees' overwhelming competitive edge on the ballfield found an echo at the box office. The Yanks led the American League in attendance for thirty-three seasons between 1921 and 1960 and accounted for more than 20 percent of total American League attendance twenty-five times over those four decades. Season after season, Yankee Stadium regularly hosted more fans than three American League teams added together; twice (1932 and 1950), the Yankees actually exceeded the combined home attendance of *four* of their putative "competitors."

Based on World Series results, the National League proved equally unable to meet the challenge from the Bronx. The Yankees recorded twenty wins in the twenty-nine World Series in which they appeared between 1921 and 1964. At the height of the Yankee Era, from 1923 to 1953, the Yanks would confront and defeat every National League team at least once. Against their intracity rivals they were especially merciless, beating Brooklyn's Dodgers five times and Manhattan's Giants four more times without a loss. In fact, the *only* National League team to take a World Series from the Yankees over that *entire thirty-year stretch* was the St. Louis Cardinals, in 1926 and 1942. Other than those two instances, the Yanks stood off the *entire* National League, undefeated. Brooklyn (1941, 1947, 1949, 1952, and 1953), New York (1923, 1936, 1937, and 1951), Chicago (1932, 1938), Cincinnati (1939), Pittsburgh (1927), Philadelphia (1950), and the Cardinals too (1928 and 1943), came, saw, and were conquered—with Chicago, Pittsburgh, Cincinnati, *and* Philadelphia unable to win a single game in their five fall contests. The balance sheet for those thirty years—eighteen pennants, sixteen World Championships—is unmatched in any other sport.

Although Yankee success has remained a constant, the identities of their prime antagonists shifted over time, but each contender would be denied in turn. The New York Giants were their first great adversary. In the early 1920s, the Giants held the preeminent place in the worlds of both New York and major-league baseball generally, which the Yankees sought to capture for themselves. But, hobbled by an ownership group that found itself ensnared in the tangled, quasi-corrupt business and political milieu from which the franchise had emerged, the Giants were left to drift, torn by internal front-office dissension and a distracted ownership, just as the Yankee challenge vigorously asserted itself in the mid-1920s. The Giants management—a holdover from an earlier era when the lines between owner and manager, on-field decision-making and player personnel acquisition, local politics and baseball politics, were blurred—simply proved unable to hold its own against a new style of team management pioneered by the Yankees, one in which spheres of authority and lines of responsibility were sharply demarcated, and owner, general manager, and field manager each had a distinct role to play in a carefully planned, entirely unsentimental model of organizational efficiency.

Even as the Yankees pushed past the Giants in the mid-1920s, a new contender for baseball's top honors emerged, surprisingly enough, from the perennially forlorn western outpost, St. Louis. Under the direction of Branch Rickey, one of baseball's few if not only geniuses, the Cardinals staked out a challenge to the Yankees that apparently was founded on a still-newer organizational model—a vertically integrated farm system. This was designed to function as an efficient processor of raw baseball talent acquired en masse at the grassroots, then carefully cultivated through the ladderlike rungs of the parent-club–owned and –controlled minor-league teams, and finally culled and harvested at the major-league apex of an elaborate pyramid of player talent. The Cardinals did indeed thrive, and Rickey's "farm system" model earned the flattery of baseball-wide imitation. But the Yankees would remain as baseball's number-one team once the Cardinal challenge had run its course—not least because the Cardinals' success was *not* that of a system, but rather that of one man's (Rickey's) exceptional, but personal, talent-spotting ability. Indeed, the Cardinal "threat" may be said to have peaked as early as 1931, just as Rickey's individual knack had transformed itself into an institutional blueprint, never to enjoy the same degree of success thereafter.

By the late 1940s, the epicenter of the National League's battle against the Yankees shifted back to New York—or, more precisely, to Brooklyn. In 1941, the Dodgers won their first pennant since 1920, but it was after Branch Rickey took over front-office management of the team in 1943 that the Dodgers emerged as the Yankees' next great antagonist. Beginning in 1947, the Dodgers established a dynasty of their own in the National League, in counterpoint to that of the Yankees. Between 1947 and 1956, the Dodgers would confront the Yankees six times in the fall, and in two other seasons (1950 and 1951), they only lost the chance to do so on the last day of the season. But until 1955, the Yankees (who had defeated the Dodgers in 1941 as well) turned back the Dodger challenge, and by the time the Dodgers finally won that year, the shadows had already fallen on their continued existence in Brooklyn.

In the 1950s, the National League's effort to contest Yankee power unfolded less on the playing field than at the negotiating tables—first in New York, then in Los Angeles, where the fate of the Dodgers would be determined. Not that the Yankees didn't hold their own, and more, on the diamond. After losing the World Series to the Dodgers in 1955, they rebounded the next year, so the final tally of their decade of almost annual head-to-head competition with Brooklyn stood at five to one in the Yankees' favor. But the true measure of their primacy was to be found in the Dodgers' inability, or unwillingness, to secure a future for themselves in New York. And when all was said and done, and the Dodgers pulled up stakes and headed west, the New York Giants were dragged along in their wake, leaving the Yankees with an undivided claim to what was far and away the largest baseball audience in the nation. None of the National League's challenges to the pretensions of the Yankee dynasty had concluded so ignominiously.

As the 1960s began, the Yankees seemed as well entrenched as ever, winning five more pennants between 1960 and 1964. Yet all was not well in the Bronx. The Yanks lost three out of five World Series in those years, including a humiliating four-game sweep by the Los Angeles Dodgers in 1963. The axis of baseball power was shifting to the National League, with such stars as Willie Mays, Henry Aaron, Bob Gibson, and Sandy Koufax outshining their American League counterparts. The pathetically but endearingly incompetent New York Mets proved an unexpectedly strong rival at the box office. In 1965, the Yankee dynasty abruptly collapsed, with the team finishing in sixth place. Worse was to come, and quickly—a last-place finish the next season. Four decades of Yankee dominance ended. Yankee management had finally failed.

Not many years earlier, it was said that "rooting for the Yankees was like rooting for United States Steel," but even as the steel giant collapsed, the Yankees rebounded. The Bronx Bombers won American League pennants in 1976, 1977, 1978, and 1981, and World Series in 1977 and 1978. A successful, if controversial, management style emerged under the unlikely direction of a Cleveland shipbuilder, George Steinbrenner. The stadium politics that doomed the Brooklyn Dodgers yielded a new lease on life for the Yankees' historic home. The business of competing under the new player procurement and retention rules ushered in by the sudden advent of players' free agency in the mid-1970s, was mastered. The Yanks won the World Series in 1996, 1998, 1999, and 2000 and only narrowly lost in 2001. In compiling that impressive, and unmatched, record amid the sweeping changes that roiled the baseball business, Yankee success in navigating the sport's fast-changing legal and economic environment counted for at least as much as their competitors' missteps. Despite a playoff defeat in 2002, the Yankees were once again being lambasted as all but unstoppable—given a considerable advantage in their available financial resources, married to a readiness to spend freely to obtain top talent. The Faustian fable of "Damn Yankees" was as timely as ever, as the team entered its second century.

From the era of Jacob Ruppert to that of George Steinbrenner, it has been the decisions and initiatives of the baseball business's "vital few"—those "individuals who have, as Joseph Schumpeter put it, changed the flow of economic life"[9]—that determined the outcome of the Yankees' efforts to gain and maintain a position of dominance in their sport over the past one hundred years. It is their story, as they battled to field winning ball teams *and* turn a profit while doing so, that will unfold in the pages that follow.

PART ONE

GOING TO "GOATVILLE"

1

THE RISE OF THE YANKEES

SHORTLY after four o'clock on the afternoon of October 10, 1923, New York Giants outfielder Casey Stengel smashed a long drive to the deep left center of the New York Yankees' massive new stadium, lost a shoe as he rounded second, and slid in to home just ahead of the throw. The well-dressed, overwhelmingly male crowd of 55,307 (men in coats, ties, and hats) set a new record for World Series attendance.[1] Earlier, Yankee fans had cheered as the home team scored three quick runs off Giant pitcher Mule Watson, whose undistinguished regular-season record had made him an unexpected choice to start the series, to take a 3–0 lead after two innings. The Giants had then quickly rallied with four runs in their next turn at bat, but in the bottom of the seventh, the Yankees evened up the game. Yankee reliever Bullet Joe Bush, who had held the Giants scoreless since the third inning, continued to blank the Giants through the eighth inning and retired the first two batters in the top of the ninth. Then Casey Stengel—a thirty-three-year-old veteran nearing the end of a playing career in which he had never hit more than nine home runs in a single season, and had not made an extra-base hit in his previous two World Series appearances—stepped to the plate.

Stengel's ninth-inning inside-the-park homer gave the Giants the lead in that first game of the third consecutive World Series between the big-city rivals. "The warped old legs, twisted and bent by many a

year of baseball campaigning, just barely held out under Casey Stengel until he reached the plate running his home run home," Damon
Runyon wrote.[2] When the Yankees went down in order in their last at
bat, the Giants won what the press immediately hailed as "the greatest
game of baseball ever played between championship teams."[3]
"Mudville is avenged at last," Grantland Rice wrote, alluding to the
"melancholy story" in which "Mighty Casey fanned the air and left
Mudville flat on its ancient back."[4]

At that moment, the Giants stood triumphantly at the pinnacle of
the baseball world. Ever since 1921, a great battle for baseball
supremacy had been waged within the precincts of New York City.
The Giants' three straight National League championships were all
matched by the Yankees in the American League. Each fall over those
three years, the World Series was played off on consecutive days—no
time was allotted for travel—and in the previous two years, the
matchup could not even have been called a "subway series," because
both teams shared the same ballpark, the Giants-owned Polo Grounds,
located just west of the Harlem River at 155th Street and Eighth
Avenue. The series showdowns between the two New York champions
were Manhattan-based affairs until 1923, when the Yankees crossed
the Harlem River and opened their own stadium in the Bronx. What
might have been a humiliating debut for the Giants in their first
appearance in the Yankees' magnificent new home had become,
instead, an occasion for the National League champions to show the
people of New York, and baseball fans everywhere, who really ruled
the baseball world, Babe Ruth be damned.

With that opening-game win, the Giants extended their World
Series winning streak over the Yankees to eight games, going back to
the sixth game of their first meeting in 1921, when the Giants rallied
from a three-games-to-two deficit to sweep the next three contests and
that year's best-of-nine series. In their 1922 rematch, the Giants

blanked the upstart challengers four straight (with one game tied). Over that stretch, the Giants had not simply been beating the Yankees; they had been utterly demolishing their rivals, shutting out the Yankees inning after inning and stopping their much-feared bats cold. So total was the Giants' dominion that the Yankees failed to score for twenty-one innings—from the third inning of Game 7 in 1921 through the sixth inning of Game 1 in 1922—and batted a measly .207 and .203 in the 1921 and 1922 series, respectively. As for the mightiest Yankee slugger of them all, Babe Ruth, after hitting a home run in Game 4 of the 1921 series, had just three hits in twenty-two at-bats through the first game of the 1923 World Series. Although the Giants lost the 1923 series' second game 4–2, they came back to shut out the Yanks in Game 3, for their eleventh win in the previous thirteen games between the two teams, going back to the third game in 1921. The Giants needed just two more wins to be champions of the world once again, and to complete baseball's first "three-peat."

"It's great to be young and a Giant," second baseman Laughing Larry Doyle had exclaimed before the war, and so it had continued to be in the first years of the 1920s, as the 1923 team swept to its ninth pennant in the twenty-one years since the National League had recognized the upstart American League. Earlier claimants to baseball's place of honor—the Chicago Cubs, Boston Red Sox, Philadelphia A's—fell off the pace in the aftermath of World War I. Of baseball's prewar dynasties, only the Giants—managed, as they had been since the summer of 1902, by the long-since-legendary John McGraw—kept winning. In that exhilarating moment of victory on October 10, 1923, when Stengel's tiebreaking home run clinched Game 1 of the series against the parvenu challengers from the Bronx, the Giants' past triumphs promised to be but prologue to an equally radiant future in which they would remain synonymous, in the minds of the sport's far-flung followers, with major-league baseball itself.

Such expectations were quickly quashed. After the two teams split the next two games, the Yankees' hitting, stifled since the 1921 series, finally asserted itself. The Yankees came roaring back, winning Games 4 and 5 by scores of 8–4 and 8–1, to take a three-games-to-two lead. In Game 6, after trailing 4–1 going into the eighth inning, the Yanks took the lead on Bob Meusel's three-run, two-out single to complete a three-game sweep to win the series, and Babe Ruth finished the series with three home runs, equaling the existing *team* record for World Series homers.

With that World Series victory, the balance of baseball power shifted suddenly across the Harlem River, from Manhattan to the Bronx, never to return. The 1923 title was the first of twenty-six Yankee World Championships, eighteen of which would be won before 1960. Three more times, the New York Giants would face the New York Yankees in October—in 1936, 1937, and 1951—and each time the Giants would lose. The two teams' final meeting (to date), in 1962—after the Giants had forsaken the town they once ruled for the windswept perils of a new home by the bay in San Francisco—ended with the same, by then familiar, outcome. The Yankees came to occupy the place in baseball's collective imagination that the Giants had once held. In time, it would even become common to hear Larry Doyle's joyous outburst misquoted as "It's great to be young and a Yankee"— the saddest testimony of all to the passing of a long-gone age when the giants of New York baseball were literally just that—the *Giants*.

IT COULD ONLY have exacerbated the Giants' distress over the devastating outcome of the 1923 World Series that no major-league club could claim less auspicious origins than the new World Champions. The roots of the Yankees lay in the Baltimore franchise of the one-year-old American League, which John McGraw had left for dead when he jumped ship in the summer of 1902 to take over the reins of the Giants. Baltimore was one of the American League's eight inaugural franchises when it mounted its challenge to the National League in 1901. Baltimore had been dropped from the National League after the 1899 season, and its sister clubs were quickly embroiled in a baseball war with the "senior circuit," which disputed their major-league pretensions. As player salaries escalated, leading stars of the National League jumped to the new league—notably, Cy Young to Boston and Nap Lajoie to Philadelphia.[5] But it was not only the stars who were on the move. Ball clubs, even at that early date, had long since come to rely on the "reserve clause" to control player costs—shorthand for the interrelated set of contractual provisions and interclub agreements that in effect, would "give to the club in organized baseball which first signs a player a continuing and exclusive right to his services."[6] From the outset, courts were generally unwilling to enforce a mechanism that, whether by contract or league rule, so drastically inhibited player mobility. With the courts on the sidelines, a club's only effective means of enforcing a claim to a player's future ("reserved") services was the mutual agreement among all major-league clubs to respect it. The American League's willingness to sign up needed talent regardless of a National League team's contract claims rendered the "reserve clause" a toothless defense against such player raiding, and seventy-four players jumped to the American League in its first two seasons.[7] Sixty percent of the 182 players appearing in American League games in 1901 had previously played in the National League.[8]

Fortified by such big-league playing talent, the new league easily held its own in this latest renewal of the baseball wars that had erupted periodically in the quarter-century since the sport had "organized" itself. In its second season, the upstarts attracted more fans than the senior circuit.[9] That year, American League attendance increased by more than half a million from its debut season, with attendance doubling for the franchise that was shifted from Milwaukee to St. Louis—the largest city, except for Chicago, to allow Sunday baseball.[10]

The Baltimore American League club was not one of the new circuit's more successful entries. Led by John McGraw, who had returned to his Oriole roots after a one-year stint with the National League Cardinals, Baltimore finished a middling fifth in 1901. Attendance averaged only slightly more than 2,000 fans for the team's seventy home games, higher than Milwaukee and Cleveland but less than half of that recorded by the league's Boston and Chicago clubs. The Baltimore treasury reported a small loss for the season, but there didn't appear to be any operational reason, whether on the field or off, for Baltimore baseball not to enjoy a second life in the new league.[11] McGraw's widow would later sum up that debut season: "The Orioles' first year in the American League was not a howling success, nor was it the dismal failure claimed by historians."[12]

Midway through the 1902 season, however, the bottom dropped out of big-league baseball in Baltimore for the second time in three years, and for much the same reason. The original Orioles of the National League had fallen victim to the emergence of "syndicate ball," in which a common ownership controlled two or more teams and manipulated players and assets to the benefit of one club, to the affiliate's detriment. The Orioles were part of a syndicate that also owned the Brooklyn club in the then-twelve-team National League.[13] Lured by the prospect of greater gate receipts in Brooklyn—which not only had more than twice Baltimore's 500,000 population on its own but had just been incorporated into the City of New York, which boasted a total population of almost three and a half million—the Baltimore–Brooklyn syndicate elected to "pool" its baseball resources in Brooklyn's favor. After the 1898 season (in which Baltimore had won ninety-six games to Brooklyn's fifty-four), future Hall of Famer, 5-foot 4-inch Wee Willie Keeler and other Oriole greats, along with manager

Ned Hanlon, were assigned to the Brooklyn Superbas, as the team was then called. Brooklyn promptly rebounded from tenth place to win the league championship in 1899.[14] The remnants of the Orioles, inspired by their boy manager, twenty-six-year-old John McGraw, and largely on the strength of the pitching of Iron Man Joe McGinnity, finished fifteen games back, in fourth place.

This finish may well have been "better than expected," given management's crassly calculated stripping of the team's best players from the Baltimore roster, but it was not sufficient to keep Baltimore in the major leagues. In the face of pressure to "cut off the dead wood," National League owners agreed to eliminate four teams from the circuit before the 1900 season: Cleveland (the weaker outpost of the St. Louis–Cleveland syndicate), Louisville, Washington, and Baltimore, with the Brooklyn–Baltimore syndicate receiving a "buyout" payment of $30,000 and the right to transfer the remaining Oriole stars to Brooklyn.[15] That Brooklyn had secured *its* claim to major-league status by forcing the Baltimore club out of baseball's top ranks was an almost-unnoticed "dirty little secret" when Brooklyn's own day of reckoning came, half a century later.

By far the largest of the excluded cities, Baltimore paid the price of being part of a Brooklyn–Baltimore syndicate that hastened to sacrifice one franchise to safeguard a more valuable metropolitan New York property.[16] Whether coincidentally or not, three of the abandoned cities represented baseball's southern frontier, each with substantial black populations, who were not regarded, or welcomed, as patrons for the all-white game.[17] This would prove to be an enduring sentiment within the sport's inner circles, still manifesting itself as late as 1946, when a major-league owners' committee expressed concern that "if Negroes participated in major league games . . . the preponderance of Negro attendance in parks such as the Yankee Stadium, the Polo Grounds, and Comiskey Park could conceivably threaten the value of the major league franchises owned by these clubs."[18] Such long-standing bigotry did indeed have long-term consequences, but they were not quite as foreseen. When the color line fell at last in 1947, not only would the relative willingness of teams to hire black ballplayers have tremendous impact on the sport's competitive balance, but the "Whites Only" sign that baseball had hung out for so long would inhibit its appeal to minority fans well after integration had belatedly come to the national pastime.[19]

Whatever the reasons for the ejection of the Orioles from the National League in 1899, the hopes of their once-rejected fans for a second life in the new American League quickly foundered. It was widely believed that American League President Ban Johnson planned to turn up the heat on the National League by transferring the Baltimore franchise to New York in 1903. McGraw, who had repeatedly clashed with Johnson, was convinced that he had no place in Johnson's vision of the team's transplanted future. In the middle of the 1902 season, McGraw preemptively struck a deal with Andrew Freedman, owner of the New York Giants, to abandon the new league and take over immediately as manager of the Giants.[20] As part of the arrangement, McGraw transferred his own stock in the Baltimore franchise to Freedman. This put the owner of the National League's Giants in the anomalous position of being the controlling shareholder of the rival American League's Baltimore franchise. Such an interlocking ownership came as second nature to Freedman, although it was only a pale substitute for the overarching model of "syndicate baseball," in which *all* teams would operate as a single business unit.[21] Freedman had only narrowly failed to win support for *that* plan the preceding winter, defeated by the last-minute intervention of one of baseball's true founding fathers, A. G. Spalding.[22] There was, however, no comparable authority to block him from having one foot in each warring camp, and manipulating the situation to his and the

Giants' advantage[23]—to the detriment of Baltimore and its own major-league aspirations.

McGraw signed on as manager of the Giants on July 7, 1902, and took the reins twelve days later. Iron Man Joe McGinnity, catcher Roger Bresnahan, and three other Orioles quickly followed their leader, as Freedman baldly shifted his Baltimore player assets to his New York City operation. With the Baltimore roster decimated, reduced to the status of a subordinate branch of a National League–centered enterprise, American League President Ban Johnson stepped in, stripped Freedman of control, and declared the franchise vacant.[24] After the Orioles forfeited one game for lack of available players, Johnson restocked the team so that it could at least complete the season, finishing, to no one's surprise, in last place.[25]

The Freedman–McGraw betrayal and the team's on-field collapse notwithstanding, estimated attendance in Baltimore reportedly increased in that hapless season (from 141,952 in 1901 to 174,606 in 1902), but it was the lowest total in the league, whereas overall league attendance rose by half a million spectators. The city's fans could see the writing on the wall. During the off-season, Ban Johnson escalated the stakes in the war with the National League and made it clear that his next move would be an invasion of the Giants' New York turf.

On the run from the unexpectedly strong business challenge presented by the new league, facing the threat of head-to-head competition in its largest market, and anxious to reduce player salaries, which had spiraled in the interleague bidding war for talent, the National League signaled its readiness to open negotiations, and baseball peace was restored early in 1903. The senior circuit agreed to recognize its rival as a coequal, and each league bound its ball clubs to respect the player reservation rights of the others.[26] The Cincinnati Peace Compact, signed at the St. Nicholas Hotel in that city on January 10, 1903, granted the American League the right to expand into New York City.

Ban Johnson, who had begun planning a move into New York during the previous season, was prepared to foot the bills until local backers could be found. In March 1903, the league sold the hollowed-out Baltimore franchise for $18,000 to a makeshift New York ownership group consisting of gambler Frank J. Farrell and unsavory former police chief Big Bill Devery, fronted by businessman-politician Joseph Gordon, who was named club president.[27] Major-league baseball would not return to Baltimore for another fifty years. Under these less-than-auspicious circumstances, the franchise that would become known as the New York Yankees made its first appearance with the opening of the 1903 season.

The transplants set up shop, quickly building a 16,000-seat playing field dubbed Hilltop Park on high ground on Manhattan's Upper West Side, the site that would be occupied after 1928 by Columbia–Presbyterian Hospital, about half a mile from the Giants' Polo Grounds.[28] And so April 1903 found John McGraw facing off against the franchise he had abandoned the year before, 200 miles to the north of their last encounter.

It proved to be a very unequal contest. The American League had landed in New York, but for the first decade and more, the Giants had little reason for concern about their own hold over the city's baseball enthusiasts. The Highlanders—as the newly arrived denizens of Hilltop Park were soon called—lagged well behind the Giants, both on the diamond and at the turnstiles. Guided by pitching great Clark Griffith, who had been hand-picked by Ban Johnson to manage the American League's critically important New York venture, the Highlanders mounted surprisingly strong pennant bids twice in their first four years in Manhattan but thereafter consistently placed deep in the second division. Attendance ran about half that of the Giants, while press and public interest in the goings-on at Hilltop Park was slight, apart from the first months of the 1911 season when the Giants themselves moved

in after an April fire forced the National League team to find temporary quarters en route to the pennant. Not even the Highlanders'
move to the "new" and expanded Polo Grounds in 1913 made much of
a difference in the team's fortunes. The shift did, however, inspire a
new nickname for the team. With Hilltop Park abandoned, the name
"Highlanders" was no longer geographically appropriate, so it gave way
to the "Yankees."

Whatever their name, the American Leaguers remained in the
shadow of the Giants, who were their Polo Grounds landlord to boot.
In 1913, as Christy Mathewson and Rube Marquard pitched the
Giants to a third-straight National League pennant, the Yankees
limped home in seventh place, their 350,000 die-hard fans rattling
around in the grandstand, which accommodated 630,000 of their landlord's paying customers. The only solace for Yankee loyalists came
when the Giants were upended in the World Series that fall (their
third such loss in a row), and McGraw capped a post-Series gathering
by firing coach Wilbert Robinson, a longtime colleague from the old
Orioles, after the two men had traded boozy recriminations over the
defeat.

In 1914, the Yankees finished in sixth place, again drawing no more
than 350,000 fans, but the great turning point in the franchise's history
was at hand. On December 31, 1914, Colonels Jacob Ruppert and Till-
inghast L'Hommedieu Huston purchased the team for $450,000. The
"two Colonels" each put up half of the record-high purchase price,
with Huston reportedly paying for his share with thousand-dollar
bills.[29] "For $450,000," Ruppert would later say, "we got an orphan ball
club without a home of its own, without players of outstanding ability,
without prestige."[30] This was true, but it was also true that the
Colonels were buying into the largest market in a fast-growing business. Interest in major-league baseball had been increasing steadily.
World Series receipts rose from $68,000 for the five-game matchup in

1905 to $320,000 for the series of the same length ten years later.[31] Total receipts for all sixteen major-league clubs in 1901, the first year of American League operations, were about $1,275,000, or $80,000 per club.[32] Ten years later, after a period that saw the forging of a more-or-less-permanent baseball peace, the institutionalization of the World Series, and important breakthroughs in press coverage, big-league baseball revenues had more than doubled, totaling some $2,750,000 to $4,000,000 in annual receipts, an average of $175,000 to $250,000 gross income per team.[33] The October day in 1903 when a New York sports page would feature the headline "English Cricketeers Win" and give lesser coverage to a World Series game had passed.[34] By 1915, the World Series had become front-page news, with a press corps of 200 covering the fall classic for an intensely interested and well-informed audience. As one reporter then wrote, "Each boy knew the abilities of the members of both teams probably better than he knew his lessons."[35] The time was ripe for Ruppert and Huston to bet on the Yankees', and the sport's, future.

Their purchase, nonetheless, certainly was a gamble, coming as it did when "organized baseball" itself was facing a strong challenge from the Federal League, an aspiring third major circuit that had just completed its first season of play. The new league comprised teams in cities that had lost major-league status during the consolidation that produced the American and National Leagues at the turn of the twentieth century—Baltimore, Kansas City, Indianapolis, and Buffalo—as well as teams that went head to head with established major-league franchises—Brooklyn, Chicago, Pittsburgh, and St. Louis.[36] After initially abjuring any intention to "poach" big-league talent, the Federal League soon was signing up players whom the American and National League teams contended were under contract, driving up salaries across the board as a bidding war ensued. The result was a sharp drop in total American and National League attendance (down one-third from 1913 to 1914) as the Federal League challenge confused and disillusioned fans, played havoc with team rosters, and subdivided key markets previously monopolized by major-league teams in the decade of peace that had followed the American League–National League peace compact.[37]

The Federal League "war" sharply depressed the values placed on major-league franchises. The year before the Federal League emerged on the big-league scene, a one-half interest in the perennially mediocre Brooklyn Dodgers had sold for $100,000. Even the year after the new league disbanded, the far more successful world-champion Boston Red Sox team, including its Fenway Park real estate, sold for only around $400,000.[38] Indeed, so dire was the upstart league's challenge that when it was repulsed with the disbanding of the league after the 1915 season, *The Sporting News*, "baseball's bible," lamented that "fans will never take the same viewpoint. . . . They know the player is no hero now and never again will he be placed on a pedestal."[39] Perhaps, however, Ruppert and Huston were fortified by their newly acquired team's own resilience amid the business turmoil of the 1914 season. Although the Yankees finished in sixth place, home-game attendance actually improved slightly over the previous year, in contrast to a decline in the Giants' attendance of more than 40 percent.

Ruppert and Huston didn't get into baseball to make their fortunes: They arrived with fortunes ready for spending, and with few, if any, inhibitions about what they spent. A few years earlier, William Randolph Hearst had done much the same thing in journalism. Ready, willing, and able to spend an unprecedented amount of money, according to A. J. Liebling, Hearst, "like a very big gambler in a very small crap game, changed the basis of the newspaper business. In the contemptuous term of the tinhorn, he froze out the ribbon clerks—he made it impossible for the man with a small bankroll to get in."[40]

Ruppert and Huston similarly entered the baseball business game with a bigger stack of chips than their putative rivals could ever hope to amass either by operating a ball club alone or by "laundering" from quasi-legal enterprises. Although grandly dubbed "the magnates" by the press,[41] baseball's first generation of owners might better be described as penny-ante players, operating a low-dollar-volume business on slim bankrolls, within a thinly capitalized economic structure. Major-league baseball's $3 to $4 million or so in income barely registered against such other recreational expenditures as motion picture and other theatrical admissions, and the sale of musical instruments, each of which yielded revenues of $167 million in 1909. These other entertainment businesses dwarfed the economic impact of the sport that pioneering baseball man A. G. Spalding was about to canonize as "America's National Game."[42] From the perspective of Jacob Ruppert, who had been elected president of the U.S. Brewers' Association in 1911, the business of baseball amounted to less than a pittance when measured against an alcoholic-beverage industry whose sales were then around $2 *billion*.[43]

Ruppert and Huston readily took advantage of the greater financial resources they could command. Within a few years of taking over the team, they spearheaded a revolution in the economic dimensions of the baseball business. From the start, the Colonels were prepared to spend unprecedented sums to acquire playing talent. The team they built demonstrated unmatched spectator appeal, drawing more than one million fans in 1920, the first time any team had broken that barrier. Only one other club in the American League (Detroit) and two in the National (Brooklyn and Chicago) would follow suit before World War II, but the Yankees enjoyed nine such bonanza seasons in the 1920s. The massive scale of the 60,000-seat stadium in the Bronx, which opened in April 1923, provided a daily reminder that the Colonels had bought into a "pastime" and turned it into a business.

The purchase of the Yankees by Ruppert and Huston also marked a sharp break with the style of baseball ownership exemplified by the Farrell–Devery regime. Although Ruppert (who had even been a four-term Tammany Hall Democratic congressman) and Huston were not without political resources and connections of their own, they held a place in society far removed from Farrell's and Devery's seamy web of associations in the netherworld where crime and the law coexisted. Farrell was a bookie and big-time gambler, a key cog in the syndicate controlled by Tammany boss Big Tim Sullivan.[44] Devery was dubbed "the most notorious police officer in New York City's history," a "bag man" for the Sullivan syndicate, which reputedly cleared more than $3 million annually from prostitution, gambling, and graft.[45] Devery earned his own distinctive place in the lengthy annals of New York City corruption lore with his patented response to questions about his allegedly illicit activities: "Touchin' on and appertainin' to that matter, I disremember."[46]

The world of Colonel Ruppert and Colonel Huston may have overlapped with that of Farrell and Devery, but only at the margins. The two Colonels' horizons were broader, their connections more respectable, their businesses emphatically legitimate. Each had arrived at a position of eminence by a different route, and they had little in common, apart from what counted most as far as the operation of the Yankees was concerned—wealth and a love of baseball. Ruppert, heir to the brewing and real estate fortune assembled by his father, was "a man of inherited wealth, social position, a patron and dilettante of the arts." Huston, his elaborately grandiloquent name notwithstanding, was "a self-made man who got his millions through his brain and brawn." His military rank had been earned through extended military service in Cuba and France; Ruppert's was a political appointment by a governor of New York on whose staff he served as a young man.[47] What would prove critically important to the future of Yankee baseball was the one thing, aside from interest in the sport, that they had in common—money, and lots of it.[48]

Taking over the family brewery (founded in 1851) at the age of twenty-three, Jacob Ruppert increased production from 350,000 barrels a year in 1892 to well over one million barrels at the onset of Prohibition. Ruppert's baseball rivals might own saloons, but he supplied them. The family fortune, enhanced by appreciating real estate investments, continued its upward trajectory under Ruppert's stewardship and was estimated at $60 million when the great Depression hit. Since Ruppert and his business survived Prohibition more or less unscathed, it is perhaps not surprising that the depression, in turn, provided an opportunity for continued, even accelerated, growth. At the time of Colonel Ruppert's death in 1939, the value of his estate was put at $100 million, including $30 million in real estate.[49]

Although the two Colonels never really got along, and their running disputes would lead to Huston's departure within a few years, it was a fortunate partnership while it lasted. Buying talented players was a common practice in the baseball business, not least by the Boston Red Sox, who would soon become its prime victims. However, the vast sums of non-baseball money that Ruppert and Huston had available provided funding for such acquisitions on an unprecedented scale. The Colonels' independent wealth also made it possible to reinvest the team's profits into baseball operations, which provided the means for continued success. Neither course of action was a readily available option for the Yankees' less financially well-endowed baseball adversaries—whether the locally oriented, gambler–saloonkeeper–machine-pol types such as Farrell and Devery, who had been (and would continue to be) fixtures in the baseball ownership ranks, or the "career" baseball men, including cross-town rivals Charles Ebbets of the Dodgers and the Brush family of the Giants, for whom baseball had been *their* primary business and source of income as they worked their way up through the sport's ranks.[50]

The money wasn't everything, however. Just as important, the Colonels introduced a new management style and structure into the sport. They successfully managed the delicate task of reconciling fandom with business acumen in operating their team. That a team owner must have an intense desire to win was, and is, a crucial ingredient to running a successful ball club, but it was just as important for the team's owners to step back and afford knowledgeable professionals the leeway needed to achieve the desired results. In the new organizational structure perfected by the Colonels, ownership supplied the sinews of baseball battle, selected the key front-office and on-field managerial personnel, and delineated and then respected hierarchical spheres of responsibility. The Yankees, who would be sold by Ruppert's estate in 1945 for $2.8 million, made up a very small part of Ruppert's total holdings—a fact that no doubt encouraged the adoption of a management structure, built on delegated authority, similar to that employed in business generally.[51] Ruppert understood this better than his partner, and it was no coincidence that the Colonels' eventual parting was precipitated by Huston's attempt to subvert field manager Miller Huggins's authority over his players.

By 1923, when Huston departed from the scene, the new Yankee model was up and running, but the circumstances that provided the team with their critical breakthrough to sporting and business success could not have been anticipated by the Colonels, or anyone else, during their first years at the team's helm. The Yankees' road to victory over the Giants in their climactic battle for baseball supremacy would, as it turned out, run through Boston.

◇

THE COLONELS BEGAN their reign by opening their checkbooks in the quest for fresh talent. In their first year of operations, they reportedly spent a major-league–leading $60,000 on acquiring players.[52] If accurate (always a question mark with regard to stories about baseball economics, then or at any time), this represented no less than one-eighth of the total sum paid by all big-league clubs for such players in the entire five years between 1911 and 1916.[53] Even a team such as the New York Giants, which was already notorious for trying to buy its way to the pennant, had never spent so freely. The expensively assembled club suited up in newly redesigned uniforms that first spring. Sports-page fashion critics adjudged the result as "batting 1.000 in the haberdashery league": blue replaced black pinstripes on the white home outfits, and, more daringly, blue, cardinal, and green stripes were featured on the "Confederate gray" roadwear, not surprisingly predicted to "command attention in every city on the circuit."[54]

Bold fashion statement notwithstanding, spending was the only statistical category in which the former Highlanders topped the standings. The 1915 Yankees finished fifth, 32½ games behind pennant-winning Boston, their eighth second-division finish in ten years, witnessed only by some 250,000 customers, less than half the attendance recorded at Fenway Park. Undaunted, the Yankees' owners continued their lavish spending over the next two seasons, highlighted by the purchase of Frank "Home Run" Baker from Philadelphia in 1916. The result was a marginal improvement on the field; they finished in fourth and sixth place in 1916 and 1917, respectively, and Yankee attendance still lagged well behind that for the Red Sox, then at their peak, and even more pointedly, behind the attendance of their Polo Grounds landlord, the New York Giants.

In 1918, while Colonel Huston was serving in the U.S. Army in France, Ruppert began to turn around the team's fortunes by hiring a talented and experienced baseball man, Miller Huggins, as field man-

ager and de facto general manager. Ruppert, and more grudgingly
Huston, deferred to Huggins's expert baseball judgment and Huggins's
authority. After deciding to spend whatever was needed to procure top
players, the Colonels made their second crucial baseball decision: to
step back and allow sound baseball veterans—Huggins as field manager and, after 1920, Ed Barrow as general manager—to make the key
personnel decisions. This set the team on the right track as far as baseball operations were concerned, but the unbounded success that followed would not have been possible without a crucial assist from an
entirely unexpected direction.

On November 1, 1916, the Boston Red Sox, who had won five
American League pennants and four World Series since 1903,[55] were
sold to two New York–based theatrical producers, Harry Frazee and
Hugh Ward. Frazee had compiled a strong track record in his own
slice of the entertainment business, rising from theater usher in his
Peoria, Illinois, hometown to Broadway boy wonder who had produced a series of hit shows, culminating in the 1910 smash, *Madame
Sherry*, by the age of thirty.[56] Frazee was confident that he could
repeat his theatrical success in the world of baseball, which he viewed
as just another branch of show business. "You can't fill a theater with a
poor attraction," he said, "and you can't interest the fans with a losing
ball club," especially in Boston, which "has been led to expect
winners."[57]

Frazee's purchase of the Red Sox set in motion a chain of events
that ultimately would bring Ed Barrow, as well as Babe Ruth, to New
York. The fortunes of the mighty Boston Red Sox and the striving
New York Yankees would be inextricably linked over the next half-
dozen seasons. In the end, the Red Sox and the Yankees had traded
places in baseball's hierarchy, and the settled ways of the sport had
been irreversibly overturned, both on and off the field.

Despite the success of the Red Sox on the ballfield, their financial affairs were in disarray when Frazee stepped in, so operating the team successfully would be a difficult proposition for even the most experienced baseball hand, which Frazee assuredly was not. In December 1911, the Taylor family, which had purchased the team in 1904 and which also owned the *Boston Globe* newspaper, sold a one-half interest in the Sox to Jim McAleer, then manager of the Washington club, backed up by Robert McRoy, American League secretary and a buddy of President Ban Johnson, for a reported $150,000. The Taylors, however, retained the Fenway Realty Trust, which owned the Fenway ballpark then under construction on land they had purchased; they also kept the remaining one-half interest in the franchise itself.[58] By the winter of 1913–14, McAleer was gone, his half interest sold for $200,000 to Joseph Lannin, who had left his native Quebec for a bellhop's job in Boston and had parlayed that humble start into the ownership of hotels, apartments, and resorts in Boston and New York, as well as a part interest in Boston's Braves. By the time Lannin sold out to Frazee, he apparently was able to deliver a 100 percent interest in the team, as well as the stock in the realty company, although the Taylors still had a claim on team income by continuing to hold preferred stock, as well as mortgage bonds against the ballpark real estate.[59]

Frazee's purchase price was dubiously alleged to be as much as $1 million in some press reports at the time.[60] Even the commonly reported, and generally accepted, figure of $675,000 (about $200,000 more than the Colonels had paid for the Yankees two years earlier), shed little light on the bifurcated structure of a transaction that would have serious consequences for the future of the team. Lannin was reported to have demanded, and received, a cash payment of approximately $400,000 from Frazee for the team and its assets, apart from Fenway Park. With respect to the ballpark, Lannin transferred the stock in the Fenway Realty Trust in exchange for a note for $262,000, payable November 1, 1919, and secured by the shares conveyed to Frazee.[61] The stock apparently also remained subject to the priority claim of the mortgage bonds, so that Lannin in effect had shifted payment responsibility to Frazee for an obligation he still owed to Taylor.[62]

The purchase was a good deal for Frazee, who (leaving aside the price of the ballpark) paid about the same price as the Colonels had paid for the downtrodden Yankees. Frazee gained a world-championship club that had been the dominant force in the American League over the previous five seasons, at a time when baseball enjoyed internal peace. Frazee took advantage of Lannin's desire to sell: "I am too much of a fan to run a baseball club and found that it was interfering with my heart," said Lannin in announcing the sale. Perhaps the shadow cast by the prospect of American involvement in the European war—made more likely in those final days of the fall's presidential election when interventionist Republican candidate Charles Evans Hughes appeared the probable winner—also played a part in Lannin's decision. There is little reason to believe that Frazee paid an inflated price in order to fulfill a dream of owning a big-league ball club and beat out rival bidders. According to Lannin, no other offers were on the table. Nor was there any reason for Frazee to overpay in anticipation of earning large sums from ownership of the team. Compared with Frazee's theatrical enterprises, baseball presented an unpromising source of profit. In an era when much theatrical activity was occurring on the road, and touring companies were a key source of income for showmen, Broadway's annual receipts alone probably totaled more than $10 million—three to five times those of all major-league teams combined. The income from one successful show was greater than the annual receipts of any single major-league club, most emphatically including Boston, which suffered from the ban on Sunday baseball.[63] At a time when a hit show could cover its initial investment in little more than one month, and bring in ticket sales of $10,000 a week for a year, no one pursuing profit would choose baseball over Broadway.

The Red Sox were riding high when Frazee took over. In 1916, they had just won their third World Series in five seasons. Their twenty-one-year-old left-handed pitching star, Babe Ruth, whom Lannin had acquired from Baltimore two years earlier, had capped a twenty-three-win season with a fourteen-inning, 2–1 win in the second game of that fall's World Series against Brooklyn. Ruth's victory gave the Red Sox a 2–0 lead in the series, which Boston went on to win for the second year in a row over their National League opponents, four games to one. Despite being hobbled by blue laws, which prohibited Sunday baseball, the Sox had consistently drawn about half a million fans a year, the best turnout for any team similarly deprived of the chance to play on the most lucrative day of the week. In 1915, the Sox had hosted a record 22.17 percent of all fans attending American League ball games.[64]

Boston fans greeted the sale with relief. Frazee's purchase averted the one shadow falling over the team's future—the prospect that Lannin's cash-starved ownership would sell off the team's key assets. Lannin had appeared to be doing just that when he sold star right fielder Tris Speaker to Cleveland for $55,000 at the start of the 1916 season. Disappointing financial results for the 1916 season had not improved Lannin's balance sheet. In that second consecutive world-championship season, Red Sox attendance had dropped almost 50,000 from the previous year's league-leading mark. Indeed, the Hub's infatuation with baseball seemed to be waning across the board. Crowds at rival Braves Field were also down that year, after a temporary fillip provided by the "miracle" title in 1914, signaling decades of perennial financial distress for the National League team, which would ultimately make Boston a one-team town. With Frazee taking over from

Lannin, the specter of further dispersal sales by Lannin, who had pleaded poverty when faced with Speaker's holdout for a higher salary, was apparently moot.

Despite their recent success, Boston's defending World Champions actually needed a thorough overhaul if they were to stay on top under their new ownership in 1917. Lannin's readiness to sell a reigning world-championship team was something of a leading indicator of trouble ahead. Winning Red Sox baseball had traditionally been the product of aggressive personnel management, conducted with a high degree of skill and ruthless pursuit of advantage. The Sox had been the only team in the American League capable of challenging the Philadelphia dynasty assembled by Connie Mack, which won four pennants in five years, starting in 1910. Mack's great team turned back a different rival each winning season—New York (1910), Detroit (1911), Washington (1913), and Boston (1914). Only the Red Sox, led by Smoky Joe Wood's thirty-four-victory season, proved able to stop the Athletics, as they did in 1912. Connie Mack's A's then rebounded quickly, and the Red Sox came to grief when Joe Wood's arm went sore and Boston dropped to fourth place in 1913.

After the 1914 season, the Athletics dynasty crumbled, as star pitchers Chief Bender and Eddie Plank jumped to the Federal League, Mack sold second baseman Eddie Collins to the White Sox for $50,000, and Home Run Baker sat out the season after failing to come to salary terms with Mack. Taking advantage of Philadelphia's sudden collapse, the 1915 Red Sox regained the pennant and then defeated the National League's surprising champion, Philadelphia's *other* team, the Phillies, four games to one, in that fall's World Series.

Boston's victory in 1915 had required a drastic rebuilding of the team that had won the 1912 title. The team that had won 105 games in 1912 was largely gone. The slide to fourth place in 1913 cost manager Jake Stahl his job midway through that season, the shortest tenure ever for a world-championship manager (apart from the Cardinals' Johnny Keane, who moved from the Cardinals to the Yankees immediately after the 1964 World Series), and made extensive personnel changes imperative. The 1915 Red Sox retained the outfield of the 1912 champions, although Tris Speaker's average slipped sixty points to .322. The infield had been reshuffled and the pitching staff overhauled since 1912. Bucky O'Brien, Hugh Bedient, and Charley "Sea Lion" Hall—who had combined for fifty-five wins in 1912 but only twenty-three the next year—were gone. Leading the new staff were Rube Foster and Ernie Shore, who each won nineteen games, and Babe Ruth with eighteen wins. Joe Wood, one of two starting holdovers from 1912, won fifteen games (a strong showing except when measured against his all-too-fleeting dominance), as did Dutch Leonard. Ray Collins slipped badly in his final season, and rookie Carl Mays got off to an awkward start in his major-league career. The reconfigured team, pieced together in 1913 and 1914, beat out the Tigers by two and one-half games, while failing to lead the league in any major team offensive, defensive, or pitching category.

In 1917, Frazee's first year as club owner, the refurbished Red Sox ran out of gas. Although they won only one less game than in the previous year, the Chicago White Sox won eleven more, and Boston finished ten games back. For the first time in four years—since the Braves had surprised their league in 1914—no World Series game was played in Boston in that first wartime autumn for the United States. The preoccupations and dislocations of wartime, combined with the Sox stumble, drove Fenway attendance down by 20 percent, the first drop below 400,000 since (fairly) reliable figures had been compiled. In his first at-bat as a "magnate," Harry Frazee had struck out.

The 1917 White Sox, like the 1913 Athletics, rank among the best in baseball history. Eddie Cicotte, at the age of thirty-three, had his first great season, winning more than twenty games for the first time (twenty-eight, in fact), pitching the White Sox to the pennant over a Boston team that had sold him during the 1912 season. The ChiSox won by outperforming the Red Sox in games against the league's better teams, beating Boston, Cleveland, and Detroit forty-two times, while Boston could win only twenty-nine from its first-division rivals (losing the season series to each). Although Boston's pitching held its own with the White Sox, their bats went cold; they surrendered nine fewer runs than the winners, who scored 100 runs more than the Red Sox. The future, however, seemed promising, with the thirty-four-year-old Cicotte unlikely to maintain his form in subsequent seasons. The Red Sox had young arms that were more than ready to renew the contest on favorable terms.

After the 1917 season, Frazee faced the same situation that Lannin had in 1913, watching a championship team falter in the drive to repeat, beaten by a truly great competitor. The Red Sox's previous management had responded successfully to that challenge under Lannin's ownership, rebuilding its way to the top without sinking too far down in the standings along the way, able to win pennants within a few years with very different rosters. This was a novel achievement—one far more difficult than that of the Tigers (1907–9) or Philadelphia (1910–14) in winning with a set lineup—and testified to exceptional personnel procurement skills. Whether or not the Red Sox could manage a similar comeback was the great challenge Harry Frazee now faced.

It was an opportunity for theater man Frazee to package a winner on the field, to plug the gaps in a production that needed just a bit of tinkering to become a hit. Frazee moved decisively to build a championship contender for the 1918 season. His method was simple but effective: buying top talent from a cash-hungry rival. In later years, of course, Frazee would be excoriated in Boston as the man who dismantled the Red Sox by selling its star players to the hated Yankees, but it was far less often remembered that Frazee assembled a good part of that team by similarly pillaging Connie Mack's Philadelphia A's. A Yankee fan might, indeed, smugly say that what goes around, comes around.

In the winter of 1917, Frazee began dealing with Connie Mack. The A's, having finished in last place three years in a row, were ripe for plucking by Frazee. Since April, the United States had been at war, with the prospect that baseball would be canceled for the duration. In past crises, Mack had always been ready to take what he could up front, stagger a while, and try to hold down losses against the chance that a brighter future might never arrive. Frazee was poised to pounce. According to his critics, he went out and bought Boston a pennant.

The last remnants of Mack's once-invincible champions were soon headed to New England, after a series of one-sided transactions. When the 1918 season opened, former Athletics player Stuffy McInnis was at first for Boston, Wally Schang was behind the plate, Amos Strunk was in center field, and pitcher Joe Bush had joined the starting rotation. In exchange, aging Larry Gardner and Tilly Walker were sent to Philadelphia, along with a reported 60,000 of Frazee's Broadway-minted dollars. The baseball press reported that Frazee was "proving himself a magnate. . . . No wonder Boston is beginning to glory in him."[65] With the switch of Babe Ruth to left field for more regular offensive duty, the 1918 Red Sox retained only Everett Scott and Harry Hooper from the 1917 starting lineup. Frazee was trying to repeat Lannin's success after the 1912 pennant by rapid rebuilding. Indeed, he outdid his successful predecessor. It took Lannin two years to restore the team to the top of the league's standings. Frazee did it in one. The 1918 Red Sox rebounded as World Champions.

It was not an unalloyed triumph. The war cast a shadow over the baseball season and dictated the outcome in crucial respects. The White Sox were decimated by the draft and by draft-deferred employment in wartime industry, which claimed leading members of the pennant-winning cast. The Red Sox lost Ernie Shore and young Herb Pennock from the pitching staff, but their rather elderly starting lineup (only twenty-three-year-old Ruth was under twenty-five) avoided Uncle Sam's grasp. When the season was precipitately halted on Labor Day, after the government issued a "work or fight" order, the Red Sox were in front of the unbalanced schedule, leading Cleveland by three and one-half games. The moves made in the off-season all testified to Frazee's desire to win and his readiness to spend significant money to do so.

The 1918 team represented an impressive accomplishment for Frazee and his new field boss and general manager, Ed Barrow. Showing a faith in the future of the game at a time when naysayers abounded, they put together an entirely revamped lineup that proved up to the job at hand, and they had managed to absorb the loss of two pitching aces to the demands of war. When the World Series ended on September 11 that foreshortened season (with a Sox win over the Cubs in six games), only Harry Hooper and Everett Scott stood (in right field and shortstop) in the same places they had on October 8, 1915, when the Sox faced the Phillies in that fall's World Series. Of the entire Boston team, only Harry Hooper had played in the 1912 World Series, just six years earlier.

With the nation at war, 1918 was an awkward time to win a World Series. Frazee and his players earned little for their efforts. Major-league attendance for the war-shortened season fell by more than 2 million admissions from the previous year. At Fenway, attendance continued to drop for the fourth consecutive season, sinking below 250,000. World Series receipts were the lowest since 1910, less than half of those taken in during the Sox's previous appearance in 1916. The winning Red Sox players took home the lowest winning shares ever, barely $1,100. Two years earlier, they had pocketed almost

$4,000 a man.[66] Winning was no doubt better than losing, but 1918 was not a year in which winning would have much effect on the bottom line.

Confident in the ability of the team they had so recently refashioned, Frazee and Barrow did little more than some fine tuning as the Red Sox prepared to defend their title when baseball's forces again deployed at full strength in the first springtime of peace. With Babe Ruth installed in the outfield as a regular, and pitching only occasionally, the Red Sox opened their 1919 campaign with high hopes for another championship. On Opening Day, one analysis found it "hard to pick a flaw in the makeup of the Boston team," and concluded that, compared to the championship team of 1918, the "Red Sox look even stronger for the 1919 season."[67]

Once the season started, almost nothing went right for Frazee's team. But the openhanded owner did not despair. The SOS went out again to ever-bountiful Philadelphia. In late June, Red Shannon was acquired from Mack to play second, along with center fielder Braggo Roth. But the Red Sox failed to revive. Newly minted outfielder Babe Ruth provided the one bright spot for the team and its fans. In the daily starting lineup for the first time, home runs flew off his bat. As Ruth's home-run total mounted, excited fans speculated about whether he would smash Gavvy Cravath's single-season home-run record of twenty-four.

Ruth continued his slugging, but the Red Sox floundered. As they struggled in sixth place, a four-team pennant race developed—but Detroit, not Boston, joined battle with Chicago, Cleveland, and New York. By early July, the four contenders were locked in the most closely bunched first division in American League history. The Red Sox were going nowhere. The moment had come for Ruppert and Huston to strike. Boston's difficulty would be New York's opportunity.

On July 13, Red Sox frustration boiled over in spectacular fashion.

That afternoon, temperamental pitcher Carl Mays, whose deceptive submarine delivery would inflict baseball's only fatality a year later, angrily stalked off the mound at Comiskey Park, where Boston was facing Chicago. Asserting that he would no longer play for a team that had provided scant support behind his strong pitching, Mays refused to rejoin the team. League President Ban Johnson expected that Frazee would suspend Mays for his lack of self-discipline, and other league team owners demanded that Mays be punished. Frazee, however, was not inclined to pay much heed to Johnson's diktat. The two men had clashed previously over Johnson's efforts to end persistent gambling in the Fenway Park grandstand, and the league president had reportedly vowed, "Frazee or gambling must go." Frazee thought that what happened in his ballpark was none of Johnson's business.[68] More important, Frazee had opposed Johnson's efforts to end the 1918 season in midsummer, and he had joined with other dissident owners to secure the continuance of play through Labor Day, with a further extension for the World Series, which the Red Sox won—Boston's fifth, and to date last, World Championship. By that season's end, Frazee was looking for the chance to break the autocratic Johnson's power over the league that he had founded and that he continued to run as his personal fiefdom.[69]

The crisis over Mays provided a fortuitous but ready-made opportunity for Frazee to put the screws on the hated Johnson, in concert with the powerful owners of the Yankees. Ruppert and Huston expressed strong interest in acquiring Mays's services, and Frazee was convinced that Mays would never rejoin his team. On July 29, he traded Mays to the Yankees for two young pitchers, Allan Russell and Bob McGraw, and a reported $40,000. A furious Johnson immediately canceled the trade and suspended Mays.[70]

It was a critical decision, but it is unfair to see the Mays trade as the first step in a systematic dismantling of the Red Sox by New

York–based Frazee in favor of the Yankees. That indictment takes the transaction out of its immediate context and owes more to hindsight than insight. In the summer of 1919, Frazee was struggling to maintain his team as a competitive force, having to make the best of a bizarre situation. He and Barrow had already made midseason moves to strengthen the club, and Frazee was now making another, giving up on a player who had already given up on him. In the face of Mays's rebellion, Frazee's options were limited. The trade was not an obviously bad one for Boston in terms of the players acquired, even apart from the substantial cash infusion that also was included. Allan Russell was a fine pitcher and had the advantage of being two years younger than the departed Mays. Although unable to arrest the Red Sox slide into the second division, Russell won ten games for them over the balance of the season, more than the nine games that Mays won for *his* new team. Frazee had not done badly after the mess that Mays had made for him.

In sending Mays to the Yankees, Frazee was not breaking up a winner, he was quelling a revolt on a losing team and arming himself with cash that could be deployed for future rebuilding. Notwithstanding Ruth's record-breaking home-run hitting, the 1919 Red Sox finished with their worst record in more than a decade. Although attendance rebounded from the disastrous wartime 1918 mark, Fenway crowds remained small, while other teams profited from the first year of a postwar boom that would quickly carry attendance to record levels. Detroit and New York (even pre-Ruth) moved to the forefront at the turnstiles, displacing the Hub. The sixth-place Sox accounted for only one-ninth of league admissions, with the number of fans attending Red Sox home games as a percentage of all fans attending American League ball games at an all-time low.[71]

The 1919 Red Sox were an inept team in need of a drastic overhaul. Frazee was prepared to take dramatic measures to jump-start a reversal of Red Sox fortunes. Any effort to do so, however, immediately collided with the loose threads left dangling from the purchase of the team from Lannin three years earlier.

The November 1, 1919, due date on the $262,000 note that encumbered Frazee's ownership interest in Fenway Park loomed ominously, and imminently, as the books closed on the disappointing (both competitively and financially), 1919 season. Given the economic realities of the game, and the unlikelihood of realizing the kind of profit that would be needed to cover the note, it is hard to understand what Frazee's expectations were when he took on that obligation, or what Lannin's were in extending it. To be sure, Frazee did not expect that the war would cut so deeply into his ability to profit from the championship club he had assembled for the 1918 season; their World Series appearance yielded less than half the proceeds that Lannin had enjoyed in 1916, no more than about $35,000 in additional gross receipts—the worst return since 1910. Perhaps, as reported in the winter of 1917,[72] he contemplated moving the team into Braves Field—whose larger seating capacity had led Lannin to transfer the Red Sox home dates for the 1915 and 1916 series there—and then selling the Fenway Park property. Perhaps he expected to be out of the baseball business altogether by the time he had to pay off Lannin, or maybe he thought Lannin would roll the note over rather than precipitate a confrontation that might end up leaving the team, in which the former owner retained an acknowledged rooting interest, with no place to play.

Speculation aside, when the November 1 due date arrived, Frazee did not pay up and Lannin declared war. Frazee justified his nonpayment by citing a provision in the 1916 sale agreement that required "Lannin to hold [Frazee and Ward] harmless from any claim or indebtedness that might exist prior to November 1, 1916."[73] Lannin and Frazee had been wrangling for some time over their respective responsibility for Boston's share of the $600,000 in payments that the two leagues had agreed to make over the next ten years to certain of the "rebel" owners as part of the 1915 settlement with the Federal League.[74] The financial stakes of the dispute were raised further in April 1919, when jurors returned a verdict of $80,000 (trebled to $240,000 by the judge in May, together with an additional award of $24,000 in attorneys' fees) against major-league baseball in favor of the Baltimore Federal League club at the conclusion of the trial in Baltimore's epochal antitrust lawsuit.[75] Frazee evidently claimed that Boston's share of that judgment was similarly Lannin's obligation under the "hold harmless" clause, and he suspended paying interest on the note, unless Lannin agreed to set off these indemnity claims—which Frazee calculated at $50,500 (his lawyers referred to $60,000–70,000)—against the balance on the note.[76] With the parties at an impasse, Frazee defaulted on the note, leaving Lannin with the right to foreclose on the realty stock and auction off Fenway Park to satisfy Frazee's debt.

And so, in the winter of 1919–20, wherever Frazee looked, he saw trouble. The team had unraveled on the field; its finances could not have been shakier; its very playing grounds were being held hostage to a debt that he was unable or unwilling to pay. And the one ostensibly bright spot in the Red Sox picture—the emergence of Babe Ruth as home-run–hitting star nonpareil—only added to Frazee's already problem-filled plate. Ruth had battled hard for higher pay the previous spring, and with his record-smashing 1919 season behind him, he insisted on a doubling of his salary to $20,000, even though two years remained on his three-year contract for $10,000 per year. Faced with Ruth's demand, Frazee and Barrow convinced themselves that Ruth, especially given the frustration, insubordination, and failure that had characterized the 1919 season, posed a discipline and morale problem that threatened the future prospects of the team. Even with Ruth and his awesome slugging, which appeared, in any event, unlikely to be repeated in what was still the dead-ball era,[77] the Red Sox had only finished a poor sixth. Ruth's own lackluster record in the opening months of the 1919 season had played a major role in dragging the team out of contention, and it made him a target for anyone seeking to pin responsibility on someone for the team's disappointing showing.

Exacerbating Boston's "Ruth problem," baseball's governing structure was in disarray that winter. The National League owners had revolted against the authority of the sport's supreme National Commission. The Yankees and Frazee were at war with their own league's president, and Frazee was supporting the appointment of a czar to rule the sport and break Johnson's power, promoting the candidacy of former U.S. President William Howard Taft for that new position.[78] The minor leagues had withdrawn from the National Agreement, which had governed their relations with the majors since 1903. If the antitrust verdict in the Federal League case survived appeal, baseball executives predicted the severing of relations between the leagues and the elimination of the reserve clause.[79] Even apart from the outcome of that case, renewed baseball war threatened to erupt, and with it the prospect of contract jumping, in defiance of the "reserve system," which had proven a paper tiger in the courtroom in previous legal confrontations over player services. If the structure of baseball broke up, whether by court decree or internal dissension, Boston might well lose Ruth—and receive nothing in return.[80]

In addition, in the immediate aftermath of the war, the economics of baseball were changing in a way that inevitably would work against Boston's prospects for renewed baseball success. In the spring of 1919, just before Opening Day, the New York legislature legalized Sunday baseball. Over the course of the season, record crowds turned out on that once-sacred day, and Yankee attendance soared to 619,000, more than 200,000 greater than for the Red Sox, and better than any previous Boston total. Puritanical Boston, which still barred its teams from Sunday play, inevitably would find it hard to keep up thereafter, now that New York had broken that all-important barrier to financial return in what was still the era of the six-day workweek.

And so, groping for a solution to myriad pressing baseball and financial problems, and hoping, however mistakenly, to restore the Red Sox to contention by removing a source of internal discord, Frazee sold Ruth's contract to the New York Yankees on December 26, 1919. It was a one-of-a-kind deal with the only men in baseball who had the cash and the credit to make it worth Frazee's while. The stated sale price was $100,000, a record sum, but that was not the full extent of the transaction. Since the money was to be paid over time—$25,000 up front, with three further equal payments over the next three years—the total payment was actually $110,000. More important, a key component of the deal for Frazee, confronting an imminent threat of foreclosure by Lannin, was Ruppert's offer to lend Frazee $300,000, secured by a mortgage on Fenway Park.[81]

The Yanks had Ruth—and the makings of a dynasty. Ruppert and Huston could not have put their money to better use, or more effectively demonstrated how they were able to take advantage of baseball's traditional way of doing things—the building of a winning team through purchase at the expense of rivals in distress. This was, of course, what Frazee had done to Connie Mack's bedraggled A's just two years earlier, but the Yankees' owners were able to deploy unprecedentedly large resources to the effort. The $300,000 loan aside, the purchase price was twice that of the highest previous payment for a ballplayer.[82] In 1919, the Ruth-less but contending Yankees had capitalized on their newly acquired right to play at home on Sundays to outdraw the Red Sox. In making Frazee an offer he could not reasonably refuse, the Colonels were contributing to the most efficient allocation of baseball resources, one that would fortuitously pay off for the entire sport when it was faced with a life-or-death struggle to survive after the potentially crippling revelations of the Black Sox scandal surfaced late in the 1920 season. Drawing on a much larger market, one that had just legalized baseball on the most lucrative day of the week, the Yankees were in a position to place a higher value on Ruth's services than anyone else, and to pay a correspondingly higher price to acquire his services. The Ruth sale offered prime proof of the economic dictum that even "a market in which freedom is limited by the reserve rule . . . distributes players among teams about as a free market would."[83]

As for Frazee, however large the sum that he had received, it was not a windfall that he invested, as baseball lore continues to hold, in his production of *No, No, Nanette*. Frazee did not produce that show until 1925, after he was out of baseball. Although it was a tremendous moneymaker, "the comedy musical hit of the 1920s—without question the most successful musical comedy of the decade," in the words of one theater historian,[84] the Ruth monies had been paid years earlier. More to the point, there were simply no significant proceeds from the Ruth deal to divert to Frazee's theatrical enterprises. The payments over time on the purchase price were hardly likely to have a significant effect on Frazee's or the Red Sox's finances, although they doubtless helped to meet expenses. As for the loan of $300,000, it simply allowed Frazee to pay off Lannin's note, as he did by settling Lannin's foreclosure lawsuit in March 1920. Whatever else Ruth's sale meant for Frazee, or the Red Sox, it did not have much impact on the wealth of either.

Nor did Ruth's departure have a negative impact on the Red Sox's fortunes on the playing field—at least not right away. The loss of Ruth did not deter Frazee and Barrow from a serious effort to put the Sox in position to rebound from the second division. Mike McNally was made regular second baseman. A big trade with the Senators brought Eddie

Foster (third base) and Mike Menofsky in exchange for Braggo Roth and Red Shannon. Tim Hendryx was purchased from the Browns to play center field. Joe Bush's arm snapped back and Waite Hoyt earned a place in the starting rotation as the 1920 Sox faced life after Ruth.

The Red Sox started the 1920 season as "the lifetime kings of the American League," with "the greatest record in baseball" over the first two decades of the century,[85] and their early season play offered hope that they were returning to form after 1919's second-division finish. One month into the season, the Red Sox actually led the league, as the Yankees, Ruth's bat notwithstanding, languished in sixth place, five games back. After Memorial Day, however, the Sox began a rapid slide down the standings. On Tuesday, June 29, the Yankees scored three runs in the bottom of the ninth to beat the Sox 6–5 at the Polo Grounds before 18,000 fans, dropping Boston below .500. By July 4, Boston had fallen to fifth place, which is where they finished in September, with the Yankees ending the 1920 season in third place.

After the surprisingly fast start, it was another disappointing year, but it was also true that, in their first post-Ruth season, Frazee's shock treatment had moved the Sox up in the standings from sixth place the previous year. Reports of fan disgust at the Ruth deal are legion, but attendance dropped off only slightly, although due to the expanded schedule (back to 154 games from the wartime 140), the decline per game was greater than the totals themselves would indicate (417,000 to 402,000). Given the great surge in attendance elsewhere—total attendance increased by a third and Yankee attendance had more than doubled—holding the line was nothing to celebrate, but the Fenway attendance figures that year do not reveal a mass revolt in the wake of Ruth's controversial departure. With or without Ruth, it was mainly Boston's continuing ban on Sunday home games that prevented the Sox from fully participating in the postwar boom.

The loss of Ruth was compounded when Ed Barrow left Boston

after the 1920 season to become general manager of the Yankees. Barrow's move filled out the management triumvirate of Ruppert, Huggins, and Barrow that would then carry the Yankees to the top and keep them there. Even without Barrow's services, Frazee was not yet ready to roll over before the emerging Yankee juggernaut. He continued to make sound baseball decisions in preparation for the 1921 season. On December 15, 1920, Frazee traded pitcher Waite Hoyt as well as Mike McNally and Wally Schang to New York. Hoyt, who had never clicked on the mound for Boston, would go on to compile a Hall of Fame career for the Yankees, but at the time, no one could say that Boston had been bested in the exchange. In the deal, Frazee acquired Muddy Ruel to catch (he was seven years younger than Schang), and Del Pratt, the key man in the trade for Boston, who could play an excellent second base, long a problem position for the team. Pratt became the fourth regular second baseman in as many years and batted .324 in 1921, combining with shortstop Everett Scott to form the best double-play combination in the American League.

The 1921 pitching staff featured Sam Jones, at last a big winner, Joe Bush, Herb Pennock, and Elmer Myers, together with an ineffective Allan Russell. Even without Hoyt, pitching was the club's strong point—the Sox gave up the fewest runs in the league. Of course, Ruth was missed at the plate, and the batting failed to back up the pitching effectively. The 1921 Sox won seventy-five games, three more than the previous year, with a slightly higher winning percentage than in Ruth's last season. As the Yankees won their first pennant, Boston could hardly take any solace in another fifth-place finish, but the path to further, if slow, improvement was clear. Frazee's task was to procure a stronger offense to match the team's more-than-adequate pitching.

It was, however, a challenge Frazee did not attempt to meet. In 1921, the patience of Boston's fans had run out. The second fifth-place finish in a row failed to stir any enthusiasm or spur hope for better

times ahead. Attendance fell by 130,000, to under 280,000. It wasn't
just the dull second-division play of a team bereft of stars (the last
hero, Harry Hooper, was now gone), and its inability to compete with
the still-vivid legacy of the team's past glories, that squeezed the
remaining vitality out of the Sox. It was also the entirely unexpected
resurgence of the Boston Braves. That season, the perennially hopeless National Leaguers put together their first winning season since
1916, and attendance at Braves Field doubled. For the first time, the
Braves attracted more fans than the Red Sox, which they had not been
able to do, despite their larger ballpark, even in their miracle season of
1914. The Braves' success did not expand the size of the Boston baseball market but rather reallocated it, at Red Sox expense, at a critical
moment in the fortunes of that Frazee-owned team.

With Barrow now in command of their front office, the Yankees
moved in for the kill. After two years of good-faith efforts to build a
contender in the wake of Ruth's sale, Frazee at last was ready to roll
over and oblige. Although Frazee did not entirely give up on his team
(he made a good trade with Cleveland for first basemen George Burns
and Joe Harris, and with Philadelphia for third baseman Joe Dugan),
after the 1921 season his dealings with the Yankees became so grossly
one-sided that they quickly brought about what the Ruth sale, legend
to the contrary, had not—the definitive destruction of the once-mighty
Boston Red Sox as a competitive ball club. If Frazee was not entirely
the patsy for Ruppert and Barrow that he appears to have become, if
it was not inevitable that the transactions in which he now engaged
would turn out to be so egregiously detrimental to his team, it would
be hard to fault a Red Sox partisan for thinking that "Goldfinger" said
it best: Once is happenstance, twice is coincidence, the third time it's
enemy action.

In the off-season between 1921 and 1922, Frazee traded the core
of his pitching staff to New York. Jones and Bush now joined Hoyt and

Mays in the Yankee rotation, along with shortstop Everett Scott, the last remnant of the 1915 championship team. Boston received a number of young players in return. The most charitable defense for the trade would be that Frazee traded away aging performance for future promise. If so, the gambit failed, and the 1922 Red Sox finished in last place. During that disastrous season, Frazee sent Joe Dugan to New York, and Herb Pennock followed the next winter. The $100,000 he received for Dugan and Pennock could not play third base or pitch the Sox out of a jam. With the Pennock trade in January 1923, the Red Sox transfusions to the Yankee system came to an end, if for no other reason than that Boston had nothing left to give. The destruction of the Red Sox was complete. Boston would finish in last place in eight of the next nine years, and ten of the next twelve. Frazee sold the team after the 1923 season. By then, Boston's Harry Frazee easily looked like the best general manager the *Yankees* ever had.

There was, however, nothing inexorable about the ultimate downfall of the Red Sox in the aftermath of the sale of Ruth. Contrary to legend, Ruth's departure had not provoked an unrelieved wail of dismay in the Hub. At the time, Boston sportswriters and baseball notables were split about the wisdom of Frazee's decision to jettison Ruth, who was seen by many as an overly demanding prima donna, selfishly pursuing his own agenda at the expense of the team. The slugger's critics cited the dismal outcome of the 1919 season to buttress their case.[86] As for the so-called curse of the Bambino, the now-prevalent idea that "for selling Babe Ruth to the Yankees, it was said, the Red Sox had doomed themselves, now and for all time [and that] for their sin, the Red Sox would never again win a World Series"[87] appears to be more of a recent invention than a genuine tradition. It is entirely unmentioned in earlier accounts of the woes that the Red Sox have indeed suffered in subsequent decades.[88] Similarly dubious is the notion that there is a long-standing rivalry between the Yankees and the Red Sox. The sad truth is that, over the ensuing decades, the Red Sox hardly registered on the average Yankee fan's mental radar. The fabled "summer of '49" aside, the two teams' trajectories were too disparate in the half century (and more) after the early 1920s for them to intersect. Any mutual "rivalry" is a very recent concoction.

Nor can final judgment be passed on Harry Frazee's stewardship of the Red Sox without acknowledging that Ruppert and Huston used the same methods that Frazee had earlier employed for the benefit of the Boston team. In the late fall of 1916, Frazee had taken over a team that urgently needed an infusion of new talent to stay competitive. He had won a championship in 1918 by spending freely to acquire talent from his economically weaker rivals, notably Philadelphia. Ruppert and Huston had then turned the tables on Boston, taking advantage in turn of Frazee's own financial distress to assemble their own winning team.

The Yankees' success was built on more than just financial strong-arming of a weaker club with a debt-burdened owner. As still remains true, money alone cannot buy baseball success. The new style of baseball management that the team's owners introduced played an equally crucial role in the rise of the Yankees by assuring the most productive deployment of monetary and personnel resources. Ownership delegated authority to general manager Barrow and field manager Huggins within carefully delimited spheres of responsibility. Ruppert accorded Barrow full control over player procurement. "For the quarter of a century that Ed Barrow sat in the general manager's chair the Yankees were a one man operation," the team's pioneering chronicler, Tom Meany, wrote. Barrow even barred the team's owners from the clubhouse after games, and Ruppert and Huston obliged. The dugout and ballfield were Huggins's turf. Barrow, for his part, stayed out of the clubhouse too, and he boasted that he had never set foot on the playing field until the day of Lou Gehrig's farewell in 1939. Barrow backed up field manager Huggins down the line, whether the challenge to the manager's authority came from Babe Ruth or co-owner Huston.[89]

In unprecedented fashion, team ownership was divorced from active control of (or interference with) baseball operations, a firewall tested when Ruppert broke with Huston in reaction to his partner's persistent second-guessing of Huggins's handling of the team.[90] The team's owners provided the sinews of baseball war, and most generously too, but just as importantly, Ruppert, in particular, imbued the organization with his single-minded pursuit of victory. "There is no charity in baseball," he said. "I want to win the pennant every year, and the bigger the margin of victory, the better." "Close games make me nervous," he once explained. But Ruppert punctiliously stepped away from the actual deployment of the forces his largesse made possible. It was Barrow's job to assemble the troops, and Huggins's to run the show on the field. Ruppert was certainly thrilled by the exploits of his stars, particularly Babe Ruth, but he was always careful to keep his distance. When Ruth visited Ruppert on his deathbed, and the colonel weakly murmured, "Babe," in greeting, it was, Ruth said, "the only time in his life that he ever called me Babe to my face."[91]

The Yankees provided a baseball example of what historian Alfred Chandler has described as "the managerial revolution in American business," in which the "modern business enterprise . . . employs a hierarchy of middle and top salaried managers to monitor and coordinate the work of the units under its control." Much like the great innovative enterprises studied by Chandler—DuPont, General Motors, American Tobacco—albeit on a much smaller scale, the Yankees would prove over time, within their own sphere of activity, "that once a managerial hierarchy had been formed and successfully carried out its function of administrative coordination, the hierarchy itself became a source of permanence, power, and continued growth."[92] Not for nothing would it later be said that "rooting for the Yankees is like rooting for U.S. Steel."

Under the leadership of the two Colonels, the best American League team of the previous era had been humbled—indeed, humiliated—along the Yankees' road to the top of the American League. As the Yankees reeled off three consecutive pennants from 1921 to 1923, only the New York Giants, the sport's leading traditional power, stood between the Yankees and baseball supremacy.

2

THE FALL OF THE GIANTS

WHEN THE Yankees emerged to challenge the New York Giants for baseball's top honors in the early 1920s, more was at stake than just a clash of teams or leagues. Two very different approaches to the conduct of the baseball business and the means of owning, staffing, and operating a big-league ball club were being put to the test as well. The Yankees thrived on an open-handed ownership and innovative management, focused with single-minded intensity on the business of baseball. The Giants were the heirs of more traditional operational habits and practices and were led by a faction-riven ownership group. Internal squabbles and legal problems diverted energy, attention, and funding from the ball club itself. In the two teams' head-to-head confrontation, it was the Giants who gave way, never to recover.

The Yankees' stunning comeback victory in the 1923 World Series signaled an enduring and irrevocable shift in the balance of baseball power—to the advantage of the upstarts from the Bronx and the detriment of the once-dominant Giants. It was nothing less than a revolution, overturning the preexisting baseball order and the Giants' well-entrenched place at the apex of its hierarchy. By the 1920s, the New York Giants had already compiled a long record as New York's premier sporting institution, reaching back to the 1880s. When the National League recognized the American League as a coequal in 1903, and thereby established the still-enduring basic structure of the sport, the Giants considered themselves the ruling power in the world of baseball. The haughty Giants only grudgingly made peace with the upstart circuit and refused to play the new league's pennant winner in 1904—the only time a World Series was canceled until the 1994 strike. In the two decades prior to 1923, the Giants enjoyed a fruitful coexistence with the recently consolidated City of Greater New York. The team provided a symbol of continuity amid an ever-changing metropolis, amassing victories on the playing fields that complemented the city's expanding hold over the nation's economic life and that similarly reinforced New Yorkers' innate sense that their rightful place in the world was on top.

The Giants quickly became the leading power in the National League, winning five pennants before America's entry into World War I and finishing in second place in four other seasons. Fans flocked to the Polo Grounds in record numbers, with the Giants leading baseball in attendance ten times in those years, both before and after the already historic ballpark burned down in April 1911 (it was then expanded and rebuilt). The Giants' attendance totals were all the more impressive considering that New York's blue laws barred Sunday home games—to the obvious financial and competitive advantage of their one serious rival, the Chicago Cubs, who faced no such limitation. The Giants were saluted as "the most spectacular team in the National League . . . whose fame has been sung for years in every household from Father Fan to Jimmie and Johnny and the rest of the male brood as they lugged to their breasts their first baseball bats, while their little sister or sisters were hugging their dolls."[1]

Although the Giants gained prominence and fashioned their identity in the years before World War I, in an era when burly and rough-hewn Germans and Irishmen dominated the playing field and thronged the grandstand, the team also acquired a patina of old-line dignity, linked to the city's increasingly tenuous Anglo-Dutch roots, which would set them apart from the parvenu success of the Yankees or the brawling provincialism of Brooklyn's Dodgers. The Giants *were* New York. By the time the Yankees emerged as challengers, the older team's origins were lost in the mists of time, its name the legacy of a long-gone manager's spontaneous exclamation in 1885—"My big fellows! My giants!" The team's original rallying cry, "We are the people," became a barely remembered echo from major-league baseball's stumbling beginnings.[2] As Harry Golden would recall, "The Giants represented the New York of the brass cuspidor—that old New York which was still a man's world before the advent of the League of Women Voters; the days of swinging doors, of sawdust on the barroom floor, and of rushing the growler," with the advertising placards on the outfield walls of the team's horseshoe-shaped ballpark similarly reflecting the facts of early-twentieth-century city life. "Last year," Golden remembered one sign reading, "Giant left fielder George Burns caught 198 flys, but Ajax Flypaper caught 19 billion, 865 million, etc. flies."[3]

Indeed, the Giants and their Polo Grounds home were so entwined with the lore and texture of the game that baseball's perennial anthem, "Take Me Out to the Ball Game," had been written one day in the spring of 1908 by Jack Norworth, a popular entertainer of the time who was inspired by reading a placard on a subway train advertising, "BASEBALL TODAY—POLO GROUNDS," and who, as the story goes, had never gone to a ball game.[4] Even Giant disasters became embedded in the marrow of the sport's emerging folklore, none more so than their loss of the 1908 National League championship to the Chicago Cubs. In first place in late September, the Giants were deprived of a crucial victory over the Cubs when Fred Merkle was called out for failing to touch second base on a game-winning hit. In what could still be described, more than half a century later, as the "single most debated, most written-about play in baseball history,"[5] Merkle was fated to be remembered ever after as "bonehead

Merkle."[6] In that tumultuous season, the Giants attracted an estimated 910,000 fans, one-fourth of the league's total attendance, setting a record that would stand until 1920.

Such setbacks, however epic, were still the exception during that glorious era, a time when all New York was said to be "baseball mad just now and thousands of wild-eyed fans are rooting for the Giants," as "the biggest crowd that ever sat around a diamond" congregated at the Polo Grounds" to cheer on their heroes.[7] Contributing substantially to the Giants' mystique was the far-from-coincidental fact that their manager—and, after 1919, part-owner—John McGraw was the dominant personality in the game. He was one manager to whom the traditional umpire's adage that managers should be ejected before players because "nobody ever bought a ticket to see a manager" did not apply—not least in McGraw's own mind.[8] "The main idea is to win" was his indomitable credo, and that he did.

Born in upstate New York, McGraw was the son of an immigrant laborer. His short stature (he was but 5 feet 6½ inches) proved no impediment, indeed spurred him on, to stardom with the Baltimore Orioles of the 1890s, compiling a .334 lifetime batting average and gaining a reputation for tough, no-holds-barred play. Taking over as manager of the Orioles in 1899, McGraw immediately impressed his players and his opponents alike with his tactical ability, leadership skills—and umpire baiting. Following a stint playing in St. Louis after Baltimore was bumped from the National League in 1900, McGraw returned to Baltimore as player-manager of the Orioles, reborn as a founding franchise of the new American League in 1901. The next year, he jumped to the New York Giants in midseason and engineered a massive infusion of Baltimore talent into his new club.

Under McGraw, soon dubbed the "Little Napoleon" by his growing band of chroniclers in the New York press corps, the Giants captured the National League pennant in 1904, repeated in 1905, then won four more times in quick succession (1911, 1912, 1913, 1917) before taking on the Yankees in three straight World Series beginning in 1921. In war, the French emperor had famously said, "The sword is always defeated by the spirit," and baseball's "Little Napoleon" agreed with respect to his own sphere of operations, once explaining: "In the first place we won the World Series because we thought we could win."[9] In those decades, no one in baseball was more widely known than the Giants manager. McGraw straddled the realms of Broadway, Wall Street, and Tammany Hall, and no less star-spangled a celebrity than George M. Cohan wrote the foreword for McGraw's memoir, *My Thirty Years in Baseball*, which he published in 1923. That there was a market for the book at all was itself a marker of McGraw's preeminent status in an era when such sports books were rare. "McGraw's circle of friends in this hippodrome atmosphere included the great and the small of the theater, the courts, the political clubs, the prize ring, the racetrack and the underworld, all somehow intertwined on Broadway as the demi-gods of public life."[10] In the hard-drinking, tobacco-chewing, brawling, manly world of baseball, McGraw stood out as its commanding personality. "There were two 'Misters' on the New York scene in the 1920s," columnist Gene Fowler wrote, "men who were always so addressed, Charles F. Murphy, leader of Tammany Hall, and John J. McGraw of the New York Giants."[11]

As the Giants prepared to fend off the Yankees' challenge to their seemingly well-entrenched status, the fact that their management structure faithfully reflected the franchise's immersion in that milieu proved to be a crippling handicap. In contrast to the well-ordered efficiency of the Ruppert–Barrow–Huggins system, the Giants' management exhibited a confusion of realms. Ever since Giant owner John T. Brush died in 1912, his heirs had been trying to sell his controlling interest in the National Exhibition Company, the corporate operator of the Giants. Brush was a career baseball man; his predecessor, Andrew

Freedman, was a politically active businessman with close ties to Tammany Hall. Early in 1919, both of these then-common characteristics of baseball's ownership profile entwined when the Brush Estate finally found a buyer. John McGraw had been trying to put together a syndicate to buy the team for some time, and he had pleaded with Brush's heir, Harry Hempstead, to give him first crack at lining up a purchaser after the estate indicated that it regarded disposing of the club as a matter of urgent interest in the unsettled aftermath of World War I.[12]

In that effort, McGraw tapped into his extensive network of sports-minded politicos and businessmen to put together an ownership slate which would enjoy solid political, as well as financial, backing at that uncertain time for the sport. In his quest to find a money man who could finance the purchase of the team, regarded as far and away the most valuable property in the sport, McGraw first enlisted baseball-loving New York City Magistrate Francis X. McQuade. A native of Manhattan, McQuade had the legal training and Tammany Hall connections that combined to put him on the bench at the age of thirty-three in 1910.[13] Widely viewed as "one of the most enthusiastic baseball fans in town," Magistrate McQuade was a notably loyal Giants fan who demonstrated his passion for the team in a variety of ways, some more savory than others. He regularly accompanied the team to spring training in Texas, "where there is no more familiar figure on Main Street in Marlin, Texas, than this same New York magistrate, garbed not in judicial ermine, but in regulation baseball togs." Nor did his rooting interest stop at the courthouse steps. In 1917, he dismissed criminal charges against McGraw and pitching star Christy Mathewson after they had been arrested for playing a Sunday exhibition game at the Polo Grounds as a benefit for a Europe-bound army regiment.[14] The magistrate was certainly an apt partner for the manager in the enterprise at hand.

Their efforts yielded a potential buyer of the Brush Estate's shares in the person of Charles Stoneham, head of a Wall Street brokerage house. It would never be clear exactly how Stoneham had been brought into the picture, or who could properly claim credit for doing it,[15] but Stoneham was a likely candidate for the role of big-league magnate. A native of Jersey City, he had recently attempted to buy the Newark ball club in the International League and had a wide range of sporting interests. Stoneham's boyhood hero was Silent Mike Tiernan, a Jersey City native who had starred for the Giants in the 1890s. "When my pop bought the club," Charles Stoneham's son and successor, Horace, would remember, "he liked to say that he'd followed Tiernan over to the Giants."[16]

In 1892, sixteen-year-old Charles A. Stoneham of Jersey City had crossed the Hudson River to start his financial career as a board boy in the brokerage house of Haight & Freese. Freese was his uncle, and Stoneham soon became a salesman. Smoothing his way in the Big City, too, were Jersey City political connections, which he parlayed into entree with Thomas F. Foley, boss of Tammany Hall. In 1913, he opened his own brokerage house. Stoneham prospered, and within a few years, Charles A. Stoneham & Co. boasted offices in eleven cities, had its headquarters at 41 Broadway, in the heart of the financial district, and offered the investing public "a private leased wire system reaching the principal curb and exchange markets of the country assuring our customers the best of service."

Yet, appearances to the contrary, Stoneham was hardly a pillar of the financial establishment. Denounced as a "pirate of promotion," he was accused in that free-booting era, before the Securities and Exchange Commission entered the picture, of running a "bucket shop," enticing the gullible with an "offer unparalleled" to "buy an income" through investments that would yield an annual income of one-half the sum invested.[17] In time, Stoneham's background on the shady side of Wall Street would come back to haunt him, and the

Giants, but when McGraw and McQuade came calling in the winter of 1918–19, all that mattered was that he had the means at hand to conclude negotiations with the Brush Estate in short order.

On January 14, 1919, Stoneham purchased the 1,306 shares of National Exhibition Company stock held by Brush's widow and two daughters—52 percent of the shares in the team—and thereby acquired control of the Giants.[18] Stoneham then sold seventy shares each to McGraw and McQuade, for a total of $100,676. Based on that valuation, contemporary estimates of the Brush sale price as exceeding $1 million were not too far off: The $719-per-share price paid by McQuade and McGraw would make Stoneham's payment to the Brush heirs $939,165. In 1903, John Brush had paid Andrew Freedman a reported $100,000 for the interest in the team that Freedman had acquired in 1895 for $40,000. If, in the age of Standard Oil and U.S. Steel, major-league baseball was not really a big business, it had, by 1919, at least become a bigger one.

The shareholders' agreement that accompanied the sales to McQuade and McGraw provided that Stoneham retained the authority to vote those shares until he acquired a majority of the Giants' stock in his own right. The three new owners also agreed, in language that invited litigation down the road, to use their "best efforts to continue each in office and the Board." Thoughts of future discord were naturally enough absent, however, as each man was installed as a team board member and company officer. Stoneham became president, McGraw the vice president while remaining bench manager; McQuade, who remained on *his* magistrate's bench, was team treasurer.

The new owners "were all drinking men, all cursing men, all fighting men," and the "management of the Giants was in the hands of a rough element," McQuade's lawyer would later say,[19] but they struck statesmanlike poses when they presented themselves to the baseball public. "The new owners," Stoneham rather grandly declared, "realize that the New York Baseball Club is something more than a private business enterprise," and that they "take possession with a keen sense of responsibility to the public of this city and of the entire country." "In its playing department," Stoneham declared, "it belongs primarily to its patrons."[20] As the 1919 season approached, it was an open question how the Giants would fare under its new leadership.

JANUARY 1919 was a perilous moment for Stoneham and his associates to assume that self-declared public trust. The future of the baseball business was, if anything, even more uncertain than it had been when Colonels Ruppert and Huston had placed their bet on the Yankees amid organized baseball's war with the Federal League half a decade earlier. The 1918 season had ended abruptly on Labor Day in the face of the Secretary of War's order to "work or fight." Playing baseball counted for neither. A nation at war had turned away from the sport as its prime audience flocked (or was dragged) to the colors, and attendance plummeted, dropping 40 percent from that of the previous year. The owners, who were up in the air about how the sport would fare as the nation demobilized, authorized a shortened 140-game season that first post-Armistice year.

Compounding all the other question marks facing the new owners of the Giants in that first year of peace, an event that made the sport a particularly risky venture unfolded in a venue well beyond the confines of the Polo Grounds—or any other ballpark, for that matter. That spring, the basic structure of the sport in which they had invested stood in the balance before the bar of justice. On March 25, 1919, in a Washington, D.C., courtroom, the trial began in the antitrust lawsuit filed by the disgruntled owners of the Baltimore team in the defunct Federal League. The plaintiffs alleged that the sport's monopolistic practices, notably the "reserve system" for controlling players, had unlawfully excluded them from the baseball business.

Appearing on behalf of organized baseball, the eminent and self-described "Philadelphia lawyer" George Wharton Pepper confidently opened his defense by asserting: "We shall contend that professional baseball is not interstate commerce. . . . We shall satisfy you that Organized Baseball is not a monopoly or an attempt at monopoly."[21] "The atmosphere of the courtroom was unfriendly to my clients," Pepper later wrote,[22] and when the trial ended the next month, uncertainty about the legality of the sport's internal arrangements was replaced by something much, much worse. Judge Stafford ruled that not only was organized baseball engaged in interstate commerce, but also that ". . . the system of organized baseball, constituted in law an attempt to monopolize the business of competitive baseball . . . in violation of the antitrust laws." All that remained for the jurors to do, as he further instructed them, was to determine whether the Baltimore Federal League club had been damaged by such acts and the amount of any such damage suffered.[23]

Given the judge's instructions, it was no surprise that the jury deliberated only briefly before reaching a verdict in favor of the Baltimore club for $80,000, which was then trebled under the terms of the Sherman Act. Headlines proclaimed: "Baseball moguls see dire changes," "Big leagues to separate," and that "Relations would be severed, too, between the majors and minors," if the ruling were upheld on appeal, which, the sport's leaders immediately declared, would be taken all the way to the Supreme Court if necessary.[24] American League President Ban Johnson denounced Baltimore's lawyers for talking like "Lenine and Trotzky." "You would have thought we were on trial in Russia," he told reporters after the verdict came in, announcing that organized baseball "was bound to appeal."[25]

Organized baseball did appeal, so the sport's first great legal tangle with antitrust law did not end with the defeat at trial. The verdict was reversed by the District of Columbia Court of Appeals in December 1920,[26] and that reversal was upheld in 1922 when attorney Pepper, by then a senator from Pennsylvania, staged a decisive rally in the United States Supreme Court, persuading the high court that organized baseball was not engaged in interstate commerce.[27] But at the time, the stinging loss in the trial court in the turbulent first spring of the postwar period, and the threat it posed to baseball's ability to control player expenses and maintain team stability, did nothing to ease any concerns that Stoneham and company may have felt about the respective risks and rewards of their new venture.

As FOR THE Giants' immediate prospects, they had finished the abbreviated 1918 season in second place, well behind the resurgent Cubs, and attendance at the Polo Grounds had fallen by half, averaging about 4,000 fans per game. When they opened the 1919 season for their new owners, half of the regulars on 1917's pennant-winning Giants team were missing, and only one starting pitcher remained in the rotation. Not surprisingly, the team played back to its 1918 (not its 1917) form, ending the season in second place once again, behind the surprising Cincinnati Reds, a first-time pennant winner. In 1920, there was more of the same, as the Giants finished second for the third straight year, this time to the oft-despised Dodgers. The nucleus of a renewed winning team, however, was starting to come together. By 1920, the team featured first baseman George Kelly, infielders Frankie Frisch and Dave Bancroft, outfielder Ross Youngs, and pitchers Art Nehf, Jess Barnes, and Fred Toney. Frisch arrived at the Polo Grounds directly from the Fordham College campus, and the "Fordham Flash" quickly became a McGraw favorite, his aggressive play and "to hell with technique, get the ball" philosophy resonating with the Giants manager.[28] "I have steadfastly tried to get college boys with natural ability on my ball clubs. Usually they arrive quicker and last longer," McGraw wrote, and Frisch fully lived up to those expectations.[29] By the fall of 1921, the Giants were back in the World Series.

The reviving Giants were well positioned to take advantage of the baseball boom, which gathered momentum as the nation returned to "normalcy" after the traumas of war and the tensions of peacemaking. Major-league baseball profit margins exceeded 20 percent in the early 1920s, a level of prosperity that was not matched thereafter, even in the years of record-setting attendance after World War II.[30] Based on contemporaneous internal financial reports submitted to the National League's board of directors by the clubs (the only reasonably reliable financial information available for the era), National League admissions income almost doubled (from $1.85 million to $3.6 million) between 1910 and 1920, with the Giants' own combined home and road ticket income increasing from $300,000 to $750,000 in those two seasons.[31]

The team's progress on the field and at the countinghouse was heartening to the team's ardent followers and new owners, respectively. However, those accomplishments were soon overshadowed by a colossal mistake in judgment in their conduct of the team's business affairs—the Giants' bungled attempt to evict the Yankees from their Polo Grounds home. In the ensuing confrontation, the Giants' "drinking, cursing, fighting men" met their match in the more refined but more disciplined, and indeed ruthless, men who were directing the fortunes of their upstart tenants. The outcome of that misfired initiative was more than simply the construction of the magnificent new Yankee Stadium in the Bronx, just across the Harlem River from the Polo Grounds. It was a sharp and self-inflicted setback to the Giants' traditional claim of supremacy in the world of New York baseball.

The story of how the Yankees came to build their own ballpark is a well-known one, part of the enduring folklore of baseball. "That the stadium came to exist at all," as one recent account goes, "was a result of a jealous fit of pique by one of the most important men in baseball in the early 20th century: John McGraw of the New York Giants. When the Yankees outdrew the Giants at the Polo Grounds in 1920 and 1921, McGraw ordered them out."[32] But a close look at the actual course of events tells a different story.

The Yankees' move to the Bronx had less to do with the slugging of Babe Ruth than with an even more important post–World War I breakthrough on the New York sports scene—the legalization of Sunday baseball. The Giants' fateful decision to evict the Yankees from the Polo Grounds came on May 14, 1920, when Ruth had been wearing Yankee pinstripes for only a month. And the decision was made for one overriding business reason that had nothing at all to do with Ruth. It was to gain control of choice Sunday dates for their own Polo Grounds home games, and not to have to share this newfound bonanza with their suddenly inconvenient tenants.[33]

The path to a new home for the Yankees in the Bronx actually owed more to Giant co-owner Magistrate Francis McQuade than to Babe Ruth. While packaging Stoneham's purchase of a controlling interest in the Giants, and securing a piece of the team for himself, McQuade was also leading the drive to legalize Sunday baseball in New York. As the onset of Prohibition loomed, public sentiment grew more sympathetic to the long-standing campaign to provide working-men with such an alternative form of entertainment. McQuade's role as "the Father of Sunday Baseball in New York" would be his enduring legacy, the lead in his obituary four decades later, long after he had been squeezed out of the Giants' front office and forced off the bench by the Seabury investigation in the 1930s.[34]

Legislation to authorize local governments to permit Sunday professional sporting events, as well as the exhibition of motion pictures, moved swiftly through the New York State legislature in the spring of 1919. In a sharp party split, the New York State Senate approved the bill by a vote of 28–22, with seven Republicans joining a solid bloc of Democrats in the affirmative. One Republican senator who broke ranks urged approval for this clean amusement to benefit the man now denied the solace of the "poor man's club"—the saloon—by the onset of Prohibition. On April 7, 1919, the State Assembly voted 82–60 to approve the bill, and Governor Al Smith signed it into law on April 20.[35]

With momentum building, the New York City Board of Aldermen was expected to exercise its option to authorize Sunday ball games right away, so that Sunday baseball would make its debut as early as the season's first Sunday, April 27, which would give the Yankees the honor of inaugurating the new amusement at the Polo Grounds. But approval was delayed for a week, until the board session of April 28, when Sunday games were authorized by a unanimous vote, provided that they started after two o'clock in the afternoon and that ticket prices would be the same as for weekday contests. Mayor John Hylan signed the ordinance a few days later.[36]

By then, of course, the baseball schedules had been drawn up for the 1919 season, which had just opened on April 23. When the Sunday green light flashed, organized baseball immediately, but diplomatically, welcomed the new opportunity with a rather pious and self-serving promise that no Sunday doubleheaders would be scheduled, to avoid any unseemly intrusion on other Sabbath activity. That said, the three New York teams hurriedly moved previously scheduled Monday games to Sunday, then prepared to play the first Sunday after the ordinance was signed.[37]

The resulting scramble over the allocation of Sunday home games would provide a preview of a continuing theme in the history of baseball. This first organized professional team sport had taken root in a turn-of-the-twentieth-century America in which the frontier had only recently closed, and an industrial, urban society was only beginning to develop. In ensuing years, the sport would struggle to accommodate the evolving social mores and technologies that would continually challenge methods of doing business that had been established in the first decade of the twentieth century, and often even earlier. Sunday baseball would be the first in a continuing line of innovations and challenges—notably radio, night games, television, and population shifts to the south and west and from cities to suburbs—that baseball would have to contend with in ensuing decades. The lack of coordinated planning, and the resulting every-team-for-itself grab for short-term gain, which marked the response to the legalization of Sunday baseball in New York, would characterize the conduct of the sport's business in later years as well.

On May 4, 1919, Sunday baseball came to New York City, with the Giants at the Polo Grounds and the Dodgers at Ebbets Field entertaining a combined total of more than 60,000 fans—the largest regular-season crowds ever to see ball games in both Brooklyn (25,000) and New York (37,000).[38] Fittingly enough, Giants-owning Magistrate McQuade, wearing his two hats, threw out the first ball at the Polo Grounds.[39] "For the first time in the history of the Polo Grounds," World Series contests aside, "the bleachers were filled and tardy fans were turned away," the *New York Tribune* reported. It was not only the size that distinguished the crowd that first Sunday, the *Tribune* took pains to report: "Up to yesterday baseball in greater New York was for the semi-idle, the floating population of New York City. Yesterday those bleachers teemed with life. The men from the docks and the factories came and they brought their wives and children. Those dark green benches held thousands of fans who never in their lives had seen a big league game."[40]

The arrival of Sunday baseball immediately revolutionized the economics of the baseball business in New York. By June, the Giants exceeded their total attendance of the previous year. Large Sunday turnouts continued for the rest of the season. By season's end, more than 700,000 fans had attended Giant games at the Polo Grounds, up from 250,000 in 1918. The Yankees also prospered, with their own Polo Grounds crowds increasing to 619,000—320,000 higher than in 1918. Even the stepchild Brooklyn Dodgers benefited from the newly legalized windfall, as their attendance increased fourfold over 1918's unbelievably low total of 83,000.

This newfound source of wealth quickly generated frustration as well as revenue for the Giants. As the unchallenged rulers of the local baseball scene, the Giants once again outdrew the Yankees in 1919— but by fewer than 100,000 fans, a narrower margin than they had grown accustomed to in a New York baseball world in which the Yanks were interlopers. Indeed, the last-minute changes in the 1919 season schedule to accommodate Sunday games had even placed the Giants at a disadvantage vis-à-vis both of their hometown rivals. While co-owner McQuade was being feted for his leadership in the campaign for Sunday baseball at a testimonial dinner, where he was presented with a diamond ring and the pen used by Governor Smith to sign the legalization law, his Giants were being shortchanged when it came to reaping the fruits of those efforts. The Giants were allotted only ten Sunday games at the Polo Grounds in 1919; the Yankees and Dodgers had twelve each.

The return of the traditional 154-game schedule in 1920—one that could be more carefully worked out in advance of the season—only increased the Giants' annoyance with the Yankees' continued presence at what was, after all, *their* ballpark. Sunday baseball was still banned in Massachusetts and Pennsylvania, so the Boston, Philadelphia, and Pittsburgh clubs desperately needed out-of-state opportunities to play on Sunday. The result was that a windfall number of Sunday home dates potentially existed for the three New York ball clubs in order to accommodate these five nearby teams, which could easily travel to the city for a one-day Sunday appearance, then immediately depart for weekday play elsewhere.

The frenetic travel schedules of the five affected Massachusetts and Pennsylvania clubs were worthy of a Marx Brothers movie. In July 1924, for example, Brooklyn played three games in Boston, then left the Hub along with the Braves to play one game in Ebbets Field. That day, the Giants interrupted a road trip to return to New York for a one-day home "stand" of their own. That same year, the Phillies interrupted an extended home stand to play a Sunday game in Brooklyn, then rushed back to Philadelphia to take on the invading Cardinals. The Giants played three in Boston, then returned to the Polo Grounds to meet the just-arriving Phillies for a Sunday, May 4, game. The two teams then moved on to Baker Bowl, after which the Phillies pushed on to St. Louis for a western trip, that one game in New York the only break in a lengthy home stand. For Pittsburgh, westernmost of the Sabbath observers, Cincinnati was the preferred port of Sunday call, and twice that year the Bucs dashed down the Ohio River to play one game on Sunday and then immediately returned home. And on one occasion, a Pirate return trip from St. Louis to Pittsburgh was routed north to provide for a one-game Sunday stopover in Chicago.

Although the 1920 schedule gave the New York/Brooklyn teams ample opportunity to take advantage of the asymmetrical scheduling provided by the blue-law–bound Massachusetts and Pennsylvania teams, the resulting riches were not shared on equal terms. With the Giants and the Yankees compelled to divide up the Sunday dates at the jointly occupied Polo Grounds, the Dodgers, as sole occupants of Ebbets Field, benefited the most. Brooklyn was scheduled to play at home on nineteen out of the twenty-six Sundays during the season, while the Giants and Yankees would divide those Sunday dates evenly, each playing thirteen Sunday home games. Especially galling to the Giants was the fact that, due to the complexities of the interlocking league schedules and the need for Sunday games at the Polo Grounds for the American League's Sunday-banned Athletics and Red Sox, *all* of the Giants' Sunday games with the Dodgers would be played at Ebbets Field, so that the Polo Grounds could be available for Yankee games with Boston and Philadelphia.

As a result, in 1920 the Giants were slated to play four Sundays against the Dodgers, each time at Ebbets Field. In those four games alone, the Dodgers would attract 83,000 fans, more than 10 percent of their total home attendance for the season, rubbing salt in the wound opened by the Dodgers' enjoyment of seven more Sunday dates than the Giants. In 1921, the same inequity, from the Giants' point of view, would prevail, even compound itself. Not only were all three of 1921's Sunday Dodgers'–Giants meetings to be played at Ebbets Field, but on two of those occasions the Giants and Dodgers would move over to Brooklyn, after playing at the Polo Grounds on Saturday, so that the Polo Grounds could be freed up for the Yankees to host the A's or the Red Sox.

In the new economic dispensation opened up by the legalization of Sunday baseball, an opportunity to schedule additional home games on Sundays was well worth a fight. The Giants' thirteen Sunday dates in 1920 accounted for more than 40 percent of the Giants' total home attendance that season. The lease of the Polo Grounds to the Yankees was no longer an asset that produced both a guaranteed annual rental of about $60,000 and a tangible symbol of the American League's subordinate status. Instead, by compelling a more-or-less-equal division of the lucrative Sunday game dates, the Yankees' lease had become a liability, cutting into the Giants' ability to maximize their share of a rapidly increasing revenue pool. As the start of the 1920 season approached, the Giants might with reason conclude that Magistrate

McQuade had made Sunday baseball a reality, that Stoneham had bought in on McQuade's representations that a sure source of increased revenue was at hand, but that Brooklyn's Charlie Ebbets was skimming the cream, and that their Yankee tenants posed an inconvenient obstacle to their own profit-making ability. One month into the new season, Stoneham, McGraw, and McQuade acted.

The Giant owners made their move on May 14, 1920, before Yankee crowds attracted to the Polo Grounds by Ruth and his teammates had much of a chance to trigger resentment or retaliation. The Yankees, as well as their new star, had gotten off to a slow start. Babe didn't hit his first home run until May 1—provoking a purple-prose effusion in the *Times* about "May Day disturbances," "Soviet uprisings among the Yankee players," and how Ruth "sneaked a bomb into the park . . . and exploded the weapon in the sixth."[41] Although Ruth's slugging was clearly exciting New York's fans, his first month in pinstripes had not yet overturned the local baseball pecking order. Even as the Giants floundered deep in the standings, they outpaced Yankee attendance at their shared home; their Sunday crowds were the biggest of the season, capped by the 33,000 attending their game on May 9.

That week, Stoneham traveled to Pittsburgh, where he joined McGraw and the team. On May 14, 1920, the two owners had a hurried conference and authorized Judge McQuade to issue an announcement from the team offices in Manhattan terminating the Yankee lease as of the end of the season.[42] The economic logic behind the decision was clear. If the Yankees could be forced out, "six or seven additional Sunday games in the [Polo Grounds] would probably net $100,000," as the *Sporting News* calculated, more than offsetting the loss of the Yankees' annual rent payment of about $60,000.[43] "The owners of the local National League club believe," another press account explained, "that the loss of [the Yankee rent] would be offset by the manipulation of schedules of succeeding years so that a greater number of Sunday games could be played in New York City."[44] Especially aggravating to the Giants was the fact that their team was being kept idle while the Yankees were drawing large crowds on Sundays at the Polo Grounds. Sid Mercer, a New York baseball writer with close ties to Giant management, wrote at the time: "The men who operate the National League team want the place to themselves. . . . A week ago the Giants laid off in Blue-Law Boston while the Red Sox appeared at the Polo Grounds, and yesterday they Sundayed in Philadelphia idleness while Walter Johnson entertained a large crowd here. Of course, the Yankees have this idleness problem when the Giants are home, but the Giants own the park."[45]

Although Stoneham had indicated when he had purchased the Giants the previous year that he had ideas about the future of the Polo Grounds, including staging other sporting events (especially boxing), which would preclude the Yankees' continued tenancy,[46] the abrupt announcement, in the middle of the baseball season, caught the Yankees flat-footed. Colonel Ruppert immediately accused the Giants of bad faith. "If we are ordered off the Polo Grounds, it will mean that our National League rivals will go back on their word," the Yankee owner charged. "One of the stipulations" of the Federal League peace settlement in 1916, Ruppert asserted, "was that the New York Nationals should grant us a long-term lease on the Polo Grounds." Although Ruppert acknowledged that this agreement had never been put in writing, and that the Yankees had been occupying the field on a year-to-year basis, Ruppert asserted: "We had a verbal understanding to that effect with Mr. Hempstead, who was then president of the Giants, and it had the approval of the National League."[47]

Whether Ruppert could rally baseball "law" to his side and enforce the unwritten agreement he cited was, however, in doubt; the Giants had timed their move to occur at a moment when the Yankees were particularly vulnerable to being bullied into submission. In that respect, the Giants' initiative again had nothing to do with Babe Ruth's recent appearance in pinstripes. It was engendered instead by an apparent weakness in the Yankees' standing within the councils of baseball, which the Giants hoped to capitalize on. The previous year, Carl Mays's rebellion had laid the foundations of the Frazee–Ruppert entente, which transformed the Yankees' competitive standing. In 1920, having set in motion a chain of events that would encourage the Giants to attack when they did, Carl Mays again played a role in Yankee history far greater than his actual contribution on the playing field.

The Yankee Colonels had responded to American League President Ban Johnson's suspension of Mays, in an effort to thwart the pitcher's transfer to New York, by going to court. The publisher of the *Sporting News*, J. Taylor Spink, later judged that "the result was a feud which for bitterness and intensity exceeded anything heretofore known in baseball."[48] The Yankees sued Johnson, seeking an injunction to bar the league president from suspending Mays. The hometown New York courts enjoined Johnson, leaving Mays free to play for the Yankees, and sharply questioned the legal basis for Johnson's unilateral decision to suspend Mays.[49]

In the court hearings on the Yankees' injunction application, evidence was introduced that Johnson had attempted to rally other team owners behind an alleged effort to force the Yankee owners out of baseball. Emboldened by their injunction against Johnson, the Yankees escalated the legal stakes. In February 1920, they sued Johnson for $500,000 in damages, claiming that Johnson had, in fact, conspired to strip Ruppert and Huston of control over the league's American League franchise. As team owners coalesced into acrimonious pro- and anti-Johnson factions, the junior circuit appeared on the verge of dissolving.[50]

The Giant owners watched the Yankee–Johnson battle closely and then found themselves dragged into the middle of it when the Yankees charged that Johnson had plotted with the Giants to terminate the Yankee lease on the Polo Grounds.[51] Stoneham did acknowledge that he had discussed with Johnson the prospect of separate ballparks for the two teams.[52] Whether or not Johnson had actually instigated the eviction, the Giants could readily have believed that they had a chance to hit the Yankees at a moment when they would not have the support of their own league's top official.

The Giants moved quickly, but not quickly enough. The feuding American League owners met on February 10, 1920, and Johnson and his supporters made their peace with the Yankees. All lawsuits arising from the Mays suspension were dropped, and Johnson's previously untrammeled disciplinary powers were made subject to review by a two-man owners' committee, one of whom would be Ruppert. But it was a truce, not a treaty, and hard feelings remained on both sides. The Yankees were even reported to be contemplating seceding from Johnson's American League and joining an expanded twelve-team National League.[53] Johnson had emerged from the battle as the clear loser. In the wake of his humiliating setback, and the continuing tensions between Johnson and his Yankee antagonists, it was not unreasonable for the Giant owners to believe that Ruppert and Huston would not have Johnson's support in fighting the eviction. The Yankees, lacking a place to play, might have to cave in and, at the least, grant the Giants a better share of the choice Sunday dates.

Stoneham, McGraw, and McQuade, however, had guessed wrong. One week after the eviction notice, McGraw and Stoneham met in Chicago with Gerry Herrmann, former chairman of Baseball's National Commission, and Ban Johnson. Herrmann corroborated Ruppert's version of the arrangement made by the Giants' previous owners with the Yankees for the long-term use of the Polo Grounds. Their recent civil war notwithstanding, Johnson fully backed the Yankees and insisted that the Giants withdraw their peremptory eviction.

The Giants had lost their wager on what Johnson would do if the Yankees were targeted. Although Johnson's wings had been severely clipped by the peace accord in February, his support of the Yankees proved so stalwart that it is unlikely that he had instigated their eviction from the Polo Grounds in a secret understanding with the Giants.[54] It is more probable that the Giant triumvirate acted on its own initiative, emboldened by the breach between the Yankees and Johnson and hoping to hit the Yankees at a weak moment. After all, the Yankees *were* vulnerable. In the immediate aftermath of the eviction, initial bravado to the contrary, the Colonels were, in fact, unable to come up with an alternative to the Polo Grounds on such short notice. Johnson, desperately trying to preserve the viability of what was, after all, still *his* American League, was not ready to abandon his league's crucial outpost in New York just when it was about to pay off.

In the face of the unexpected united front of Ruppert and Johnson, and with the prospect of a breakup of the American League dashed, at least for the moment, by the settlement in February, Stoneham and McGraw backed away from the fight they had initiated. On May 21, Stoneham and McGraw surrendered. From Chicago, Johnson wired Ruppert, who had remained in New York, that, "in conversation with Mr. Stoneham yesterday, he agreed to allow your club to continue at the Polo Grounds. Next Thursday he will be in New York and will then arrange the details with you."[55] The Yankees had held off the Giants' attack and would be able to stay on at the Polo Grounds, pending construction of a ballpark of their own, which they were free to undertake when and how they pleased.

Having realized the impossibility of relocating for the 1921 season, and thankful for the breathing space provided by Johnson's forceful intervention, Ruppert and Huston were determined never again to be at the mercy of the Giants—or, for that matter, of Johnson, with whom they would soon be battling once more. The Colonels promptly accelerated their previously halfhearted efforts to build their own ballpark. With the two leagues at odds over the future governing structure of the game, the American League prepared to protect itself in the event of open hostilities with the senior circuit, which would render joint occupation of the Giants' Polo Grounds impossible. At a special meeting in August 1920, the American League's team owners agreed that the Yankees should acquire their own grounds, but the owners rebuffed the bid by the league's wealthiest team for financial assistance in building a new ballpark.[56]

As Ruppert and Huston cast about for an alternative to the Polo Grounds, the first site they had in mind—that of the Hebrew Orphans' Asylum between Amsterdam Avenue and Hamilton Place and 136th and 138th Streets on Manhattan's Upper West Side, about a mile south of the team's original Hilltop Park home—would cost $1.5 million for the land alone. Well served by mass transit, surface cars along Amsterdam Avenue, the elevated on Ninth and Sixth Avenues with stops at 135th and 140th Streets, and the subway at 137th and Amsterdam, the site was more accessible to midtown Manhattan than the Polo Grounds. Acquisition only awaited, the Yankees thought, the asylum's move to the suburbs, which had been delayed by the war.[57] The Colonels, buoyed by their team's unprecedented success on the field and at the gate in 1920, were not wedded to any particular site. When a deal for the asylum location fell through, the Yankees pushed ahead with relocation plans.

◇

TURN-OF-THE-twentieth-century Giants owner Andrew Freedman's ties to the Democrats' Tammany Hall political machine have been credited with impeding the efforts of the transplanted Baltimore franchise to find a suitable New York ballpark site back in 1902–3,[58] but this time ex–Democratic machine Congressman Ruppert could easily match—indeed, trump—the Giants' political clout. After the 1920 season, acquisition of a site for a new Yankee ballpark proceeded apace. In February 1921, the Yankees announced the purchase of 11.6 acres at the intersection of 161st Street and River Avenue in the Bronx as the site for their new home. Elaborate plans were published for a triple-decked grandstand "which will surpass in capacity any structure heretofore built for the accommodation of lovers of baseball."[59] The proposed site was served by the Sixth Avenue elevated and the Lexington Avenue subway, and the public was assured that "automobilists, too, will find the new park easy of approach by several channels." The press also reported that "an effort will be made by the owners of the team to induce the New York Central railroad authorities to agree to put in a station near the grounds, which are quite near to the tracks of that line"—the one element of the plan that did not fall into place, and which remains on the agenda of current thinking about the future of Yankee Stadium.[60] The Yankees closed on their purchase in May, for a reported price of $600,000, and construction began immediately.[61] The ballpark was completed in time for the opening of the 1923 season. The Bronx Bombers would go on to make their rather grandly named Yankee Stadium the closest thing that baseball would have to a cathedral.

At the time, the Giants' attempt to evict the Yankees struck some observers as quixotic. Commentators noted that the interleague compact on avoiding conflicting dates in two-team cities would likely bar scheduling more Sunday Giants games at the Polo Grounds, even if the Yanks were compelled to relocate. If each enjoyed its own park, the two would both be New York teams, and the "Chicago rules"— under which one team was generally on the road while the other was at home, even though each had its separate ballpark—would likely prevail.[62] However, the Cubs and the White Sox did play on the same days on occasion, and the Giants might reasonably expect that forcing the Yankees into their own grounds would allow the reallocation of some National League Sunday dates from Brooklyn to the Polo Grounds and, at the least, that not all of their Sunday games with the Dodgers would be played at Ebbets Field.

Moreover, in the aftermath of the potentially devastating jury verdict in the Baltimore Federal League case (holding that organized baseball was an illegal monopoly), and the tenuous truce in the American League's civil war, Giant expectations that existing interleague arrangements would collapse were hardly unwarranted, although they would not be fulfilled. The Black Sox scandal, which broke at the end of the 1920 season, compelled the major-league clubs to stifle their internal rivalries and submit to the iron rule of federal Judge Kenesaw Mountain Landis, named the first Commissioner of Baseball in January 1921, in order to regain public confidence. That same winter, the life preserver thrown the sport by the District of Columbia Court of Appeals' reversal of the verdict in the Baltimore Federal League case in December 1920 similarly militated against any imminent breakup of the baseball "monopoly." Taken together, these developments ensured that the preexisting division of home-game dates between Giants and Yankees would continue whether or not the two shared one ballpark. As the Yankees completed construction of their new stadium in early 1923, the Giants made a final effort to win approval to schedule Sunday games at the Polo Grounds when their ex-tenants were playing in the Bronx, but their proposal was rejected.[63] In the end, the Giants had gained no advantage in Sunday scheduling from the Yankees' departure from the Polo Grounds after the 1922 season.[64] Before too long, the struggle over Sunday game dates, which had triggered the Yankees' departure from Manhattan, was all but forgotten.

The always pugnacious John J. McGraw had scoffed at the Yankees' move to the Bronx. "They are going to Goatville," he said, "and before long they will be lost sight of."[65] But the new Yankee home proved a tremendous success from the start. The stadium's Opening Day on April 18, 1923, was a gala affair.[66] Colonels Ruppert and Huston hosted Baseball Commissioner Landis, who blazed the trail that millions would follow in subsequent seasons by taking the IRT subway to the game. New York Governor Al Smith threw out the first ball, and John Philip Sousa conducted the National Anthem. American League President Ban Johnson, whose feud with the Yankees' owners had played a key part in leading the Yankees to the Bronx, pleaded illness and stayed away, but his absence hardly dampened the festivities. The "official" attendance of 74,414 represented blatant puffery by the Yankee front office: The new stadium had a seating capacity of about 60,000, and there were "patches of bald spots in the bleachers."[67] Although it remains part of the stadium's enduring lore, the inflated estimate was questioned at the time and authoritatively debunked decades ago.[68] Even if the crowd numbered "only" 55,000–60,000, it was the largest ever to see a baseball game, and considerably larger than the capacity of the Polo Grounds. Even more impressive crowds quickly materialized, and that fall's World Series found the stadium hosting what was, as Grantland Rice described at the time, "undoubtedly the greatest assemblage that ever saw a ball game."[69]

The Yankees did not disappoint their fans on that first Opening Day at Yankee Stadium, beating Boston, 4–1. Fittingly, the winning runs were tallied on a three-run homer by Babe Ruth. That the opposition for the Yankees' debut in their new home was furnished by the picked-over remnants of the once-mighty Red Sox team, and that Babe Ruth was the game's hero, must have proved especially gratifying to the New York fans and excruciating to Boston's. Rubbing salt into those New England wounds was the presence of Red Sox owner Harry Frazee, as one of the Colonels' honored guests. As Frazee stood at attention while the Yankees' 1922 American League pennant was raised above the great stadium's outfield, the damnation of the Red

Sox owner—probably the *one* thing on which Boston's bitterly divided partisans and antagonists of Sacco and Vanzetti could have agreed—was complete.

As the years passed, and the Yankees irrevocably pulled ahead of the Giants in the battle for pride of place in the New York baseball hierarchy, Ruppert's own verdict on the circumstances that led the Yankees to the Bronx was far closer to the mark than McGraw's errant prophecy. "The Yankee Stadium is a mistake," Ruppert said. "Not mine, but the Giants."[70]

THOUGH THE Giants lost their impetuous gambit to improve their allocation of the choice Sunday dates, the first years of the Stone-ham/McGraw/McQuade era were good ones indeed. Despite that mis-step, the Giants dominated the National League in the early 1920s, winning an unprecedented four straight pennants, the first in 1921. The box office responded in kind. The Giants set a team attendance record of 973,000 in 1921, topping the mark set the previous year by 50,000 and dipping only marginally the next year to 945,000. By 1923, team presi-dent Stoneham, having wound up his brokerage operations and sold off his Havana gambling and racing interests, was poised to devote his full attention to the Giants. As the team threw off a steady stream of profit (averaging $200,000 a year in that period)[71] and declared a four-for-one stock dividend, Stoneham responded to the Yankee Stadium challenge with his own building initiative. The Polo Grounds was fully enclosed with a double-decked grandstand, increasing its seating capacity to 54,555.[72] The resources appeared to be at hand to ensure a successful future for the team, on and off the field.

Even as the Yankees celebrated their 1923 come-from-behind World Series triumph, it was by no means apparent that the Age of McGraw had ended. The next year, the Giants repeated as National

League champs and the Yankees faltered, finishing second to the Washington Senators, the sentimental favorite of every fan who cheered the fact that, after 373 wins and eighteen frustrating seasons, the great Walter Johnson would finally have a chance to pitch in the World Series. In Washington, D.C., on October 4, 1924, Johnson took the mound for the Senators, in the first World Series game played outside the five boroughs of Greater New York since October 12, 1920 (when Cleveland had hosted the Dodgers). Rebounding from their series loss the previous year, the Giants confounded the home fans' yearnings and defeated the Senators (and Johnson) in twelve innings. Four days later, in the series's fifth game, the Giants, this time at the Polo Grounds, beat Johnson again, with a three-run rally in the bottom of the eighth inning, and McGraw's men stood within one game of their third series title in four years. At that moment, the star of New York Giants baseball appeared to shine as brightly as ever.

It proved, though, to be a heartbreaking replay of the 1923 series for the Giants and their fans. The Senators, back on their home grounds, tied the series with a win in the sixth game, and the next day, the Giants team again walked off the diamond as World Series losers. With the Giants leading 3–1 in the eighth inning of the deciding game, a ground ball skipped over the head of rookie third baseman Freddie Lindstrom, scoring two runs to tie the game. In the ninth inning, Walter Johnson was unexpectedly called in from the bullpen and proceeded to pitch four scoreless innings. In the bottom of the twelfth inning, yet another ball hopped over Lindstrom and rolled safely into left field, scoring the series-winning run. It was, Giant veteran Heinie Groh recalled, "Fate, that's all. Fate and a pebble." At long last, Johnson had a World Series victory. McGraw had suffered a second consecutive crushing defeat.

The narrow margin of that 1924 defeat was easily dismissed by Giants partisans as an unfair fluke, but over the succeeding seasons, the Giants fell victim to problems that could not be so easily blamed on an ill-placed pebble. The team, having won an unprecedented four consecutive league pennants, seemed poised for continued success. The only starter over the age of thirty-one was third baseman Heinie Groh, and Lindstrom was more than capable (World Series mishaps notwithstanding) of stepping in if Groh faltered. The pitching staff was the youngest in the league. The 1924 Giants had led the league in hitting, home runs, and runs scored. John McGraw's force of personality certainly had not ebbed. First baseman Bill Terry was, along with Lindstrom, a rising star. Still, appearances deceived, and, the Giants were about to tumble.

The pitching unraveled quickly. Within four years, the team's four top starters would all be traded away, as their combined sixty victories in 1924 dwindled to nineteen only two years later. Future Hall of Fame outfielder Ross Youngs died suddenly in 1927, at the age of twenty-nine. Second baseman and team leader Frankie Frisch was traded for Rogers Hornsby in 1927. Hornsby, although a great hitter, was in turn dispatched after only one difficult season, while Frisch would star for St. Louis's Gashouse Gang for another decade. McGraw, approaching the three-decade mark as a major-league manager, with his roots in an increasingly distant baseball era, was starting to lose his grip on a new generation of players and had begun to tire of the managerial responsibilities he had discharged for so many years.

When McGraw had become a part-owner of the team in 1919, he had expressed a desire eventually to exchange his place in the dugout for one in the front office. Former Giant pitching great Christy Mathewson was hired as McGraw's assistant pitching coach and designated managerial successor.[73] But Mathewson soon succumbed to tuberculosis as a result of being gassed during wartime service in France. He retired to upstate New York to recuperate and died prematurely in 1925. Nor did Rogers Hornsby qualify as a prospective manager. He quarreled with the Giants' owners and swiftly departed from the Polo Grounds, as McGraw continued to direct the team from the dugout, without an obvious replacement at hand.

The Giants finished a badly beaten second in 1925, then fell to fifth place the next season, for their worst finish in ten years. Although they would rebound slightly and finish in the first division once again in the next few years, it was the Yankees who dominated the New York baseball scene for the balance of the decade and beyond. Starting in 1926, the Yanks finished in first place three years running. They would win the World Series in 1927, 1928, and 1932, and they would sweep four straight World Series titles from 1936 to 1939. The Giants of John McGraw would not win another pennant before his retirement midway through the team's sixth-place 1932 season. The Giants would win pennants again—as early as 1933 in fact—but they would never again dominate New York or their league, or the baseball world. At best, they would be very good; at worst, they would be awful. Most of the time, they would just be ordinary. And after 1922, they never again would beat the Yankees.

As the Giants and Yankees swapped places in the record books, their financial ledgers reflected a similar turnabout. Even before the Yanks bade farewell to Coogan's Bluff, they were outdrawing their resentful landlord.[74] The post–World War I baseball boom was good for the Giants, but it was better for the Yankees. The same pattern continued after the Yankees moved to the Bronx. With the exception of 1925, the year of Babe Ruth's great bellyache and the Yankees' only second-division (seventh-place) finish in the *half-century* between 1918 and 1965, their attendance exceeded that of the Giants every year until 1945. (Thereafter, Yankee attendance bested that of the Giants each season until the Giants fled west in 1957.) The excitement generated by the move to Yankee Stadium, and the resulting expansion of the seating capacity of the Polo Grounds notwithstanding, neither team did as well after the Yanks moved out as they had during the last years of their coexistence at the Polo Grounds. Perhaps, however, some of the apparent downturn was due to more accurate counting and stricter enforcement of fire regulations, rather than an actual decline in fan interest. The Yankee team attendance mark of 1,289,000 set in 1920 stood until 1946, and although the Giants never broke the one-million-fan barrier in the great post–World War I boom, their own record attendance of 973,000, set in 1921, was not surpassed until 1945.

Within their respective leagues, the Yankees held their own but the Giants did not. In the early 1920s, the Yanks were responsible for between one-fifth and one-quarter of the total home attendance in the American League, and they maintained that drawing power over the next three decades, with the exception of the dismal years of wartime baseball.[75] The Giants lost the similarly dominant role in National League crowd appeal that they had enjoyed in the early 1920s, a position they had held since the first years of the century. After 1923, the Polo Grounds' proportional share of total National League attendance fell off by 25 to 30 percent, and the Giants found their attendance figures outpaced first by the Cubs and then by the Dodgers.[76]

Numbers bandied about over the years in the sporting press about baseball economics always need to be taken with a (large) grain of salt.[77] The best available figures for team finances in the 1920s and 1930s come from the team financial information reported to the 1951 congressional inquiry into baseball's allegedly monopolistic business practices. Those authorized team accounting statements document the Yankees' economic preeminence, as do the reported attendance figures.[78] In the period 1920–25, the Yankees accumulated total profits of $1,700,000, almost twice those of the Giants. Thereafter, the Giants fell irrevocably behind the Yankees in the war in the counting house, as well as on the diamond.

In one financial category—the amount of dividends paid to shareholders—the Giants outdid the Yankees, but this did not enhance the team's future as a viable competitive entity. The Stoneham/McGraw/McQuade regime eagerly tapped into the income stream generated by its ball club. Between 1920 and 1930, $2 million in team profits funded $1.5 million in dividends, three times the retained earnings that were then plowed back into the club. Even apart from these substantial dividends, the team advanced Stoneham $280,035 in "loans," which were entirely unsecured and apparently were not even memorialized until after the fact.[79]

In contrast to Stoneham's free-and-easy way with his club's finances, Colonel Ruppert's stewardship of the Yankees was far better calculated to ensure long-term success for the team, as opposed to short-term rewards for its owners. In the 1920s, the Yankees recorded profits of more than $3.5 million and paid *no dividends*. The entire sum was available to reinvest in an already dominant club and strengthen it even further for the future.[80] Ruppert played the business and the sport of baseball to win, but he did not rely on his team's earnings as a source of personal income. His Giant rivals, less wealthy to start with, most certainly did. Stoneham made money from his team, but Ruppert built a dynasty. It was emblematic of the differences in ownership objectives and styles that exposed the fatal weakness of the New York Giants in their doomed struggle to remain the kings of the baseball hill. And just when the Yankee challenge gathered full strength, Charles Stoneham's checkered past caught up with him, accelerating the Giants' woes. Even as his team prepared for their World Series showdown with the Yankees in 1923, Stoneham was facing federal criminal charges in connection with the transfer of his customer accounts two years earlier to firms that had quickly fallen into bankruptcy.

The brokerage business from which Stoneham had emerged to buy the Giants had existed in the twilight of legality that characterized the operations of the Consolidated Exchange. The firms of the Consolidated represented the successors to the old-style "bucket shop," which had passed from the scene on the heels of a court decision that its operations constituted illegal gambling. The firms of the Consolidated (including Stoneham's), although still denounced as bucket shops by the crusading press and the established exchanges, developed practices in response to the law to differentiate them from the true bucket shops of the earlier era. Stock would actually be purchased upon order by a customer; then it might be sold immediately under a fictitious name—thus washing the sale—leaving the firm in possession of the margin deposit but without the stock to satisfy a customer's demand for same. The firm would itself have to go into the market to buy stock at a later date should a customer so demand—or make good on the customer's gains out of its resources, offset of course by the interest payments charged on the balances in the customers' margin accounts. Sometimes stock would be bought and held, the margin accounts would be charged interest, and the stock would be "borrowed" by the firms' principals for "short selling" against clients in a manner proscribed even by the lax securities laws of pre–Crash Wall Street.[81]

Whether or not a firm stayed on the right side of the law, however narrowly, while remaining solvent, depended on a falling market. This would allow enough selling out of customer margin accounts, whether real or fictitious, to permit settling up with the few winning customers. It would also allow a successful return on the illegal practice of trading against customer securities. The shadowy ethos of this double-dealing enterprise was not, in fact, far removed from that of Stoneham's new venture, major-league baseball, in which gray rumors of ballplayer gambling and game fixing would mutate into public scandal after the 1919 World Series.[82]

After his purchase of the Giants, Stoneham began to extricate himself from the brokerage business by transferring his customer accounts. In January 1921, Stoneham agreed to transfer all of the stock held in 3,000 Stoneham customer accounts to other brokers. Stoneham sent a letter to his customers advising them of the proposed transfers of accounts and recommending their acceptance: "We have investigated Hughes & Dier who have exhibited their ability to take over your accounts."

However, the account transfers did not go smoothly. Hughes & Dier (as well as its successor, E. D. Dier) was undercapitalized. Stoneham had never requested an audit of Dier, despite his assurances to his customers, and he evidently had ignored increasing evidence of Dier's financial difficulties. By April 1921, Dier was unable to take over some of the securities that had been formally transferred in March. Within a year, the Dier firm collapsed, unable to satisfy more than $4 million in liabilities to customers.

In July 1922, another successor brokerage firm, E. M. Fuller & Co., also failed. In the ensuing bankruptcy court proceedings, investigators probed the relationship, if any, between Stoneham and the Fuller concern after 1921. Stoneham denied having any continuing link to the Fuller firm, but evidence was presented that he paid $147,500, by checks drawn on the National Exhibition Company (the ball club's corporate entity) to the order of his old mentor, Thomas F. Foley, former New York sheriff and a member of the Fuller firm. Stoneham testified that the payment was a loan. A grand jury, however, concluding that the money represented part payment for a one-quarter interest in the firm, indicted Stoneham for perjury on August 31, 1923.[83] This was bad enough, but worse quickly followed. On January 11, 1924, Stoneham was charged with conspiracy to defraud, arising out of the transfer of accounts to E. D. Dier.[84]

The interlocking worlds of politics and fast-talk finance, which had raised Stoneham up, now dragged him down, and the Giants took the fall as well. The team desperately needed an ownership able to concentrate all of its attention and resources on meeting the challenge from the Bronx, but that was precisely what Stoneham could not do. Stoneham had fallen afoul of Tom Foley's bitter foe, newspaper publisher William Randolph Hearst, who thundered in his papers against the bucket-shop operators who failed to execute trades for customers and in effect sold them short by waiting for declines in the market.[85] The financial fallout of his efforts to divest himself of the brokerage operations, which had made possible his purchase of the Giants, had placed Stoneham in the line of fire of the Hearst press crusade against the Tammany Hall chieftains, one of whom—Magistrate McQuade—had, of course, installed Stoneham in the Giants' executive offices in the first place.

When Stoneham's trial started in January 1925, the prosecutors contended that he had run a bucket shop that had failed to execute purchase orders, and that he had fraudulently transferred accounts to E. D. Dier, knowing it lacked the resources to satisfy customers whose stock positions had increased in value, while pocketing a substantial payout based on the dollar value of the $2 million transferred margin accounts.[86] Stoneham had assured his customers that Dier was a trustworthy and financially responsible firm, but witnesses for the government testified that Stoneham had made no investigation of Dier's affairs, and that even a minimal inquiry would have revealed Dier's lack of financial responsibility and bucket-shop modus operandi.

According to the prosecution, Stoneham had for some time been a leading figure in this sort of unscrupulous brokerage enterprise. He allegedly had profited from a long period of declining prices but was ready to unload accounts when he anticipated a rise in prices, and he found in Dier a fellow buccaneer who was ready to make a bet that the market was headed the other way. The judge, for one, was convinced that both Stoneham and Dier had "bucketed orders outrageously," but in that pre–SEC era, he could only urge that the state authorities take action. As to the federal charge, that depended on proof of conspiracy, and the jury in the end accepted Stoneham's defense that he had acted in good faith in transferring accounts to the Dier firm. The Giants owner was acquitted on February 27, 1925.

The acquittal saved the Giants for Stoneham. While the jury deliberated, circus owner John Ringling and Ruppert's former Yankee partner Colonel Huston were preparing a bid to purchase the team, in anticipation of Stoneham's involuntary departure from the baseball scene. Although that possibility was forestalled by his courtroom victory, Stoneham could not turn his undivided attention back to the Polo Grounds. He remained under indictment for perjury, ensnared in the bankruptcy of another successor firm, Fuller & McGee, as an alleged secret partner and co-debtor. According to their own lawyer's later account, "Ed Fuller and Frank McGee . . . were likable roughnecks, lacking in all moral scruples, . . . ready to handle any racket which would bring in 'jack,'" who found sanctuary in gangster Arnold Rothstein's Upper West Side brownstone after their firm collapsed.[87] Stoneham's denial that he was their secret partner had led to the perjury indictment.[88] Although that indictment would be dismissed in 1927 and the bankruptcy proceedings would be settled that same year, former customers of Stoneham's brokerage eventually won restitution in the civil courts for conversion of securities and fraudulent transfer of accounts.[89]

From 1923 to 1927, these criminal and civil proceedings had been Stoneham's most pressing order of business. In the meantime, the Giants had lost the commanding position they had held in the National League, as the balance of power in the senior circuit shifted westward, to Chicago and most especially to St. Louis. Then, just as *these* legal problems were overcome, internal team troubles bubbled over to further divert Stoneham's, and McGraw's, attention from the urgent task of improving the faltering ball club's performance.

From the beginning, Stoneham, in addition to drawing a salary of

$45,000 per year as team president, had used the Giants as a personal piggy bank, without much regard for formalities or concern about separating personal and business affairs. The proliferation of legal proceedings that had engulfed him only increased his recourse to the Giant coffers. In January 1925, he borrowed $125,000 from the team, bypassing team treasurer McQuade. When McQuade confronted the majority owner and demanded documentation and security, an angry Stoneham executed personal notes and pledged about half of his shares in the Giants, valued at $311,183.

McQuade had instigated this showdown at a tense moment—just as Stoneham's criminal trial on the Dier indictment opened. Perhaps McQuade feared the impact on his holdings if Stoneham were to be convicted and then barred from ownership, leaving the team holding the empty bag on his debts. His back to the wall, Stoneham had bowed to McQuade's demands, but in December 1928, after all pending criminal charges against him had been dismissed, he joined forces with McGraw to strike back at the rebellious McQuade. In an apparent effort to keep McQuade in line thereafter, the Giants' board voted to replace McQuade as treasurer with Leo J. Bondy, Stoneham's personal lawyer, when McQuade's term expired in several years' time. When McQuade continued to demand that Stoneham make interest payments on his outstanding loans from the team, McQuade was removed as treasurer at a special meeting of the board of directors in May 1928, and then replaced as a director at the annual shareholders' meeting that November. According to McQuade's later testimony, Stoneham was blunt about the change: "I told you to lay off me, and that is the result."[90]

For a team's owners to fall out was hardly unusual. A few years earlier, the Yankees' Colonels had themselves parted ways over a long-simmering dispute about Miller Huggins's performance as manager.

But Ruppert and Huston handled the dissolution of their partnership quietly and diplomatically. No announcement of the change in command was made until after Colonel Huston had the pleasure of joining Colonel Ruppert in presiding over the opening of Yankee Stadium, although he had been bought out some months earlier. And that fall, Huston cordially toasted his former partner, congratulating Ruppert on the Yankees' first World Championship at a victory celebration in a New York hotel.

Nothing about the discord in the Giants' front office followed this model of discreet conflict resolution. McQuade sued Stoneham for breaching their original agreement and demanded that he be reinstated and awarded any lost salary as damages. The ensuing high-profile legal battle was waged over the next six years, in courtrooms from lower Manhattan to Albany. It ended with no clear victor, and with the team itself as the ultimate loser.

After an initial dismissal of McQuade's case was reversed on appeal[91] in December 1931 Stoneham was once again defending his conduct in a downtown New York courtroom.[92] The trial provided a very public forum for the former partners to air a decade's worth of bad blood. As charges and countercharges flew back and forth, it was clear that there had never been much harmony in the Giants' executive suite. The defense offered a litany of McQuade's alleged misdeeds to justify his removal. Witnesses testified that the magistrate had bad-mouthed Stoneham to minority shareholders, had scalped tickets to Polo Grounds events, had improperly collected a cut of the proceeds from the Dempsey–Firpo fight, and had cursed Stoneham and waved his fists when Stoneham refused to award the concession contract to a friend.

John McGraw, allying himself with Stoneham against the man who had brought the two together a dozen years earlier, offered some of the most pungent testimony—to the delight of the press. The Giants manager and part-owner testified that McQuade had hoped Stoneham would go to jail, saying, "If that guy goes to Atlanta, we will get the ballclub," and had also told McGraw: "If the only way we can get Stoneham's stock is when he is dead, I'm going to put a pill in Stoneham's soup." Somewhat irrelevantly, but undeniably juicily, McGraw testified that the magistrate had punched Mrs. McQuade in the face when she forgot the key to their hotel room during a spring training trip to New Orleans in 1920. "I would say," McGraw summed up, "that when McQuade is in one of his rages, he is not in full possession of his faculties." As Stoneham put it when he took the stand, McQuade was a ranting, cursing, table-thumping partner who "didn't care what anyone else got so long as he got his."

The case made great press and cast an embarrassing spotlight on a sporting enterprise that the three partners had once pledged to conduct as a public trust. But the lurid picture that McGraw and Stoneham painted of McQuade failed to carry the day. The trial judge brushed aside the charges of personal misconduct and ruled that McQuade had been improperly ousted from his position with the club. McQuade was awarded back pay of $10,000 a year since his termination, although his demand to be reinstated to his position with the team was denied. The judge was unwilling, reasonably enough, to saddle the team with such a bitterly divided management.[93]

Stoneham appealed, but the court's appellate division unanimously affirmed the results of the trial, across the board. The majority owner pressed on, and in 1934, New York's highest court handed McQuade a total defeat. The Court of Appeals decision turned on a point of law that did not reflect well on any of the litigants: that McQuade's agreement with his partners that they use their "best efforts" to continue him in office as treasurer was illegal. At the time the agreement was made, McQuade was a city magistrate who was barred by law from serving as an officer of a private business, such as the Giants.[94] "The plaintiff can recover no compensation for loss of opportunity to perform services forbidden by law," the court ruled.

For McQuade, who had resigned from the bench in 1930 just ahead of being removed for misconduct by the celebrated Seabury investigation into corruption among judges and elected officials in New York City, it was a bitter blow, mitigated, however slightly, by a more successful subsequent suit to force the city to pay him a pension.[95] It was an ironic turn of events indeed. McQuade's politically connected judgeship had secured the legalization of Sunday baseball and had brought Stoneham into the Giants' picture in the first place. According to the Court of Appeals, it was precisely that status which barred his claim.

With the McQuade case finally concluded, Charles Stoneham, for the first time in the dozen years since 1922, could follow the action at the Polo Grounds without anxious glances toward the courthouses downtown. It proved, however, too late for him to have much of a chance to turn his full attention to the Giants. Less than two years later, Stoneham died in January 1936. It was too late for McGraw, as well. On June 3, 1932, with the Giants mired in sixth place, McGraw resigned as manager, turning over the team to his first baseman, Bill Terry. And it was, by then, also too late for the Giants themselves. As their front office self-destructed, the once preeminent team never recovered its footing after the fourth successive pennant and near–World Championship in 1924. In a final but fleeting bow to the time when McGraw had dominated the sport, news of the Giants manager's resignation eclipsed coverage of Lou Gehrig's four-home-run game that same afternoon, but this could not disguise the fact that it was Gehrig's Yankees, not the once-mighty New York Giants, who were now the reigning kings of the baseball mountain.

PART TWO

THE RESIDUE OF
DESIGN?

Interlude

NEW YORK TO ST. LOUIS

IN THE FIRST quarter of the twentieth century, the New York Giants had dominated the National League, winning ten pennants. The St. Louis Cardinals, manning baseball's distant western frontier on the Mississippi River, were as far removed from the Giants competitively as they were geographically. The Cardinals compiled the worst win–loss record in the sport over the first two decades of the century, finishing last or next to last in eleven of those twenty seasons. Nick Adams, Ernest Hemingway's fictional alter ego, talking baseball with a friend late in the 1917 season, wondered whether the Cardinals would ever win a pennant in his lifetime. To see a World Series game, it seemed to them, you had to be in New York or Philadelphia.[1]

After 1924, the Giants were shuffled back into the National League pack. In the following decade, the competitive balance of the National League would shift in a radical new direction, as the very unlikely St. Louis Cardinals forced themselves into the top tier of senior circuit teams. In six years, beginning in 1926, the Cardinals won four National League pennants and took the Giants' place as the Yankees' primary antagonist. More important, the Cardinals revolutionized the structure of organized baseball. St. Louis general manager Branch Rickey invented the "farm system," a network of Cardinal-owned or -controlled minor-league teams that created a centrally directed, vertically integrated pipeline of player talent leading to the major-league club. Under Rickey's leadership, the Cardinals not only proved capable of beating the Yankees on the playing field but also were even able to change the way the Yankees conducted their own baseball business. By contesting the Yankees' dominance, despite the disparity in the two teams' financial resources, the Cardinals set a winning example for two recent Yankee rivals, the Arizona Diamondbacks in 2001 and the Anaheim Angels in 2002.

◇

IN A LEAGUE that had been dominated by the free-spending New York Giants, and at a time when that city's even more open-handed Yankees were beginning to consolidate their own more enduring grip on baseball's top honors, the emergence of the Cardinals marked an apparently revolutionary change in the sport's traditional power balance. Previously the second team in the major league's smallest multiteam city, Rickey's Cardinals offered a counterexample to the thesis, as prevalent then as now, that teams in large cities, with their big bankrolls, hold an insurmountable edge over their smaller, less wealthy competitors. In the 1920s, Rickey turned what we would nowadays call a "small-market team" into a leading competitive force, and in the process he invented the farm system. As was so often true in the history of innovations in the baseball business, this fundamental change in baseball's organizational model, and the resulting transformation in the relations between the major leagues and the minors, was not the outcome of baseball-wide planning or decision-making. Rather, it was undertaken on one team's unilateral initiative. Rickey's creation of the farm system—the first

achievement listed on his plaque in the Baseball Hall of Fame—
has long been credited with the rise of the Cardinals to the
sport's top ranks. It was the explanation offered by Rickey, and it
has been accepted ever since, not least by the major-league
teams that quickly followed his lead.

In fact, however, the Cardinals' own rise to baseball's top tier
owed much more to fortuitous events and Rickey's individual
abilities than to his new system, no matter how well designed.
Rickey's innovative methods were not a stark alternative to the
expenditure of money as a means of building a ball club; they
represented instead a different way of spending that money.
Even more pointedly, Rickey built his winning ball club before
the farm system made a significant contribution to his team.
Although Rickey's innovation was widely copied, it was not a
blueprint for parity between small- and large-market teams.
Even the Cardinals actually derived limited returns from the
baseball revolution Rickey engendered. The Cardinal revolution
ran out of steam, leaving the Yankees reigning supreme. The
unique circumstances that allowed Rickey to build a winner in
St. Louis militated against successful imitation elsewhere. And
Rickey's own efforts failed to provide a launching pad for a Cardinal challenge to the Yankees that could sustain itself over time.

3

THE PROBLEM

O N FRIDAY, November 13, 1931, the nation's sports pages carried a small story all but lost amid the reports on the next day's big football games—Wisconsin against Ohio State, Notre Dame versus Navy, NYU against Fordham (a game that would attract 78,000 fans to Yankee Stadium), among them—steeplechase racing at Pimlico, and the opening of the National Hockey League season in Toronto's new Maple Leaf Gardens. "Newark Club Is Acquired by Ruppert, Owner of Yankees," the *New York Times* recorded. "Chain store baseball, frowned upon by Commissioner Landis, ever since its inception but nevertheless exploited with signal success by the St. Louis Cardinals, was believed to have enlisted another powerful ally yesterday with the announcement that New York Yankee owner Jacob Ruppert had purchased the Newark club of the International League." It was the Yanks' first acquisition of a minor-league team. "Baseball men," the *Times* continued, "regarded it as the beginning of a course that sooner or later must be accepted by all major league teams in view of the pronounced success of the world's champion Cardinals."[1]

One month earlier, the Cardinals had stormed out of baseball's west to win the World Series. Not only had no National League team been able to do that since the Cardinals themselves in 1926, but they had beaten one of baseball's all-time greatest teams, the Philadelphia A's of Simmons, Cochrane, Foxx, and Grove, who were gunning for a third straight world title. Not only a great triumph for the team and its league, it was immediately hailed as a victory for an entirely new system for producing winning ball clubs.

That system was conveniently encapsulated by the story of the Cardinal player who all but won the World Series single-handedly: twenty-seven-year-old rookie outfielder Pepper (for "pepper pot") Martin. Batting .500 and stealing five bases, Martin, who had only broken into the Cardinal starting lineup in June, thoroughly dominated the series, with fearless base running that demoralized the heavily favored Philadelphians. No less a figure than Baseball Commissioner Kenesaw Landis saluted Martin after Game 7, saying, "I'd rather trade places with you than any other man in the country."[2]

Martin, "the Wild Horse of the Osage," hailed from the poor scrub plains of Oklahoma, part of the Southwest hinterland that produced a steady stream of talent for St. Louis over the years. That spring, he had presented himself at the Cardinal camp in Bradenton, Florida, arriving a tattered mess after riding the rails from home (he was almost tossed out of the sedate team hotel before he identified himself). Not that Martin's appearance in the Cardinal lineup was a fluke: It followed a lengthy apprenticeship in the interlocking network of minor-league teams that Cardinal executive Branch Rickey had assembled—a baseball odyssey that carried Martin from raw recruit to World Series star, rung by rung up the baseball ladder, from Greenville to Fort Smith to Rochester to Houston and finally to St. Louis.[3]

The Cardinals, in winning a World Series and besting the handcrafted A's—patiently assembled by Connie Mack with his time-tested technique of "cherry picking" top prospects from independent minor-league teams and trading for the rest—appeared to be teaching its rivals a lesson in baseball management. The example provided by the 1931 Cardinals in large and Pepper Martin in particular immediately led baseball's St. Louis–based bible, the *Sporting News*, to prophesy:

"If the Eastern clubs do not watch . . . St. Louis with both eyes well opened, they may be forced back into even greater obscurity."[4] That the Yankees, mightiest of the "eastern clubs," had acquired a farm club of their own ratified an emerging baseball-wide consensus that *the* key to that half decade of Cardinal success was the farm system that Branch Rickey had been assembling in the decade since his return to the Cardinal front office after service in World War I.

By 1928, the Cardinals had created a network of five wholly owned farm clubs, with two more on deck. No other major-league club had followed suit. Six (including the Yankees and the Giants) owned no minor-league teams at all, and five had but one each. None of the others owned more than two. Only the Cards boasted a fully functioning farm system.[5] (By 1940, Rickey's system would encompass thirty-three teams and 600 players.)[6] Although criticized repeatedly as Rickey's "chain gang" by Commissioner Landis and others, the new system inspired more emulation than denunciation. When the Cardinals won the 1928 pennant, their second in three years, the *Sporting News* paid tribute to "a baseball organization that operates almost nation-wide, through its subsidiary clubs" and to the "man who can not only run one ball club and make it a winner, but who through his ability, vision and energy can make a string of them go—Branch Wesley Rickey." "No man in baseball in the last quarter century, with the possible exception of Judge Landis and Babe Ruth," sportswriter and pioneering baseball historian Fred Lieb wrote in 1944, "has left so deep an impress on the game as Branch Rickey," who had "devised a method whereby the poorer clubs could cope on equal terms with the more opulent ones."[7]

Baseball men, by their rush to adopt Rickey's methods, voted with their checkbooks that the farm system was the key to the unlikely rise of the Cardinals to the top of the big-league heap, and posterity has agreed. A team that had compiled the lowest cumulative winning per-

centage in the National League over the first two decades of the twentieth century, and had been the "second" team in baseball's weakest
two-team city, had won pennant after pennant and beaten the very
best the American League could field against them—the Yankees'
Murderers' Row and Connie Mack's last great Philadelphia team—in
World Series play.

But the roots of Cardinal success did not, in fact, lie in the organization's farm system. The great 1931 World Series win actually marked
an ebbing of the St. Louis tide, the ending of an era for the Cardinals
as well as the A's. After 1931, the Cards fell off the pace, with only one
more peacetime pennant (in 1934) until 1946, and thereafter no additional pennant until 1964. Rickey's 1931 Cardinals had more in common with their Philadelphia opponents than is generally recognized,
and they reflected the genius of the scientist, not the science. The rise,
and decline, of the Cardinals demonstrated that the man, and not the
"system," was responsible for St. Louis's very improbable baseball success story. Inspired by the lessons apparently taught by Rickey, other
teams built their own farm systems. Indeed, the ensuing depression
era made major-league financial support for economically struggling
minor-league teams imperative, but Rickey's unique talents could not
be so easily duplicated. Yet there was no better example of the limited
contribution that a farm system could make to the success of a major-
league team than that provided by Branch Rickey and the St. Louis
Cardinals.

◇

IN THE WINTER of 1918–19, Major Branch Rickey, late of the U.S.
Army's Chemical Warfare Service, returned to baseball's western front
from Europe's, resuming his peacetime duties as president of the Cardinals and taking up the job of field manager besides.[8] Redbird
prospects could not have looked less encouraging. The team was com-

ing off a last-place finish in the abbreviated 1918 season, which had ended on Labor Day. Not too many fans had actually witnessed the Cardinals' ineptitude: Attendance had barely exceeded 100,000 for the entire season. The franchise was broke, having been haphazardly funded by short-term loans guaranteed by the team directors. Years later, Rickey remembered what awaited him upon his return to the Cardinals: "The St. Louis club went a second year with the same uniforms. . . . I went without my salary to meet a payroll. . . . My wife objected to the use of the family rugs in my office. . . . I am not proud of some of these things that had been done in that day."9

The team's performance in the 1919 season was entirely consistent with its tradition of impecunious ineptitude. In that abbreviated 140-game postwar campaign, the Cardinals won only fifty-four games and finished seventh, 40½ games behind pennant-winning Cincinnati. Total season attendance was 167,000, the lowest in big-league baseball, whose overall attendance had doubled over the previous season. The crosstown Browns of the American League were thriving by comparison, with a fifth-place finish and almost 200,000 more fans in attendance. Branch Rickey's Cardinals were the second team in a two-team city that could realistically support only one big-league team.

The Mound City proudly claimed to be one of only five cities represented in both major leagues, a distinction it retained until the Browns left for Baltimore in 1954, but its status as a two-team city was always precarious. The shift of the American League's Milwaukee franchise to St. Louis before the start of the new circuit's second season in 1902 had brought a quick lift at the gate and provided a convenient, centrally located western (as it then was) forum for the Sunday games that were barred in the big eastern cities. Although this two-team status came just in time for the 1904 World's Fair and ratified St. Louis's standing as the nation's fourth largest city (it had moved up from fifth place in 1890 by dint of Brooklyn's absorption into New York in 1898), St. Louis was already beginning to slip out of the top tier of American cities.

Population growth was slowing, as the new immigrants who crowded into Chicago and the other metropolises of the Northeast and Upper Midwest largely passed by St. Louis. The city's boundaries were confined within cramped limits that had been fixed in the decade after the Civil War and would never be expanded to capture any suburban growth. The city's traditional industries were beginning a long decline; the new automobile-production–driven economy centered on the Great Lakes would push Cleveland and Detroit past St. Louis in population by 1920. The proud turn-of-the-twentieth-century dreams of the Mound City's "One Million Population" club would remain frustratingly elusive, as the city fell toward the bottom of the rankings of the nation's ten most populous cities.[10]

From the start, St. Louis was by far the smallest multiteam venue in the major leagues. Its two teams shared a metropolitan-area population of 828,000 in 1910, not much more than one half of Boston's. Over the years, that disparity grew. By 1920, St Louis's population had fallen even farther behind that of the other four two-team cities,[11] and St. Louis's weakness as a two-team city became more and more evident as the years passed. The predictable result was that average attendance for the Browns between 1910 and 1920 was second worst in the American League (only ahead of the Senators), and the same was true for the Cardinals (only the Braves fared worse).[12] The problem persisted in the ensuing decades, as each team's attendance, relative to performance, would consistently be the worst in its respective league.[13]

As early as 1918, the Cardinals were reportedly planning to move across the state to Kansas City, as the major leagues had concluded that two teams in St. Louis were at least one too many.[14] Those doubts never disappeared. Thirty years later, the Cardinals' then-owner again

said that one of its teams would have to move, and the Browns' management had seriously, if not very practically, considered fleeing to the
West Coast in 1941.[15] The St. Louis teams were tapping into the smallest population numbers to be found within 100 miles of any major-
league ballpark, smaller even than what was available to the teams
(Washington, Cleveland, Cincinnati) located in smaller metropolitan
areas (as defined by the census bureau), and those were one-team
cities, in any event.[16] On a per-team basis, the Cardinals and Browns
of the late 1940s enjoyed the smallest potential fan base in the major
leagues.

In St. Louis, the total baseball audience tended to be inelastic, a
stable figure that, in view of the noncompetitive finishes regularly produced by the local clubs, did not expand or contract much. It was just
divided up differently, depending upon the respective showings of the
local teams.[17] Sunday baseball had been legal for decades (a major reason that the American League had mounted its invasion of the territory back in 1902), and no quick fix was available to increase paying
audiences. Bereft of the natural rivalries that might swell otherwise
soft gates—such as when the Brooklyn and New York teams or the
Boston and New York squads or the Pennsylvania teams met on the
field—the Cards had only one possible way to set turnstiles spinning—
by winning—and then only at the expense of the Browns, their American League rivals for the St. Louis baseball dollar (or quarter).

Operating a ball club in St. Louis involved a harsh competitive
struggle to gain the larger share of a finite pie, as Branch Rickey well
knew when he returned to the baseball wars in 1919. The manager's
perch in the Cardinal dugout was only the latest stopping point in the
thirty-eight-year-old Rickey's baseball travels, which included experience with the crosstown Browns as player, manager, and executive.
Beginning his professional career as a catcher in Lamar, Wyoming, in
1903, Rickey moved up to Dallas in the Texas League in July and

ended the season on the roster of the Cincinnati Reds, but he didn't see big-league action. Demoted to Dallas after he refused to play on Sundays, Rickey was acquired by the Chicago White Sox late in the 1904 season, before they quickly traded him to the St. Louis Browns. His third big-league team was the charm, and Rickey made his first appearance on a major-league diamond catching one game for the Browns in 1905.

In 1906, Rickey appeared in sixty-four games, mostly catching but also playing the outfield and pinch-hitting, batting .284 for the fifth-place Browns. The next season he was traded again, this time to the New York Highlanders. Demonstrating that his solid play the previous year was a fluke, Rickey had a batting average below .200 for the fifth-place New Yorkers and some of the worst catching ever recorded—he allowed thirteen stolen bases in one game against Washington, an American League record, en route to an incredibly bad fielding average of .911. Not surprisingly, his baseball address the next season was the University of Michigan, where he coached and enrolled in law school, earning his degree in 1911.

Two years later, Rickey was out of baseball, practicing law in Boise, Idaho, when St. Louis Browns owner Colonel Robert Hedges asked him to scout the Pacific Coast for the Browns. By 1914, he was working full time for Hedges as the club's secretary and field manager. That year, Rickey managed the club to a fifth-place finish (going hitless in two pinch-hitting appearances, which marked the end of his undistinguished career as a player) and sixth the next—both modest improvements over the previous half decade, in which the Browns were consistently in or near the American League cellar.

When the 1916 season rolled around, the Browns appeared to have survived the Federal League war in relatively good shape on the field, but the losses on the business side were severe. Attendance dropped to 150,000 in 1915, the lowest ever, more than 100,000 below

1914's already anemic total. Help, however, was soon at hand. In December 1915, a 90 percent interest in the Browns was sold to Philip de Catsby Ball for a reputed $525,000. Ball had owned the St. Louis Federal League team (the noneuphonious Sloufeds); his acquisition of the Browns was part of the peace treaty that ended the Federal League war.[18] Before he sold the club, Hedges had signed Rickey as his assistant. Ball first stated that Rickey would not be retained, arguing that Rickey's contract with Hedges was not binding on the new ownership. In the end, Ball decided to discharge Rickey as field manager and keep him on in the front office with control over player personnel decisions.

With a leg up provided by the dissolution of the St. Louis Federal League club and the assignment of its player contracts to the Browns, de facto general manager Rickey had sixty-two players from which to assemble a squad for the 1916 campaign. Evidently he chose well, and, in 1916, as baseball stumbled back into its conventional orbits after the Federal League challenge, the Browns finished fifth, a respectable twelve games off the pace, the second best finish in the team's history. More to the point in the zero-sum game for baseball success in St. Louis, the Browns more than doubled their attendance to 335,000— their best total ever and 110,000 higher than the Cardinals, who tied for last place in the National League, 33½ games behind the pennant-winning Cubs.

In February 1917, the Browns gathered for spring training in St. Petersburg, Florida. Rickey was ready to build on the foundation for success that had been laid the previous year, subjecting the team once again to his innovative training routines. After a mile-and-a-half walk from hotel to ballpark, along a rough, sand-strewn road, the Browns were driven to exhaustion by the rigorous schedule of running and sliding drills and batting practice. The pitchers worked with a unique Rickey innovation, "pitching strings" outlining a three-dimensional strike zone, in order to hone their skills at nicking the corners of the plate. Afterward came the long walk back to the hotel. Although Rickey did not impose a curfew, the exhausted players retired early, as he confidently expected. Breakfast was served at 8:30 the next morning, after which the team's daily training routine would begin again.

Before Rickey had a chance to see whether or not these practice methods would pay regular-season dividends in the performance of his Brown players, his own career path took an unanticipated turn. James C. Jones, the attorney for St Louis's *other* team, the Cardinals, which was struggling for survival in the wake of the Federal League war and the resurgence of the Browns, approached Rickey that spring with a proposal that he switch sides in St. Louis's intramural baseball competition.

The Cardinals had been owned since 1911 by Mrs. Schuyler Britton. "A woman has no business in baseball," National League owners had said when Cardinal owner Stanley Robison had died (inconsiderately, as far as they were concerned), leaving control of the team to Mrs. Britton, his niece. Although Mrs. Britton exerted her influence through the mediating presence of her husband, who represented the Cardinals at league business meetings, owner pressure to force her out of the game had continued unabated.

When the Federal League war ended in the winter of 1915, one of the clauses of the peace treaty provided that the owners of the St. Louis Federal League franchise would be entitled to purchase one of the existing St. Louis franchises. National League owners seized the opportunity to force out Mrs. Britton, telling her that "it would be good for the game for her to get out of baseball." The owners had misjudged their woman. Although she had decided to dispose of her baseball holdings, Mrs. Britton resolved not to yield to such naked chauvinism, so she refused at the time to bow to her resentful peers' pressure tactics.

Two years later, however, attorney Jones came calling on Rickey to tell him that Mrs. Britton, tired of the continued drain on her resources that the Cardinals presented, was ready to sell the team. According to Jones, the Cardinals might well be sold to out-of-town interests: Rickey and Jones and, indeed, every baseball fan in and outside St. Louis, knew that a year earlier, the Baltimore Federal League ownership had offered to buy the Cardinal franchise and move it to Baltimore as their share of the peace accord. Rebuffed, they had turned to the courts for redress. In the first months of 1917, their antitrust action against organized baseball was working its way through the calendar of the U.S. District Court in Philadelphia, headed toward an apparently imminent trial.[19] Although the Cardinals had been saved from the Feds earlier, the National League team might still be lost to St. Louis—unless Rickey was willing to step in and provide baseball savvy credibility for a new local ownership.

True, Mrs. Britton was asking $350,000, which, as far as Rickey knew, greatly exceeded any previous offers. But, Jones told Rickey, a group of local businessmen working with Mrs. Britton's personal attorney had secured a purchase option open until March 3. They intended to finance the purchase by a public offering of stock in the Browns. To seal the deal, Jones said, they needed Rickey to agree to become president of the recapitalized club.

Rickey, after securing what he believed to be Ball's green light (including, in Rickey's later account, Ball's promise to provide tactical assistance "to help you on that contract"), signed on with the new Cardinal ownership at a salary of $15,000 per year and a promise of full operating authority. Rickey also purchased 200 shares of the 7,000-share stock offering, which, at $25 per share, raised $175,000. On May 2, 1917, the St. Louis National League Baseball Club was incorporated, and Mrs. Britton received $175,000—half of the total purchase price, with the outstanding balance carried as a liability of the new corporation.[20]

Rickey's entry into the Cardinal front office proved to be not as smooth as he had expected. Ball turned around and tried to block Rickey's move, apparently as a result of some intense lobbying from American League President Ban Johnson.[21] Rickey would come to believe that Johnson ordered Ball to keep Rickey in the American League, lest his unique talents provide critical ballast to National League prospects in the baseball war that Johnson anticipated.

Whatever the accuracy of Rickey's rather self-flattering explanation of Ball's—and Johnson's—motivation, the Browns went to court and tried to obtain an injunction against Rickey's switch, but without success. Rickey was unappeased by his legal victory, still furious that Ball had broken his word by denying that he had ever consented to Rickey's negotiations with the Cardinals. Forty years later, Rickey would recall what he regarded as Ball's reneging in characteristically melodramatic fashion: "I wish I had gone out of baseball at that moment. I was overwhelmed by mortification and shame at hearing a man of big business and responsibility feel obliged to say such a thing. . . . I didn't speak to Mr. Ball for many years."[22] And so, in 1917, Rickey took the Cardinal helm, the team's fortunes in his hands, although any glimpse of the shape of the Cardinals' baseball under his tutelage would be deferred by the outbreak of war, the curtailment of the baseball season in 1918, and Rickey's own departure for military service. Not until the spring of 1919 would Rickey get his chance to turn things around for his new team.

At the time, Rickey's move from the Browns to the Cardinals looked like a risky leap from the promising to the hopeless, all the more so since Rickey was putting his own savings on the line, or at least that of his parents, who mortgaged their Ohio farm to bankroll

Rickey's Cardinal stock purchase.[23] As the 1917 season opened, the Browns appeared to have the financial firepower and newly won fan support to hold the upper hand in the battle for local baseball dollars.

The Cardinals, trailing the rejuvenated Browns both on and off the field, their very future in St. Louis at risk, had turned to Rickey in desperation. The team had had only two first-division finishes (a third and a fourth) since the turn of the century. Home attendance was consistently dismal, well below 300,000 every year since 1912. This was generally lower than anywhere else in the league, apart from Boston. But Boston's weak National League team had to compete against the mighty Red Sox for local support; the Cardinals had failed to take the measure of the mediocre Browns. And Boston's "Miracle Braves" had just won the 1914 pennant, pushing past the Cardinals at the box office as well as in the standings. Nor was the enthusiasm the Redbirds failed to generate at home offset by the appearance of fans in the rest of the circuit anxious to see the Cardinals perform. In the one year for which roughly accurate road attendance figures can be computed (1910), the Cards trailed the field.[24] When Rickey took over, the Cardinals were probably the least financially successful team in major-league baseball.

To make the task of running the Cardinals even more daunting, there was an additional, and ineluctable, obstacle that the heavens themselves placed in the way of building a better baseball club in St. Louis—the weather. It was said that St. Louis teams had to be several notches better than the opposition if they hoped to contend for a pennant, otherwise they would not be able to withstand the wilting, humid St. Louis summer heat over a seventy-seven-game home campaign— every game played, of course, under the merciless sun. Players who, as thankful visitors, had come off the Robison Field or Sportsman's Park grounds already looking forward with expressions of deliverance to their next stop on the circuit—wherever it was—dreaded the prospect of putting on Cardinal or Brown home whites. Chick Gandil, on the

Washington trading block after 1915, openly declared that he would not go to his rumored destination in St. Louis. It was another obstacle with which Rickey had to contend, and a particularly frustrating one because it was immutable, as he turned his attention back to baseball upon his return from France in December 1918 and made his plans for the 1919 season and beyond.

◇

WHEN RICKEY celebrated his return from the war by taking on the role of Cardinal field manager in addition to his front office duties, he promptly confirmed Phil Ball's doubts about his skills in that capacity. The 1919 Cardinals won just fifty-four games, only three more than the previous year, and twenty-eight games fewer than the eighty-two won in 1917. The team finished in seventh place, 40½ games behind the league champion Cincinnati Reds.

"It is not a joy continuously to experience the emotions of defeat," Rickey remembered. "I did not like it. . . .What can I do about it?" Rickey later said he had asked himself, "I have no money. We owe $175,000. We have a reserve list of 23 players. How can I get more players?"[25] Rickey's response was the development of a new model for a baseball organization. Accepting the harsh fact that a team in St. Louis—what we would now call a "small-market" team—was at a competitive disadvantage with those in larger markets, especially New York, where higher attendance would generate greater revenues that could be applied to the purchase of top minor-league talent, already fully trained from the highest classification clubs in the minors. To circumvent the power of the big spenders, Rickey set out to implement a new method of player procurement based on Cardinal control of talent, from sandlots to the majors.

Rickey later said that he "was a comparatively young fellow . . . at the inception of the farm system in St. Louis in a day when it was customary for three or four clubs to divide the honors of pennant winning from year to year. Those clubs were regarded as wealthy clubs, as distinct from, let's say, three or four poorer clubs." And "some of those poorer clubs, one notably the St. Louis Club, were at the bottom. . . .They were the door-mat for the successful clubs, economically and artistically on the field, to step upon to enter into high-favored competition."[26]

Running a team like the Cardinals, Rickey explained, had always been a self-destructive enterprise: "In order to stay solvent, those clubs were compelled to sell their players wherever they could for the most money in order to pay administrative salaries and players' salaries and keep its franchise and operate." In Rickey's later appraisal of the Cardinal predicament, relayed through a sympathetic reporter, the Cardinals had been ensnared in an iron cycle of failure, "because the team was inept few people cared to pay to see it play; because few people cared to see it play, there was not enough money to acquire players who would make it less inept."[27] As Rickey explained:

> *It was felt at that time that these so-called richer clubs were some-what sympathetic with the annual position of these poorer clubs and sympathetic with their need of funds, conscious, of course, that they needed an eighth club to complete the circuit in the league, and you were able, perhaps, to get without too much negotiating a satisfactory price for your players; and the result is, the record and the history will show, that during those years . . . they have to sell their good players to continue solvent, and they forfeit their artistic work; they forfeit a good team standing, and stay perennially in the second division.*[28]

Rickey's objective was to establish a secure pipeline for developing talent, with the Cardinals directing the entire course of a player's career by means of ownership and operation of a series of minor-league teams. The process by which these players, as well as the reserves who subbed for them, reached the major leagues would be based on a few fundamental principles. First, use your scouts to beat the bushes, especially Charlie Barrett, the "king of the weeds." Second, hold open tryout camps for eager talent seeking a chance to make the big leagues, boys whose attitude was readily familiar to Rickey and Barrett, "because we had tried so hard as kids in Texas. We had gone hungry to play. We had slept with the pungent leather glove under the pillow, awakened at dawn and walked the miles. And all we asked was a chance. . . ."[29] Third, exploit Rickey's contacts in the college ranks to generate additional tips on talent. These methods would allow the Cardinals to tap into a great reservoir of young, unproved talent. Within a few years, the team would be looking at 4,000 prospects a year.

In 1919, Branch Rickey began putting his new system in place. As Rickey remembered it, "For a pittance, I forget the price, I bought half of the stock or ownership in a little Class D [actually Class C] club in Arkansas. . . . And then came Houston and then came Syracuse. And it all paid off. The farm system is the only vehicle that a poor club has available to it to use to mount into respectability competitively," Rickey proclaimed.[30]

Rickey's plan involved nothing less than a revolution in the structure of organized baseball, and it posed a fundamental challenge to the sport's established order. Rickey's business model was logical and elegant, but it confronted two not-inconsiderable obstacles to its implementation. Like any enterprise (or, indeed, economy) seeking to take off into self-sustaining growth, it required both a favorable institutional setting and a stock of sufficient start-up capital. However, Rickey's vision involved a direct assault on the existing laws of organized baseball and required initial expenditures that the threadbare coffers of the Cardinals did not have. The realization of Rickey's plan would require a considerable amount of luck.

◇

THE LEGAL OBSTACLES facing Rickey were the product of two decades of ongoing responses by the sport's governing councils to the untiring efforts by major-league teams to build an inventory of playing talent in excess of the numbers that could be carried on their rosters at any one time, talent that was not yet ready for big-league competition. Tension inevitably arose between the formal rules, on the one hand, and the "primary and basic purpose in the efforts of all clubs in regard to almost everything they have done to get a great team," as Rickey later put it, on the other.[31] When Rickey took over operation of the Cardinals, the supreme maker and enforcer of the sport's laws was the National Commission, which regulated the world of organized baseball under the terms of the accord that had resolved the National League–American League war in 1903, and the subsequent National Agreement entered into between the major and the minor leagues.[32] The commission's permanent members were the presidents of the two major leagues and a mutually selected chairman.

Under the National Agreement, the minor leagues, which were grouped together in the National Association of Professional Baseball Clubs, submitted to the authority of the National Commission and joined with the major leagues in accepting a set of rules governing player personnel transactions. The most important of these rules was the institution of a player draft, giving teams in higher classifications— including the majors—the right to select players from the roster of a lower-level club at a set price during a fixed period of time at the close of the playing season. The key to the draft was the baseball-wide acceptance of the twin cornerstones of the free assignability of player contracts and the right of clubs to reserve the future services of players, which afforded the team holding the contract of a player in any one year control over the future direction of that player's career.[33]

If the existence of the draft placed the minors in a subordinate position, the rules, as a whole, protected a considerable sphere of autonomy for minor-league organizations, which in turn imposed serious restrictions on the ability of Branch Rickey to implement his novel system. These rules reflected what was, relative to later years, the substantial power of the minor leagues vis-à-vis the majors. After all, the International League franchise in Baltimore and the American Association teams in Milwaukee inherited audiences that had very recently hosted major-league clubs—the two 1901 American League franchises that, as the acts of war, had been shifted to St. Louis (1902) and New York (1903), respectively. They had been "big league" towns until very recently, and a number of other "minor league" cities—including Louisville, Columbus, Toledo, Rochester, and Syracuse—had also previously been a part of the major-league circuit. The rules, as originally promulgated and then elaborated in the first decade of the National Agreement's existence, also reflected the fact that minor-league clubs were the more-or-less-exclusive transmission belt between the majors and the untapped talent reserves lying beneath the house of organized baseball. The majors rarely reached out directly to tap that pool. Instead, players typically were signed by a minor-league club, then shepherded upward until at some point in the informal, and unorganized, path toward the majors, they were purchased by a big-league club for immediate service.

One rule in particular had fatal implications for Rickey's postwar plans for the Cardinals. The no-farming rule (Article VI, Section 4) of the 1903 National Agreement had long been a focus of controversy and an invitation to evasion. Its very enactment testified to the already existing practice of "lending" a player to the minors for further seasoning, with the strings being held by a big-league club. The rule stated: "The practice of farming is prohibited. All right or claim of a Major League Club to a player shall cease when such player becomes a member of a Minor League Club, and no arrangement between clubs for the loan or return of a player shall be binding between the parties or recognized by other clubs."[34] Despite the sweeping language of the rule's preface, the rule was specifically designed, and applied, to outlaw the one particular practice that the remainder of the section's language addressed: that of major-league clubs "lending" a player under contract to a friendly, or at least complaint, minor-league team for temporary service, subject to recall by the major-league club in accordance with its own needs. The rule was intended to prevent a team from controlling more players than actually required at any given time, from keeping a stock of players in inventory against the future, as it were. But the teams, always interested in having a surplus of talent at hand, sought ways to avoid the black letter—and, indeed, the intent—of the no-farming rule.

The most popular trick for evading the no-farming rule was the optional assignment, by which a player was optioned to a minor-league team, subject to recall at will by the major-league team. This proved so prevalent that the National Commission decided to regulate rather than ban it. In 1907, the commission limited the number of times a club could option a player; four years later, the commission, responding to pressure from the minor leagues, whose competitive integrity and financial viability were being undermined by having so many of their players subject to unilateral recall at a preset price, limited a major-league club to a maximum of eight optional assignments at one time.

The no-farming rule, combined with the increasing limitation on optional assignments, left a big-league team that identified a player with major-league potential, but who was a number of years away from being ready for the big leagues, with only limited means to control his future. First, the player could be signed directly to a major-league contract and then optioned out for more seasoning. However, a club was allowed no more than three options for each player, as long as the player was recalled to the big club at some specified date late in the season and then carried on the team's reserve list over the winter and into the spring. The optionees counted against the team's thirty-five-player reserve limit, which was set after 1912–13. This posed a problem for Rickey, who wanted to corral and develop fresh talent in excess of the numbers that this method allowed. Nor, of course, did Rickey want such unproven prospects to count against the legal limit on his major-league roster.

Alternatively, the perversely named (as indeed many such tended to be in various walks of life) "gentlemen's agreement," which was necessarily verbal and consequently not without risk, might be made with an independent minor-league operator. A big-league team would, on paper, assign a player to a minor-league team unconditionally, or simply recommend prospects to a friendly minor-league team for signing. In reality, the minor-league club would have to agree to sell the player to the major-league team at a fixed price and not to deal with anyone else. The problem for Rickey and his fellow major-league executives was that not all minor-league operators honored their unwritten obligations. Instead, talented players, free and clear of any written competing claims on their services, would often find their way to the highest bidder. Nevertheless, despite the risks, records of player transactions show that major-league clubs did establish regular relationships with particular minor-league franchises. The practice—"secret, covert, illegal, and, therefore, undesirable," in Rickey's later description[35]—certainly existed.

Finally, a major-league club might acquire control of a minor-league team and thereby command, without the necessity of verbal or written agreements, the movement of its players from, in effect, subsidiary to parent organization. Charles Ebbets of Brooklyn and Charles Somers of Cleveland had previously experimented with this approach, acquiring several minor-league franchises.

The National Commission had construed the preface to the no-farming rule as a mandate to act against transactions that, arguably, did not come within the literal language of the rule, but that violated its spirit, and the commission relied on its rule-making authority to promulgate its interpretations of the agreement. In the face of perceived abuses in major–minor-league player relations, it periodically took corrective action, albeit more for the protection of the rights of minor-league clubs than the players themselves. The wholesale purchase and draft of minor-league players each fall was believed to tie up the player market and prevent competitors from having a fair crack at talent. An investigation by the commission after 1909 determined that apparently excessive numbers of players were being reserved by the big leaguers, with most teams reserving more than forty players and eight clubs reserving more than fifty. The revised National Agreement (adopted July 20, 1912) limited major-league clubs to thirty-five player reservations, except during the heart of the playing season (May 15 to August 20), when the limit was set at twenty-five.[36] To complement these new limits, the commission expanded the waiver rule, barring an outright assignment to the minor leagues without providing all other major-league clubs from putting in a claim for the player at a fixed price, although the waivers were revocable.

Once player limits were adopted in 1912, however, concerns about limiting major-league control over minor-league players were no longer adequately addressed by the specific language of the farming ban. In particular, the emergence of working agreements and outright ownership of minor-league clubs tested the readiness of the National Commission to extend its reach beyond the specific definition of farming provided in section 4 of the National Agreement.

The working agreement posed a pointed challenge to the commission's efforts to extend the reach of the ban on farming. The farming ban clearly meant to strike, and did strike, at the "gentlemen's agreement." The response, pioneered by the New York Giants in 1905 and then employed by others, was for a major-league team to conclude a "working agreement" with a minor-league club. Under such an arrangement, the Giants provided a minor-league outfit financial assistance, as well as help in assembling a roster of players who would be signed to minor-league contracts in exchange for an option to purchase, at a fixed price, one or more players at the conclusion of the year. Under this baseball version of sharecropping, the literal injunction of the farming ban—that no arrangement between clubs would be permitted "for the loan or return of a player," and that the major-league right or claim to a player would "cease" upon assignment to the "farm"—was heeded. Under the working agreement, the major-league club had no prior right or claim that would have to "cease" under the rule, and no loan or commitment had been made to return a particular player.

The National Commission did not interpret the phrase, "the practice of farming is prohibited," to bar the working agreement. But the commission did draw a line when it came to outright ownership of minor-league teams by big-league clubs. Brooklyn had acquired the Newark team in the International League, and Cleveland the Toledo club in the American Association. In May 1913, the commission ordered major-league teams to divest themselves of minor-league franchises that they owned, on the grounds that such a practice was "antagonistic of the rights of other major league clubs to recruit their teams and preventive of the promotion of the players."[37] Although this language anticipated the criticism that would be directed at Branch Rickey's proliferating farm system in later years, and a prominent minor-league official later claimed that the ruling represented an application of the no-farming rule to "a method of accomplishing in a wholesale way a thing that was prohibited as to an individual case,"[38] the ruling did not rely on the no-farming rule. Instead, the commission cited subsections 2 and 3 of the National Agreement's preface, which had, in the spirit of the federal Constitution, set out the objects of baseball's fundamental document:

2. *Protection of the property rights of those engaged in baseball as a business without sacrificing the spirit of competition in the conduct of the clubs.*

3. *Promotion of the welfare of ballplayers as a class by developing and perfecting them in their profession and enabling them to secure adequate compensation for expertness.*

Whatever the basis for the ruling, it represented a crippling obstacle to any attempt to create a completely integrated major–minor-league organization. Neither the legally unenforceable gentleman's agreement, nor the legal, but restricted, working agreement—both dependent on the goodwill of a formally independent junior partner— provided the centralized control over a player's career and hierarchical framework to channel the best talent toward the majors, which Rickey desired.

At a moment when the New York teams enjoyed the windfall proceeds of legalized Sunday baseball to ante up ever-greater sums in the bidding for baseball talent, the odds against Rickey's bid to build a winning team in a small-market city were only lengthening. Even before the Yankees made their epochal purchase of Babe Ruth, the New York Giants made an all-out effort in the spring of 1919 to purchase the Cardinals' own Rogers Hornsby. Although Rickey stoutly resisted the Giants' escalating offers (reportedly from $150,000 to $175,000, then to $200,000, up to $250,000, and finally to $350,000),[39] the unprecedented price the Giants were prepared to pay underscored the ways in which the teams with the biggest bankrolls were likely to hold sway in an era when those bankrolls were growing larger.

The chances that the big-money teams would be able to throw their weight around even more aggressively was exacerbated by another development in the aftermath of World War I. Early in 1919, the minor leagues repudiated the National Agreement, after failing to secure an end to the player draft, through which major-league clubs could acquire top-tier minor-league talent at fixed, noncompetitive prices. With the demise (at least temporarily) of the draft, the Cardinals could not emulate Rickey's earlier practice with the Browns of drafting large numbers of well-scouted players each fall and then attempting to direct their assignment downward. The richest clubs would have an obvious advantage if such top prospects in the high minors were subject to a bidding war for their future services.[40] Rickey would have to move quickly to forestall this further threat to a small-market team's ability to compete effectively in the player market with the sport's more affluent organizations.

However, the chaos that descended over organized baseball during the 1919 season, which led to the collapse of the National Commission, offered Rickey a fortuitous, but only briefly open, window of opportunity to break free of previous constraints on his innovative plans.

4

THE OPPORTUNITY

BRANCH RICKEY'S opportunity to build a countervailing force to the brute power of large-market-team money was, as it happened, provided by an entirely unrelated battle that broke out between the Philadelphia A's and the Boston Braves over the contract of a journeyman pitcher (who never played for the Cardinals) named Scott Perry. Perry was a six-foot, right-handed junk-ball pitcher with erratic control who came out of Corsicana, Texas, to pitch three full seasons and patches of four others in the major leagues. The spring of 1917 found Perry pitching for Atlanta in the Southern Association, after an unsuccessful stint in the majors. Perry had made his major-league debut two years earlier, giving up five hits and three earned runs in two innings for Rickey's St. Louis Browns. A more successful, but almost as brief, stay with the Chicago Cubs followed in 1916, and he began the 1917 season with the Cincinnati Reds, but an earned-run average of 6.75 drove him off the Reds pitching staff by early May and back to the minors.

Late in May, the Atlanta front office conditionally sold Perry to the National League's Boston Braves.[1] The teams agreed that the Braves could acquire Perry for a thirty-day trial upon payment of $500; if they liked what they saw, an additional $2,000 would buy Perry's contract free and clear. Perry reported to the Braves on June 1. But—and it would prove to be of great importance—the Braves did not immediately forward the promised $500, and Atlanta didn't press the point.[2]

As the trial period passed, a frustrated Perry didn't see any front-line action. On June 17, he suddenly deserted the Braves. In a move that revealed that hapless major-league team's relative standing in the baseball world, he next turned up pitching for a semipro baseball out-fit in Joliet, Illinois. Being more attentive to fiscal details than the Atlanta front office, Perry had made sure to draw, and cash, his June paycheck before taking off. In short order, the cables began flying between Boston and Atlanta. Atlanta demanded payment in full of the $2,500 purchase price, contending that the trial/purchase assignment had shifted the burden of loss in these circumstances to the Braves. The Braves took a hard line and refused even to make good on the unpaid $500 down payment, let alone the full purchase price. The National League president advised the National Commission that Perry had deserted Boston and had been placed on Boston's ineligible list. Atlanta turned to the National Commission for relief.

The authority of the "Supreme Base Ball Court," as A. G. Spalding had dubbed it, was already under assault when Atlanta appealed to it in the spring of 1917. Two years earlier, National League owners had reacted violently to a commission decision awarding the rights to University of Michigan first baseman George Sisler to Branch Rickey's St. Louis Browns, rejecting Pittsburgh's claim to his services, based on the National League club's acquisition of a contract that Sisler had signed with a minor-league team before enrolling in college. The Browns prevailed by a 2–1 vote, with the majority ruling that the contract relied on by Pittsburgh was unenforceable because Sisler signed it while still a minor.[3] Pirates owner Barney Dreyfuss was outraged, and he all but declared open war on the commission, particularly its original and still presiding chairman, Cincinnati Reds owner Gerry Herrmann, whom Dreyfuss blasted as a traitor to *their* National League and the tool of American League President Ban Johnson. But Dreyfuss, however grudgingly, accepted the ruling as final and then watched in dismay as

Sisler became an instant star with the Browns while the Pirates dropped to the bottom of the second division.

The dispute over Perry sharply escalated the smoldering conflict between the leagues, which Chairman Herrmann had to try to ameliorate. Herrmann first advised Boston that, in view of the trial assignment, Perry did not belong on their ineligible list and that Boston should release Perry to Atlanta, which would carry Perry on its ineligible list and moot the dispute about payment of the second installment. This tentative ruling did not address the issue of the down payment and its refund. To expedite resolution of Atlanta's immediate grievance, and to induce Boston to make the delinquent down payment, Herrmann, on August 1, 1917, advised the Braves that, taking into consideration the terms of the transaction, if Perry returned to organized baseball, the National Commission would, "in my judgment," recognize Boston's preemptive right to acquire the rights to Perry's contract upon payment to Atlanta of the balance of the purchase price. Herrmann thereby personally committed himself to a course of action in the event Perry tired of the sandlots.

The Braves, having received this assurance, were notified on August 6, 1917, of the formal decision of the commission. Boston would have to give Atlanta the "down payment" of $500 but did not have to pay the $2,000 balance. The ruling said nothing about the rights of the parties in the event of Perry's return. The Braves, after their appeal was dismissed (along with Atlanta's on August 30), paid Atlanta the $500 but had Herrmann's private assurance that, by so doing, they would retain an option to acquire Perry's contract.

Perry's status continued to simmer on baseball's back burners during the off-season. Relying on Herrmann's unofficial opinion, the Braves placed Perry on the reservation list (listing him as an "ineligible player") that they submitted to the National League office at the close of the 1917 season. National League Secretary John Heydler, however, informed the Braves that Perry did not belong on their list and that he was still the property of the Atlanta club. The Braves, wishing to avoid placing Perry in a contractual limbo, checked with Atlanta and learned that Atlanta was indeed reserving Perry's contract. The Braves acceded to this state of affairs, but as events would show, they relied in doing so on Herrmann's assurance that they held an option on Perry's future services, which they believed they had acquired by making the $500 payment.

Up to this point, the controversy between the major-league Braves and the minor-league Atlantans posed no serious problem for Herrmann. Nor did it raise any question about the future of the National Commission, but matters were about to escalate sharply. Late in spring training 1918, Atlanta sold Perry to the Philadelphia A's. Atlanta's president asserted that the National Commission's finding of the previous year—and specifically its failure to order consummation of the deal with Boston and full payment—left Atlanta free to dispose of Perry's contract as it wished. Herrmann's assurance to the Braves, after all, had been private. From Atlanta's viewpoint, the Braves had *not* been awarded any future rights to Perry, and most particularly had not been ordered to pay Atlanta the money required to secure title to Perry's contract. And in Philadelphia's Connie Mack, known as the "slender schemer" as well as the "tall tutor,"[4] Atlanta found a man ready to take his chances on Perry's legal status as well as his pitching ability—Connie was always looking for live arms, on the cheap.

The Perry case then returned to the National Commission for the second time in June 1918, when the Braves filed their claim to Perry, who had unexpectedly blossomed into an ace of the A's pitching staff, and challenged Atlanta's right to dispose of his contract. Augmented by the secretary of the National Association and the president of the Southern Association (as provided in commission rules when a minor-league club was involved in a dispute), the National Commission once again dug into the tangled affairs of Scott Perry.

National Leaguers braced for the worst, fearing that Herrmann would again side with his old friend from Cincinnati, Ban Johnson, and vote against his own league. The Sisler case would not repeat itself. Garry Herrmann had boxed himself in. In light of his assurances to the Braves the year before, Herrmann had no choice but to break with Johnson. On June 12, Herrmann voted to award Perry to the Braves upon payment to Atlanta of the contractual balance of $2,000 within thirteen days.

The vote was 3–2, Johnson and the president of the Southern Association dissenting. The majority recited the history of the dispute between Boston and Atlanta and quoted from the communications between Herrmann and the Braves, including Herrmann's advisory opinion as to the rights of the parties in the event Perry sought reinstatement in organized baseball. The commission majority concluded that any determination in 1918 of Atlanta's, and by extension Philadelphia's, rights to Perry was subject to the commission's final adjustment of the 1917 controversy—i.e., the final determination of Boston's rights. The commission decided: "Payment of consideration for the release of such [an ineligible] player is not enforceable until his reinstatement and entrance into the service of the purchasing club." The purchasing club was Boston, and the commission gave it the right to complete that purchase if it desired.

The decision inspired a wave of criticism, with the *Sporting News*, always close to Johnson, blasting it. The National Commission was on the defensive, and over the next week it offered supplementary support for its decision, which seemed, in the first instance, to be rooted primarily in the informal, and not legally binding, commitments that Herrmann had made to the Braves. Herrmann explained that the Braves' down payment had given them a "sort" of equity in Perry's contract; alternatively, and more technically, he argued that the transfer agreement between Atlanta and Philadelphia had never been filed, pursuant to the rules, with the National Commission; and that Philadelphia had neglected to seek the permission of the commission before negotiating with a contract-jumper on the ineligible list.[5]

No matter how Herrmann dressed up his ruling, Mack and Johnson, were not buying. The A's were playing in Chicago when news of the June 12 decision broke. Although Johnson denied any collusion with Mack, the A's arrived at the next stop on their road trip—Cleveland—ready to escalate the battle. As the National League owners congratulated themselves on evening the score with their upstart rivals, Mack readied his counterattack. On Monday morning, June 17, attorneys for Philadelphia appeared in the Court of Common Pleas in Cleveland and filed a suit for an injunction restraining any interference with their title to, and use of, the services of Scott Perry. Mack's lawyers walked out of court with the injunction, even as Perry was having a rougher time on the League Park mound, giving up six runs in a losing effort. But, win or lose, to the burning anger of those in the National League who had abided by the baseball code to keep family disputes within the family, and thereby lost claim to the great George Sisler, Perry remained the property of Connie Mack, by order of Judge Moran.[6]

Mack's defiance, and the conviction among National League owners that the hand of Ban Johnson lay behind it, marked the point of no return for the National Commission as baseball's governing body. National League President John Tener immediately resigned from the commission, effectively crippling its ability to act. When the National League owners declined to break relations with the American League and refuse to play in the 1918 World Series, Tener resigned as league president on August 6. He was succeeded, on an interim basis, by John A. Heydler, league secretary since 1902, who had earlier stepped in during an emergency in league affairs when President Harry Pulliam had committed suicide in 1909 (victim, many thought, of the stress brought on by the dispute arising from the infamous Merkle play during the Cub–Giants pennant playoff the year before). Heydler was formally elected president on December 10, 1918, and took his place on the National Commission.

With the Perry injunction in force, and the commission's award of Perry to the Braves a dead letter, the commission now stood bereft of authority. Its power had been shown to reach only as far as a ball club would voluntarily accede to it, and no farther. Although Boston and the A's settled the Perry case in October 1918 (the A's paid the Braves the $2,500), Mack's act of defiance had fatally compromised the commission's claim to govern organized baseball.

Amid this crumbling edifice of internal baseball law, Branch Rickey returned to the Cardinal front office in 1919. With the National Commission reduced to impotence and on the verge of total collapse, the already porous ban on major-league ownership of minor-league franchises was no longer a deterrent to Rickey's ambitions. While the commission awaited its formal death sentence, and major-league owners plotted and counterplotted over contending proposals to revamp baseball's government (and then had to face the crisis that erupted with the revelation, as the 1920 season ended, of the Black Sox scandal), the commission was unable to enforce any of its earlier no-farming orders. It was this sudden vacuum in the governing councils of the sport that provided Rickey with an unanticipated opportunity to turn long-incubated theory into practice.

In the course of 1919–20, the National Commission disintegrated. Baseball law was more or less in a state of suspension until the Major League Agreement was adopted on January 12, 1921, replacing the 1903 National Agreement and creating the office of commissioner. During this interregnum, Rickey made his first moves to implement his new ideas about player development. And when the new Major League Agreement addressed the "farming" issue, it would do so only in precise and limited terms: "player loan prohibited." The more general declaration of the 1903 agreement, that "the practice of farming is prohibited," was eliminated. Moreover, the sole Commissioner of Baseball, who replaced the three-man National Commission, was barred from interpreting agreement provisions other than to resolve disputes between the leagues. Rickey's ambitions would be safe in the reorganized baseball world that emerged under Commissioner Kenesaw Mountain Landis, and would survive the new commissioner's own lengthy, but largely fruitless, guerrilla war against Rickey and his system. Major-league baseball's first season under the new dispensation was Scott Perry's last, but by 1921 he had played his own considerable, if accidental, role in the realization of Branch Rickey's grand design.

ALTHOUGH THE collapse of the National Commission, and its ban on minor-league team ownership, provided the institutional opening for Rickey to proceed with his venture, his ambitions would have remained unrealized had it not been for the availability of newly found financial resources that enabled him to take advantage of that opportunity just when he needed it. The actual scope, and limits, of Rickey's achievement can only be understood by recognizing that the funds were available to turn the Cardinals into a winning ball club *before* the farm system made a significant contribution to the team's fortunes.

Simply put, and contrary to his later pronouncements, Rickey's initial moves required substantial expenditures by the standards of the day. The Cardinals' investment in the Syracuse minor-league team cost $25,000, and the purchase of an interest in Houston (18 shares of 100) required $15,000 (although the Cards did acquire Fort Smith for a nominal amount). Adding the purchase, in the winter of 1919, of pitcher Jesse Haines from Kansas City, at $10,000, Rickey spent a total of $50,000–55,000, in that first postwar year. This was a considerable expense for a team that, as the 1919 season ended, had trailed the league in attendance for two years running. Rickey could undertake these initiatives only because he had carefully attended to the account books, as well as the box scores.

Following the 1919 season, St. Louis had responded to the plight of the Cardinals by providing Rickey with new financial support. The team issued 4,000 new shares of stock, increasing the stated capital of the club by $100,000. More important, Rickey also found, in automobile dealer Sam Breadon, the partner he needed in order to fund his ambitions. Breadon is the uncelebrated hero in the Rickey-dominated St. Louis baseball saga, but he was vital to the team's rise to baseball power.

Breadon's first contact with the business of Cardinal baseball had come a few years earlier, when he attended a banquet at the Mercantile Club, drawn by the prospect of seeing up close a number of the Cardinal players he had watched perform on the ballfield. By the time he left the function, he had made the first of a series of loans to the team. In 1917, Breadon agreed to buy $2,000 worth of stock (eighty shares) in the team that had just lured Rickey to its front office.[7]

For Breadon, that investment was just the beginning. The reorganized Cardinals were carrying a debt of $175,000 to Mrs. Britton on the unpaid balance for the team assets that she had transferred to the new Cardinal corporation. The stock offering had raised only $175,000 (7,000 shares). When Breadon began attending stockholder meetings, and saw how parlous the Cardinals' books were, he recognized that without infusions of additional resources, the original investment would be lost. Within a year, Breadon had lent the corporation $18,000 and had acquired a seat at the directors' table.

Breadon's increased stake in the Cardinals' future did not go unnoticed by his fellow directors; they recognized that Breadon was ready to divert his energies from the automobile business. In December

1919, attorney James Jones offered him the presidency of the club. Breadon accepted, on condition that the board be reduced from twenty-five directors to a more manageable five. Jones worked out a compromise, and the board was reduced to seven. It was a sufficient basis for Breadon to agree to become team president in January 1920. Rickey was then elected vice president, retaining control over player personnel.

◇

BREADON had come a long way from an impoverished childhood in New York. His schooling had ended in the eighth grade, and he had struck it rich in the automobile business in St. Louis in the early years of the twentieth century, becoming known as "Singing Sam, the Selling Man." As a boy, he remembered, he had never been able to attend a big-league ball game: "When I was a kid, even the 25¢ bleacher admission at the Polo Grounds, and the 10¢ to go up there on the El, represented big money." By the mid-1920s, he held majority control of the Cardinals, which he would maintain until November 1947. When he died two years after selling the club, a longtime observer remembered him as "a man nobody knew . . . a tight-fisted, hard-boiled businessman, cold-blooded by nature and a fellow who drove a hard bargain, no matter if it hurt his best friend."[8] Indeed, the relationship between Breadon and Rickey would have its rough patches, notably in 1925 when Breadon fired Rickey as field manager and replaced him with Rogers Hornsby. And Rickey would leave the club in 1942 after a dispute over Breadon pay cuts for club employees, but it proved a successful partnership for two decades.

Breadon was also a fan; he had played baseball as a boy and enjoyed donning a Cardinal uniform and working out with the team in the spring throughout his tenure as owner. In a favorite story, he related how an unknowing rookie, reporting to training camp one day in the late 1930s, observed Breadon out on the field. "He stood around watching us for several minutes and then left to go into the clubhouse. Getting inside, the first thing he said was, 'Well, there are a couple of old buzzards out there that I know I can beat out for a job.'"[9]

Far from being the forlorn "basket case" of baseball lore, the Cardinals were poised to enter the 1920s with new leadership, a recapitalized financial structure, and a broad base of support in the civic-minded St. Louis business community. The first major decision of the new regime was selling the team's ramshackle Robison Field, the last wooden ballpark in the majors. Breadon later described the sale as "the most important move I ever made for the Cardinals. It gave us money to clean up our debts and something more to work with. Without it we never could have purchased the minor league clubs which were the beginning of our farm system."[10] The city needed a site for a new high school, and the local trolley company needed land for a turnaround, so $275,000 ($200,000 from the city and $75,000 from the trolley company) poured into the Cardinal coffers. The Cardinals became tenants of the Browns in recently remodeled Sportsman's Park, at an annual rental of $20,000,[11] and Rickey finally had available the money to begin building his long-mooted farm system.

Rickey's key aide in that effort was his chief scout, Charlie Barrett. Barrett liked to say that "the easiest assignment is to look over players in Class AA and Class A. In leagues of this classification the players are almost finished. They are just a step behind the majors."[12] But doing that kind of easy talent-spotting was not Barrett's assignment when he began working for the Cardinals and Rickey in 1919. Rickey had a different itinerary in mind for the already well-traveled Barrett.

Barrett had been a scout for the Browns since 1910, working with Rickey after 1913 and staying with that team until Rickey left for the Cardinal front office in 1916, when Barrett took a job with Detroit. In

1919, Barrett negotiated his release from his Detroit contract and took a cut in pay to work for Rickey again. On Rickey's instructions, his job was no longer simply scouting for players; it also involved looking for minor-league franchises that might be interested in forging an ongoing relationship with the Cardinals as a means of ensuring financial security amid the post-Armistice business downturn.

It was a propitious time to be trolling for such candidates, as minor-league teams struggled to recover from a severe postwar economic recession. The year 1918 had seen the abrupt cancellation of baseball seasons everywhere for all leagues from majors to Wisconsin–Illinois; and even before that campaign, demands on manpower and fast-changing economic conditions had reduced the minor leagues to a low ebb of activity. The total number of minor leagues operating fell to nine in 1918, half the number playing the previous year, which, in turn, was just half the number existing in 1914. After half a decade of hard blows, the prospects for the minors did not look promising in the winter of 1919.

As it happened, Charlie Barrett's friend Blake Harper owned the Fort Smith franchise in the Western Association. The association was going to reopen in 1920 after three inactive wartime years. Prospects for the resuscitated league were uncertain. After talking to Harper, Barrett realized that Rickey's proposition might well be received favorably by the Fort Smith owner. The Cardinals, Barrett explained, were looking for the opportunity to acquire part ownership in a minor-league team. If Harper would be willing to entertain a proposal, Barrett suggested he accompany him to St. Louis to discuss it further with Rickey. Barrett brought him to St. Louis, where Rickey committed the Cardinals to finance a one-half interest in the Fort Smith club. When Harper left, the lowly Cardinals were, very quietly, half owners of the Class C Fort Smith club.

That spring, while the Cardinals trained in Brownsville, Texas,

Rickey met the owners of the Houston club in the Texas League. He purchased 18 percent of the club (18 of 100 shares) for $15,000, shaking hands on the deal and pledging that the Cardinals money would be forthcoming shortly. The Cards continued to acquire Houston club stock, increasing their holdings to a 75 percent interest for an additional outlay of $47,500, and acquiring control of the team. Over the course of the 1920 season, Rickey made a sustained approach to Memphis in the Class A Southern Association, but in the postseason he learned that Sam Breadon had concluded his own deal to purchase a half interest in the Syracuse club in the International League (AA), so he worked Syracuse into his plans, backing away from Memphis.

These acquisitions entailed initial capital expenditures and ongoing expenses, but in the early 1920s, the income of the Cardinals parent club was on the rise. Rickey's adventure in baseball empire-building coincided, not coincidentally, with the very moment when the dimensions of the baseball balance sheet suddenly expanded, the sport enjoyed its first great boom, and attendance and revenues surged upward. In 1920, the Cardinals edged up from seventh to sixth place, finishing just four games shy of .500. Cardinal attendance doubled, passing the 300,000 mark for the first time since reliable figures became available. The Cardinals home attendance of 326,000 produced a record home-game income of $212,000, twice the estimated 1910 income. Road-game earnings reached new levels, too, enhanced by the legalization of Sunday baseball in New York, where the Cards played three—two in the Polo Grounds, which attracted 54,000 fans between them, and one in Brooklyn. On the road, the Cards played before more than 500,000 fans and earned $118,000.[13] Total Cardinal income from attendance then amounted to $330,000, against $195,000 ten years earlier.

That 1920 marked a point of transition for Cardinal finances was borne out in the following seasons. In 1921, profits jumped to more than $200,000, reflecting a slight increase in attendance but, much more important, the proceeds from the sale of Robison Field—proceeds that permitted the liquidation of the outstanding indebtedness to Mrs. Britton to be carried out painlessly, sheltered by the nonrecurring real estate transaction. The next year, although having to fall back on ordinary income sources, the Rickey–Breadon team continued to be in the right place at the right time. In the city's most glorious baseball season yet, St. Louisians responded with daily enthusiasm to the unprecedented performance of both of their teams. The Browns dominated the headlines, making their greatest peacetime run for a pennant, falling one game short. George Sisler hit .420 and Ken Williams led the league in home runs with thirty-nine (a record until 1932 for a non-Yankee American Leaguer). The Browns' run at the top thrilled 712,000 fans, who just about doubled the team's previous top mark. The Cardinals—winning eighty-five games for a club record, finishing tied for fourth and featuring Rogers Hornsby's National League record-setting forty-two home runs, together with a .401 batting mark (best in the league but only second best in his city)—almost held their own in this intracity battle. Although they still played second fiddle to the Browns in their hometown, the Cardinals set their own attendance mark with 538,000 admissions, and the Cards cleared $136,000 in profit for the year.

In the early 1920s, Cardinal earnings had been sufficient to liquidate the Britton debt as well as to cover the cost of acquiring substantial ownership interests in the three minor-league franchises around which Rickey would expand and extend his farm system. The team also reported an overall profit for these years, which was exceeded in their league only by the Giants and Pittsburgh. Indeed, the Cards' earnings provided an economic advantage beyond what the raw numbers alone indicated. Unlike other teams, the Cardinal management retained and reinvested its earnings. While the Giants paid $50,000 of their profits and Pittsburgh $74,000 of theirs to shareholders, the Cardinal board, firmly dominated by Breadon and Rickey, did not declare dividends. With Cardinal stock widely scattered in hundreds of minuscule holdings, shareholder pressure for dividends was nonexistent. The men who *did* own a substantial amount of stock did not need dividend payments. Rickey took a very large salary, and Breadon retained enough outside interests to generate income without requiring cash flow from his Cardinal investment.

It didn't hurt that Breadon's investment had been made with much less money than Charles Stoneham had needed to buy the Giants. Breadon had acquired a majority of Cardinal stock in 1923 for $90,000, compared to the $960,000 Charles Stoneham had paid for his majority stake in the Giants four years earlier. For Stoneham and for Barney Dreyfuss of Pittsburgh, the ball club was their major business activity, and dividends were a prime source of personal income. Cardinal dividends stayed at very low levels compared to those of the Giants or the Pirates, or any of the other teams such as Brooklyn and Chicago, which in time emerged at the head of the National League financial class. It provided an important advantage.

Fueled by this income stream, the Cards separated themselves from the lower-tier, have-not teams with which they had been lumped in the past. Everyone's boat had been lifted by the first wave of the postwar baseball boom, but by 1923, the Phillies and the Braves had returned to the poverty of the permanent second division. The Cards, by contrast, were ready to make a run at the top, leaving these erstwhile rivals behind. Rickey's visionary ambitions for himself, his team, and his system provided the motivation, but it was the more mundane fact that the Cardinals were armed with the requisite financial resources that made the Cardinal assault possible.

5

THE AMBIGUOUS PAYOFF

B Y THE TIME the 1921 season opened, Rickey had put together the beginnings of his long-planned farm system. The role the fledgling farm system would play in making the Cardinals competitive on the field remained to be tested. The pieces of Rickey's ultimate design were falling into place, but what was most striking about Rickey's stewardship of the Cardinals was that, without too much spending and without the advantage of large-scale farming operations, he fielded a contending team in 1921. Paradoxically, the Cardinals, in practice, were thereby "prematurely" breaking the cycle of defeat, which, according to Rickey's theory, only a well-stocked farm system could overcome.

Rickey's inspired improvisations were preempting the self-assigned task of Rickey the methodical planner. The keystone of the newly competitive Cardinals was second baseman Rogers Hornsby, a pre-Rickey acquisition, purchased on August 20, 1915, from the Denison, Texas, Class D team, for $500. This was the discovery of a lifetime, and it was not realistic to expect it ever to happen again. The rest of the infield had come together in the haphazard way that characterized National League teams bold enough to challenge the era's superpowers. First baseman Jacques Fournier had been picked up from Los Angeles in the high minor Pacific Coast League in 1920. Fournier had played in the American League for half a decade after 1912, before

being demoted to the minors, where Rickey had found him. Shortstop
Doc Lavan had been acquired the previous year in a trade with Washington. Rickey had known him from his years with the Browns and had
traded for him from the Athletics in 1913. Milt Stock played third. The
Giants, who had drafted him in 1911, had traded him to the Phillies
when he came up against their third and final option in 1914. The
Phillies had passed him along to the Cards. Assembling the Hornsby/
Lavan/Stock/Fournier infield combination owed nothing to either the
careful nurturing of young talent or the expenditure of large sums.

The same was true of the Cardinal outfield, manned by acquisitions from teams in the high minors and discards of weak big-league
clubs. The pitching staff was just as much a product of such traditional
team-building maneuvers. Bill Doak was the veteran in point of service, a Cardinal hurler since 1913. He had come on board abruptly
when his Interstate League disbanded on July 14, 1913, and he had
pitched through the bleak years before 1921. Bill Sherdel was
acquired from Milwaukee in 1918. In 1920, in his one major purchase,
Rickey bought the contract of Jesse Haines from Kansas City. Haines
had six years of organized ball behind him and two unsuccessful
attempts to crack the Detroit and Cincinnati rosters. In 1921, Rickey
rounded out the staff, acquiring Bill Pertica from Los Angeles and Jeff
Pfeffer from Brooklyn.

This patchwork team of castoffs and discarded veterans (seven of
whom had played in organized ball for more than a decade without
making a mark anywhere), led by the great Hornsby, compiled a stunning 87–66 record in 1921 and signaled the rising fortunes of Cardinal
baseball. The team stayed up near first place through August and finished in third place, beaten by only seven games. It was their best
finish ever, by a good half-dozen games. Rickey had turned the Cardinals around. To reach the next level, however, the team would have to
overcome the entrenched powerhouse that barred the way to a

National League pennant: the resurgent New York Giants. The Giants had the league's deepest pockets—ready, willing, and able to outplay their competitors on the field after they had outspent them off of it. A classic clash of baseball cultures loomed.

After John McGraw's 1919 team fell nine games short of the surprising Reds, the veteran manager and new part-owner, backed by the record-breaking crowds delivered by Sunday baseball, set to work refashioning the ball club. McGraw turned to the league's doormats to find Giants-in-waiting. The Cards balked at surrendering Hornsby for cash, and McGraw backed away from the one deal that the Cards would have likely approved, a second-baseman swap that would have brought Frankie Frisch to St. Louis.[1] Frisch had stepped off the Fordham College campus and onto the Polo Grounds infield in 1919, and Rickey had had his eye on him from the beginning. But McGraw knew that the "Fordham Flash" was the key to the championship club he intended to build, and he refused Rickey's proposal, turning to the rest of the second division in his quest for talent.

Scavenging among baseball's have-nots was standard operating procedure for McGraw. Trades with the Boston Braves, Cincinnati Reds, Philadelphia Phillies, and Chicago Cubs had brought pitchers Jess Barnes, Fred Toney, Slim Sallee, and Phil Douglas to New York, as well as shortstop Dave Bancroft. Outfielder Earl Smith was acquired from Rochester in the International League, in exchange for no fewer than seven inferior players. The Giants were also free spenders in the talent market, paying the Braves $55,000, the first major expenditure of the Stoneham/McQuade/McGraw regime, to obtain left-handed pitcher Artie Nehf in 1919.

The rebuilding Giants faced a crucial challenge in 1921. The Giants had finished second to Brooklyn in 1920, a result that, combined with the financial windfall the Dodgers took home from their four home Sunday games against the New Yorkers, spurred extraordinary efforts to take the flag the next year. Adding to the pressure was the fact that the Giants could see, when the 1920 returns came in, that the Yankees were poised to supplant them in the baseball hearts of New York.

Yet when the 1921 season opened, the most imminent threat facing the Giants came from an entirely unexpected direction. The heretofore lowly Cardinals rushed into contention, along with the Pirates, and McGraw fought back in customary fashion. On July 1, 1921, the Giants initiated what remain the most sweeping and one-sided midseason trades in National League history. McGraw had a willing accomplice in William Baker, owner of the Phillies, former New York City police commissioner, and a fellow habitué of McGraw's Broadway circle. The series of related transactions began with the announcement that the Giants had sent Goldie Rapp, Curt Walker, and Lee King to the Phillies in exchange for Johnny Rawlings and pitcher Red Causey. Judged as a straight exchange, the terms were not overly unfavorable to the Phillies. Causey proved ineffective for the Giants; Rapp and King hit little for the Phils. The key men were Walker and Rawlings. In Walker, the Phillies obtained a solid .300-hitting outfielder. Rawlings, in New York, was reunited with his Philadelphia double-play partner, filling the gap left by the retirement of Larry Doyle and allowing Frisch to stay at third base. But a few weeks later, it became clear that there was more to the deal.

On July 26, New York announced the acquisition of Emil (Irish) Meusel from the Phils as part of the previously announced trade, in exchange for an additional payment of $30,000. Casey Stengel also came to the Giants, to complete the transaction. The final balance was clearly in favor of New York. The Giants had obtained starting players at second base and in the outfield, plugging a gap left by retirement and reuniting a great infield combination. The Phillies had pocketed a sizable amount of cash, but the arms and legs and bats the Phillies had also gained did them scant good; thereafter, they would not rise above seventh place until 1929.

McGraw had thereby assembled the team that would win the pennant that year and put him back on top. The only regular on that team who had been a Giant before 1918 was first baseman George Kelly. And of all the talent that made up the Giant champions of 1921, only George Kelly, Frank Frisch, and Elmer Smith had begun their major-league careers in Giant colors. Everyone else had been acquired by trade or purchase from another major-league roster, and most came from the league's weaker franchises. Only Phil Douglas, acquired from Chicago, had come from a contending or solvent organization.

The 1921 Giants victory was a triumph of the rich and powerful, founded on acquisitions from other big-league clubs. Yet Branch Rickey built his own first competitive Cardinal team that season in much the same way, which mirrored league-wide player procurement practices. Of the National League's 112 front-line players in 1921, sixty-two had come from other major-league clubs and only thirty-five had come up directly from the minors.[2] On that year's Giant team, nine of their fourteen regulars had prior major-league service, and the Cardinals similarly deployed eight starting players acquired through transactions at the big-league level. The Giants were just better able to accomplish their goal, fortified by cash reserves that other teams did not possess, and so were in a position to pry more prime talent from less affluent clubs. Although the Cardinals had faltered in the end, the groundwork had been laid, by dint of Rickey's mastery of traditional team-building methods, to make St. Louis a winner, not just a competitor.

Even as they rolled to victory in 1921, the Giants hit the high-water mark for their steamroller personnel-procurement methods. In June of that year, Commissioner Landis, in his first major decision on nongambling matters, advised Heinie Groh, then a Cincinnati hold-out, that he would play either for the Reds in 1921 or for no one else; Landis would not approve his reinstatement as a player for any team other than the Reds. Groh, who was angling for a trade to the Giants, capitulated. As it turned out, when the season ended, he did go to the Giants after all, but Landis had flashed a caution sign, although he did allow the deals with the Phillies that the Giants made as a substitute for the Groh deal.

The next season, matters came to a head. In July 1922, the Giants bolstered their pitching staff by purchasing right-handed pitcher Hugh McQuillan from the floundering Braves for a reported $100,000. The Braves were stuck in last place, having failed to play up to the previous year's respectable fourth-place finish. Owing to the dis-favor into which the post–Ruth Red Sox had fallen, the Braves seemed to have a chance to forge enduring ties on the Hub's baseball heart. Indeed, at the height of the 1921 season, 40,000 fans had jammed Braves Field, the second time in a week that record crowds had thronged the huge ballpark, which had, ever since its completion in 1915, stood as a mostly empty monument to the extravagantly mis-guided hopes fired by the 1914 miracle.

In the first months of the 1922 campaign, McQuillan had lost ten of fifteen decisions and sported an excessively generous (even by lively ball standards) earned-run average over 4.50. He was hardly helping the hapless Braves; but he could, McGraw knew, reinforce the Giants down the stretch. With their pitching bolstered by McQuillan's improved form (he won six games and lost five for New York), the Giants won the pennant. But they paid a price. League owners promptly adopted a rule restricting player transactions between league clubs after June 15 and before August 31. The midseason replacement door, at which the Giants had knocked regularly and successfully in past years, had been closed.

With the Giants' traditional (and to many abusive) team-building methods under attack, Rickey enjoyed an enhanced opportunity to extend the accomplishments of his 1921 team. In 1921, he had fielded a competitive team playing by the "old rules," including the major purchase of Jesse Haines. The Cardinals' key asset was Rickey's unmatched eye for potential talent, especially for players who had failed in previous major-league stints but who would justify the second, or even third, chance at the major leagues that Rickey offered them. There was talent aplenty among the ranks of former big leaguers who had dropped back into the minor leagues. About 15 percent of the regulars in the National League in 1921 were in their second (or more) tour of major-league duty. Although the lordly Giants shunned their services, preferring either proven major-league or expensive, seasoned minor-league talent, such "retreads" could hold their own when given the chance, as Rickey's acquisitions demonstrated.[3]

But however astute his dealings were in this "used player" market, and however resolutely Rickey and Breadon withstood the monetary blandishments offered by the Giants for a player such as Hornsby, Rickey was convinced that an entirely fresh pool of talent would have to be tapped to move the Cardinals up from first-division contenders to league champions. With money in hand from the fortuitous ballpark sale and the recapitalized Cardinal corporation, Rickey set out to find the talent to stock his incipient empire.

Large-scale tryout camps were instituted, "three years," Rickey recalled, "ahead of all the other clubs." Young men, some with talent and more without, flocked to St. Louis for the chance to show their stuff, performing under Rickey's carefully appraising eye. Here Rickey hoped to find the raw material for his projected assembly-line method of signing, cultivating, and harvesting top talent, keeping them securely in the Cardinal fold throughout their development. By 1926, Rickey could claim to have succeeded in his challenge to baseball's traditional team-building practices, as the Cardinals won the baseball World Championship. On that championship team, only Jess Haines, Rogers Hornsby, and Bill Sherdel remained from the third-place squad of 1921. Everyone else—Fournier, Doak, and Mann, as well as Stock and Pertica (Rickey's reclaimed spitballers)—was gone.

The backgrounds, not just the identities, of the players on the 1926 team also differed from their predecessors. Completely absent from the starting lineup (except for Haines) were the minor-league reclamation men who had played so large a day-in-and-day-out role in 1921.[4] Most of the players on the 1926 team, just as the Rickey model would have it, had come to the Cardinals directly from the minors. An impressive ten of the fifteen regulars saw their first major-league action in a Cardinal uniform, and the same was true of seventeen of the twenty-four men on the World Series roster. But it was also true that the balance of the team had been assembled in tried-and-true fashion, through a series of player trades that had been engineered after the start of the 1925 season and had certainly paid prompt dividends.

They were remarkable deals, testimony to Rickey's great ability to size up talent. The first was surely the most important. Catching was a Cardinal weakness in the mid-1920s, and former catcher Rickey certainly knew the importance of filling the position adequately if the team was to contend. Rickey found the answer to the catching gap in a foul tip, which, midway through the 1924 season, had smashed through an old, banged-up, twisted mask and fractured Bob O'Farrell's skull. O'Farrell, regular catcher for the Cubs, didn't play much for the rest of the season and, after the winter layoff, had a sputtering start the next year. Playing infrequently, he was hitting .182 after seventeen games.

Rickey seized the moment. In exchange for O'Farrell, he could offer the Cubs (who had Gabby Hartnett ready to step into the regular catching spot) Mike Gonzales as a dependable source of relief for Hartnett, along with third baseman Howard Freigau. He made the deal. Rickey's faith in O'Farrell was amply rewarded. The catcher hit .278 for the Cardinals the rest of the 1925 season; in 1926, he batted .293 and was voted the National League's Most Valuable Player on that first Cardinal World Championship team.

After the 1925 season, Rickey set out to retool that season's fourth-place club for a drive at the pennant. In December, he returned to the Cubs and acquired right-handed pitcher Vic Keen (coming off a weak 1925 showing 2–6 and 6.26 ERA), in exchange for shortstop Jimmy Cooney, who would be replaced by Specs Toporcer. The 1926 season opened with the winning team not yet in place. Only in June were the final moves made to complete the eventual pennant-winning roster.

On June 10, 1926, the Cardinals were in fifth place but only two games behind the league-leading Reds in a very tight pennant race. Beating the June 15 intraleague trading deadline by just one day, Rickey surprised Cardinal fans by trading local boy Heinie Mueller to the Giants in exchange for Billy Southworth. This wasn't just a popular local hero who was being traded away; Mueller was also a poster boy for Rickey's much-trumpeted revolution in baseball talent-spotting. Mueller had been one of his first tryout-camp products, a young man who had stamped himself on Rickey's mind, with aggressive and untested assurances that he was as good an outfielder as Speaker, a base runner as Cobb, and a hitter as Home Run Baker. He carried himself, Rickey remembered, "with the stolidity and stubbornness of the indefatigable German." Mueller had stepped off a St. Louis sandlot and broken into the Cardinal lineup in 1920, the very first of the sandlot kids to wear the Redbird cap. But he had been dogged by bad luck. His 1925 campaign had been interrupted by a broken bone in his foot, and his 1926 start was slow. Rickey's patience was exhausted. The thirty-three-year-old Southworth had the experience and leadership needed by the Cardinals, the youngest club in the league.

The next week, Rickey completed his midseason maneuvers with a surprising deal, the kind of move made only by a club knocking on the pennant door. The Cardinals needed pitching. By June 21, Vic Keen had more than justified the trade made for him that winter by winning eight of his ten decisions and teaming up with the even more effective Flint Rhem (who was then 10–1) to pitch the Cards into the thick of the pennant race. But it was evident another strong starter would help.

One afternoon in mid-June, the already legendary Grover Cleveland Alexander, in his sixteenth major-league season, was intercepted by Cub freshman manager Joe McCarthy in the doorway to the visiting team's clubhouse in Philadelphia. The thirty-nine-year-old Alexander, who hadn't pitched in a month, had made McCarthy's managerial debut as difficult as possible. Now McCarthy laid down the law, flatly telling Alexander that he knew he was drunk again—which the *Sporting News* euphemistically described as "apparently the worse for wear." It was the sixth time in ten days, and McCarthy ripped into Alex, telling him not to suit up and barring him from the locker room. McCarthy ordered the pitcher to report directly to the Cub offices in Chicago and told the press: "Any player may drink and enjoy life and get away with it if he is winning. But he hasn't been winning for me." The Cubs front office backed up the rookie manager and placed Alex and his big salary on waivers.

At the $4,000 waiver price, Alexander was a steal—if he could stay sober. Cardinals manager Hornsby conferred with Rickey, a man bound to be worried by Alexander's lack of discipline. Hornsby had reason to believe he could handle Alexander: His third-base coach was Bill Killefer, Alexander's catcher on the Phillies when the great pitcher had won thirty or more games three years in a row a decade earlier.

Killefer told Hornsby he could hold Alex in line, so Alexander became Cardinal property on June 22.

The veteran donned a Cardinal uniform ready to pitch for a team that was playing winning baseball and had just completed a very successful eastern swing. The prospect of seeing Alex pitch for a contending team fired up St. Louis fans as never before. On Sunday, June 27, a doubleheader against the Cubs, featuring Alexander's debut as a Card in the opener, attracted a massive crowd that began forming before eight in the morning. The police barely maintained control. Forty thousand fans (37,190 paid) jammed the Sportsman's Park enclosure, well in excess of its stated capacity of 34,000, and 10,000 more reportedly were turned away. Alexander, flashing his familiar assortment of curves and hard-pitched fast balls, all coming off his still-effective half-side arm motion, delighted the throng by pitching his new team to a win.

Rickey's and Hornsby's and Killefer's faith was more than repaid. Alexander won nine games in a pennant race that the Cardinals won by two. To cap off his comeback, in the seventh game of that fall's World Series, Alexander strode in from the Yankee Stadium bullpen, immersed in the shadows of the low, late-afternoon October sun that was already becoming a familiar setting for World Series drama, and struck out Tony Lazzeri with the bases loaded in the bottom of the seventh. He then pitched his experienced way through the eighth, walking Babe Ruth with two out in the ninth, and saving it all for the Cardinals as Ruth was thrown out attempting to steal second. A World Series title had come to the banks of the Mississippi River for the first time.

WHEN THE Cardinal celebrations ended that winter, attention drifted back to the men who had done so much to assemble the team that had won the title—to Rickey and Hornsby and Breadon, of course, but also to Charlie Barrett and to the players he had scouted and signed, as well as his daring decision to spend all of $2,500 on Les Bell. That was a lot of money, Barrett remembered, at a time when he had to wait three months for a salary check.[5]

By 1927, it was all different, according to Barrett. The Cardinals had become a big organization. They didn't bounce his paychecks anymore, they had even built an extensive farm system. Barrett peered down into that system and saw an endless stream of player talent flowing upward toward St. Louis: "Six great outfielders developing for us in the minors, 14 pitchers, 3 third basemen, 4 shortstops, 2 second basemen, 3 first sackers." "I think," he confidently concluded, "the Cardinals are pretty well fixed for young players," naming a few. There was Lefty Weather from Nokomis, "another Jim Bottomley"; Harry Layne at Peoria, "another Ray Blades"; and a pitcher named Cunningham was "a real prospect" at Syracuse. Pepper Martin, too; the names rolled off Barrett's tongue, promising future success for the parent club.

There were skeptics about what Rickey claimed to be doing, most notably and not surprisingly, the Giants' John McGraw. One spring day, he listened to umpire Bill Klem's animated description of the Cardinal camp where, Klem told McGraw, "I saw the greatest thing in my life today . . . they had 78 young ballplayers working out." McGraw said he had heard about it, without any apprehension. "It's the stupidest idea in baseball," he said to Klem. "What Rickey's trying to do can't be done."

McGraw had a point. Rickey's farm *system* was irrelevant to the development of the 1926 Cardinals. Rickey's first championship team was the product of skilled detail work by a master baseball hand with an unerring knack for detecting talent, not of an assembly-line method of mass player production. In building that club, Rickey had honed in on a group of players of unusual ability, most of whom came from the hinterland that surrounded St. Louis, the southwestern flank of major-league baseball's geographically unbalanced stockade. With an unusually high number of the regulars on the 1926 team having been brought to St. Louis directly from the minor leagues, it is understandable that Rickey and Barrett could conclude that they had accomplished a baseball revolution. But, at the time, the Cardinal "farm system" was more of a slogan than a reality, given the small scale of its operations and the unusual abilities of the players involved.

The progress of Rickey's first set of "farm boys" to the big club in St. Louis was extraordinarily rapid. Jim Bottomley, signed in 1920, was playing for the Cards by 1922. Les Bell, purchased in 1922, was brought up to St. Louis the next year, then was optioned twice before sticking for good in 1925. Ray Blades signed in 1920, was lent that year to independent Memphis under a gentleman's agreement, was optioned twice to Houston, then brought up for good in 1922. Terry Douthit, signed off the Berkeley campus in 1923, needed one year at Fort Smith before being brought up to the St. Louis spring roster in 1924, then was optioned twice (St. Joseph and Milwaukee) before sticking with the Cardinals in 1926. Tommy Thevenow was bought from Joplin for $4,000 in 1923 and optioned twice before final recall in 1925. Specs Toporcer, signed by Syracuse, was optioned once, staying with St. Louis in 1922. Flint Rhem, seasoned by college ball, needed a brief assignment to Fort Smith in 1924 before being recalled for the first and last time later that season. And Chick Hafey, who followed in Douthit's wake from California, needed only one year at Fort Smith before being brought up to the Cardinal roster for two optional assignments to Houston and Syracuse successively, then being recalled permanently in 1925.

Of the minor-league recruits who constituted the bulk of the 1926 club, the only man who needed more than three full or partial seasons in the minors for seasoning was Art Reinhart, who took six years to reach the St. Louis club after the Cardinals first signed him in 1919. In any event, the route of most of these players to the Cardinals would have been possible without any recourse to the theory of interlocking control that Rickey had preached as a necessity, and then put into practice. It could have been accomplished simply by following the revised option rule that accompanied the ratification of the new major league–minor league National Agreement in 1920–21; it allowed a major-league team (although limited to eight optional assignments at any one time) to option the same player twice before an assignment downward was treated as an unconditional release. This liberalized option rule allowed the Cardinals to maintain control over the raw talent that was signed in the first wave of player development activity that had accompanied the timely influx of cash into the Cardinal coffers in the early 1920s. Branch Rickey's "chain store" model of baseball player development was a solution to a problem that had largely been resolved just as it was being implemented.

The Cardinals of 1926 did not need the long apprenticeship in the minors, the step-by-step advancement up the rungs of competition before being ready for major-league competition, which the farm-system model was designed to provide for a club anxious to retain control over that player beyond the limits of previous option rules. Apart from the special case presented by Art Reinhart's extended stay in the minors, the home-grown Cardinals were ready for limited duty on the big club within one year of signing, and then, when further tutoring was called for, the two options permitted under the revised rules were sufficient to maintain Cardinal control.

Of the 1926 Cardinals, Thevenow, Blades, Holm, Toporcer, Rhem, and Bottomley all found their way to Sportsman's Park through use of the optional assignment, as though the farm system didn't exist; they were ready for the majors in two years, and Rickey treated them that way, not holding them on minor-league rosters even though he controlled those clubs. These men were signed directly by the Cards and then optioned out for experience. After just two options had been exercised, they were ready for the majors.

With Hafey, Bell, and Douthit, Cardinal control of a minor-league club did assist in bringing their talent to flower in Cardinal uniforms. Douthit, after starting out at Fort Smith, was brought onto the Cardinal spring roster of forty in 1924, and his future availability to the Cardinals was assured by use of the optional assignments to St. Joseph and Milwaukee in 1924 and 1925, respectively—options, that is, to two clubs that were not under Cardinal control. The only role of the Cardinal organization in Douthit's rise was to provide a first landing at Fort Smith, which, of course, was the way the system was intended to operate, and why Rickey wanted a Class C club at the outset of his work. But had Fort Smith not existed, the gap no doubt would have been plugged—either by a gentleman's agreement or by more rapid development. Bell's case is similar: His only year in the Cardinal organization outside of the option network was his first, 1922–23, when he was brought from Lansing under Cardinal direction for Syracuse. After that, he appeared on the Cardinal 1923 roster and was optioned to Houston. The next year he was optioned to Milwaukee, and in 1925 was a Cardinal for good. For Hafey, as with his fellow collegian Douthit, Fort Smith was the first nonoptional spot he played under Cardinal direction, and that was only for one season. After that, the optional-assignment track was followed.

The key to Cardinal success lay not in the availability of subsidiary farms on which to plant a "quantity" of players from which to harvest the select but, instead, in the aggressive scouting of talent outside of, and at the lower rungs of the ladder of, organized professional baseball. The men who made it to the Cardinals in 1926 had playing ability that was noticed almost immediately upon their introduction to the Cardinal organization. Talk of "mass production" of ballplayers was irrelevant. Rickey was dealing in quality, not quantity.

The 1926 Cardinal team reflected changing baseball-wide talent acquisition methods, more than the implementation of Rickey's innovative theories. The rising tide of prosperity in the 1920s made the sale of proven talent less necessary even for bottom-drawer clubs. As the pool of available major-league talent dried up, the entire league increasingly looked to the minors for personnel. Even with respect to the minor leagues as a source of talent, patterns of recruitment were changing. In contrast to Rickey's 1921 team, the 1926 Cardinals fielded no regular player who had been sent down to the minor leagues after having failed in a previous major-league tour of duty. The chances of finding players who deserved a second chance was diminishing, as demonstrated by a comparison of the major-league castoffs playing in 1926 with those active in 1921.[6] Although pitchers were still promising candidates for a second or third chance—as witness Charlie Root of the Cubs and Dazzy Vance of the Dodgers—successful salvage jobs had become less likely. The teams that still relied on the leavings of other major-league clubs were the second-drawer ones. A tight connection was evolving between competitive success and the acquisition of talent at lower levels. Along with the Cardinals, the Pirates and even the Giants staked their bids for success on similar practices. Rickey's hard work was well timed, but it was not unique.

Thus, the 1926 Cardinal team was largely a product of its time, as indeed the 1921 team, pieced together through baseball's *then*-current player-procurement practices, had been. By fielding a team of players without previous major-league experience, St. Louis was less of a pioneer than a participant in an overall trend in player procurement. In 1926, sixty-two of the 123 regular players in the National League were playing for their first club in the majors; fifteen had been "reclaimed" from the minors; and forty-six had been acquired through trades at the big-league level—a reversal of the ratios that had prevailed at the beginning of the decade. Rickey's *bête noir,* the Giants, had built their championship clubs of the early 1920s around men ruthlessly picked off the rosters of weaker major-league clubs. McGraw's 1926 team, by contrast, counted eleven out of sixteen regulars who had come to the Giants directly from the minors. This new balance of forces was identical to that of the Cardinals.[7]

AFTER 1926, the Cardinals remained at or near the top of the National League for several seasons. Falling short of the 1927 pennant by just 1 1/2 games to Pittsburgh, the Redbirds came back to take the flag in 1928, won again in 1930, and repeated in 1931. In 1926 and 1928, they faced the Yankees in the fall; in 1930 and 1931, it was the Philadelphia A's. The Cards won once and lost once against each American League opponent. With four pennants in six years, they had emerged as the league's dominant franchise. Every victory solidified the economic position of the once-insolvent team, which now stood near the top of the baseball world, financially as well as competitively. The steady stream of World Series revenue amounted to more than $600,000 in those triumphant seasons. Even as much of the baseball world, along with the nation at large, was being battered by the great Depression, Rickey had the resources to make possible the "mass production of ballplayers" on an ever-larger scale. If "quantity" truly mattered in Rickey's equation for winning baseball, the pieces were now in place to yield the desired outcome.

The remarkable team that Rickey had assembled in 1926 provided the foundation for those further successes. Only one major addition to the 1926 squad was made before the 1927 season. It was, of course, the result of a tremendously important transaction—the trade of Rogers

Hornsby in December 1926 for Frankie Frisch and Jimmy Ring of the New York Giants. Eight years after Rickey had first suggested exchanging Hornsby for Frisch, the move was made. Rickey's early judgment about Frisch was more than vindicated. Frisch played superbly in 1927 and 1928, overcoming an initially skeptical reception in St. Louis and readily filling the gap left by the departure of the greatest hitter in National League history. No Cardinal fan ever had any reason to regret the trade.

In 1927, the defending World Championship team, more or less intact apart from the Frisch–Hornsby swap, fell just short of the top. That season was a turbulent one, and not only because of the acrimonious dispute that erupted behind the scenes after Hornsby was traded to the Giants. Hornsby had to dispose of his Cardinal stock, and a dispute with Breadon over its valuation was only resolved by a special meeting of National League team owners in April.[8] On the field, problems abounded as well. Tommy Thevenow broke his ankle. To fill in for him at shortstop, Rickey turned not to a farm-bred youth from the vaunted farm-system talent pipeline, but instead to thirty-six-year-old Rabbit Maranville, who had played for Brooklyn the previous year. To take up the catching slack left by O'Farrell's diminished ability and increasing years, Rickey reacquired thirty-four-year-old Frank Snyder, whom the Cardinals had traded to the Giants in 1919. So fortified, and benefited by a truly unexpected twenty-one-game season from forty-year-old Grover Alexander, the Cards came up 1 1/2 games short at the finish, as Pittsburgh won what would be its last pennant for thirty-three years.

Breadon and Rickey each reacted to that loss in characteristic fashion. Breadon fired Hornsby's replacement as manager, Bob O'Farrell. By now, Breadon had divorced himself from the automobile business, becoming a full-time baseball man. The price for his increased involvement in team affairs would be paid most directly by

Cardinal field managers, who could never rest easy with an impatient owner looking over their shoulders, ever ready to make a change. Despite their on-field successes, the Cards would go through six managers in the decade following 1926. Rickey could sit back and watch the on-field musical chairs with some detachment, but he could foresee the day when *his* number, too, would come up for cancellation. He started buying Cardinal stock again (having sold his original stock to Hornsby when Breadon had terminated him as field manager in 1925), as a hedge against any problems with Breadon down the road.

Rickey responded to defeat in 1927 by seeking out new talent to punch up the somewhat ragged lineup. As the Cards regrouped for the 1928 season, reinforcements were needed at catcher, the infield, and the outfield. The time had come for the farm system, which now included a fourth team (Danville of the Three I League), to produce. But when help arrived, it did not come from within Rickey's expanding organization.

For the infield, Rickey turned to the Braves and obtained second baseman Andy High, the type of raid on a weak club that was a specialty of nemesis McGraw. To catch, Rickey acquired Jimmie Wilson from the similarly hapless Phillies. For the outfield, O'Farrell was shipped to New York in exchange for George Harper. To bolster the pitching, Rickey, who certainly was not counting on another twenty-one wins from Alexander, acquired Clarence Mitchell from the Phillies as part of the Wilson trade. Syl Johnson was brought up from the minors to pitch, but he was not a Rickey farm-system product either. The Cards had drafted him from minor-league Vernon, after he had been released in 1925 by Detroit (which had purchased his contract from Portland in 1921 for $40,000 and had then optioned him out for two seasons).

Far from advertising the benefits of the Rickey farm system, the

1928 team contained only one regular who had joined the Cardinals
after 1925 other than through an acquisition at the major-league level.
The 1928 team, which won the National League pennant by two
games over the Giants before losing the World Series to the Yankees
in four straight games (New York's second successive World Series
sweep), had been assembled by the time-honored practice of cherry-
picking talent from the weak links in the National League circuit, *not*
by the exertions of that ever-expanding pool of farm boys, who were
percolating through the Cardinals' talent pipeline.

In 1928, the Cardinals won the league pennant by getting maximum
mileage out of a patchwork assortment of veteran ballplayers. It was
not a team likely to enjoy many—if indeed any—more years of success.
The next season, the team fell apart, with second-year manager Bill
McKechnie, who was fired in June, as the first casualty. The core of the
aging pitching staff—Haines, Sherdel, and Alexander—contributed only
thirty-two wins (down from fifty-seven in 1927), and their earned-run
averages soared from around three or fewer runs per game to almost six
for Sherdel and Haines, and nearly four for Alexander. Maranville had
been traded to Boston, replaced by Charley Gelbert, who was called up
from Rochester after three years in the Cardinal organization. Ernie
Orsatti, who had played split optional seasons for the Cards in 1927 and
1928, moved into right field, as Wally Roettger and Wattie Holm
slumped badly. The team finished in fourth place, twenty games behind
the Cubs, playing the season under three different managers. The
lineup featured three position players who were survivors from the initial wave of minor-league talent in the early 1920s, two from the Rickey-
bred generation of 1927, and three who had been acquired through
trades. The pitching was even less of a tribute to the expanding farm system, with only Fred Frankhouse raised to be a Cardinal.

The whole point of the Cardinal experiment was to provide an
internal source of supply from within a rapidly growing organization,

and new ballfields for its minor-league clubs rose across the country—from Houston to Danville to Rochester—valued at $1 million in real estate and improvements.[9] Yet, contrary to expectations and theorizing, very little major-league talent emerged from the Cardinals' minor-league network to shore up the badly beaten 1929 team. The Cardinals won their third pennant in 1930 because the old arms came through. Johnson and Rhem and Haines, and an even older pitcher, Burleigh Grimes, led the way. They were joined by Wild Bill Hallahan, a product of the farm system, but one who had been exposed to the major-league draft after having been assigned "outright" for two final minor-league seasons once his options were exhausted. Grimes was in his fourteenth season when he was obtained from Boston in mid-June, in yet another talent raid on a second-division club. The thirty-seven-year-old Grimes won thirteen important games for the Cardinals, second only to Bill Hallahan. Backing up the pitchers were the veterans Bottomley, Douthit, and Hafey, as well as trade products Wilson and Frisch, joined by Sparky Adams (acquired from the Pirates) at third base. By comparison, the farm system was making only a limited contribution, with Charley Gelbert at shortstop and outfielder George Watkins, who had worked his way up to the Cardinals after five minor-league seasons. Right field remained a revolving door, as Holm, Harper, Orsatti, and Watkins all failed to match the hitting power of their predecessors.[10]

Rickey's astute trades were far more responsible for replenishing the Cardinal talent pool after 1926 than the farm teams, but in 1931, this changed. That year's great team still featured trade products (Frisch, Adams, Wilson, and Grimes) and the fruits of the first incredibly successful years of the Rickey regime, as well as the seemingly indestructible Jess Haines, in his last productive season. Joining these holdovers was a considerable mass of young talent, raised according to Farmer Branch's scientific methods of cultivation, notably including

center fielder Pepper Martin, first baseman Rip Collins, and Paul Derringer, Rickey's first truly farm-bred pitching star. With Derringer winning eighteen games and Bill Hallahan nineteen, a rejuvenated Flint
Rhem returning to the Cardinals after two years in Houston and Minneapolis, and Allyn Stout (winner of six and loser of none) up from
Houston, the Rickey blueprint appeared to be fulfilled—just as he had
outlined it almost twenty years earlier, when he first talked to Robert
Hedges in the Browns' office at Sportsman's Park about raising
ballplayers from scratch.

In 1931, after years of relative drought, rich streams of young talent did seem at last to be arriving at their intended major-league destination. But in the victorious Cardinal clubhouse on that October
afternoon after the mighty Philadelphia A's had been defeated, there
were still many players whose procurement did not conform to any
Rickey theory. There was Frisch, of course, and Adams, Wilson, and
Grimes, who had won the series's seventh game. All were veterans who
had vital talents that could not necessarily be raised down on a baseball farm, however shrewd the planting.

Even the farm-system products on that team were not clear-cut
testimonials to any "science" of player development. Hallahan, who
had failed in his first two tries with the Cards and then survived one
year in the Texas League without being drafted, had been saved for the
Cardinals by that good fortune. Collins had been purchased by
Rochester from a club in the low minors—certainly an astute transaction, but just as certainly not an easily repeatable one. Pepper Martin
himself did not represent the sandlot pickup that Rickey envisaged as
the benefit of his open-tryout system. The 1931 series star had been
purchased in his second year in organized ball and assigned to Fort
Smith. Martin had taken his first steps in organized baseball on his
own, and as soon as other teams imitated the scouting practices of the

Cardinals, the chances of making such a find in the lower minors would necessarily diminish.

In fact, for the Cardinals, 1931 proved more of an end than a beginning. After suffering through two subsequent rebuilding years, St. Louis won the National League pennant in 1934 and took the World Series from the Tigers. But they did not win another pennant until 1942, repeating in the war-depleted seasons of 1943 and 1944. Cardinal dynastic hopes that were stirred in 1931 were not fulfilled. Bad trades and bad luck intervened to derail Rickey's ambitions. After 1931, players were lost through questionable deals—for instance, pitcher Paul Derringer and first baseman Jim Bottomley were traded to Cincinnati after the 1932 season. By order of Baseball Commissioner Landis, who was waging a relentless but inconclusive guerrilla war against "chain store baseball," catcher Gus Mancuso was declared a free agent in 1932 as was Pete Reiser in 1938.[11] And the worst of luck came in the form of Dizzy Dean's sore arm. Other teams built up farm systems, a move hastened by the economic crisis that struck the minor leagues during the depression. The Cards lost any advantage they had ever enjoyed. By the middle of the 1930s, the National League entered a period of unusually competitive equilibrium. The senior-circuit pennant was won by five teams in the eight years starting in 1934, and a sixth team, Pittsburgh, ran a very close second one year. Whatever else Rickey had achieved, his Cardinals had not gained a secure spot at the top of their league.

NOT THAT the Cardinals' vanquished 1931 World Series opponent, Connie Mack's Philadelphia A's, offered an alternative path to future success. The first years of the Great Depression had been a second Golden Age for Mack. Born Cornelius McGillicuddy six months before the Battle of Gettysburg, Mack was, by the 1930s, in the third decade of his half-century career as founder, manager, and part-owner of Philadelphia's American League franchise. As hard times battered Philadelphia with a fury that was exceptional even amid the nation-wide economic collapse, Shibe Park provided a measure of psychic, if not material, relief. The A's won three consecutive American League pennants starting in 1929, an accomplishment no American League team (other than the Yankees) would match until the twice-transplanted heirs of the A's, bedecked in the garish green and yellow hues chosen by Charlie Finley for his Oakland team, pulled off the feat in the early 1970s.

Philadelphia's depression-era champions had their roots in the demise of Mack's first great A's team, winners of four pennants in the five years from 1910 to 1914. Over time, a myth developed, cultivated by Mack himself, that Mack had broken up that first great team by design, concluding that the fans had grown tired of perfection, that too much talent on the field had generated too much boredom among the fans. As Mack would remember it, "The local fans had been staying away from Shibe Park in droves and yawning with boredom when they read of another Athletic victory."[12] In fact, the A's led the league in attendance in 1910 and 1911, finished third behind the White Sox and the Red Sox in 1912 (when the Boston team took the pennant), and finished second to the White Sox in 1913 as they regained the flag. What did precipitate the downfall of that great team, as well as a sig-nificant decline in attendance the next year, when the A's repeated as American League champions, was the well-bankrolled assault of the Federal League. Only after two of Philadelphia's top pitchers, Chief Bender and Eddie Plank, jumped to the new league in 1915 did Mack unload the rest of his stars. The result was disaster on the field, accom-panied by record low attendance averaging 2,500 per game, an abysmal figure that made the previous season's discouraging mark look good. Making a bad situation worse was the rather humiliating fact that the A's National League–rival Phillies rallied from a sixth-place finish in 1914 to win their first (and, until 1950, only) pennant in 1915, also topping the A's in attendance for the first time, almost tripling their 1914 gate of 138,000.

Beginning in the early 1920s, Mack began rebuilding, player by player, the club that had monopolized the American League cellar for seven straight years after 1915. By 1925, the A's were back in the first division, finishing second to the Senators and drawing record crowds of 869,000. In 1929, all the pieces were in place for a renewal of the club's winning ways. The 1929 A's won the league pennant by eighteen games, and defeated the Cubs four games to one in the World Series. In that last pre-depression season, the A's drew 839,000 fans, third best in their league and fifth best in baseball. The team attracted 18 percent of the total league box office, the best mark ever for a Philadelphia team, and a better showing than the raw numbers alone suggested, because Pennsylvania remained the last holdout against Sunday baseball after Massachusetts lifted the ban that season. That barrier, which wouldn't fall until 1934, cost the A's twelve to fourteen lucrative dates and as many as 200,000 to 250,000 annual admissions during those glory years.

Even as the A's were winning the 1929 World Series, the stock market was sliding downward from its mid-September peak; within two weeks of the baseball triumph, the market had crashed. Baseball attendance held up in 1930, even setting a record in the National League that year, but thereafter it collapsed, along with the nation's business system. It was tough luck for the A's, who were unable to reap the full financial reward that their on-field success might otherwise have delivered, but they did a fair job of holding on to their pre-depression patronage. The 1930 club drew 721,000, and the 1931 club attracted 627,000, second only to the Yankees in each of those seasons—and still without the fillip of Sunday games.

But 1931 ended the six-year stretch in which the A's—first contending, then prevailing—outdrew every team in their league except the Yankees, and every team in the National League other than the Giants and the Cubs. With crowds came profit. The A's earned more than $1.1 million from 1925 through 1931; only the Yankees, the Cubs, and the Giants were more profitable. But even as the pressure for Sunday baseball was building, with the prospect of greater profit and a diversion from depression malaise, Connie Mack was pulling the plug. The A's found themselves abruptly at a dead end as a competitive ball club on the field and a box-office attraction at the gate.

In 1932, the A's faltered on the playing field, falling to a badly beaten second to a resurgent Yankee team that won 107 games under second-year manager Joe McCarthy. After more or less holding their own in the first seasons after the Crash, baseball finances now felt the full force of the depression, which drove down total 1932 attendance to a bit above 6 million—4 million below the mark set just four years earlier. The A's suffered with everyone else—indeed, suffered more than its rivals—as Philadelphia attendance fell by a third in 1932 and then by a third again the next year (dipping below 300,000). Operating revenue, derived almost entirely from home and road gate receipts, fell from $966,000 in 1929 to $311,000 in 1933. Although expenses (chiefly player salaries) were cut sharply, the tide of red ink could not be contained. For the second time, Mack "broke up" his ball club.

Complaining as he had twenty years earlier—unfairly then and unfairly again—that his winning team was "too good for Philadelphia," Mack blamed a high payroll and tight finances. In fact, the team was starting to slip (the A's finished second in 1932, ten games behind the resurgent Yankees), and a rebuilding task loomed. The onset of the Great Depression was not necessarily fatal to such an effort. The Washington Senators, whose attendance and income had fallen in tandem with the A's after 1930, and which had started from a much lower base, managed the wherewithal to capture the flag in 1933. And the Detroit Tigers, playing in a city that was hit even harder economically than Philadelphia, put together a consistently winning team in the mid-1930s, with attendance tripling between 1933 and 1934 as the Tigers took their first pennant since 1909. The years 1932 and 1933 were difficult for everyone in the major-league-baseball business, but as the examples of the Tigers and Senators showed, those years' losses did not require a team to throw down the hand and cash in the chips.

Yet that is what Connie Mack and the A's did. Raising cash appeared to be the sole object of the off-season maneuvers that step-by-step dismantled the team that Mack had so carefully built up and led to the top. The team's slide from contention became a free fall to the bottom of the second division by the 1935 season, and Mack topped it off by selling whatever playing assets he still had left. Slugger Jimmie Foxx and pitcher Johnny Marcum went to the Red Sox for $150,000 in December 1935, followed a month later by Doc Cramer and Eric McNair for another $75,000. The Red Sox failed to buy a pennant, but the A's had surely done their best to sell one. Mack's team would not finish any higher than seventh place in the standings until a wartime fifth in 1944, would not win more games than they lost until 1947, and would lose 100 games or more six times before leaving Philadelphia in 1955.

That Mack was more or less forced to "monetize" his playing assets to keep his franchise afloat was not the result of lean times alone. It was just as much—if not, indeed, more—the reflection of the way he had managed the team during the preceding years of plenty. Income had fallen off sharply, from $966,000 in 1929 to $311,000 in 1933; in that latter year, all that averted financial catastrophe was the $250,000 netted from player sales, which brought the books almost into balance and left the team with only a slight loss ($20,000). After all, the depression was driving down payrolls across the board. Mack tightened the belts of his players, cutting payroll from $255,000 in 1929 to $166,000 in 1933, from second highest in the league (after the Yankees) to fourth, on the way down to seventh by decade's end. Even with that reduced payroll, the A's remained competitive, a pitcher or two away from challenging for the pennant again.

What doomed the depression-era A's was the lack of reserves in team finances—no acorns in the storehouse against the punishing winter that had struck baseball and the nation. Mack and his co-owners had soaked the earnings out of the club during the good years. Profits hemorrhaged out of the team's capital account and into dividend checks. From profits of $1.1 million earned between 1925 and 1931, $400,000 in dividends had been paid—$250,000 in 1931 alone, a last-minute bonanza reaped even as Mack bemoaned the pressures placed on the team. It was the last dividend the Philadelphia club would ever pay. By the end of the decade, the club was on life support, with Mack's stock pledged as security against $85,000 in loans from the American League, a charity case kept going to round out the schedule.[13] Mack had steered a disastrous, and ultimately fatal, course for the fortunes of American League baseball in the City of Brotherly Love. When the time came for major-league baseball to "rationalize" the distribution of its franchises to better fit the changing geographic patterns of Eisenhower-era America, it was no surprise that Philadelphia's American League team would be declared expendable and the A's would be packed off to Kansas City in 1955, to close the first wave of expansion.

◇

As THE A's sank and the Cardinals faltered, the New York Yankees gathered their strength for a return to the commanding position in the baseball world they had first gained a decade earlier. The first years of the Great Depression had been difficult for the aging Bronx Bombers. After winning six pennants in eight seasons starting in 1921, the Yankees then won only one (in 1932) over the next seven years, their least successful run until the late 1960s. Unlike Mack, who was dipping deeply into the till, the ever-so-prudent Yankees, with an ownership not dependent on baseball income, earned $1.9 million and paid no dividends during those years. While first Philadelphia and then Detroit set the pace in the American League, the cash-rich Yankees made the transition from the managerial regime of Miller Huggins to that of Joe McCarthy. Babe Ruth's departure after the 1935 season sealed an end to one era, just as Joe DiMaggio's arrival in 1936 marked the start of another—one in which the Yankees would be more dominant than ever, winning four consecutive World Championships between 1936 and 1939. Apart from Lou Gehrig at first base and Tony Lazzeri at second, the 1936 team represented a total makeover from the 1928 Yankee champions. With shortstop Frank Crosetti, catcher Bill Dickey, and pitchers Red Ruffing and Lefty Gomez on board by 1932, the addition of DiMaggio provided the spark that propelled the Yankees to a position of superiority that they would then maintain, more or less continuously, for the next thirty years—a record unmatched by any team in any sport. Not only that, but DiMaggio's presence in the Yankee lineup, added to that of Lazzeri and Crosetti before him, and Phil Rizzuto and Yogi Berra thereafter, created a solid base of Italian-American fans for the team—even extending into the heart of Dodger-mad postwar Brooklyn to include a young Rudy Giuliani—which endures to this day.

By the late 1930s, the Yankees were back where they had been when the Cardinals had first emerged from the National League pack to challenge them. It would be the Cardinals, not the Yankees, who fell back thereafter. Through all the future years, when the Cardinal empire grew to embrace thirty teams and 600 players, all the years when Branch Rickey could count fifty and more former Cardinal farmhands on the rosters of his competitors, the Cardinals never matched the marks they had already set in the half-decade beginning in 1926. Those marks had been set not with the end products of a mass production of ballplayers, but instead with a team that reflected the exceptional talents of one man. It was Rickey who had negotiated the trades that made those pennants possible, and it was Rickey who had found players with such great abilities that they could make it to the big leagues without the apprenticeship his farm-system model contemplated. In its greatest era, the Cardinals were actually a small-scale operation whose successes bore the handcrafted imprint of Branch Rickey.

Between 1926 and 1934, the Cardinals established themselves as the first small-market team to compete consistently at baseball's top levels. Although they ultimately proved unable to break the ongoing hegemony of the Yankees, the prototypical large-market team, this was a singular achievement. Rickey demonstrated that a small-market team could win, at least for a time, but he did not teach lessons that were readily exportable to similarly situated teams not blessed with a management of comparable genius. Almost half (nine) of the total of twenty appearances by small-market teams in the World Series through the 2000 season were recorded by the Cardinals in the two decades after 1926, during the Rickey and immediate post–Rickey eras.[14] Perhaps that is—finally—changing. Despite recent alarms over the supposedly increasing stranglehold of the best-funded teams on winning baseball, recent seasons have witnessed an unusual resurgence for baseball's have-not teams. Small-market or low-payroll teams—such as the Atlanta Braves, Minnesota Twins, Houston Astros,

Arizona Diamondbacks, Anaheim Angels, Oakland A's, Cleveland Indians, and Seattle Mariners, as well as the St. Louis Cardinals themselves—filled thirteen of the sixteen spots in the playoffs of 2001 and 2002 and provided the World Series winners in both years.

In assessing the place of the Cardinals in the National League's more than eighty-year struggle against the New York Yankees, it is easy to posit Rickey's Cardinals as the antithesis of Ruppert's Yankees, with the former winning through organizational innovation, the latter through massive spending. But this overly schematic dichotomy exaggerates the differences between the two teams' paths to success and obscures what they had in common. Money alone did not win pennants for the Yankees, nor did the farm system deliver championships for the Cardinals. For money also played a crucial role in the Cardinals' own history, by providing the wherewithal for Rickey's initial expenditures in acquiring proven talent and assembling the beginnings of a network of farm clubs. And if the essential foundation for ongoing Yankee triumphs was its front office's astute, efficient, and victory-oriented management, the true secret of the Cardinals was Rickey's own personal skill as a discoverer and developer of ballplayers, not the farm system that he, and his team's money, had built as the fruit, not the seed, of success.

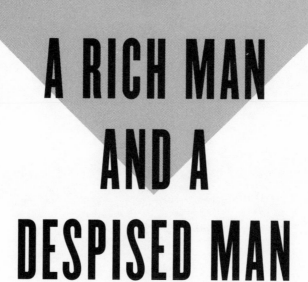

PART THREE

A RICH MAN
AND A
DESPISED MAN

Interlude

ST. LOUIS TO BROOKLYN

I N 1943, the Yanks topped the Cardinals in the World Series four games to one, gaining a two-two split in their twenty-year-old rivalry. Over the remaining war years, the Cards would do a better job than the Yanks in holding onto a place at the top of the baseball pack. They would win pennants in 1944 and 1946 and win the World Championship both years as well, while the Yanks, mortal for once, would barely cling to the first division. After the 1942 season, Branch Rickey and Sam Breadon parted ways, and Rickey left St. Louis for Brooklyn, to become president and general manager of the Dodgers. The Cardinals had been the dominant team in the National League from the mid-1920s to the mid-1940s, and they were the only National League team to win a World Series from the Yankees between 1923 and 1955. But within a few years, the Cards were destined to fall by the wayside, while the Yanks would regroup and come back stronger than ever.

Starting in 1947, the Yanks would win eleven pennants over the next thirteen years. After 1946, the Cards would not win another pennant until 1964. Any postwar challenge to the Yanks would come not from the banks of the Mississippi but rather from much closer to home, just a subway ride away, from the

177

Borough of Brooklyn, with a significant assist from the Yankees' first great rivals, the resurgent New York Giants.

Never before had the Yanks faced such a sustained challenge for supremacy on the ballfield. Between 1947 and 1956, the Yanks faced the Dodgers in six World Series. And it could easily have been two more had the Dodgers not lost two pennants on last-inning home runs on the last day of the season—the first, in 1950, was hit by Dick Sisler of Philadelphia's "Whiz Kids"; the second, and more renowned, was Bobby Thomson's "shot heard round the world," which gave the New York Giants the 1951 National League flag. The postwar Yankees of "Old Reliable" Tommy Henrich, Joe DiMaggio, Joe Page, Charlie Keller, and Joe Gordon seamlessly gave way to the team of the mid-1950s, starring Mickey Mantle, Bill Skowron, Hank Bauer, Gil McDougald, and Whitey Ford, with Hall of Fame catcher Yogi Berra and shortstop Phil Rizzuto linking the two lineups. Managed after 1949 by Giant and Dodger retread Casey Stengel, the Yankees proved fully capable of turning back all challengers from the senior circuit, whether from Brooklyn, New York, or Philadelphia.

◇

ONCE AGAIN, the prime architect of a challenge to the Yankees was Branch Rickey, this time operating out of the Dodger front office. The key move during Rickey's eight-year tenure in Brooklyn was the decision to break baseball's color line. Within the National League, integration upset the traditional hierarchy of power. Jackie Robinson's signing had immediate and far-reaching consequences for the game on the field. The Dodgers leveraged their readiness to sign up black ballplayers into a decade of unprecedented success. Together with the New York

Giants, who were similarly in the forefront of baseball integration, this advantageous tolerance secured National League pennants for New York City in eight of the ten years after 1947. Meanwhile, the St. Louis Cardinals, based in a segregated border state, hesitated to sign black players and did not integrate until the 1954 season. After 1949, the Cards faded swiftly from contention and would not again make a serious run for the pennant until 1963.

From 1947 through 1956, winning National League baseball was virtually a New York City monopoly. Over that decade, the Dodgers won six National League pennants and the Giants two. Brooklyn fans had the good fortune to cheer on such great players as Jackie Robinson, Duke Snider, Gil Hodges, Roy Campanella, Carl Erskine, Carl Furillo, Don Newcombe, Preacher Roe, and Pee Wee Reese. Their exploits, notable as they were at the time, loom even larger in retrospect, thanks largely to Roger Kahn's memoir, which managed to secure for "the boys of summer" a more vivid place in baseball's collective memory than that enjoyed by the Yankee teams that defeated them in five of their six World Series encounters. For their part, the New York Giants of Willie Mays, Monte Irvin, Alvin Dark, Eddie Stanky, Sal Maglie, Bobby Thomson, and Don Mueller, managed by Leo Durocher, rewarded the faith of the fans who had stood by a franchise that had long since ceded its place as the city's, and the sport's, premier franchise. When the Dodgers and the Giants met in a playoff for the 1951 National League pennant, Brooklyn fielded four future Hall of Famers and New York two, with yet another, manager Leo Durocher, in the coaching box. In addition to 1951's "Miracle of Coogan's Bluff," memorable Giant moments included journeyman outfielder Dusty Rhodes's two-game winning pinch-hit home runs in the 1954 World Series,

which sparked a 4–0 series sweep against the Cleveland Indians
and Willie Mays's great catch in deepest center field on a tower-
ing drive by Indian slugger Vic Wertz in the first game of that
series, not to mention just the sight of Mays playing stickball with
neighborhood kids in the streets of Harlem. These provided
imperishable images for the sport's archive of memory. Mays's
exploits—at bat, in the field, and on the bases—exhausted sportswriters' arsenals of superlatives. In a decade when Mickey Mantle and Duke Snider competed with Mays for the title of best
center fielder in the city—and the world—honest Dodger and
Yankee partisans knew, at least in their heart of hearts, who was
really most deserving of that honor. "All of a sudden," Murray
Kempton wrote a few years later, "you remembered all the
promises the rich have made to the poor . . . and the only one
that was kept was the one about Willie Mays. They told us then
that he would be the greatest baseball player we would ever see,
and he was."[1]

FROM THEIR baseball Olympus in the Bronx, the Yankees surveyed their rivals without fear. The Dodgers had capitalized on
their readiness to break the color line and draw on the talents of
black ballplayers even as the complacent and lordly Yanks
remained lily white for eight years after Jackie Robinson's debut.
Defiantly, the Yanks bucked the tide that had doomed the Cardinals. The Bronx Bombers beat the Dodgers in each of their
four fall showdowns between 1947 and 1953, which was the Yankees' last World Series appearance as an all-white team. Counting their 1941 series win, the Yanks were five-for-five in their fall
showdowns with Brooklyn's Bums when they closed out the 1953

contest in six games, scoring the game- and series-winning run in the bottom of the ninth.

To the Yankees, Brooklyn's baseball heroes might even have looked like a team that had something of a gift for coming up short when it counted. Even apart from their accumulating skein of World Series defeats, the Dodgers had also managed to blow a 13½-game lead to the Giants in 1951, and then lose the resulting playoff. They had similarly lost the previous year's pennant to the Phillies, a team that was playing under a severe self-imposed handicap. In that fourth season after the arrival of Jackie Robinson, the Philadelphia "Whiz Kids" would be the last all-white team to win a National League pennant.

As for the Giants, the Yankees put an end to their miracle season of 1951 by winning the final three games of the World Series that year to beat them four games to two. And the Giants' astonishing 1954 World Series sweep of a Cleveland team that had won a league-record 111 games that year only underscored the Yankees' status as the American League's indispensable instrument in the battle for baseball's World Championship.

When the Yanks did finally succumb to the Dodgers in 1955, it proved to be only a temporary setback. The Bronx Bombers came back to win the World Series in 1956, after dropping the first two games to the Dodgers. Aided by Don Larsen's perfect game in Game 5, the Yanks closed out the series with a 9–0 romp in Game 7, the last time they would ever play in Ebbets Field.

By then, more was at stake than the standings of the clubs on the playing field. In their final decade in Brooklyn and New York, the fortunes of the Dodgers and the Giants intersected with three of the most important developments in American society in those years: the civil rights revolution, the movement of population from inner city to suburb, and the rise of the Sunbelt. By leading the way in bringing black talent into the previously all-white sport, the Dodgers, followed closely by the Giants, had parlayed the first into a formula for success on the ballfield. The two other trends would have less felicitous consequences for the Yankees' two intracity rivals. Playing in ballparks that were widely condemned as outdated relics of the streetcar era, the Dodgers and the Giants found themselves locked into an aging infrastructure that was ill-suited for their increasingly suburban fan base. The accelerating westward movement of population, and particularly California's fast-growing prosperity and prominence, highlighted the increasingly suspect pretensions of a self-proclaimed "national pastime" that remained (notwithstanding recent franchise shifts to Milwaukee, Kansas City, and Baltimore) confined to the nation's northeast quadrant. The conjunction of the quest for new playing facilities with the prospect of new economic opportunities on the West Coast would prove fatal to the two teams' long histories as local institutions.

Even in the midst of Brooklyn's one great championship season, the future of baseball in the borough had begun to unravel. By the time the 1958 season rolled around, the Dodgers not only had been beaten on the field, they had abandoned Brooklyn altogether, taking the Giants with them. The National League's postwar challenge to the Yankees would end with the most crushing defeat possible.

6

THE CASE AGAINST BROOKLYN

THE LAST WEEK of January 1957 was a quiet time at an uncertain moment in the often-tumultuous history of the Brooklyn Dodgers. The excitement of the previous year's dramatic pennant race had subsided, as had the trauma of yet another World Series defeat at the hands of the Yankees. The acrimony and mutual recriminations stirred up by the Dodgers' December trade of Jackie Robinson to the hated New York Giants, and Robinson's subsequent retirement, were stilled for the moment. The controversy that had been simmering over Dodger owner Walter O'Malley's efforts to build a new stadium in downtown Brooklyn had been muffled into occasional mentions on the back pages of the New York papers. On January 28, the Dodgers announced the hiring of tramp-like circus clown Emmett Kelly to personify the team's bedraggled but feisty "Brooklyn Bum" cartoon image. The reason, O'Malley wryly explained to bemused reporters, was "to relieve tension at Ebbets Field."[1]

Indeed, as the opening of spring training for the 1957 season approached, nothing less than the future of the Dodgers as a winning ball club, or even a Brooklyn ball club, was at stake. In 1956, the Dodgers had proven vulnerable to the Yankees on the diamond. In 1957, Brooklyn would prove just as vulnerable to an attack on its continued viability as a home for major-league baseball.

The Dodgers had flown Brooklyn's flag in baseball's major leagues ever since 1890. After the American League's 1903 move into New York City, in competition with the National League's existing New York and Brooklyn franchises, the three teams had waged a unique three-sided battle for local baseball honors. Over the years, their players contributed far more than their share to the sport's record books, although one may wonder whether the "memorable moments" ballot distributed by major-league baseball during the 2002 season, on which the Dodgers, Giants, or Yankees figured in ten out of the eleven pre-1958 highlights, testified more to persistent New York media bias than an entirely dispassionate assessment of baseball history.[2] The glory had by no means been shared equally. The Giants had triumphed first, the Yankees most often, and, for much of the time, the Dodgers had triumphed not at all. The emergence of the Brooklyn Dodgers as the Yankees' preeminent rival in the late 1940s marked a sharp break in the fortunes of a team that had long been overshadowed by its competitors across the river.

As the Yankees began their rise to baseball dominance in the early 1920s, the Dodgers had fallen to the bottom of the baseball heap. After winning the National League pennant in 1920 (and losing the World Series to Cleveland), Brooklyn would not win another league title for twenty-one years, recording fourteen second-division finishes in the intervening two decades. Brooklyn's contribution to a baseball era highlighted by the Yankees' "Murderers' Row" and the Cardinals' "Gashouse Gang" was the "Daffiness Boys," who "batted out of turn and stole bases with the bases loaded; runners passed each other on the paths, sometimes in opposite directions, fielders got skulled by fly balls, and two base runners often wound up occupying the same sack"—not to mention the perhaps apocryphal time that three Dodger runners wound up on third base simultaneously. It was a hapless age, but not without humor in adversity, as in the oft-told story about the fan who left a game early and reported that the "Dodgers are ahead and they've got three men on base," only to be asked, "Which base?"[3]

The "Daffiness Boys" fit comfortably into the mental image of Brooklyn that was disseminated first by vaudeville, then by radio and the movies, to the nation at large. These mass-entertainment media turned Brooklyn itself into something of a national joke; its inhabitants and the "deses and dems" of their stereotyped "Brooklynese" dialect were favorite foils for comedians desperately seeking surefire laughs. Increasingly overshadowed by the cosmopolitan pretensions of Manhattan since its incorporation into New York City in 1898, its home-based cultural and economic institutions relentlessly eclipsed by those just across the river, the Brooklyn of the 1930s was readily perceived as the impenetrable, and indecipherable, world unto itself portrayed by Thomas Wolfe in the short story "Only the Dead Know Brooklyn." In baseball terms, the nadir came in the spring of 1934, when Giant manager Bill Terry sneered, "Brooklyn—are they still in the league?" in response to a reporter's question about how the Dodgers would do that season.

Even at the time, Terry's gibe backfired. That year, the sixth-place Dodgers knocked the Giants out of a pennant by taking two crucial games from them in the last days of the season. More important, within a few years the Dodgers began a dramatic rise out of baseball's lower depths. After several more second-division finishes, the Dodgers bolted into third place in 1939 and then won their first pennant in two decades in 1941. A heartbreaking World Series loss to— who else?—the Yankees, forever after blamed on catcher Mickey Owen's dropped third strike on a pitch that would have tied the series at two games each, could not blunt the accelerating momentum of the Dodger revival. Yet as Brooklyn pushed past the Cardinals in the late 1940s to monopolize the top spot in the National League, the Dodgers, much like their home borough, held on tightly to the underdog self-image, gamely battling against the sport's, and society's, establishment.

Given the Dodgers' string of postwar pennants, fans of the truly downtrodden teams of the late 1940s and early 1950s—the Pirates, the Cubs, the Senators, and the Browns—could find Brooklyn's increasingly anachronistic "us against the world" protestations either irritating or amusing. As the opening of the 1957 season approached, the Dodgers looked back on a decade in which they had posted the best record by far in the National League, winning 112 games more than the Braves and 123 more than the hated Giants.[4] There was, however, frustration as well as satisfaction for Dodger fans in those years of triumph. Frustration came from Brooklyn's nagging habit of losing close pennant races—in playoffs to the Cardinals (1946) and the Giants (1951), and on the last day of the 1950 season to the Phillies. Then there was the team's history of World Series losses—never, until 1955, winning a World Series in seven previous fall appearances. Most of all, there was the accumulating record of failure against the Yankees, personified in the persistent inability of Brooklyn's ace pitcher Don Newcombe to defeat the Yanks.

Appearing in three World Series (1949, 1955, and 1956), Big Newk, who was winning almost 75 percent of his regular-season games in that time span, lost four games without a win against the Yankees, running up a combined earned-run average of 8.59. The low point occurred in Game 7 of the 1956 World Series, after the Dodgers had come back from Don Larsen's perfect-game win for the Yankees in Game 5 to even things up with a 1–0 win on Jackie Robinson's tie-breaking single in the bottom of the tenth the next day. In the series's deciding game, Newcombe was driven from the mound after giving up five runs in three innings to increase his earned-run average for that series to an incredible 21.21. He left the ballpark before the game was over and spent the night in seclusion. In the winner's locker room, Yankee pitcher Whitey Ford graciously defended Newcombe against the charge that he "choked" in big games, but Yankee fans no doubt gloated over the ignominious failure of their rival's mound star, and Dodger fans took little solace in the twenty-seven wins that Newcombe had recorded during the regular season.

The Yankee–Dodger rivalry extended beyond the win–loss columns. The Yankees were the team par excellence of the Eisenhower era's gray-flannel-suited organization men, for whom rooting for the Yankees was, indeed, comfortably akin to rooting for U.S. Steel. Independently wealthy Yankee owners Dan Topping and Del Webb, who had purchased the team from the estate of Jacob Ruppert in 1945, continued the hierarchical corporate management style pioneered by their predecessor, delegating responsibility for running the team to General Manager George Weiss, much as Ruppert and Huston had relied on Ed Barrow. For Topping and Webb, the Yankees were a sporting proposition. Although they certainly expected results, the team was not *their* primary business, as it was for the owners of the New York Giants and the Brooklyn Dodgers.

The appropriately pinstriped Yankees were as image-conscious as any Fortune 500 corporation. Yankee Stadium had the aura of a shrine, complete with tombstone-like monuments to Yankee luminaries standing in deepest center field, and the annual Old Timers' Day tribute to the widows of Babe Ruth and Lou Gehrig. Lest the image be tarnished by the hint of scandal, the organization practiced brutal damage control when necessary. In the spring of 1957, the Yankees quickly traded away one of the team's most popular players, Billy Martin, after embarrassing stories of a brawl involving a group of Yankees celebrating the shortstop's birthday at the Copacabana nightclub were splashed across newspaper front pages.

The upstart, integrated, and manifestly imperfect Dodgers offered a "politically correct" alternative to the remorselessly efficient Bronx

Bombers, who had continued to field an all-white team for years after Jackie Robinson entered the game. No one confused the Dodgers with a soulless corporate leviathan. The Dodgers' cartoon image as a "Brooklyn Bum" was a far cry from the Yankees' star-spangled, top-hatted iconography. That a raffish epithet could still be embraced as a point of reverse-perverse pride by a team with an increasingly suburban fan base, and which now performed like baseball royalty, encapsulated the split identity of the Brooklyn Dodgers in the Eisenhower years.

True, too much can be made of the currently prevalent notion that Dodger fans were socially conscious proletarians, in contrast to the well-heeled suburbanites who rooted for the Yankees. Julius and Ethel Rosenberg cheered on the Dodgers in their *Death House Letters,* but Communist Party leader Earl Browder was a Yankee fan who enjoyed spending the occasional afternoon at Yankee Stadium as a respite from his service to the revolution. The city's working classes provided loyal patrons for the stadium's 30,000 general-admission and bleacher seats and thirsty customers for broadcast sponsor Ballantine's far-from-premium brew.[5] But there *was* an underlying basis to the notion that, despite their great success on the playing field, the Brooklyn Dodgers were not the fully enrolled members of the baseball establishment that the New York Yankees had been for so many years.

The crux of the matter was geography. The Yankees represented New York, the Dodgers represented Brooklyn. By the 1950s, the team was an increasingly vestigial reminder of the time when the National League was young, New York City was confined to the western shores of the East River, and Brooklyn was an independent entity—the fourth largest city in America, in fact, trailing only New York City (which then consisted only of Manhattan and the Bronx), Chicago, and Philadelphia. Brooklyn would surpass Philadelphia in population as early as 1910, but by then its pretensions to independence had been clipped.

Instead of being the nation's third largest city, after 1898 Brooklyn was merely one of five boroughs of the City of Greater New York. A franchise that was a relic of the gaslight era found itself cast in the role of the champion of a constituency that was not the political master of its own fate, or of that of the Dodgers. Whether or not Brooklyn would continue to claim its own place in the national pastime would be determined by *New York*, not *Brooklyn*, policymakers. These might well prove unsympathetic to the parochial concerns of a borough that had become a backwater.

In the winter of 1956–57, the *Brooklyn* Dodgers confronted not one, but two, intersecting, and intensifying, crises. First, the Dodgers' decade-long reign as the dominant team in the National League was under sharp attack. The 1956 pennant race had been far tighter than the previous year's. The 1955 season had been a one-sided romp, with Brooklyn leading the league on all but two days of the season, clinching the flag on September 8, and finishing thirteen games ahead of second-place Milwaukee. On Labor Day 1956, by contrast, the veteran Dodger team trailed the Milwaukee Braves by 3½ games. Only a tremendous stretch drive, with wins in fifteen of their previous twenty-two games (including a no-hitter in the season's final week by onetime nemesis Sal "The Barber" Maglie), allowed Brooklyn to squeeze past Milwaukee by one game, and the Cincinnati Redlegs (as the "Reds" had officially renamed themselves in 1953, at the height of the McCarthy era, over local protests that "we were Reds before they were")[6] by two, and capture the pennant on the season's last day.

The closeness of that contest, in contrast to the cakewalk the previous season, highlighted the overriding reality facing the Dodgers: The team had become old. The average age of the starting lineup was over thirty-one, the oldest in baseball, and no one was getting any younger. No regular, other than second baseman Jim Gilliam, had played back to his 1955 level. For catching star and three-time

National League MVP Roy Campanella, the breakdown was truly appalling: Campy's batting average fell from .318 to .219, his home runs from 32 to 20, his runs batted in from 107 to 73. Duke Snider led the league with a team-record forty-three home runs, but both his average and run production were well below his 1955 marks. As a unit, the team batting average dropped from a league-leading .271 in 1955 to a fourth-best .258. True, thirty-seven-year-old Jackie Robinson, no longer a regular, turned in a better performance at the plate than in 1955, and his tenth-inning hit in Game 6 of the 1956 World Series gave the Dodgers a 1–0 win and kept their series hopes alive in a must-win situation. Robinson was still a great clutch player, but he had decided to retire before the 1957 season, even before the team forced his hand by trading him to the Giants. The fabric of the team that had played together as a unit so long and so well was beginning to unravel.

Going into the 1957 season, the Dodgers appeared destined to slip away from the top and enter a period of rebuilding, as the previous job of plugging stray gaps—especially at third base and left field—now had to expand to a thorough overhaul. The time was approaching when the team would be short of glamorous, pre-sold stars and long on fresh-faced, unproven youth who were sure to flounder—at least for a while—as they tried to take over for Hodges, Snider, Campy, Robinson, Furillo, and Reese. When the 1957 season got underway, the consensus of sportswriters picked the Braves, not the Dodgers, to take that year's pennant.[7]

Brooklyn's fans would have counted themselves lucky if that was the only challenge looming. A second crisis, one that threatened the future of the Dodgers as a Brooklyn institution, was even more pressing. For several years, Walter O'Malley had been trying, first privately and then publicly, to win local governmental support for the construction of a new stadium for the Dodgers in downtown Brooklyn. By January 1957, those efforts were being crushed between the conflicting visions and priorities of the Dodger owner and New York officialdom, and O'Malley had begun scouting out Los Angeles as a future Dodger home.

As the 1957 season unfolded, and the Dodgers struggled to hold off the Braves on the field, Brooklyn would find itself equally hard-pressed by Los Angeles in the battle for the team itself. By the end of the season, the Braves would be the winners of the National League pennant (and go on to defeat the Yankees in the World Series), finishing eleven games ahead of the third-place Dodgers. Brooklyn would lose out to Los Angeles in the struggle over the team's future home. Not only that, the Giants would join the Dodgers in making the move to California, leaving the nation's largest city—and its financial, cultural, and media capital—a New York Yankee monopoly.

For the third time, the Yankees would witness the implosion of a preeminent competitor from baseball's senior circuit. The Giants had fallen back amid the turmoil that beset a dysfunctional front office in the 1920s. The Cardinals' guerrilla war against baseball's established player-procurement practices had failed to perpetuate itself as anything more than the handcrafted extension of the individual genius of Branch Rickey. The Yankees would now watch from the sidelines as the Dodgers would fight and lose a political battle for survival on their home turf. On January 20, 1957, the *New York Times* carried the schedule for the upcoming season under the heading, "Day by Day with the Three New York Baseball Teams."[8] That headline would never appear again.

THE FLASHPOINT of the crisis that would deprive Brooklyn of its beloved "Bums" flared up, sad to say, at the hallowed intersection of McKeever Place and Sullivan Street, the site of the Dodgers' Ebbets Field home since 1913. No one could deny the immense amount of baseball history—good, bad, and bizarre—that had been made at the Dodgers' ballpark. Ebbets Field was where a bird flew out of Casey Stengel's cap, where an irate fan (lately released from jail) had assaulted umpire George Magerkurth, where Hilda Chester had rallied the faithful with her cowbell, where Cincinnati's Johnny Vander Meer had celebrated Brooklyn's first night game in 1938 by pitching his second-straight no-hitter, where the first televised major-league game had been played (in 1939), and where Dodger third baseman Cookie Lavagetto had broken up Bill Bevens's bid for the first World Series no-hitter with a game-winning double in the ninth inning of the fourth game of the 1947 series. On April 15, 1947, the old ballpark had even been the scene of "real" history, not just baseball history, when Jackie Robinson had broken the sport's "color line." Up until the end, even those who bemoaned its lack of creature comforts had to concede that "a visit to Ebbets Field is always entertaining," and that "no baseball park is more fun, for the Dodger fan shows his affections or his outspoken displeasure with a continuing riot of noise."9

But one day, although no one could say precisely when, Ebbets Field had become old, and a cherished tradition had become an inconvenient obsolescence to a growing number of critics. Whether the critics were right or wrong might not have mattered, were it not for the fact that Walter O'Malley, the Dodgers' president since 1950, was among those who believed that Ebbets Field had outlived its usefulness as a suitable venue for major-league baseball.

There had been storm signals along the way. In September 1941, the overwhelming demand for tickets to the first World Series in Flatbush in a generation precipitated talk about playing Brooklyn's home games in Yankee Stadium, which could accommodate crowds of 70,000, twice the capacity of the Brooklyn ballpark. After the war, Dodger management watched enviously as night after night, Sunday after Sunday, crowds of 50,000 and more flocked to the Polo Grounds and Yankee Stadium, selling 20,000 more tickets than the Dodgers could on any given day. Desperately trying to make up for seats that weren't there, O'Malley's predecessor, Branch Rickey, had instituted a separate admission policy for morning–afternoon doubleheaders on major holidays, at a ferocious cost in goodwill. The resulting animosity could still be detected years later in Dick Young's "obituary" for the Brooklyn Dodgers, in which the *Daily News* columnist recalled the "unpopular but undeniable success of Branch Rickey."[10] The New York State Legislature even voted to ban the separate admission policy, and it took all the political muscle the Dodgers could muster to induce Governor Thomas E. Dewey to veto the bill. It was a dead-end anyway, a desperate expedient at best, and when Walter O'Malley became the team's principal owner in 1950, he made a favorable first impression on the team's fans by immediately abandoning it.

So well known was Rickey's predilection for such financial corner-cutting that even a far more inspired Rickey innovation, the integration of baseball, has rather unfairly been similarly ascribed to a bottom-line–oriented motivation of the man dubbed "El Cheapo" by a suspicious New York press.[11] Indeed, Walter O'Malley evidently subscribed to this cynical theory as well, explaining on one occasion to Roger Kahn that "Rickey's Brooklyn contract called for a salary plus a percentage of the take, and during World War II the take fell off. It was *then* Rickey mentioned signing a Negro. He had a fiscal interest."[12] If so, Rickey was likely disappointed, since the signing of Jackie Robinson did not significantly boost Dodger attendance, which was already tops in the league, even in 1947, his first season, and it did nothing to arrest the decline over the course of Robinson's playing career. After 1947, attendance at Ebbets Field, as well as at the Polo Grounds and in major-league baseball generally, fell sharply.[13] By 1955, the World Champion Dodgers would share one distinction with the last-place (by thirty-eight games) Pirates—they were the only teams in the National League drawing fewer fans than in the last pre-war season of 1941. Rickey's integration initiative proved no magic formula at the box office.

Whether in the realm of penny-pinching tactics (the separate admission policy) or enlightened grand strategy (the breaking of the color line), Rickey's efforts to overcome the structural limitations of the Dodgers' historic home failed to yield a durable solution. Indeed, as the Dodgers fought their way into, or to the margin of, every World Series for the next decade, the limited size of the grandstand became an accelerating source of exasperation. As the baseball boom withered after 1950, the Giants and Yankees no longer were drawing their fifty thousands regularly and no longer were the envy of the baseball world, or of Dodger management. But, come fall, there was no way to ignore the simple fact that playing World Series games in Ebbets Field was costing the Dodgers (and their inevitable opponents, the Yankees) a great deal of money.

Even the Dodgers' first-ever World Series victory in 1955 was not without its shadow of fiscal regret. After losing the first two games, the Dodgers had rallied to win the series in seven games, the first time they had beaten the Yankees after five losses in the fall classic. Highlighted by Jackie Robinson's steal of home (although Yogi Berra would claim, then and always, that Robinson had really been out), Duke Snider's record-tying four home runs, Sandy Amoros's great catch, and Johnny Podres's shutout pitching in the deciding game, the series provided the most exhilarating experience in Brooklyn baseball history for the team's fans, whose long-suffering battle cry had been "wait till next year." But for the team's ownership, the balance sheet on the series was more complicated. The gate receipts for that series, in which the middle three games were played in Brooklyn, spelled out the opportunity costs imposed by Ebbets Field. For that series, the Dodgers and the Yankees each earned approximately $330,000 from the live gate.

Had the seating capacity of Ebbets Field been equal to that of the 65,000-seat Yankee Stadium, earnings for each team would have exceeded $405,000, an increase of $75,000.[14] Multiplied by the six World Series that the Dodgers co-hosted in Brooklyn during that decade, the total dollar cost to each team exceeded $500,000. Even those perspicacious writers who had learned to tap cautiously on their typewriter keys when the source of a team financial story was Walter O'Malley could not dispute the arithmetic lesson taught by these simple, easily accessible figures.

It was not simply Ebbets Field's limited seating capacity that suggested that it was out of step with the times. The playing field itself was confined by the dimensions of the available real estate. Its layout was economical of space and defiantly unsymmetrical in design. Deepest center field was just 403 feet distant from home plate, compared with over 460 feet in Yankee Stadium and 483 feet in the Polo Grounds. Built in the dead-ball era, when home runs were few and pitchers, throwing what were then legal spitballs, held an edge over the batters, distances to the fences hardly mattered. By the 1940s and 1950s, though, the park seemed to many observers too small for the muscular game being played.

The Dodgers front office, even as it loaded up the team with power hitters—notably, Duke Snider, Gil Hodges, and Roy Campanella—who could profit from the proximity of the park's outfield fences, subscribed to the conventional wisdom that the small and irregular dimensions distorted the game. It was certainly true that no one would ever see in Ebbets Field a counterpart to the grandiose, even monumental, shrine over which the Yankees ruled in the Bronx. Indeed, many Dodger fans celebrated the contrast.

There was still more to the critics' indictment of the historic Brooklyn ballpark. The compact two-tiered grandstand created a basic structural problem. Pitched steep and close to the field, it was, as a result, riddled with posts that obstructed views. Many fans were left with a somewhat sour memory of that great game they had *almost* seen. This was a persistent source of complaints, with the resulting intimate relationship to the field below being insufficiently unappreciated until the next generation's mode of post-free, more gently tiered stadium seating arrangements made clear what had been lost. At the time, there was a unanimous feeling that something had to be done about those posts. Even when Brooklyn was in its most desperate hour of need, and the last-ditch fight to save the Dodgers was clearly being lost, veteran Brooklyn Congressman Emanuel Celler couldn't help interrupting his indictment of O'Malley as a double-dealing liar to complain, "When I want to see a game in Brooklyn, I have to sit behind a post."[15]

Ebbets Field's amenities, such as they were, also reflected an earlier, less affluent time. O'Malley always recalled, with apparently unfeigned horror, his first inspection of the rest rooms at Ebbets Field. Few things seemed to him more shortsighted than Branch Rickey's refusal to endorse O'Malley's proposal to spend $250,000 to improve ladies' toilet facilities.[16] He lost that battle to what he described as Rickey's "old-fashioned thought that it was not going to put another customer in the park to have ladies' toilets there," but he added it to his lengthening list of grievances about Ebbets Field.[17]

The shadow of obsolescence had also fallen on the historic ballpark's location after 1950. In the first decades of its life, Ebbets Field had seemed to be a particularly happy setting for a ballpark. When built, it lay just at the fringe of settlement, but growth quickly spurted around and beyond it, snugly enclosing it within the comfortable embrace of urban bonhomie. On the leisurely afternoons that provided the typical setting for baseball before World War II, Ebbets Field enjoyed an enviable, and profitable, location. Daytime baseball was largely a walk-in business, the casual haunt of men and boys who, on that particular day, had nothing better—indeed, nothing much at all—to do, and Ebbets Field could draw nearby residents to the grandstand. Crowds were small but steady, and these weekday games moved the season along between the big weekend attractions, which, in good times, filled the team's coffers.

Although Ebbets Field was accessible by foot from its friendly neighborhood and by subway from the farther reaches of the city, it was preeminently the proliferating trackage of Brooklyn's trolley cars that gave the Dodgers their name and bound Ebbets Field into the life of Brooklyn. Even when, after World War II, the city began ripping up the tracks and cutting streetcar service, dozens of lines continued to trundle their way through Brooklyn, waging a gallant but hopeless battle against the forces of progress and petroleum. But you could, at least for a few years after the war, still get to Ebbets Field easily enough along the surface tracks. Flatbush Avenue cars ran out of downtown— just as they had for generations—past the Long Island Railroad depot at the tangled and already blighted intersection of Atlantic, Fourth, and Flatbush Avenues, then slid through the clutter of Grand Army Plaza and rolled on by the Brooklyn Botanic Garden, where a stop left you just a few short blocks from the ballpark. From the beaches, Coney Island Avenue service would bring the fan up to Park Circle at the southwest corner of Prospect Park, where a transfer could be made to a trolley that made a half circle around the park and passed alongside Ebbets Field by way of Franklin Avenue. It was the twilight of a waning era that had not, however, entirely ended.

It had been a good location for a Brooklyn ballpark for a very long time. But, that changed too, and very quickly, as a plausible case was built in the 1950s against the location of the Dodgers' home field. The increasing number of night games played beginning in the late 1940s made easy accessibility to a small but hardy pool of neighborhood regulars less important when measured against the enhanced attendance requirements for profitability in a more expensive age. Then, too, the ballpark's immediate neighborhood was becoming increasingly run-down, and fans became steadily more concerned about crime and safety issues. Walter O'Malley himself fell to worrying about it, recalling, "My mother-in-law and my wife wouldn't go to Ebbets Field unescorted because of the hoodlums and the purse snatchers."[18] The increasing black population of the ballpark's surrounding neighborhoods was a source of undoubted, if rarely articulated, concern for the team's owner and, indeed, its traditional patrons.

The most pressing problem of all with Ebbets Field and its long-established location was inadequate automobile access and parking. No one said it more sharply than O'Malley himself. "The Dodgers had earned their nickname when the fans dodged trolleys to get to the ball-park," he remembered, but "now the public was on wheels."[19] At Ebbets Field, there was not nearly enough space to handle the cars that now thronged its environs. Traffic patterns along the area's quiet residential streets were difficult at best, but they became murderously clotted as game times approached. The area's parking lots could accommodate barely 700 cars, and as they filled up, the jockeying for on-street parking began in chaotic earnest. Ebbets Field had lived by the trolley, and now, if O'Malley was right, it was going to die by the car. And more dispassionate observers agreed. "Be prepared for heavy traffic and inadequate parking facilities," *Sports Illustrated* warned potential patrons.[20]

In fact, the need for the spectator sport of baseball to accommodate the automobiles being driven by an ever-increasing number of its prospective spectators was not a novel issue. Thirty years earlier, 6,000 cars had jammed the environs of Yankee Stadium on its Opening Day in April 1923, and "traffic for miles around was at a standstill for an hour and a half" before a World Series game in October.[21] That fall, the *Sporting News* warned: "Such a big percentage of a ball club's patronage comes to it by automobile that the pressing problem is to find parking space," so "the fan is demanding of the ball club that it furnish not only a seat in the grandstand, but also parking space for the automobile"—this in 1923![22] Nothing had happened since then to cause O'Malley to doubt his diagnosis. Ebbets Field's Old Age was announcing itself with a hardening of the traffic arteries. But as he prepared to act, perhaps even O'Malley was surprised by the unanimous chorus of assent that rose up to echo his assault on the Dodgers' hallowed and historic home. Yet that's what happened. O'Malley's own self-interested condemnation of Ebbets Field was heartily seconded by nearly everyone else who had a say in the matter.

Day after day, Dodger fans read that Ebbets Field was "an inferior ballpark," "outmoded," "smallish," and, in an especially ripe rhetorical leap, "a hallowed but decaying goat shed."[23] Even Brooklyn's soon-to-be-defunct hometown newspaper acknowledged: "It is a widely held belief that Ebbets Field . . . is too small," and "prohibitive construction costs make it unlikely that this condition can be corrected in the foreseeable future."[24] It was "old and dirty" and inaccessible from midtown Manhattan, according to baseball's venerable "bible," *The Sporting News*.[25] Arthur Daley of the *New York Times* approvingly quoted former Dodger pitcher Billy Loes's complaint that pitching in Ebbets Field was "like pitchin' in a phone booth," and looked forward to a new age of standardized, symmetrical ballparks, with the Dodgers and Giants "no longer forced to play in the cramped, outmoded confines of the Polo Grounds and Ebbets Field, a pair of architectural monstrosities from a baseball standpoint."[26] "The park is certainly not beautiful, nor especially neat," one widely read "spectator's guide" to the big-league ballparks said of Ebbets Field, adding, "Rest rooms and concessions are too few and too far between to handle large crowds. Ushers growl if not tipped."[27] By comparison, at Yankee Stadium, "concessions are everywhere" and "rest rooms are sufficient and usually clean," although there, too, "Ushers dust seats, linger till tipped."[28]

One descriptive adjective was used so often and so predictably that the proverbial Man from Mars dipping into the sports pages of the *New York Times* could be forgiven for thinking that the name of the Dodgers' ballpark was "antiquated Ebbets Field."[29] Would that the Dodgers had had a left-handed batter with the consistency of the writers and compositors who drummed this talismanic watchword into the heads of New York's power elite. Although there would be rigorous debate aplenty when the time came to settle on the shape of the Dodgers' future after Ebbets Field, at the very outset of the discussion, the high ground of necessity was conceded to Walter O'Malley. From the beginning, everyone who had a say in the matter agreed that Ebbets Field had to go.

There had indeed been a sharp decline in attendance at Ebbets Field since the great years of the late 1940s. The average season attendance of 1,600,000 for the first four postwar years (1946–49) was down by one-third to an average after 1950 of a little more than 1,100,000. All too often, Ebbets Field looked like a "deserted village."[30] Even during the last weeks of the 1956 season, as the Dodgers were engaged in a "to-the-death struggle with the Milwaukee Braves for the pennant," in which "the championship may hinge on a single pitch," Ebbets Field was generally no more than half full, and Sal Maglie's crucial no-hitter against the Phillies on the night of September 25 was witnessed by only 15,200 fans. "Is that civic pride?" Arthur Daley asked. "Is Brooklyn really the wackiest and most fanatical baseball town in the country? Don't think that [construction of a new ball park] will solve the problem. The new 'home . . .' will provide more seats to stay away from. It's a cinch that Milwaukee fans would not react in such indifferent fashion."[31]

In hindsight, however, the case against Ebbets Field was not as open-and-shut as O'Malley and even most of his critics made it out to be at the time. As one ordinary fan, powerless against the tide of "informed" opinion, put it the day O'Malley pronounced the sentence of death on the ballpark, "a lot of Brooklyn people have been going there for a lot of years—and liking it—win, lose or draw."[32] Ebbets Field, whatever its defects, simply was not *that* old. Before baseball expanded to Milwaukee, Kansas City, and Baltimore after 1953, Ebbets Field was actually the third youngest ballpark in the National League, one year older than Chicago's Wrigley Field, two years older than Boston's Braves Field. As for the American League, only Cleveland's Municipal Stadium and Yankee Stadium had gone up after the Dodger home grounds. Rather than being an antiquated poor relation, Ebbets Field had been built at the end of the great wave of privately financed steel-and-concrete construction that, in the years bracketed around 1910, had transformed the face of major-league baseball. It was a ballpark that summed up the then-existing state-of-the-stadium art.

It was also forgotten, or ignored, that due to a series of renovations at several intervals since the ballpark had been opened in 1913, the 32,000-seat capacity of Ebbets Field was not out of line with prevailing standards (see Table 3.4 in the appendix). Rather than being unusually small, the Brooklyn ballpark actually contained the typical number of seats to be found in National League ballparks of the time. True, its capacity did appear to be cramped when set against the more commodious stands that dotted the American League landscape, but considered in its National League context, Ebbets Field fit right in, and not unfavorably in terms of the revenue it could generate.[33] The Polo Grounds was considerably bigger (its great patches of empty seats more and more apparent in the years after 1951), and so too, although by a lesser margin, were Wrigley Field and the Braves' two homes in Boston and Milwaukee. But Ebbets Field was larger or the same size as all the rest—not that anyone took notice of this at the time—and even today, blanket indictments of Ebbets Field's exceptionally small size are still handed up.[34] It remains a bum rap, especially given the trend to the downsized, more intimate ballparks that have recently been built, replacing the 50,000-plus multipurpose stadia of the 1960s and 1970s with baseball-only parks seating about 40,000 fans. In Houston, Pittsburgh, and Cincinnati, the fans of the new millennium have been given a simulation of what Brooklyn's fans were told was hopelessly out of date half a century ago.

Ebbets Field, however, suffered from the fact that the most relevant point of comparison was not any of its sister National League ballparks, but rather the Yankees' massive stadium in the Bronx. Had the Dodgers enjoyed less success, the comparison would not have been so pointedly adverse to Ebbets Field, and it more likely would have enjoyed a longer, if less glorious, existence. The Dodgers' head-to-head competition with the Yankees on the playing field highlighted the self-evident disparity between Yankee Stadium and their own more modest home in Brooklyn. With a capacity less than half that of the Yankees' home, Ebbets Field was bound to leave thousands of World Series fans frustrated by the limited number of seats available, and it also cost both Dodgers and Yankees substantial potential revenues. Yankee Stadium was a powerful, if silent, witness to the perceived deficiencies of Ebbets Field.

Then, too, the 1950's—today an era that is itself subject to nostalgia without end—was a bad decade for tradition. Perhaps Ebbets Field's misfortune was that it became "ancient" and "antiquated" and "obsolete" too soon. On June 12, 1967, a *Sports Illustrated* article summed up the case against Boston's Fenway Park in terms eerily familiar to anyone who had followed the earlier debate over the Brooklyn ballpark. Fenway attendance hadn't topped one million since Ted Williams's retirement in 1960, and it had fallen below 700,000 in

1965 before barely reaching 800,000 in 1966. The root of the problem, the magazine pronounced, was "ancient, obsolete Fenway Park with its 33,524 seats, its totally inadequate parking facilities and its Great Wall in left field."[35] Red Sox owner Tom Yawkey had rebuffed proposals to increase capacity by adding a second deck a decade earlier, saying that lagging local baseball interest in the wake of the departure of the Braves did not justify the expense.[36] Yet at the very time that the pundits and apparently the fans had turned thumbs-down on "ancient, obsolete" Fenway Park, Boston's "impossible dream" year was already underway, as the Red Sox would go on to win the 1967 pennant, draw almost 1,700,000 fans, and provide an entirely unexpected new lease on wildly successful baseball life in Fenway for three decades more (and counting). That thirty-year reprieve would show that a ballpark built in 1912 did not pose an insurmountable obstacle to success on the field or at the gate.

It was a stay of execution that Ebbets Field did not enjoy.[37] It was Ebbets Field's bad luck that the Dodgers were owned by a man who was a true visionary, capable of seeing and seizing opportunities from which others shied away, opportunities that might not even be there at all. Walter O'Malley's concept of a new stadium in the heart of downtown Brooklyn was, for good or ill, perhaps a decade or more ahead of its time. It anticipated the wave of new construction that swept over the baseball world in the mid 1960s, as did his model of a symmetrical, spacious, and sterile replacement for idiosyncratic and cramped Ebbets Field. In Cincinnati, Philadelphia, St. Louis, and Pittsburgh, among other traditional baseball towns, new multipurpose municipal stadiums replaced vintage ballparks, as governmental agencies intensified their efforts to rehabilitate depressed inner cities. Perhaps Brooklyn, too, would have been able to hold on to the Dodgers, given a similar delay in O'Malley's pursuit of a new home for his team.

Or perhaps not. No project elsewhere entailed the massive redevelopment of a still-functioning commercial hub that O'Malley's plan required. None of the new stadiums were privately owned, one of O'Malley's key demands. And each, of course, was undertaken with the cautionary example of Brooklyn's loss of major-league baseball in the absence of such a project—an example very firmly fixed in the minds of the decision-makers. That sobering experience, by definition, was not available to guide—or, some would say, intimidate—those who would be called upon to consider the future of the Brooklyn Dodgers.

◇

WHETHER OR not Ebbets Field was really as obsolete as its critics charged, there could be no question that, by the mid-1950s, the map of major-league baseball was badly out of date. The traditional alignment of the two leagues—sixteen teams crowded into ten cities in the nation's northeast quadrant—had endured beyond all reasonable expectations, repelling all challenges in the half century after it had been fixed once and for all by the transfer of the Baltimore American League franchise to New York City in 1903. It had been, after all, an improvised structure, thrown together in haste and devised in large measure to meet the immediate demands of the trade war then raging between the National and American Leagues. Only the prolonged stasis induced by the Great Depression, followed by the insistent agenda of world war, had kept it intact for so long.

"It's too bad," Giants manager John McGraw told the local newsmen crowded into his Los Angeles hotel suite one winter afternoon in 1931, "that a city as large as Los Angeles is kept out of the big leagues on account of geographical conditions. It is a big league city at heart."[38] Two decades later, major-league baseball's exclusion of Los Angeles and San Francisco, two of the nation's eight largest metropolitan regions, was even more incongruous. A "national pastime" that did not encompass these cities would be increasingly hard-pressed to retain that cherished title. Wedged between the Atlantic and the Mississippi, the Mason–Dixon line and the Great Lakes, the baseball nation was fast losing touch with the real one.

This was more than a crisis of image for the "national pastime." It was an economic crisis as well. The relative size of the markets being tapped by the major leagues was shrinking as growth accelerated beyond the bounds of the traditional circuit. One-fourth of the American people still lived in the environs of major-league baseball in 1950, a proportion that had held steady for decades. But the westward trend of population growth was threatening to reduce that ratio to barely one-fifth, as registered in the 1960 census, unless baseball got on the move itself.

Shortly after World War II, representatives of major-league baseball recognized the "tremendous potentialities" of the Pacific Coast for major-league baseball and concluded that the Los Angeles and San Francisco Bay areas offered "rich opportunities for major league expansion." However, their 1947 report proposed no course of action to realize that objective.[39] Los Angeles and San Francisco were the obvious—and far and away the most desirable—candidates to crack baseball's half-century-old mold. It did not, however, work out that way. More immediately pressing problems arose, shoving aside any long-term expansion plans. Emergency preempted strategy. When the baseball landscape finally buckled in March 1953, it did so under short-term pressures and with a move that was entirely unexpected until just days before it was made.

The Braves' move to Milwaukee just before the opening of the 1953 season shattered the fifty-year-old alignment of major-league clubs, but it had been an ad hoc, spur-of-the-moment decision, taken when club owner Lou Perini abruptly learned that his claim to the Milwaukee territory (where the Braves had a farm team and which Perini had been eyeing as a *possible* escape route for some time) would be lost—the Browns were preparing their own move there—unless he acted immediately. Perini had been ready to absorb at least another season of financial reverses in Boston—where 1952 attendance had dropped to an unbelievably low 280,000 (more than one million down from the total just four years earlier), and the club had lost more than $500,000—to see whether Boston fans would support a team that was, as he knew, on the verge of substantial improvement on the field.[40] The next year, the St. Louis Browns fled to Baltimore. In 1955, the first round of "musical franchises," which reduced the ranks of baseball's multiteam cities from five to two (New York and Chicago), ended as the Philadelphia Athletics breached the Mississippi frontier of major-league baseball and headed to Kansas City.

The attractiveness of Milwaukee, Baltimore, and Kansas City did not account for these shifts; dismal conditions in Boston, St. Louis, and Philadelphia did. Problems back home drove the teams away, and they settled where they could, in convenient havens with ready-built ballparks, crusading newspapers, and openhanded politicians. They were expecting something better than what they had left behind, but they were by no means aiming for the best. The Braves, the Browns, and the Athletics had escaped the past, but they did not thereby point the way to an abundant future. Indeed, two of the three expansion pioneers, the Braves and the Athletics, would move on again to new homes (in Atlanta and Oakland, respectively) not much more than a decade later.

IN FACT, baseball had long ago mapped out and discarded these reclaimed territories. Each had been a major-league city in the years before consolidation and realignment reduced the reach of big-league baseball from three leagues with twenty-six teams in twenty-two cities in 1884 down to two leagues of sixteen teams bunched into just ten cities in 1903 (see map on page 207). Kansas City, isolated as it was at

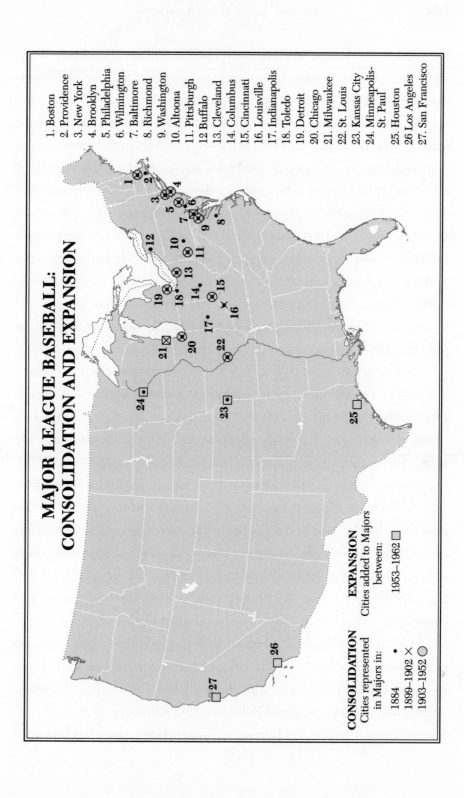

MAJOR LEAGUE BASEBALL:
CONSOLIDATION AND EXPANSION

1. Boston
2. Providence
3. New York
4. Brooklyn
5. Philadelphia
6. Wilmington
7. Baltimore
8. Richmond
9. Washington
10. Altoona
11. Pittsburgh
12. Buffalo
13. Cleveland
14. Columbus
15. Cincinnati
16. Louisville
17. Indianapolis
18. Toledo
19. Detroit
20. Chicago
21. Milwaukee
22. St. Louis
23. Kansas City
24. Minneapolis-
    St. Paul
25. Houston
26. Los Angeles
27. San Francisco

CONSOLIDATION
Cities represented
in Majors in:

1884   •
1899–1902   ×
1903–1952   ◯

EXPANSION
Cities added to Majors
between:

1953–1962   ▢

the gateway to the sparsely populated western plains, had been eliminated from the big-league roster early on. But Baltimore and Milwaukee had clung to big-league status up until the final cut.

Between 1900 and 1903, four cities had lost their major-league
teams. First, Louisville and Buffalo disappeared from the list when the
National League reduced its complement of twelve teams to eight
after the 1900 season. Then, Milwaukee and Baltimore were gone
after the American League—which had embraced these National
League castoffs in 1901—regrouped its forces in order to wage more
effective war on the senior circuit.[41] And although they had been made
under the special pressures of immediate and passing circumstances,
the decisions to eliminate these cities had been well enough founded
so that over the next fifty years, baseball hardly noticed—nor was it
hurt by—their absence from the close-knit big-league scene.

They were not missed. Baseball had guessed right about the future
patterns of growth and power, calling even the close ones correctly:
Pittsburgh over Louisville, Detroit over Buffalo. By the time baseball
finalized its circuits, Louisville, Buffalo, and Milwaukee were already
losing the battle of relative importance, never to be as significant in the
twentieth century as they were in the closing decades of the nineteenth. Even Baltimore, the only city among the ten largest in the
country to be shut out of the majors by the new map, had little to com-
mend it beyond simple numbers. The sport, after 1903, could stake
out its claim to be the national pastime, secure in the belief that its flag
was planted in the nation's leading centers of trade, commerce, and
enterprise.

The "fit" that baseball achieved with the country at large held up
over time, too. In 1903, the ten cities of the major leagues were home
to one out of every seven Americans. Fifty years later, they still were.
Even without the presence of Baltimore, Milwaukee, or Kansas City—
not to mention Buffalo or Louisville—major-league baseball had kept

in step with the nation for the first half of the twentieth century. These years were dominated by the industrial urban heartland of the North and the Upper Midwest that major-league baseball had staked out as its turf.

It was the rise of the Far West in the decade after World War II that finally shattered this equilibrium. It had taken fifty years, but a massive shift in population, wealth, and influence suddenly challenged an earlier age's landscape of power, as reflected in the baseball map. California marked the emerging frontier of growth and opportunity in post–World War II America in just the way that the great cities of the North and Midwest had done when major-league baseball was young. But when the Athletics decamped for Kansas City in 1955, organized baseball still lacked any hard ideas about how it was going to extend its reach to the Pacific Coast. Only on one point about the future course of expansion did there appear to be consensus in baseball's ruling councils. "From now on," Baseball Commissioner Ford Frick told the press in March 1956, "instead of switching franchises from one city to another as has been done, there will be true expansion. . . . The franchise switches that have been made . . . came about because of financial necessity. Now every big league franchise is in a solid position. Every town is secure."[42] But, as Brooklyn was about to find out, not "secure" enough.

7

STADIUM GAMES

I F "ANTIQUATED" Ebbets Field became "Exhibit A" in the case against the future of the Dodgers in Brooklyn, the lead prosecutor was team owner Walter O'Malley, who more or less singlehandedly pushed the case to trial. As it happened, O'Malley *was* a lawyer by trade; his initial contact with the team's business affairs had come about through the intercession of one of his trust-company clients in the early 1940s. Until then, neither the Dodgers nor Brooklyn had then been the focus of his professional life. "I never practiced law in Brooklyn," he took pains to emphasize years later. "I worked in the Lincoln Building on Forty-second Street in Manhattan."[1]

It was a carefully chosen distinction, a revealing attempt to distance himself from the borough he had, in the end, abandoned. O'Malley and Brooklyn, he seemed to be saying, had not been identities after all, a clarification that provided a useful thread for untangling the story of the last days of the Brooklyn Dodgers. Walter O'Malley's own initial rendezvous with Brooklyn had been, after all, an accident of hard times and busted opportunities.[2] "My roots are in Brooklyn" became his cry of reproach to those who would later doubt his professed reluctance to move the Dodgers away from their historic home, but this was not actually true. The way stations of the O'Malley family as it ascended the gentle ladder of upward mobility included Manhattan, the Bronx—where Walter was born in 1903—and suburban Hollis in Queens, but no part of the Borough of Brooklyn. In later years, his speech "would be called pure Brooklyn," but only by those "who didn't recognize a perfect blend of Bronx and Queens intonations with a sprinkling of Long Island on top."[3]

Edwin O'Malley, Walter's father, was a businessman active, among his other enterprises, in the political business of Tammany Hall. When his faction in the tangled world of Democratic clubhouse politics held power during the years of machine rule between 1917 and 1933 (which bridged the reform mayoral terms of John Purroy Mitchel and Fiorello La Guardia), Edwin O'Malley became a public servant as well. But even when a political power play forced him from office as New York City Commissioner of Markets amid a splash of scandal-mongering headlines, Edwin kept his eye fixed on the future of his family and strove to parlay his up-and-down career into expanded opportunities for Walter, his only child.

Edwin provided well. Walter attended prep school before being sent out of the city—no ordinary chance for even a well-off young man of the time—to the University of Pennsylvania. That wasn't the end of the training intended to equip Walter for more in life than a regular Democratic clubhouse and the long climb, at best, to a tarnished prominence that such a launching point might provide. So Walter entered Columbia Law School, with the boat his father gave him to mark his Penn engineering degree snugly tied up in its slip. From Columbia, there need be no limit to his reach.

There had always been money in the O'Malley family. Then, suddenly, there wasn't. The stock-market crash hit Edwin hard. Walter, forced to work days now, switched schools and graduated from Fordham in the depths of the depression. A Fordham night degree in law counted for little. The dreams of the great world lying in wait at his impeccably credentialed feet were gone.

Walter made the best of it—and more. After being admitted to the

New York bar, he continued the engineering work on which he had depended for support during his time at Fordham. Seizing the moment, he devoted his law practice to bankruptcy work. The O'Malley law office was in midtown Manhattan, and Walter was among a coterie of Jewish and Catholic lawyers who made the most of their exclusion from the legal profession's rigidly Protestant Wall Street precincts. Together they struggled to make a living through the depression, gaining whatever footholds they could in the field of law— real estate, entertainment, antitrust, probate—that, unbeknownst to them at the time, would make their fortunes in the years of prosperity that would follow World War II. It was then, however, that they would be ready to gain full recompense for their skills and their creative legal thinking. Among others who would make their mark, the lawyer who devised the framework for the real estate syndications that changed the postwar face of the city established his office in the building that housed O'Malley's own quickly growing firm.

Manhattan provided O'Malley's working environment, but his personal life was anchored in Brooklyn, where he had settled with his bride at the onset of his law career. Along with his wife, Kay—whose voice could not rise above a soft whisper after the pre-wedding removal of a cancerous larynx—there he raised his children, one son and one daughter. Over the years, O'Malley's own ties to Brooklyn grew beyond those of family alone: He became a director of the Brooklyn Borough Gas Company in the mid-1930s, and, in time, his legal work in pursuit of the impecunious debtors of the Brooklyn Trust Company led to the bank's placing him on the board of one of its more prominent defaulting customers, the Brooklyn Dodgers.

O'Malley's Brooklyn associations steadily accumulated as the years passed. The causes he came to serve were Brooklyn ones: general chairman of the United Hospital Fund of Brooklyn, director of Brooklyn's Swedish Hospital (a bow to his wife's ancestry), chairman of the

Board of Brooklyn's Froebel Academy, director and vice president of the Brooklyn Club. His ascendancy in the Dodger hierarchy—from club counsel in 1943 (succeeding Republican presidential candidate Wendell Willkie), to ownership of one-twelfth (1944), one-fifth (1945), and one-half (1950) of the club's stock, ousting Branch Rickey as president of the team that year as well—kept pace with those charitable and civic activities. O'Malley's identification with the borough was anchored by the brownstone he maintained on venerable St. Mark's Place, a few blocks from Grand Army Plaza.

When O'Malley became president of the Dodgers in 1950, he gave up his Manhattan law practice. Thereafter, the Dodger team offices at 205 Montague Street served as the base for all his operations. To a significant extent, therefore, O'Malley's Brooklyn "roots" were not much more than a decade old when he cited them as proof of his bona fides in his thinking about a new Brooklyn home for the Dodgers. More to the point, it was a bad time to be putting down such "roots" at all.

The Great Depression had killed Brooklyn as a business center, stopping new construction flat and stranding the borough's only skyscraper, the Williamsburgh Savings Bank (completed in the unfortunate year of 1929), in a low-rise cityscape. The war did not revive Brooklyn as a commercial center, nor did the peace, as expansion and growth simply leapfrogged over the borough's decaying downtown. Manhattan institutions either assumed the commercial and consumer functions that had formerly been discharged by downtown Brooklyn's shops and offices or farmed them out to smaller epicenters of trade closer to the changing distribution of a metropolitan population that was increasingly getting around by car. The postwar private sector simply wrote off Brooklyn's downtown.

The processes of change, having fatally wounded Brooklyn as a marketplace, also struck hard at Brooklyn as a community. In the course of the 1950s, a massive exchange of populations transformed the sociological map of the borough. A wave of black migration from the feudal South, much of it channeled through the overcrowded streets of Harlem before passing along the route of the IND's A train under the river to Brooklyn, shattered traditional lines of segregation, first in Bedford-Stuyvesant in the late 1930s and 1940s, then, after the war, in Crown Heights, East New York, and Brownsville. Pushed, certainly, by the intrusion of a different race of people, but pulled, too, by the better housing opportunities opened up by good times, older residents of the borough abandoned familiar turf to make new homes in the just-opened reaches of southeast Brooklyn, in Queens, and on Long Island as well. The rate of mobility was dramatic as neighborhoods "changed" (in the language of the day) in two or three years, sometimes less. Amid these rapid shifts of population, which gave no indication of abating, Walter O'Malley also cut the tie that had bound him to Brooklyn. In the early 1950s, he gave up his home on St. Mark's Place and moved his permanent residence out to his summer house in Amityville, on Long Island. It was a decision that reflected what was happening all across Brooklyn. Everything was in flux. For anyone who held investments in Brooklyn, most emphatically including Walter O'Malley, the only certainty about the future was that it would be different from what had gone before.

These rapid changes highlighted a structural weakness in the very nature of the Borough of Brooklyn itself. It might be true that, in the realm of the imagination, and notwithstanding its geographical proximity to the Manhattan that was, for all intents and purposes *the* City, Brooklyn remained a place apart. Turning down a job offer from the *Brooklyn Eagle* in the mid-1940s, the Philadelphia-based sportswriter Red Smith "decided that Brooklyn was farther from New York than Philadelphia was."[4] As Brooklyn-born Norman Podhoretz would put it, "one of the longest journeys in the world is the journey from Brooklyn to Manhattan."[5] But if Brooklyn was a city "in fact," it was not a city "in law," a distinction that made a fateful, perhaps decisive, difference when Brooklyn confronted a threat to the continued existence of its last remaining emblem of independence, its major-league baseball team. By the 1950s, the Brooklyn Dodgers baseball team was a vestigial remnant of the long-since-vanished independent City of Brooklyn, just as much a fish out of water as the singularly monumental Williamsburgh Bank tower. Over the years, all of the other appurtenances of "major league" status had disappeared, in an inexorable process triggered by the surrender of municipal sovereignty in 1898. The fate of its preeminent cultural institution, the Brooklyn Museum, was emblematic of this downward trajectory. Designed by McKim, Mead & White, architects of so many of New York's great institutional buildings—including Pennsylvania Station, Columbia University's Low Library, and the Morgan Library—the museum had the misfortune to be launched in the year before Brooklyn's "declaration of dependence." "As a borough in the larger metropolis, support for the museum waned," and only one-fourth of the original design was realized, a truncated symbol of the price paid by Brooklyn for consolidation into the City of Greater New York. In the 1950s, even as the Dodgers enjoyed unprecedented success on the playing field, the full bill on Brooklyn's subscription to that metropolitan vision came due. The great gibe about Brooklyn said it all: "Brooklyn is the biggest city in the world without a railroad station, a daily newspaper, or a regular left fielder."[6]

The newsprint that announced the daily place in the "Standing of the Clubs" claimed by "BROOKLYN" or "BKLN" or, when space was short, "BKN," was the one remaining recognition of the status once rightly due what had been the nation's fourth largest city, as Brooklyn had been in 1898. But Brooklyn's independence had long since been sacrificed to the glory of Greater New York. By 1955, the National League of Professional Baseball Clubs, alone among worldly institutions, continued to accord the vanished City of Brooklyn recognition as a separate juridical entity. For scheduling purposes, the National League placed the Dodgers in the league's eastern division, along with the Manhattan-based New York Giants. As a result, home games for each team were slated on the same dates whenever the season called for east–west matchups, thereby dividing fan dollars and interest in a unique contravention of the fundamental rule of baseball's geography, which generally prohibited such conflicting playing dates for teams in the same city. For the National League, at least, Brooklyn was not part of New York, but, for the world at large, it was.

No one was more attentive to Brooklyn's postwar woes than Walter O'Malley. "We have lost our newspaper. We have lost our department stores, we haven't built a new office building, a real one, a new theater or a new hotel since 1929," he said in 1957, as he prepared to take the Dodgers west, insisting that Brooklyn was yet "an old place" that "I just happen to love."[7] Indeed, as Brooklyn declined, the Dodgers' own ties to its ancestral home were fraying. Fans by the hundreds of thousands were moving out of Brooklyn, their continued loyalty to the team increasingly vicarious and detached from the place itself.[8] The team's great broadcaster, Red Barber, who had done so much to popularize the game and the team with his ingratiating commentary, in which he referred to on-field arguments as "rhubarbs," run-scoring rallies as "tearin' up the pea patch," and loaded bases as being "FOB" (i.e., "Full of Brooklyns"), lived in Manhattan, commuted to Ebbets Field, and hardly tarried once a game was over. Asked by an adoring fan to reminisce, in later years, about sandlot baseball in Brooklyn, Barber's indifferent response made clear that he had not the slightest interest in the subject.[9] By the mid-1950s, O'Malley himself lived on Long Island. This displacement was not entirely new. In his memorable campaign stop at Ebbets Field in 1944, Franklin Roosevelt had proclaimed himself a Dodger fan, while acknowledging that he had never been to Ebbets Field before.[10] The increasingly "virtual" nature, as we might label it today, of so much of the team's support did not augur well for baseball's future in Brooklyn.

Yet, as the 1950s reached the halfway point, Brooklyn still had the Dodgers, and the prospect of a divorce between the two appeared unthinkable. But even as the team was running away with the National League pennant in 1955 on the way to its first, and only, World Championship, the Brooklyn Dodgers' moment of truth had suddenly arrived. When the decision time came, the team's millions of fans, near and far, would have no say in determining the Dodgers' future, and the people of Brooklyn would learn that the one thing worse than not having a regular left fielder was not having any kind of left fielder at all.

IN THE WANING days of the existence of the *Brooklyn* Dodgers, Walter O'Malley would say that he had decided as early as 1947[11] that Ebbets Field, as it then stood, could not house the Dodgers much longer. Locked into his unpleasant partnership with Branch Rickey, and unable to assume responsibility for management of the ball club, O'Malley took the initiative in studying possible improvements for the ballpark. He arranged for the team to commission a design for enlarging the field's seating capacity. The solution sketched out was the construction of a new grandstand in right field, which would enclose the entire playing area with two tiers of seats. But the right-field wall backed up against busy Bedford Avenue, which was responsible for a serious traffic of cars and trucks, along with the happily bouncing home-run balls catapulted out there first by Dolf, later by Gil or Duke. The simplest solution, O'Malley decided, was not practical.

It was a decision the more easily made, since O'Malley soon had something much better in mind for the Dodgers than simply remodeling Ebbets Field. By the early 1950s, he settled on what he then thought was the perfect location for an all-new Dodger home—the intersection of Atlantic and Flatbush Avenues in downtown Brooklyn, on the site of the deteriorating depot of the Long Island Railroad, surrounded by a network of subway stations that, in their ensemble, handled every rapid transit line in the city system (see map on page 219). Here was Brooklyn's transportation nexus, and here, too, was a cluster of leading Brooklyn institutions—the Academy of Music, the Central Brooklyn YMCA, and the lonely tower of the Williamsburgh Savings Bank. This, O'Malley decided, was the place to build a new stadium for the Brooklyn Dodgers.

It was an audacious decision, entirely at odds with the history of ballpark construction in New York City. Each in their turn—the Giants under Brush, the Dodgers under Ebbets, the Yankees under Ruppert—had been driven, by the price of land and the accelerating congestion of urban life, farther and farther toward the margins of the city in order to find land cheap enough and extensive enough to build a ballpark. O'Malley proposed to break that pattern and return baseball to the central city.

A full forty years earlier, commercial realities had driven Dodgers owner Charlie Ebbets to the site that would become Ebbets Field.[12] Before building the field in 1913, the Dodgers had played their home games in Washington Park, alongside the Gowanus Canal, between Third and First Streets and Fourth and Fifth Avenues, about one-half mile south of Brooklyn's downtown. It was an industrial district of coal yards and stone works, of construction sheds and transit power stations, its interstices filled in with a motley collection of brick and frame houses. The grandstand of the ballpark could handle about 12,000 fans. Desiring a bigger ballpark, Ebbets did the only thing that occurred to him: He cast his eye in search of property even more distant from the borough's densely developed downtown area.

Ebbets's attention drifted, in the years just after 1910, across

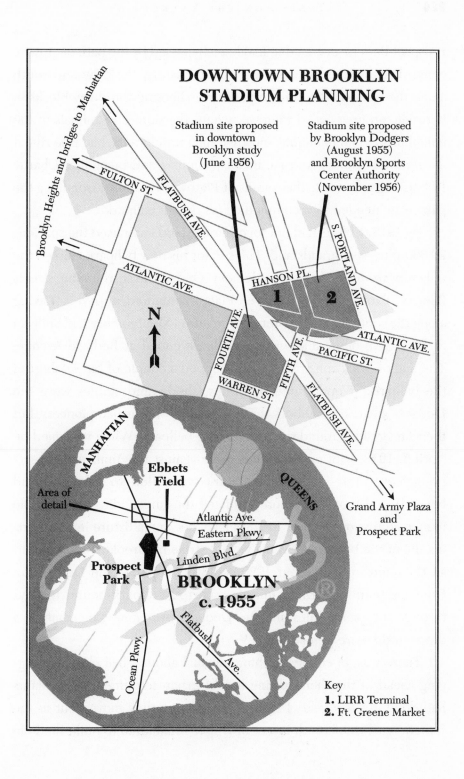

DOWNTOWN BROOKLYN STADIUM PLANNING

Stadium site proposed in downtown Brooklyn study (June 1956)

Stadium site proposed by Brooklyn Dodgers (August 1955) and Brooklyn Sports Center Authority (November 1956)

Brooklyn Heights and bridges to Manhattan

FULTON ST.

FLATBUSH AVE.

ATLANTIC AVE.

N

HANSON PL.

S. PORTLAND AVE.

1   **2**

FOURTH AVE.

FIFTH AVE.

ATLANTIC AVE.

PACIFIC ST.

WARREN ST.

FLATBUSH AVE.

Grand Army Plaza and Prospect Park

MANHATTAN

QUEENS

Ebbets Field

Area of detail

Atlantic Ave.

Eastern Pkwy.

Prospect Park

Linden Blvd.

BROOKLYN c. 1955

Ocean Pkwy.

Flatbush Ave.

Key
1. LIRR Terminal
2. Ft. Greene Market

Prospect Park to an area that had been bypassed by the path of growth, which had proceeded eastward along Eastern Parkway and south along the eastern edge of the park, overshooting the dusty blocks in between, an area called Pigtown, where the domestic animals of the neighborhood's inhabitants, mostly Italian immigrants, had free run of its unpaved streets. And so, inconspicuously and incognito, Charlie Ebbets began to make the rounds of Pigtown, carefully assembling the parcels he needed to accommodate *his* dream ballpark.

By 1913, Ebbets had put together the land and raised the spacious 20,000-plus–seat grandstand. The site for his new ballpark marked the unkempt frontier of urban settlement. One of the surrounding streets (Cedar Place—later McKeever Place) remained unpaved. Paving along the southern and western boundaries (Montgomery and Sullivan Streets) gave out just where the ballpark ended at Bedford Avenue. The line of brick construction still stopped a couple of blocks short of the ballpark. Wood frame buildings, sheds, and stables were the Dodgers' nearest neighbors.[13] The Dodgers were urban pioneers, but their fans readily found their way to the ballpark. When it opened on April 5, 1913, with an exhibition game against the Yankees, Ebbets's brand-new, state-of-the-art ballpark was filled to capacity (and beyond), and thousands more thronged the surrounding area, unable to gain admission. Ebbets Field quickly became a fixture in the sporting life of the borough. Even a violent strike by Brooklyn Rapid Transit trainmen in September 1920 could not separate the Dodger fan from his team, as armed guards escorted ballpark-bound trolleys through the picket lines and the Dodgers overcame Cincinnati in a down-to-the-wire pennant race.[14]

There was, of course, nothing unusual about a ball club leapfrogging ahead of the then-existing line of urban settlement. The Giants had done it a few years before Ebbets when they moved out to the remote reaches of 155th Street in Upper Manhattan to build the Polo

Grounds, as would the Yankees ten years later, when they forded the Harlem River and crossed into the Bronx. To get the large parcel of land needed, club owners had no choice but to reach beyond the frontier of development and build on the edge of growth.

Like Ebbets before him, O'Malley could not afford to buy downtown land. When faced with the cost barrier, Ebbets had simply retreated along the line of least expensive resistance out to Pigtown. After all, in Ebbets's time, the job of land acquisition, construction, even what passed for city planning,[15] remained the preserve of private capital. The law of the market prevailed, and a team owner could get only what he could pay for out of his own pocket. Four decades later, O'Malley thought there was an alternative purchase mechanism he could use to obtain a ballpark site that was otherwise beyond his means.

In the early 1950s, O'Malley embarked on a series of highly confidential and (although a number of newspaper publishers attended some of the sessions) leak-proof meetings with city officials,[16] in which he sought governmental assistance for his stadium plans. The Dodger owner explained that, as a private businessman, it was simply impossible to assemble, in the private market, at the price of $1 million (the amount he had allocated for land in his proposed $6 million construction budget), these heavily used, centrally located parcels in Brooklyn's central business district. The only way to obtain sufficient contiguous acreage for the stadium in that area, and to divest existing owners and users at an affordable price, was by resorting to the sovereign power of condemnation. "Of course," lawyer O'Malley knew, "the ball club very properly does not have the legal right to condemn land."[17] His solution to that potential obstacle was to link the construction of a new Dodger stadium to a comprehensive plan for the redevelopment of the entire surrounding neighborhood, so that the eminent-domain powers of the sovereign city could be made to serve the real estate demands of his Dodgers.

O'Malley could cite an impressive inventory of publicly useful works that would be tied in to the stadium project, including the relocation of the "old, inefficient" Fort Greene meat market (which would, he said, "bring the price of meat down five cents a pound in Brooklyn"); the building of a new Long Island Railroad terminal with improved track alignments so that modern air-conditioned trains could come into Brooklyn, instead of what he called "the Camp Yaphank troop trains"; eliminating a "traffic intersection that was terrible"; providing parking facilities, not just for the ball-game crowds but also for neighborhood office workers and shoppers; "and all of this would have magically left enough acres of land on which a ballpark could be built."[18]

Under O'Malley's proposal, the Dodgers would pay the city about $1 million for the land condemned and seized by the city under its eminent-domain powers and would build a ballpark "at the cost of the owners of the Brooklyn ball club, not one penny of which would be paid by the city of New York." In proposing this initiative, O'Malley insisted that the Dodgers were not coming to the city "with our hats in our hand."[19] "I want to own my own ballpark," he said,[20] but "we need the help of the city to acquire the necessary land at a reasonable price."[21]

O'Malley's repeatedly professed readiness to pay a "reasonable price" for the land obfuscated the crux of the financial issues raised by his plan. He was offering to pay $1 million—at most $1.5 million—for title after the city had acquired the parcel he wanted (the LIRR terminal and the meat-market property) through eminent-domain proceedings. It was evident from the start that, even at condemnation prices, the cost to the city amounted to several times the best Dodger offer of $1.5 million, and when that expense was finally calculated, the condemnation cost was put at more than $9 million.[22] The essence of the O'Malley land-acquisition proposal was that the city should condemn that property and then turn it over to him at a sharp markdown, with the approximate difference between the city's acquisition cost and the "markdown" resale price to the Dodgers being $8 million—or 90 percent of the city's expense.

Yet even that multimillion-dollar subsidy was just the beginning of the investment in taxpayer funds that would be required if the Dodgers were to implement their plan "to build the ballpark we want in the location we want," in O'Malley's deceptively simple phrase. City Planning Commissioner Robert Moses had bluntly challenged O'Malley in their private discussions: "If you need only three and one half acres of land, if you have one million dollars in the bank, if you have railroad easements, if you really want to stay in Brooklyn, why don't you buy the property at a private sale?"[23] This was, however, a somewhat disingenuous question, because the fundamental problem that O'Malley faced was not the impossibility of going into the private market to acquire the property he needed, as Charlie Ebbets had done forty years earlier without driving up prices.[24] The real problem standing in the way of O'Malley's proposal was that his plan required a massive redevelopment project—one entailing public expenditures for much more than just the acquisition of the ballpark site.

A new meat market and railroad depot would have to be built, and the bankrupt Long Island Railroad, already in debt to the state, would not be able to do that under its own depleted steam. Traffic improvements in the area would be necessary—and expensive. The cost of the parking garages that O'Malley casually penciled into his plans as a city responsibility was not toted up, but the figures on similar work elsewhere promised that the tab would be high. The city's consultants would later estimate a construction cost of $6.5 million.[25] One preliminary estimate of the tab *to the city* for the site acquisition and related improvements that would be needed to build and support a stadium in downtown Brooklyn came to $20 million.[26] For the Dodgers to build at Atlantic–Flatbush would require the city (or other public agency) to incur costs of more than $10 million, in addition to land-acquisition expense for relocation of the market, road improvements, and covering LIRR tracks.[27] When an overall estimate of the cost involved in the downtown stadium project was finally made—taking into account the vast array of related improvements that O'Malley's chosen location would entail—it priced out at $55 million, with the city's share at more than $40 million.[28]

Although O'Malley was ready to incur the expense of stadium construction and was not, as continues to be alleged, demanding that New York build a stadium for him, O'Malley's claim, (echoed by his defenders) that "I have never asked the city of New York to build me a ball park, to give me land, to give me a subsistence or a subsidy," hardly presented a complete picture of the financial implications of his proposal.[29] A Dodger-built and -owned stadium would require an unrecouped multimillion-dollar public investment in the site, a politically unpalatable reality that O'Malley obfuscated at the time. To conclude that "the evidence indicates that O'Malley was prepared to purchase land and construct a stadium," for which purpose "he needed the cooperation of the city government—not to build him a stadium but to condemn private land, compensate the original owners and then sell the property to the Dodgers,"[30] understates the extent of the public subsidy that O'Malley's plan required. It was not a proposal calculated to gain the approval of city officials struggling to proceed with a backlog of depression- and war-deferred projects, and facing an overwhelming array of social-service and educational demands on public monies. In the fall of 1955, New York Mayor Robert F. Wagner, Jr., had advised the City Planning Commission to give top priority in the next year's capital budget to four "vital areas": education, pollution control, transit (mostly for the Second Avenue Subway), and waterfront development, with the "utmost care" to be used in selecting particular projects for funding.[31] The Board of Education was seeking at least $1 billion in construction funds over the next decade from a city that was already crashing against its statutory debt limit.[32] Within the councils of government, there were many who wondered about the propriety of devoting large outlays of scarce funds to a project in Brooklyn, on behalf of a sports franchise that was privately owned and of primarily local significance.

Given the limited resources of the city, O'Malley had only one potential card to play in his quest for public financial support for his initiative. Funding for the acquisition of urban property was available for federally assisted slum-clearance projects under the program known as Title I (in reference to the section of the 1949 Housing Act that created it).[33] The Title I program authorized expenditures for "slum clearance," with the newly cleared properties available for resale at marked-down prices to private developers. In New York City, the Title I program was yet another fiefdom in the astonishingly comprehensive planning and construction empire ruled over by Robert Moses, who had added the housing portfolio to an already overflowing slate of responsibilities for highways, bridges, parks, and other assorted public works, on both city and state levels. Moses had made the Title I program—enacted to encourage private construction of new housing in run-down sections of America's cities—an unprecedented instrument for the wholesale renewal of large patches of the city, notably on Manhattan's West Side.

When Walter O'Malley came calling, New York's premier "master builder" and "power broker," Robert Moses, was in his fourth decade in government service, which began as a state park official under New York Governor Al Smith in the 1920s. In the 1930's, Moses, while retaining his state responsibilities, became New York City Parks Commissioner and chairman of what would become the Triborough Bridge and Tunnel Authority. In 1942, he was named to the city Planning

Commission; after World War II, he was appointed City Construction Coordinator—all in all an unprecedented, and unduplicated, concentration of power over virtually all of the region's transportation, recreation, and housing infrastructure.[34] If, however, O'Malley expected Moses to respond to the Dodgers' downtown-Brooklyn agenda with the ruthless creativity that characterized the planning czar's pursuit of *his* own objectives, O'Malley was doomed to disappointment. Moses drew an unyielding line against O'Malley's plans, taking the kind of principled position that his critics contended was frequently absent when it came to projects closer to his own heart. "We have told you," he reminded O'Malley in the summer of 1955, "verbally and in writing that a new park for the Dodgers cannot be dressed up as a Title I project. . . . Let's be honest about this," he continued. "Every conference we have attended over several years began with a new Dodger ball field as the main objective with other improvements a peripheral and incidental purpose."[35] By the middle of August 1955, O'Malley's behind-the-scenes efforts to secure support for his proposal had failed.[36]

ON AUGUST 16, 1955, the Brooklyn Dodgers were leading the National League pennant race by fifteen games, their momentum unchecked since opening the season with ten straight wins. The Milwaukee Braves stood a distant second and the Giants were lagging in third place, en route to one of the worst records ever compiled by a defending World Champion. Competition was a stranger to the National League that summer, and talent ran thin. None of the other five teams in the league would finish the season with a winning record.

Individual performances were unimpressive by historical benchmarks for batting and pitching prowess. National League batting champion Richie Ashburn of the Phillies would end the season as the league's only batter hitting over .320. For the first time in ten years, no one would hit more than forty doubles. Willie Mays's thirteen triples and Billy Bruton's twenty-five stolen bases paced the circuit, the lowest marks by leaders in those categories since the war. Though Willie Mays, freed of the disciplines of team play by the Giants' hapless record, was swinging with abandon on his way to fifty-one home runs, it was a lonely peak in a year of dull underachievement. Even the great Stan "The Man" Musial was affected, at least relatively speaking: His batting average slipped all the way down to .319, twenty-five points below his lifetime mark.

It wasn't that National League pitching was so overpowering. Only Philadelphia's Robin Roberts and Brooklyn's Don Newcombe won more than seventeen games. The Dodger pitching staff's earned-run average was the highest recorded by a league leader in a quarter of a century. Only Sam Jones of the Cubs struck out more than 160 batters.

Such mediocrity on the field was hardly calculated to excite baseball fans, and indeed it did not. Attendance dropped across the league. Only fanatical Milwaukee, still in the first blush of its love affair with the Braves, bucked the downward trend. Even in league-leading Brooklyn, attendance sagged, threatening at midseason to end up below the one million mark for the first time since the Battle of the Bulge. In Brooklyn, at least, anticipation and talk and the promise of excitements to come could be focused on the approaching fall collision with—who else?—the Yankees. For the fans of other clubs, there was absolutely nothing to look forward to. Only the schedule's legislated routine carried the teams along the slow currents of obligation to season's end.

It was during the midsummer doldrums of a season, a city, and a sport that Walter O'Malley met the press on August 16, 1955, and took his heretofore-secret battle for city assistance in building a new Dodger ballpark to the city's sports fans—and voters. He opened the bidding by pronouncing a sentence of death on Ebbets Field.[37] "I love

Ebbets Field," O'Malley proclaimed, "but our days at Ebbets Field are numbered." "We plan to play almost all our home games at Ebbets Field in 1956 and 1957," O'Malley assured Dodger fans, as he announced that the team would also play seven "home" games at Roosevelt Stadium in Jersey City in each of those years. "I am willing," he stated, in the gallantly beleaguered tones that would become familiar in future months, "to stand the gaff" at the old park for a few more years, but "not past 1958." "We'll have a new stadium shortly thereafter," he insisted.

O'Malley said little that afternoon; he was discreet and guarded about his post–Ebbets Field plans for the Dodgers. "The Dodgers have been trying to get a suitable site in Brooklyn since 1948 and for the last four years have been in the plan-drawing stage," he disclosed. He made it clear that he thought he had a rightful claim on the city and the state for help. Horse racing, O'Malley said, had found a way to strike an alliance with the state to carry out *its* plant-improvement program, and such improvements were, O'Malley said, absolutely critical to the future well-being of the Dodgers. "Our fans require a modern stadium with greater comforts, shorter, walks, no posts, absolute protection from inclement weather, convenient rest rooms and a self-selection first come, first served method of buying tickets." "Baseball," he continued, "with its heavy night schedule now is competing with many attractions for the consumer's dollar and it had better spend some money if it expects to hold its fans. I shudder to think of this future competition [from horse racing] if we do not produce something modern for our fans."

That the Dodgers were headed toward their fifth pennant in nine years did nothing to relieve the gloomy prospects for the franchise as a business operation, according to the team's owner. Dodger attendance, O'Malley said, had been steadily decreasing since 1947, a decline that had accelerated in the previous two years with a drop-off of more than 150,000. The total for 1955, he projected, based on attendance to that date, would not pass one million. The consequences of that decline at the gate were reflected on the team's ledger. O'Malley, circumspect and wary, alluded cryptically to "declining revenues," but other club officials told reporters that the Dodgers would lose money in 1955. The root of the problem, O'Malley said, lay in the team's outmoded ballpark, with its inadequate parking facilities and relatively inaccessible location, whether by automobile or public transportation.[38]

For some time, O'Malley had been painting a dire picture of the future prospects of the Dodgers as a competitive team, given the perceived limitations of Ebbets Field as a place for doing baseball business. The prime threat came from Milwaukee, where the Braves had been drawing record crowds since their move from Boston just before the start of the 1953 season.[39] Speaking to Roger Kahn in Milwaukee during the Braves' inaugural season in their new home, O'Malley said, "They're going to draw a million customers more here [Milwaukee] than we will back in Brooklyn . . . we can't afford even a few years of this. The Braves will be able to pay bigger bonuses, run more farm teams and hire the best scouting talent. The history of the Brooklyn club is that you're either first or bankrupt. There is no second place."[40] O'Malley repeated the same message of doom to writer Ed Linn a few years later, asking, "How long can we compete on an equal basis with a team that can outdraw us 2 to 1 and outpark us 15 to 1? . . . If they take in twice as many dollars, they'll eventually be able to buy better talent. Then they'll become the winners not us."[41] The Braves in their new home in Milwaukee were outdrawing the Brooklyn team by two to one in their county-built, low-rent stadium—an edge that O'Malley then and later said meant that, "in five years, the . . . Braves would have ten million more dollars to spend in baseball than us." "They," O'Malley claimed, "would have a lock on the pennants."[42] According to

O'Malley, "It would be only a question of two, three, four or five years before Milwaukee would be the Yankees of the National League and Brooklyn would be the Washington."[43]

This message of doom was, from O'Malley's standpoint, one more useful nail in the coffin of "antiquated" Ebbets Field, but it was based on a self-servingly skewed analysis of the two teams' comparative finances. Although the Braves' attendance surged after the move to Milwaukee, and Brooklyn's stayed relatively flat, Milwaukee was not about to steamroll the Dodgers financially, as the economic information gathered by a congressional committee in the summer of 1957 would reveal.[44] The Braves, despite their substantially greater gate receipts, simply did not hold a significant financial edge over the Dodgers. The great equalizer was television.

Commercially sponsored Brooklyn Dodgers home television baseball broadcasts had begun in 1947, as New York, which then had five of the twenty-five television stations in the entire country, led the way into the television age. The Dodgers, along with the Giants and the Yankees, eagerly embraced the new medium—and revenue source—showing none of the trepidation that had earlier kept radio out of New York's ballparks until the eve of World War II, well after it was a staple everywhere else. In 1950, the critical year in television's penetration of the New York market, home TV-set ownership soared from 875,000 to 2,000,000, reaching more than half of the area's homes. Dodger television-rights revenues increased accordingly, to $340,000 that year, and then again to more than $500,000 in 1953. By 1956, television and radio income swelled to $888,000, accounting for almost 30 percent of total Dodger income.[45]

The Dodgers parlayed their television money into income leadership over a Milwaukee franchise that was outdrawing the Brooklyn team by *one million* at the gate. The crucial edge was provided by the Dodgers' vastly greater television and radio income, the result of their much larger media market and of the Braves' decision to televise (in contrast to their practice in Boston) only a very limited number of games. The 1956 Braves, who finished second, may have been backed by County Stadium's nightly forty thousands, but the Dodgers who beat them were just as surely supported by their nightly—if unseen and distant—hundreds of thousands, who smoked Luckies and drank Schaeffer and who, while relaxing easily in their favorite armchairs, were underwriting that margin of superiority out on the playing field.

Brooklyn, along with the New York Giants, was pioneering a new model of baseball economics in the 1950s, compiling a balance sheet far more dependent on television and radio income than that of any other team in the league. The money from the new medium provided a crucial cushion against the crash in live attendance that hit the entire baseball world after 1950, the last time as many as five National League teams drew one million fans until 1957. As attendance fell sharply in the first half of the 1950s—by more than 1.5 million in the seven stable franchises (that is, apart from Milwaukee) between 1950 and 1955—the infusion of television income allowed the Dodgers (and the Giants) to buck the general trend toward lower incomes and to post higher revenues in the middle of the decade than at the beginning.[46] At a time when the other National League teams were deriving about 10 percent of their income from television and radio broadcasts, the Dodgers and the Giants were earning about 30 percent of their income from that source. It was an entirely new method of doing baseball business—a sharp contrast, ironically enough, to the traditional reliance of the newly minted Milwaukee Braves on the live gate.

And, it was a successful method, too. Adding all revenue sources together, Dodger income matched in 1955, and exceeded in 1956, that of the Braves. Brooklyn's balance sheet, unlike Milwaukee's, did include World Series income in those years, but with those post-season receipts excluded,[47] the two teams stood in a roughly equivalent financial position.[48] In terms of the future competitive balance between the teams, the Dodgers were spending more than the Braves on minor-league player development, and they continued to have the where-withal to do so.[49]

Even with seats behind posts, and a lack of parking, fans in the mid-1950s were still making their way to Charlie Ebbets's ballpark in numbers that remained among the highest in baseball. The Dodgers had attracted more than one million fans to Ebbets Field every season since 1946. From 1946 through 1956, they had led the National League in attendance five times, and finished second in the years when they did not. That Ebbets Field remained a viable venue for major-league baseball was confirmed by a sudden revival in Dodger attendance figures in 1956. Fueled by the first close pennant race since 1951—and the first season-long chase since the Dodgers–Cardinals duel of 1949—attendance at Ebbets Field spiked sharply upward. The Milwaukee Braves emerged as sustained challengers, the successor rival to the fading Cardinals, plugging a big gap in the Dodger account books. Average attendance per game rose toward the levels of the preceding decade; the season's total home attendance (including the 150,000 fans attending the seven "home" games the Dodgers played in Jersey City's Roosevelt Stadium)[50] passed the 1,200,000 mark. It was a stunning reversal, tribute to a hot pennant race and the rise of new rivalries, and it proved that Dodger baseball at Ebbets Field was still an attractive proposition, provided there was an attraction to see. As late as the 1957 season, facing imminent deser-tion, more than one million Brooklyn fans paid their way into the historic ballpark.

Nor was the decline in attendance from the record-setting levels of the late 1940s accompanied by any noticeable disaffection or estrangement on the part of the team's famously devoted fans. Even Duke Snider's petulant blast in 1955—"Brooklyn fans don't deserve a pennant"—hardly diminished the affection in which the Duke of Flatbush was held by his subjects. In large part, the decline from the record attendance marks of the late 1940s was just the local variant of the dominant theme of major-league baseball after 1950—an across-the-board drop in attendance after the frenetic years of the postwar boom. There were also other, more technical explanations for the abruptness of the decline in Brooklyn. For one thing, there had been a reduction in the number of dates played at Ebbets Field over the years, as O'Malley had broken with Rickey's aggressively grasping management style and again scheduled single-admission doubleheaders at the Dodger home grounds after he took control of the club, decreasing from seventy-nine in 1949 to sixty-six in 1955. Dodger attendance also suffered from the lag in competition after 1950, and especially from the self-destruction of a traditional rival (and leading gate attraction), the St. Louis Cardinals. Once a team whose visits to Ebbets Field outdrew even the Giants, the Cardinals of the mid-1950s, a thoroughly mediocre team despite all-time great Stan Musial's continued stellar play, were barely outdrawing the Cubs or Phillies. No contender to Dodger power emerged to pick up the slack, until the Braves in 1956.

Such considerations had no place, needless to say, in O'Malley's campaign for a new ballpark to replace Ebbets Field. Escalating the stakes from the start, O'Malley warned on August 16, 1955, in his first public pronouncement on the Dodgers' future, that, although a shift to another city was not necessarily foreshadowed, "such a change . . . is not impossible at some future date." As a shocked city reeled from this apparently sudden threat to the Dodgers' future existence in Brooklyn, O'Malley moved quickly to focus attention on his own ideas about a new home for the Dodgers. Meeting the press the next day, along with Brooklyn Borough President John Cashmore, at the team's Montague Street offices, O'Malley announced that he had the funds

available "to purchase the land and pay the costs of building a new stadium . . . but we do need help from the city to acquire the necessary
land at a reasonable price."[51] He was keeping faith with the borough,
he would later say, because "I am crazy enough to be willing to put $5
million into an old place I just happen to love."[52]

As Borough President Cashmore explained O'Malley's proposal,
the Dodgers were interested in building their own stadium "if an adequate site can be made available" just to the east of the intersection of
Flatbush and Atlantic Avenues, the land primarily occupied by the
Long Island Railroad station.[53] It would, Cashmore continued, tie into
an area-wide improvement program, and he duly recited the litany of
proposals and new uses that city officials had been batting around with
O'Malley for years. The Dodger stadium, Cashmore tried to indicate,
would be incidental to a general program of necessary public
improvement. He was deliberately casual about its place in the
scheme: "If we can eliminate the traffic bottleneck and further make
it possible for a modern railroad depot . . . there is a possibility that
there will be enough land for the Dodgers to purchase on which they
could build the dream stadium O'Malley has in mind." It was all very
tentative, of course. "I do not know," Cashmore reflected, "if all these
things can be worked out, but I certainly believe it is worth a trial." A
few hours later, the team released sketches of the proposed stadium at
the intersection of Atlantic and Flatbush Avenues, with the railroad
station relocated underground and changes in the adjacent streets.
O'Malley's design showed two circular decks with 50,000 seats enclosing a neatly symmetrical playing field with regular, spacious dimensions—330 feet down each foul line, 400 to center—that marked a
clean break with the cramped idiosyncrasies of Ebbets Field.[54] Within
days, O'Malley would be insisting that, far from being just one idea for
consideration, this was the *only* "practical site for a ballpark in Brooklyn,"[55] the only place in which the Dodgers would invest, the only

Brooklyn location in which he would build—in short, the only accept-able site for a new Dodger stadium. "This is not a threat," he said, but even as his public campaign for a new home was just getting underway, he announced, "We're down to what we believe is our last chance."[56]

Almost immediately, O'Malley received a return on his investment in publicity. Up until then, New York Mayor Robert F. Wagner, Jr., first elected in 1953, had been buffeted by the constant flow of municipal business that crossed his desk demanding his immediate attention, and he had spared no time for the Dodgers and their plans. In Wagner's first term, the city built new schools, hired additional teachers, expanded hospital and health care facilities, and increased the number of police and firefighters. As mayoral historian Chris McNickle has concluded, it was "a distinguished record."[57] Faced with a multitude of urgent claims on the city's purse in the summer of 1955, Wagner was struggling to balance the city's budgets for the upcoming fiscal year, and spending in connection with a new ballpark for the Dodgers held a low priority.

The behind-the-scenes talks with O'Malley had been left, as such questions of planning and public works routinely were, to Robert Moses and his staff. Wagner's improvised style of crisis management left little spare time for long-range planning, so most planning deci-sions fell by default into the tireless hands of Robert Moses—backed up, as always, by a team capable of fast and decisive, if not always reli-able, work. The Dodger stadium proposals had constituted such a del-egable item on the city's planning agenda. Yet the power Moses exerted over city planning in the Wagner administration was not sim-ply a consequence of the mayor's absorption in the more pressing affairs of a city besieged by endless emergencies. It also reflected Moses's ability to produce the kind of results that Wagner wanted, and this reliance on Moses's undeniable talents made the type of direct appeal that O'Malley wanted to carry to the mayor in the face of

Moses's own veto a dubious proposition at best. Wagner, who desperately needed Moses, was inclined to back him up. It was a relationship of real dependency that O'Malley would now try to challenge.

With O'Malley's announcement, the ball was suddenly, and very publicly, in the mayor's court. Declaring that he was very anxious to keep the Dodgers in New York, Wagner said that he would meet with O'Malley later in the week and would then explore possible ways in which the city might assist the Dodgers' efforts to acquire the downtown property they coveted.[58] There was "trouble in Brooklyn," a *Times* editorial warned on August 19, albeit in rather mock-apocalyptic language:

> *Catastrophe looms in Brooklyn. . . . A crisis has blown up of a dimension to be tackled only on the highest level, in a place and at an hour reserved only for the gravest of problems: Gracie Mansion at 9:30 o'clock in the morning—this morning. Whether Mayor Wagner will be equal to the emergency—the saving of the Dodgers for Brooklyn through city help in finding a site for a new ball park to improve on Ebbets Field—no one can now foresee. But the man is clearly at the turning point of his political career.*[59]

When O'Malley met with Mayor Wagner, along with Robert Moses and Brooklyn Borough President Cashmore, on August 19, 1955, the sharp East River wind off Hell Gate rattled the awnings hung over Gracie Mansion's waterside terrace—"Hurricane Dodger," O'Malley called it—and Wagner had to strain to catch what O'Malley was saying. New York, he told the mayor, speaking as one German–Irishman to another, Democrat to Democrat, Dodgers owner to Giants fan, was faced with the prospect of becoming a one-team city. "The problem," he warned, "is bigger than the Dodgers alone." If the

Dodgers moved, O'Malley said, the Giants would have to leave town, too, given their heavy dependence on Dodger games for attendance.

Speaking up over the din, O'Malley made his pitch. He emphasized the urgency with which he viewed the situation, insisting that come what may, the Dodgers would be out of Ebbets Field by 1958. He told Wagner that he was already negotiating the sale of the old ballpark with the intention of taking back no more than a two-year lease from the prospective buyer. That, he said, was his deadline.[60]

Once again, O'Malley explained his need for city assistance. The Dodgers, he said, were prepared to invest their own dollars to buy the necessary land and to build the stadium at the Atlantic–Flatbush site, and the construction itself would be undertaken at the sole expense of the team. But with only $1.5 million available to buy the land, he needed the city to make up the difference between that and the (unspecified) total acquisition cost. After all, O'Malley said, "Other cities have gone further. They've built the ballparks and rented them to clubs. Other cities, can't understand why we can't do it and they can." And, he continued, with the funds available under the Title I slum-clearance program, the fiscal instrument was at hand whereby the city might be able to pass along the lion's share of the costs all the way to Washington.[61]

That day on the terrace, O'Malley finally had the chance he wanted—to make a personal pitch to Wagner, in the full glare of the attention of the baseball-loving public, about the Dodgers, their problems, and their alternatives if the city failed to come through in the clutch. The press barrage had gained him that much after his behind-the-scenes lobbying had failed, but it wasn't as though he had Wagner out there all by himself. When the meeting got around to specific proposals and hard numbers, Wagner was more than ready to hand the floor to Robert Moses.

After having rebuffed O'Malley in private for some time, Moses had no trouble doing so again in public. Indeed, the very public nature of the meeting was itself a signal—in the characteristically secretive and behind-the-scenes processes of New York City decision-making— that nothing would be accomplished that day. In a replay of their private dialogue earlier in the month, Moses asked O'Malley to justify the city's condemning land for the benefit of the privately owned, very-much-for-profit commercial enterprise that was the Brooklyn Dodgers. Even apart from such legal issues, Moses insisted that the price O'Malley proposed to pay to the city was far too low. As for Title I support, Moses said he could not see any way to shoehorn the type of development proposed by the Dodgers—utterly lacking in substantial housing construction—into the guidelines of that program. At best, to get city backing for O'Malley's plan would require surmounting extremely tangled legal and financial problems, and it was clear that Moses wouldn't be making that task any easier. Nor was there any confusion about what was at stake. O'Malley said that the Atlantic–Flatbush location was "our last chance in Brooklyn," and Moses agreed that there was "no prospect of an alternative Dodger location in Brooklyn."[62]

To govern is to defer, Mayor Wagner might have said. The heretofore-behind-the-scenes impasse over O'Malley's plan was now in full view of the ball-game–going, taxpaying, and voting public. Wagner hesitated to shut the door on all efforts to get the Dodgers what they wanted, but there seemed no doubt in Wagner's mind that when all was said and done, the Dodgers would not abandon Brooklyn or New York. The mayor's complacency was shared by his constituents, who reacted with surprising passivity to the escalating crisis. After all, the imperfections of Ebbets Field in the eyes of Walter O'Malley (and others) had not prevented the Dodgers from imposing mastery over the rest of their league on the diamond; nor had it prevented the

Dodgers from attracting more than a million fans to their home games in every season (apart from wartime 1943–44) since 1941, in an era when that mark was the gold standard for attendance. Furthermore, it had not prevented the Dodgers from being the most profitable team in baseball, as revealed by figures released toward the end of the ensuing controversy. The Brooklyn Dodgers of the 1950s bore no resemblance, in any of these categories, to the uncompetitive and poverty-stricken franchises that had fled Boston, Philadelphia, and St. Louis in recent years. That the Dodgers might actually move appears to have been simply beyond the imagination of the team's fanatically devoted fans.

In the aftermath of the Gracie Mansion meeting, a fallback plan quickly won across-the-board acquiescence. Two days later, Wagner proposed that the city's key governing body, the Board of Estimate, fund a survey of the proposed downtown Brooklyn stadium area and leave to future study the exploration of some means of clearing the land and building the stadium.[63] Within a week, the board did so, authorizing $100,000 to survey the site desired by O'Malley—although the authorizing resolution simply placed the money at Borough President Cashmore's discretion and made no express mention of the Dodgers.[64]

For O'Malley, it was a sharp setback. His meeting with Wagner and Moses had failed to reverse the city's adverse private reaction to his plan. As newspapers mounted their editorial platforms and the leaders of big business gained the mayor's ear and the opinions of the man in the street poured into the mayor's mailbox, it was quickly apparent that O'Malley had miscalculated very badly if he expected to win the ensuing political battle. The editors of New York's quality press, a prestigious force unique to the city, the *Times* and the *Herald Tribune*—the only ones that mattered to a Democratic mayor intent on building a record of fiscal responsibility—immediately took a hard line against any public subsidy to the Dodgers. "It cannot be expected," the *Times* lectured, "that the city will make any outright gift of land to professional baseball."[65] The city's corporate elite, for its part, saw no reason for the city to extend itself financially on behalf of a fellow capitalist while they were groaning under the burden of self-described "overtaxation."

Perhaps Democrat O'Malley expected that. But out on the streets and sidewalks and stoops, in the candy stores and luncheonettes, around barbecue grills in the yards behind the two-family houses of Bensonhurst and Queens, far beyond the editorial offices and board-rooms with their particular traditions of civic responsibility and fiscal prudence, reactions were not favorable either. Right away, the situation was sized up—in terms more acute than much of the news coverage in subsequent years, in which the cost issue was underplayed or fudged—as a naked grab by O'Malley for unwonted public succor. Of course, there were voices raised in support of *whatever* the Dodgers wanted—some from such distant outcroppings of the borough as Norfolk and Baltimore—but in the main (to judge from the letters on file in the city archives), the opponents of any Dodger designs on the city's treasury were in the majority.

The letters came from the taxpayer "disgusted" by his own high property levy and opposed to seeing public funds in any amount going to the support of a private business; from the homeowner who had been battling persistent basement flooding for more than seven years and was skeptical "that the world was coming to an end because the Brooklyn Dodgers do not have a park large enough"; from the "avid baseball fan for over twenty years" who thought that any money spent on the Dodgers could be expended more usefully on the children of the city; from the Brooklyn dentist who considered it the height of "audacity, gall and imprudence" for O'Malley not simply to ask the city for help, but even to specify exactly what he wanted; from the man who asked, "Has anyone calculated how many thousands of people live in the area involved . . . is it just that thousands of people should be made homeless so others can have more comfort to enjoy watching their favorite sport?"; and, speaking for many, the "Brooklyn resident" who made it clear that he wasn't having any of the Dodgers' blustering—"If they are so dissatisfied with the support Brooklyn is giving them, let them get the hell out of Brooklyn!"[66] It was hardly what Walter O'Malley wanted, or expected, to hear. Indeed, the Dodger owner's evident misreading of political and public opinion was so great as to invite the suspicion, then and since, that O'Malley's sights were set on a move out of Brooklyn from the start of his public campaign for a new ballpark.

The basic political reality was that there was not a sufficient city-wide consensus to support the downtown Brooklyn stadium project. Brooklyn's borough president was on board, which was necessary, but not sufficient, for O'Malley's strategy to succeed. The powers of the borough presidents had been under siege for a long time, and in that summer of 1955, work moved forward on a new city charter that promised to strip them away almost entirely, but John Cashmore—along with his four fellow borough chief executives—still possessed one fundamental, if informal, power.[67] The borough presidents stood at the sluice gates for local public works, armed with a traditional veto power that would be respected by their peers when appropriations came up for approval before the Board of Estimate.[68] When the time for decision came and the Board of Estimate (made up of the mayor, the City Council president, the controller, and the five borough presidents) retreated into its always-closed business sessions, everyone turned to the borough president whose domain was affected, and his veto would provide the negative lead to a board that exercised power according to a long-established tradition of unanimity. O'Malley had to have Cashmore on his side even to get his plan under discussion when those doors closed. But it would not be the politicians—or people—of

Brooklyn who would decide the fate of the Dodgers; it would be the city as a whole. And neither Cashmore nor O'Malley (or, indeed, Brooklyn) had the power to carry the day.

The one concrete result of the Gracie Mansion meeting was New York State's creation of a new public entity, the Brooklyn Sports Center Authority, in the spring of 1956. The authority was vested with what Mayor Wagner described as "broad powers" to undertake a comprehensive work of renewal in the area around the LIRR depot, including construction of a new terminal, market relocation, traffic improvements—and the building of a new home for the Dodgers. The project would be financed through the issuance of bonds by the authority.[69]

The legislation had a rough ride to passage. Commissioner Moses publicly questioned the agency's ability to finance the stadium project.[70] In the New York City Council, members challenged the shrinking of the city's tax rolls by the creation of yet another public authority that would—in Manhattan Councilman Stanley Isaacs's words—"invade the city and seize large parcels of property," and for a project that, far from serving the general weal, was just "an effort to take care of the Dodgers."[71] State legislators were similarly skeptical, and the Republican-controlled Senate authorized the measure passed with just two votes to spare, with one Republican leader saying that, all in all, "It stinks."[72] Even its proponents downplayed its effectiveness. To all objections in the Legislature, the stock answer had been that the law, as Mayor Wagner said when he proposed the legislation in the first place, was "merely an enabling act," which did not commit anyone to do or to pay or to build anything.[73] It was "merely permissive," Wagner again emphasized, after the authority proposal had won City Council approval.[74] On April 21, 1956, on the steps of Brooklyn's Borough Hall, New York Governor Averell Harriman donned an ill-fitting

In the first decades of the twentieth century, John McGraw (RIGHT) of the New York Giants was baseball's dominant personality, and the team's Polo Grounds home (BELOW) was the game's premier venue.

Team owners, including the Yankees' Jacob Ruppert (fifth from left), the Cardinals' Sam Breadon (sixth from left), the Giants' Charles Stoneham (ninth from left), and the Red Sox's Harry Frazee (eleventh from left) watch Judge Landis sign his contract as Commissioner of Baseball in 1920.

Ban Johnson, the American League's founder and long-time president, moved the league's Baltimore franchise to New York in 1903.

The purchase of Babe Ruth, shown here hitting a home run at the Polo Grounds on June 26, 1920, from Boston made the Yankees instant contenders, but it was a dispute over Sunday game dates with their New York Giant landlords that triggered the Yankees' eviction from that historic ballpark, not Ruth's slugging.

Faced with eviction from the Polo Grounds, the Yankees built their own great stadium across the river in the Bronx (TOP, in a preliminary drawing); it opened in April 1923 (ABOVE), with Commissioner Landis (second from left) joining the Yankees' Colonels (Jacob Ruppert, left, and T. L. Huston, center) and Boston owner Harry Frazee (second from right).

Changing of the guard: John McGraw shakes hands with Babe Ruth during the 1922 World Series.

The Giants' Casey Stengel scores the winning run in the first game of the 1923 World Series with the Yankees, the Giants' high-water mark in their losing struggle for baseball honors against the American League upstarts.

Jacob Ruppert and Yankee General Manager, Ed Barrow, who followed Babe Ruth from Boston to New York, look on as Ruth signs his contract for the 1927 season.

The two architects of the rise of the St. Louis Cardinals from "worst to first" in the National League: (ABOVE, LEFT) General Manager Branch Rickey and (ABOVE, RIGHT) team president Sam Breadon (right), in the uniform he liked to don for the spring training workouts he enjoyed even into his seventies.

ABOVE: Cardinal second baseman and manager Rogers Hornsby crosses home plate in the sixth game of the 1926 World Series, en route to a seven-game win over the Yankees. The Cards would be the only National League team to defeat the Yankees between 1922 and 1955.

LEFT: Branch Rickey followed up the Cards' 1926 World Championship by trading Hornsby (left), the team's star, manager, and part-owner, to the Giants for Frankie Frisch (right), a move that shocked St. Louis fans but laid the groundwork for further Cardinal success.

LEFT: In 1943, Rickey moved from St. Louis to Brooklyn (shown here at the season opener at Ebbets Field), where his greatest accomplishment was breaking the color line by signing Jackie Robinson (BELOW, outside Ebbets Field on April 16, 1947).

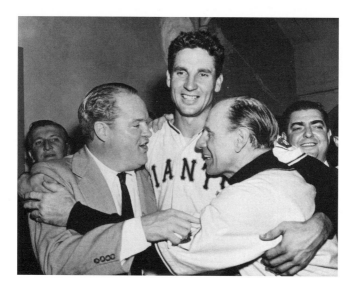

ABOVE: Giants owner Horace Stoneham, manager Leo Durocher, and home-run star Bobby Thomson celebrate the team's 1951 play-off win over the Dodgers. BELOW: Yankee manager Casey Stengel surveys his team's personnel chart.

ABOVE, LEFT: Not even Stengel's fortune-telling skills, displayed at a 1954 baseball writers' dinner (center, with Brooklyn Dodger owner Walter O'Malley on left and manager Walter Alston on right), could have predicted the Dodgers' departure from Brooklyn within four years (ABOVE, RIGHT)—a move that was expedited by the actions of Cubs owner Phil Wrigley (left) and the Braves' Lou Perini (second from left).

On February 20, 1957, Walter O'Malley and the Brooklyn Dodgers flew south to spring training for the last time; the next day, O'Malley announced the acquisition of Los Angeles franchise rights.

ABOVE: On October 4, 1955, Brooklyn Dodger fans and players celebrated the team's first World Series win after seven losses. BELOW: Two years later, they were headed to California, along with the Giants, shown leaving the Polo Grounds for the last time on September 29, 1957.

What if they broke a record and hardly anybody came? Roger Maris hits his sixty-first home run on October 1, 1961, before 40,000 empty seats in Yankee Stadium.

In 1964, CBS acquired control of the Yankees from Colonel Ruppert's successors, Dan Topping (left) and Del Webb, and installed network executive Michael Burke (right) as president.

In his most notable accomplishment, Mike Burke won city support for the renovation of Yankee Stadium. Joe DiMaggio looks out over the building site in 1974.

But it was CBS's successor, Cleveland shipping executive George Steinbrenner, who was in charge when the stadium reopened in 1976, the Yankees' first pennant-winning season since 1964.

The baseball business was built on an exemption from the antitrust laws that was won in a 1922 Supreme Court case argued by Senator and "Philadelphia lawyer" George Wharton Pepper (ABOVE, batting in a pickup ball game outside the Capitol) and successfully defended against all subsequent challengers, including that mounted fifty years later by former Cardinal outfielder Curt Flood (BELOW, right).

ABOVE: A new era in baseball labor relations spearheaded by Players Association Executive Director Marvin Miller (center) was marked by a series of work stoppages and, most notably, an arbitration ruling overturning the sport's long-standing reserve clause, as baseball's business practices remained the subject of continuing judicial and legislative oversight. BELOW: Commissioner Allan "Bud" Selig testifies before the Senate Judiciary Committee in November 2000.

ABOVE: In 2000, free-agent acquisition Roger Clemens pitched the Yankees into the first "subway series" since 1956. BELOW: With Yankee owner George Steinbrenner and General Manager Joe Torre flanking New York Mayor Rudy Giuliani, the Yankees closed out the century celebrating their twenty-sixth World Championship.

Dodger cap and signed into law the bill creating the Brooklyn Sports Center Authority.[75]

Whatever the criticisms it faced, the new authority was the *only* politically viable mechanism to keep the Dodgers in Brooklyn. It immediately became clear, however, at least to those in the know, that its prospects for success were slight, because it was not a financially viable one. An attempt to broaden the power base for this very Brooklyn project by garnering appointees to the three-member board with city and statewide reputations and clout failed, and its members eventually were designated by Walter O'Malley.[76] Assisting them[77] as consultant was Emil Praeger, who was more than just a man with "diversified experience including the design and construction of stadia," as the authority described him in its first report.[78] He was O'Malley's own consulting engineer, and his designation was hardly likely to appease the suspicions of those who viewed the authority as nothing more than a Dodger boondoggle.

The O'Malley hand could indeed be seen in the site that the authority selected for the ballpark in the report it issued in November 1956. A city-financed study, undertaken after the 1955 Gracie Mansion meeting, had recommended that the ballpark be built across the street from the railroad terminal, requiring the demolition of hundreds of units of tenement housing but not interfering with existing rail operations. There was, however, no chance at all that the city would ever condemn and clear the residential blocks—however decrepit—to consummate a distress sale to private citizen O'Malley. Even the most egregious and questionable of the Wagner–Moses urban-renewal projects—the redevelopment of Manhattan's Upper West Side—may have unduly enriched private developers and driven residents from homes that fell under the wrecker's ball, but at least it resulted in the construction of new housing. This was an equation that balanced in New York's political and planning calculus. An urban-renewal program that demolished established business and residential premises for a baseball stadium would not. The authority finessed this problem, but bruised the sensibilities of those who had underwritten the earlier report, by shifting the location of the proposed stadium from the site designated by the city's own survey (which had been handed to the authority as a working paper) to the Long Island Railroad station, on the other side of Flatbush Avenue, O'Malley's preference all along (see map on page 219).[79] To support *its* recommendation, the authority included a sketch that was none other than the sketch released to the press by the Brooklyn Dodgers back in August 1955.

Watching from the sidelines, Robert Moses remained a relentless, and politically adept, opponent of the authority and a sharp critic of its flimsy financial underpinnings. In response to the authority's November 1956 report, Moses promptly suggested to Mayor Wagner that the city allocate $100,000 for a preliminary study of the costs of public improvements that would be necessary and an additional $15,000 (together with $15,000 for expenses) for the authority to engage consultants ("such as Madigan–Hyland") to determine whether the Sports Center could be self-liquidating. There would be no need, Moses said, for the authority to engage the larger staff contemplated by its proposed budget until the authority had determined whether or not it could sell the bonds it planned to issue to finance construction.[80] It was a reasonable proposition, and the Board of Estimate quickly agreed. On December 28, 1956, the city authorized $25,000 for a bond feasibility study, and a further $100,000 for more general engineering studies of the impacted area.[81]

The authority's moment of truth came in early 1957. On January 31, 1957, consulting engineer Michael J. ("Jack") Madigan sent the chairman of the Brooklyn Sports Center Authority a memorandum that summarized a recent meeting with O'Malley, concerning the terms under which the Dodgers were prepared to occupy a proposed publicly built stadium in downtown Brooklyn. Madigan had bleak news to convey to Chairman Charles Mylod. The Dodger boss would only agree to subleasing full operating rights to a publicly owned stadium, paying a fixed-sum rental ($500,000) in exchange for sole management of the facility and a full claim on all rental and concession income.[82] "Mr. O'Malley," Madigan continued, "appears to be less interested as a tenant . . . indicated by his offer of an extremely low rent amount which he would be willing to pay."[83]

Madigan calculated, however, that a $15 million stadium bond issue with a twenty-year term ("appropriate for this type of facility") and an interest rate of 4 percent ("the lowest possible rate"), would require annual net income of $1,100,000 to service its debts—more than twice what the authority would receive under O'Malley's proposal. And, as Madigan further pointed out, "From experience, I know that in the event of open-market revenue bond financing, investment bankers would insist on coverage of at least two times—requiring a net income of $2,200,000 per year." With stadium revenue limited to the $500,000 O'Malley would pay for exclusive rights to operate the facility, "net revenues sufficient to provide minimum coverage of revenue bond financing cannot be realized," Madigan concluded, adding that "the realistic approach to the problem would be to recognize the impossibility of financing the stadium through open-market revenue bonds."[84]

That fatal message was carefully concealed at the time. Chairman Mylod accepted Madigan's assessment "that a formal report by us which will be negative would have a most unfavorable effect." No public statement was made. In the months to come, the fate of the Dodgers would inspire public debate, anguish, and controversy as the community belatedly awakened to the prospect of actually losing their beloved Bums.

New York officialdom had been dead set against Walter O'Malley's original proposal that the city condemn the necessary real estate and sell it to him at a sharply discounted price for construction of a privately owned ballpark. Madigan's calculation—that a publicly owned Brooklyn stadium could not be financed based on the rental the Dodgers were willing to pay—sealed the fate of the *Brooklyn* Dodgers.

IN JUNE 1957, Congress launched the second wave of hearings into baseball's business practices, which had commenced six years earlier. Although baseball's continued immunity from the antitrust laws was again the focus of the proceedings, the controversy over the future of the Brooklyn Dodgers claimed its share of attention. This was not surprising, considering that the committee's chairman was Brooklyn's Emanuel Celler. When his turn at the witness table came, Walter O'Malley attempted to deflect the committee members' ire over the Dodgers' threatened departure from Brooklyn by pointing the finger at local government for its supposed lack of support. New York City had "built a wonderful home for the fish out at Coney Island," he said. "They charge 60 cents to see the fish, but we can't do anything for the Dodgers." According to the Dodger owner, construction of a new stadium in Brooklyn had been sabotaged:

> *I said "sabotage." . . . It developed that a lot of fellows who voted for [the authority] figured we would never get the Republican votes from upstate New York to get the thing through in Albany . . . but weren't willing to back up their vote with money for appropriations. The Sports Center Authority came in for a quarter of a million dollars for their study.*
>
> *To this day they are about to receive the total magnificent sum of . . . $5000 to keep the Dodgers in Brooklyn. . . .* [85]

O'Malley's self-serving accusation was not persuasive to his congressional interlocutors and does not hold up any better in retrospect. The more prosaic, and less incendiary, reality was that the downtown Brooklyn stadium project failed because no viable mechanism existed to finance its construction. O'Malley's negotiations with the authority revealed that he had no intention of proposing any arrangement for a Dodger tenancy that would enable the authority to be financially viable.[86] The record does not support one sympathetic writer's conclusion "that the Dodger president was receptive to a number of proposals for a new stadium as long as the site remained in Brooklyn."[87] The fact that O'Malley was not willing to pay the price for use of the stadium stipulated by the authority's financing requirements suggests indeed that O'Malley never believed in the efficacy of the authority.

For the Dodger owner, the authority had, at best, served as a stalking horse for his unwavering objective, the construction of a privately owned stadium in Brooklyn. It was a way to keep a hand in the game *until* the city folded and he could get what he really wanted, the purchase of city-condemned land, at a sharply discounted price (in O'Malley's parlance, a "reasonable price"), on which he could build *his* stadium. With the January 1957 collapse of the financial assumptions behind the Sports Authority concept, O'Malley had called the city's bluff—or vise versa—but to no avail. The failure of the Sports Center Authority plan failed to generate any momentum behind the Dodger owner's original proposal. The Brooklyn Dodgers had reached the end of the line.

Robert Moses's opposition has often been viewed as the decisive reason for the failure to build a new home for the Dodgers in Brooklyn. If Moses can be held responsible for the "fall of New York," how much easier to pin the primary responsibility on him for the far simpler task of driving the Dodgers out of town. Robert Caro, the master builder's relentlessly critical biographer, had no doubt that Moses single-handedly killed the project. Neil Sullivan agreed that Moses's "antipathy to the Dodgers' proposal" doomed any chance of success, a charge seconded by Michael Shapiro in his recent account of the Dodgers' "last good season." O'Malley himself had attempted to deflect the ire of his critics toward Moses in his testimony to the Celler Committee.[88] And it was certainly true that Moses consistently brought to bear his unstinting opposition to O'Malley's plan at every critical stage in the downtown Brooklyn stadium's half-life and slow death. With his support, perhaps a new Brooklyn stadium would have been built, although by the late 1950s, Moses was racking up defeats as well as victories in pursuing his plans.[89]

But Moses's power was founded on the fact that he was not a lone wolf; he served as, in the description of a recent historian, "the loyal instrument" of a widely shared (not least among New York's liberal political elites) vision of urban redevelopment. As a recent scholar has written, "Moses operated within the grooves of municipal policy. Much of what Moses accomplished rested on forty years of agreement about the future of the city."[90] The key to O'Malley's failure was that Moses was hardly alone in opposing O'Malley's stadium project. There was simply no significant political support for a public subsidy for a privately owned stadium operated by a profit-making enterprise. Indeed, it would be hard to find any New York politician outside of Brooklyn who supported it. Even in Brooklyn, there was considerable opposition. House Judiciary Committee Chairman Emanuel Celler questioned the propriety of governmental financial assistance to the highly profitable Dodgers and subjected O'Malley to a sharp cross-examination at his antitrust subcommittee's hearings in June 1957. City Council President and former Borough President Abe Stark was a particularly outspoken opponent of the Dodgers' plans. A Brooklyn retailer whose political ambitions had been advanced by the famous "Hit Sign, Win Suit" that his clothing store placed on the Ebbets Field outfield wall, Stark charged that "Dodger management has maintained a cold war of silence and evasion toward the people of New York while engaging in a warm flirtation with the mayors of the Pacific coast. . . . What sort of Frankenstein monster are we creating," he asked, "which today can reach out and threaten the right of the people of New York to watch their own baseball teams?"[91]

Furthermore, Moses came forward with a reasonable and more economical alternative to the downtown Brooklyn plan, a municipal stadium on city-owned land in Flushing Meadows in Queens, the future site of Shea Stadium. Flushing Meadows was conveniently located for both urban and suburban fans, and Moses calculated that a stadium there could even be built on a self-liquidating basis.[92] Dramatically less expensive than the overall costs of the O'Malley plan,[93] the Flushing Meadows stadium project was, in terms of the city and the region as a whole, a feasible undertaking, one that would deliver the Dodgers from Ebbets Field yet keep them more or less "at home," in a location that was readily accessible for their own increasingly dispersed fan base.

Simply put, both in his challenge to the feasibility of the stadium's proposed bond-issue financing, as well as to the desirability of the downtown Brooklyn site, Moses was right—as, indeed, he so often was. As the city's study had concluded, "In light of the estimated costs of the project and with conventional open-market revenue bond financing without an acceptable guarantor, the likelihood of the project being financially feasible is remote."[94] Nor was downtown Brooklyn a sensible ballpark location, even assuming that it could have been financed and built. O'Malley's "dream" ballpark was an ill-conceived solution to the problems the Dodgers faced in the mid-1950s. Perhaps in the years immediately after World War II, when Walter O'Malley first envisaged the LIRR terminal site as the ideal home for the Brooklyn Dodgers, the location made logistical sense. Private cars were still scarce, families remained crowded into the old prewar neighborhoods as the generations doubled up while waiting for new housing to catch up with unprecedented demand; the routines of an incipient affluence were not yet ascendant over the amusements of a more stringent past. It was in that setting that O'Malley decided, "My first choice was Atlantic and Flatbush . . . because we have a maximum of subway stations. Every subway line in the city of New York has a station that would be on the property."[95]

Over the ensuing years, O'Malley stood by that initial decision, but Brooklyn and the city changed, and he had to advance new arguments to support a choice that made little sense when measured against the problems he had originally diagnosed. By the middle of the 1950s, O'Malley laid the blame for declining attendance at Ebbets Field on the acute lack of parking facilities around the old ballpark. The public, O'Malley admitted, was "on wheels," yet the 2,500 parking spaces that were, according to the traffic engineers, the maximum that could be jammed into the congested downtown site would hardly be sufficient to satisfy the accelerating taste of the public for automobile travel. "Subway fares were falling off," O'Malley noted a few years later. "Fewer people were riding the subways because they were riding in automobiles—and we couldn't park 'em."[96]

The Atlantic–Flatbush site was simply not the right solution for the problems that had led the Dodgers to seek an alternative to Ebbets Field in the first place. The location was hard to reach by car (far more difficult than either Yankee Stadium or the Polo Grounds) from other parts of the city. No expressway ran within one mile of the site, and just the vision of thousands of ballpark-bound cars strung along the cramped right-of-way of the Brooklyn–Queens Expressway (one of Robert Moses's less felicitous works) is torture enough (as is driving it now, even without ball-game traffic). Then the cars drawn toward the Dodger Stadium would have to fight their way across murderously congested surface streets and finally attempt to squeeze into parking garages whose size strained the optimum for even moderately difficult entrance or exit. Few would make a second trip.

The city's traffic consultants questioned the placement of such a "major traffic generator" in the middle of an already heavily trafficked neighborhood, and they described the site as "relatively inaccessible because of a lack of major arteries." It was noted that the stadium site presupposed the end of weekday afternoon baseball games, still something of a summertime staple in the city, to avoid rush-hour traffic jams, and the same would necessarily be true of the twi-night double-headers that were counted on later in the season for making up games postponed during the raw days of early spring.[97] As one critic said, it would be "like building a baseball stadium in Times Square."[98]

There was, however, no reasonable alternative means to get to such a downtown Brooklyn ballpark for millions of fans caught up in the burgeoning age of the automobile; the family car busily rearranged the social maps of borough and city and suburb. The frontier of growth in the city itself now lay in the outlying stretches of Brooklyn and Queens, the Bronx and Staten Island too—off and beyond the subway lines dug in an earlier age. The ring of older settlements girdling downtown was undergoing a dual process of depopulation and racial change, neither of which was promising from the point of view of someone selling tickets. Moving the Dodger ballpark to downtown Brooklyn meant moving it against the grain of growth to a location even harder to reach by car than Ebbets Field itself.

That was true for the new areas of postwar development within the city. It was, of course, even more true for the new suburban world, relentlessly expanding across recently idle stretches of Long Island, Westchester, and New Jersey. The Long Island Railroad was a theoretical alternative for fans from Nassau and Suffolk, but it was hardly a practical one. Service was already falling off by the middle of the 1950s, and fares were escalating. The expense and aggravation of buying a passel of round-trip tickets for a family outing at the ballpark was not likely to be much of an inducement for attendance. For fans in the other suburbs, not even the chimera of the railroad existed. They would come by car or they would not come at all.

O'Malley's Atlantic–Flatbush stadium would exacerbate congestion in an already crowded part of the city and provide no impetus to the rehabilitation of the neighborhood. A ballpark's bulky, desolate, occasionally frenetic and noisy presence would be more likely to spur deterioration than to arrest or reverse it. The proposal answered no urgent city-planning needs. But O'Malley, from beginning to end, would insist that "the Atlantic and Flatbush solution . . . is the only thing I have been fighting for," and reject any alternative.[99]

The city has been faulted for responding with insufficient alacrity to the prospect of losing the Dodgers.[100] This misses the point. New York officials did not bungle O'Malley's Atlantic–Flatbush initiative through negligence or lethargy. The problem, from O'Malley's point of view, was not that the city did not respond to his proposal quickly or decisively, but that it did not respond with the answer he wanted to hear. Nor can it fairly be said that New York City officials "could have taken measures to keep the two teams in New York but chose not to." The Dodger owner's argument, as echoed by one baseball historian, that "through urban renewal provisions specified by Title I . . . , businesses could have been relocated and the land made available to the Dodgers," was fundamentally flawed.[101] The governmental acquisition of land in downtown Brooklyn for transfer to the Dodgers simply did *not* fit, legally or politically, within the parameters of even the most creative uses of Title I funds. Razing the Long Island Railroad terminal and adjacent commercial structures would not constitute "slum clearance"; constructing a baseball stadium in the area would not fulfill the purpose of the statute by providing new housing. Given the nature and scope of O'Malley's demands, taking the measures required to meet them was not legally, politically, or fiscally possible.

It was O'Malley who set in motion the "crisis" over the future of the Brooklyn Dodgers. Indeed, it was O'Malley who discovered that there was a "crisis" at all. When he stuck to his consistent and sincerely held agenda, he settled the fate of Brooklyn baseball. O'Malley insisted that the Dodgers would not play ball in Ebbets Field after the 1957 season; that the Dodgers would only build a privately owned ballpark in downtown Brooklyn on the site then occupied by the Long Island Railroad station; that government would have to provide a massive subsidy for the Dodgers' "private" construction project; and finally that the failure to meet his terms would lead to the loss not only of the Dodgers but of the Giants as well. In the end, it was O'Malley's intractability with regard to this vision—together with the fortuitous fact that Los Angeles was ready, willing, and able to hand him *exactly* what he wanted— that eliminated any prospect for the Dodgers' ballpark wish list to be fulfilled in New York. That the New York Giants turned out to be ready to move to California along with the Dodgers provided a further blow to Brooklyn's chances to remain a major-league town. The double shift alleviated the concerns of other team owners who might have balked at the scheduling and travel complications entailed by a single franchise's shift to the Pacific Coast, half a continent beyond the National League's half-century-old Mississippi River frontier.

The construction of a new city-owned stadium in Flushing Meadows in Queens was the one legally and politically feasible means available to keep the Dodgers, and the Giants, in New York. O'Malley was not interested. "They are not the Brooklyn Dodgers . . . if they are not in Brooklyn. . . . They are something else, they are the Long Island Redskins . . . ," he said with a straight face. "If the Dodgers have to get out of Brooklyn, whether it is 5 miles or 5000 miles, they are no longer the Brooklyn Dodgers."[102]

8

FROM EAST TO WEST

BY JANUARY 1957, Walter O'Malley was indeed looking at the prospects for a new Dodgers home well beyond the confines of Brooklyn, Queens, or Long Island. O'Malley had met with representatives of Los Angeles who had come trawling for a big-league franchise at the previous fall's World Series in New York.[1] Coming east in an attempt to interest the downtrodden Washington Senators in a move west, Los Angeles County Supervisor Kenneth Hahn received a surprisingly sympathetic hearing from the owner of the National League champion Dodgers, who was about to sell Ebbets Field to a real estate developer, taking back only a short-term lease. Stopping off in Los Angeles with the Dodgers, en route to Japan for a series of exhibition games right after the end of the World Series, O'Malley had coyly cautioned the locals, "You don't want an inartistic ball club [like the Senators] out here."[2] The Dodgers, O'Malley clearly intimated, were a far better prospect.

Executing a move to Los Angeles required O'Malley to proceed along several fronts, and to line up a number of critical allies. The first task was, perhaps, the simplest: securing the baseball territorial rights to Los Angeles. These were held by Phil Wrigley, owner of the Chicago Cubs and of its top minor-league franchise, the Angels of the Pacific Coast League, as well as the Wrigley Field ballpark in south-central Los Angeles. The previous fall, O'Malley had parried questions about a possible move to Los Angeles by saying, with reference to Wrigley, "I wouldn't be guilty of invading a friend's territory."[3] Once his negotiations over rental terms with the Brooklyn Sports Center Authority had broken down early in January 1957—"I was told," O'Malley said, "that the rental would have to be not the substantial sum I mentioned but a minimum of a million and a quarter to a million and a half a year—O'Malley "called Mr. Wrigley and said, 'Phil, will you sell me Los Angeles?' The jig was obviously up."[4] "I bought the Los Angeles Club," O'Malley added, "when I had every sound reason to believe that there would be no solution in Brooklyn."[5]

O'Malley followed up his initial call to Wrigley with an unannounced trip to Los Angeles in January. There he inspected several potential ballpark sites, including a largely vacant, city-owned tract of land in centrally located Chavez Ravine, just north of downtown.[6] Easily accessible by a network of freeways that girdled the area, Chavez Ravine had previously been the site of a "hidden village" of Mexican-American immigrants, which had been condemned and largely cleared in the early 1950s for a proposed public-housing project. The project had been canceled amid charges of Communist infiltration of the local housing agency; its disposition had been a headache for local government ever since.[7] O'Malley clearly liked what he saw. When Wrigley came to New York in early February to accept an award from the New York baseball writers for—ironically—"meritorious service," O'Malley told him that he was ready to purchase Wrigley's Los Angeles baseball properties.[8]

On February 20, 1957, O'Malley and a number of Dodger players flew to Florida from New York as spring training got underway. The next day, O'Malley stepped before the Brooklyn Dodgers press corps and announced that he had obtained Wrigley's Los Angeles franchise and ballpark, in exchange for $2 million and the Dodgers' Fort Worth minor-league farm team. Wrigley hardly needed the money, and he had even said a few years earlier that he considered his Los Angeles baseball holdings to be more valuable than his major-league team in Chicago.[9] Wrigley had long been an advocate of expansion to the West Coast,[10] so there is no way to account for Wrigley's acquiescence to O'Malley's proposition without assuming that O'Malley promised Wrigley that he would be bringing major-league baseball to Los Angeles. "I sold out," Wrigley explained when O'Malley announced the deal on February 21, 1957, "primarily because I felt that the move would give Los Angeles a better chance to become a major league city sooner. All the evidence points to a move to Los Angeles."[11] Clarence "Pants" Rowland, president of the Angels and a longtime Chicago baseball fixture, called it a "sacrifice play": "Mr. Wrigley felt that people in Los Angeles were blaming him for failure of the city to get major league baseball. He was willing to sacrifice his property to speed up arrival of big league baseball on the coast."[12]

In Los Angeles, there was no doubt about the meaning of the O'Malley–Wrigley territorial swap. County Supervisor Kenneth Hahn announced that he had been assured that the Dodgers "will be here within a year or two."[13] O'Malley was similarly blunt: "The deal we made with Phil Wrigley assures us of territorial rights in Los Angeles if such a move becomes necessary." He baldly asserted that the Dodgers "would feel no compunction about moving away from New York. . . . Where we would move should be obvious."[14]

Having staked his claim to the Los Angeles territory so far as the ground rules of baseball were concerned, O'Malley's next task was to win the political battle that had been lost in New York—to obtain the governmental support necessary to build the stadium he wanted to build, where he wanted to build it, on the terms he was willing to pay. In Los Angeles, unlike New York, O'Malley held the whip hand. His timing was perfect. The team he could offer Los Angeles was the reigning National League champion. It was the very last moment that he would have been able to negotiate against the vibrant backdrop of glory lent by "the boys of summer," who were playing with diminished, but still competitive—and marketable—skills. The team was good enough to be a desirable catch for its boosters in Los Angeles, yet not quite good enough to win the 1957 pennant (let alone the World Series)—an event that would have made the desertion of Brooklyn even more of a black eye for baseball than it was.

Los Angeles, driven by an outspoken ambition to secure a place in the world alongside New York, quickly proved that it was willing to go to any lengths to land a major-league baseball team. The simple question facing Los Angeles, according to Mayor Norris Poulson, was "Are we going to be a bush league town or are we going to be major league in everything?"[15] Parochial politics, O'Malley complained, had blocked his plans in New York. "If the man in Queens won't vote for this to be done in Brooklyn," O'Malley explained, "and the man in the Bronx won't vote for it, then Mr. Moses gets disgusted with the whole thing and says let's put them over in Flushing Meadows." Driven by big-league dreams, which New York had taken for granted for decades, Los Angeles proved far more receptive to O'Malley's agenda. "The people from Los Angeles showed," he said, "they had political unanimity. The Republicans and the Democrats, and the publishers of the papers" grouped themselves around O'Malley, ready to run interference.[16] Mayor Poulson, untaxed by an overabundance of official responsibilities,[17] was always available to pitch in, a nice contrast to the distracted attentions of Mayor Wagner in New York. And Walter O'Malley was ready, willing, and able to parlay Los Angeles's intense interest in snaring the Dodgers into agreement on precisely what he had tried and failed to secure in New York: a privately owned ballpark on the site of his choice that the city would convey to him at a "reasonable price."

In later years, Mayor Poulson would claim that O'Malley had

demanded that Los Angeles build a ballpark for the Dodgers. The contemporary evidence, as well as the denial by Poulson's coventurer, Supervisor Hahn, does not support this contention.[18] In fact, O'Malley consistently pushed for a privately constructed and owned Dodger Stadium in Los Angeles.[19] In early May 1957, when O'Malley flew to Los Angeles to close the deal, Poulson and Hahn offered him a publicly built stadium on the Chavez Ravine site. The LA officials were so confident that O'Malley would jump at their offer that they drafted an advance press release announcing the decision to build a public stadium, which would be leased to the Dodgers, as their chosen mechanism for bringing the Dodgers to Los Angeles.[20]

To their obvious surprise, O'Malley demurred, scrawling a handwritten "vetoed in toto" across their proposal. In Los Angeles as in New York, O'Malley was simply not interested in what he would disparagingly refer to as a "political ballpark," and he strongly objected to the suggestion that *only* a public stadium could be built on the city-owned land at Chavez Ravine.[21] In place of what the city and county had proposed, O'Malley dictated a detailed "strictly confidential" ten-point outline of the offer that "the city and county should be prepared to make" to bring the Dodgers to LA.[22] Under the terms proposed by O'Malley,[23] the Dodgers would finance the construction of the stadium, and own and manage it, but the city and county would have to grade and provide the land on which he would build it and undertake construction of access roads. As an end run around the apparent illegality of an outright gift or long-term, nominal-cost lease of Chavez Ravine, O'Malley would transfer his own recently acquired Wrigley Field property to the city in exchange for the city-owned Chavez Ravine site.[24] When O'Malley returned to Brooklyn, the terms for a new stadium for the Dodgers in Los Angeles were in place.

There remained one piece of outstanding business, but on it hinged the ability to consummate the Dodgers' move to the West

Coast. Major-league baseball had only recently expanded beyond its traditional western frontier on the Mississippi, and then by only a few hundred miles, to Kansas City. St. Louis remained the most westerly city in the National League, as it had been for half a century. If one team jumped to the Pacific Coast, there were bound to be concerns from other club owners about the increased travel expenses and scheduling complications (in the pre–passenger-jet era) involved in road trips to California for a series of games against one opponent.[25] It was calculated that travel expenses would double, requiring a sharp increase in attendance to cover the added cost to the visiting team.[26] The easiest way to overcome such objections was to make a West Coast trip more cost-beneficial by arranging for another team to make a move along with the Dodgers. One National League owner who was *very* interested in the Dodgers' fate had said earlier that "Brooklyn wouldn't move to Los Angeles without assurances that another National League club would go to San Francisco." From day one of his campaign for a new Brooklyn ballpark, *O'Malley* had said that if the Dodgers moved, the Giants would have to follow; in May of 1957, he turned to the Giants' owner, Horace Stoneham, to complete the game plan for a move to California.[27]

THE RIVALRY between the Brooklyn Dodgers and the New York Giants was one of the glories of the world of baseball, unsurpassed in intensity and passion for players and fans alike. It remained as fierce as ever into the 1950s, fueled by the bitterly fought 1951 pennant race and playoff, and the Dodgers' out-and-out hatred of Giant (and former Dodger) manager Leo Durocher. In September 1953, Brooklyn right-fielder Carl Furillo had charged the Giant dugout and knocked Durocher down in retaliation for being hit by a Ruben Gomez pitch. In 1955, Sal "The Barber" Maglie's inside pitches set off a round of rough base-running in which Jackie Robinson crashed into Giant second baseman Davey Williams covering first on a bunt, and later faced a hard-sliding Al Dark barreling into third.[28] No wonder that Robinson's abortive trade to the Giants in the winter of 1956 came as a shock to fans of *both* teams.[29]

Walter O'Malley knew as well as anyone that this still-smoldering baseball war was an extremely valuable business as well as intense sporting proposition. When he had first met with Los Angeles Mayor Poulson at the Dodgers' Vero Beach spring-training camp in early March 1957, O'Malley had said that a transplanted Dodger franchise wanted that rivalry to continue.[30] As the Dodgers' plans to move to Los Angeles took shape, one of New York City's greatest baseball traditions was about to reveal itself as an Achilles heel.

ON THE AFTERNOON of October 3, 1951, Red Smith sat in the Polo Grounds press box and typed, "Now it is done. Now the story ends. And there is no way to tell it. The art of fiction is dead. Reality has strangled invention. Only the utterly impossible, the inexpressibly fantastic, can ever be plausible again."[31] Down below, Dodger fans sat in stunned silence as Giant fans surged around the center-field clubhouse calling for their heroes to take their bows.[32] Moments earlier, the press loudspeaker had announced, "World Series credentials for Ebbets Field can be picked up at six o'clock tonight at the Biltmore Hotel," but Bobby Thomson had just hit the "shot heard round the world," and those credentials would be going unclaimed.[33]

On that day, no one would have predicted that within just a few years, "Now the story ends" could serve as the headline for a story on the Giants' farewell to the Polo Grounds and New York, and not only the lead for a classic account of the single greatest moment in New York Giants, perhaps all of baseball, history. The Giants, beginning their

fourth decade under Stoneham family ownership, had been prime beneficiaries of the postwar baseball boom, setting a team attendance
record in 1947. In 1951, the Polo Grounds hosted more than one million fans for the seventh consecutive year, matching the Dodgers in setting that league record. Dividends continued to flow regularly to the
team's owners, as they had over the previous thirty years.[34]

Although after the late 1940s, attendance at the Polo Grounds
began declining, the Giants, like the Dodgers, took early advantage of
the increasing revenues provided by the new medium of television.
The Giants earned $250,000 for television and radio rights in 1950,
second only to the Dodgers—a sharp increase from the $87,500 in
pre-television broadcast income received just four years earlier.[35] The
team that the Giants fielded in 1951 was well worth viewing, whether
live or on television. The Giants followed closely behind the Dodgers
in breaching baseball's color line. When the two teams clashed in that
epic 1951 playoff, the Giants squared off against the Brooklyn
Dodgers of Jackie Robinson, Roy Campanella, and Don Newcombe,
with a lineup bolstered by Monte Irvin, Willie Mays, and Hank
Thompson.

Still, when Bobby Thomson stepped to the plate that October
afternoon, the Polo Grounds crowd numbered only 34,320, less than
two-thirds of capacity. Never mind the millions who swore ever after
that *they* had been there, the Giants had not even been able to attract
a full house to their 55,000-seat ballpark for the climactic game of their
incredible season. The lack of witnesses was commented on at the
time and has now entered literary lore, thanks to novelist Don
DeLillo.[36] The attendance that day was even smaller than the less-
than-capacity crowd the previous day. Even as headlines announced,
"Baseball Fever Grips City 3d Day," the press and the Giants front
office scrambled to explain the disappointingly small turnouts, specu-
lating that an "assumed sell-out cuts size of crowd" for Game 2, and

that threatening weather had held down the crowd still further for the decisive struggle.[37] On the field it was an epic, once-in-a-lifetime drama, but the rows of empty seats in the grandstand signaled a gathering storm for the Giants.

After the 1951 season, Willie Mays left for two years in the U.S. Army, and the 1952 and 1953 teams proved no match for the best teams that the Dodgers ever fielded in Brooklyn, the "boys of summer" turning in peak performances and winning the pennant by 4½ games in 1952 and thirteen games in 1953—a year in which they won a team-record 105 games. Following their fairly close second-place finish in 1952, the Giants fell far off the pace in 1953, finishing fifth, thirty-five games behind the Dodgers. The next season, Willie Mays was back, and the Giants won it all, beating out the Dodgers by five games for the pennant, then, taking the World Series in four straight games from the seemingly unbeatable Indians, winners of an American League record 111 games. It was, however, a victory that marked an ending, instead of a beginning, for the New York Giants.

The Giants simply collapsed thereafter—on the field and at the box office. Only a handful of defending champions compiled a worse record than that posted by the 1955 Giants, who finished the season in third place, a distant 18½ games behind the pennant-winning Dodgers. The next season, having jettisoned a suddenly tired and disinterested Leo Durocher, the Giants sank completely out of sight, finishing in sixth place, twenty-six games off the lead, and scoring fewer runs than any National League team in five years. Willie Mays just wasn't enough, but with pitcher Johnny Antonelli off in the U.S. Army, he was all that these final editions of the New York Giants had.

Increasingly, the sounds of silence echoed grimly in the vast recesses of the Polo Grounds. At the peak of the postwar baseball boom, with the novelty of night baseball regularly attracting crowds of 50,000 and more to the Harlem ballpark, the eleven contests with the

Dodgers were good for more than 400,000 admissions alone in 1947. That year, a record 1,600,000 fans attended Giant home games. Within two years, however, Giant attendance was down to 1,200,000 and barely exceeded one million in 1950 and 1951. By 1953, only about 800,000 fans paid their way into the Polo Grounds.

The World Championship season of 1954 saw attendance rebound to 1,155,000, more than one-third of whom attended the Giants' eleven games with the Dodgers, but there was no carryover into the next year, when attendance sank back to the 1953 level before collapsing to 629,000 in 1956. This was half the attendance claimed by the Dodgers, and 300,000 lower than any other team in the National League; attendance increased in every other ballpark in the league. It was the Giants' worst peacetime mark since depression-ridden 1933, and third worst since 1918. Weekday afternoon Polo Grounds "crowds" averaged fewer than 3,500. Especially galling, and worrying, was the fact that an increasing number of the Giants' home "fans" were likely Dodger partisans infiltrating behind enemy lines. In 1955 and 1956, about 40 percent of *total* Giants home attendance occurred during the team's eleven Polo Grounds games against Brooklyn. As the team sank in the standings, not even Willie Mays, who was establishing himself as arguably the best, and undoubtedly the most exciting, player in the game, could prevent this implosion at the gate.

True, the Giants had been dogged by some bad luck as attendance declined. In 1951, they had played the bulk of their home schedule before their late August and September stretch run, which carried them to their playoff win over the Dodgers. When excitement was at its peak, the Giants had the misfortune of having only *three* Polo Grounds games scheduled after Labor Day. In 1956, the Giants' front office attributed that year's dismal turnstile count to a flurry of rainouts, including the loss of three games with the Dodgers and several Sunday dates, which cost the Giants 200,000 in admissions.

The Giants also suffered from choices of their own making. Horace Stoneham remained committed to long-standing business practices that contributed to the long-term attendance drop. By the middle of the 1950s, the Giants were playing more weekday-afternoon games than any team in the National League (other than the Cubs, who played no night games at all). The Dodgers bowed to the changing times and accepted the fact that afternoons in the affluent society yielded more pressing tasks than a grandmother's funeral at the ballpark. In 1947, the Dodgers had played thirty-four games on weekday afternoons, the Giants twenty-six. By 1956, O'Malley cut his weekday-afternoon schedule to nine games. The Giants held the line, playing twenty-one games under God's lights that year and drawing significantly smaller crowds as a result. Stoneham's increasingly outdated scheduling was probably costing the Giants more than 100,000 admissions a year.[38] Whatever the extenuating circumstances, there was no mistaking the fact that at the typical mid-1950s game at the Polo Grounds, more than 40,000 of its 55,000 seats were empty.

Bad luck and conservative scheduling aside, the Polo Grounds ballpark itself was a prime culprit in the case of the disappearing Giants fan. After all, the Polo Grounds, which dated back to 1911, was even older than "antiquated" Ebbets Field. There were undeniable problems with the historic Giants ballpark as a venue for either the sport or the business of baseball. The dramatically odd dimensions of the playing field—the legacy of the dead-ball era, 257 feet to right field, 279 feet to left, but a colossal 483 feet to center—distorted the playing of the game and placed a nerve-racking strain on pitchers to avoid the errant pitch that could be popped into the neighborly corner seats by any batter at all. The intriguingly intimate distances down the lines always threatened to skew front-office strategy toward the signing of "pull hitters" to take advantage of the local terrain—a tendency that invariably resulted in disaster (much as it had for Red Sox management when it succumbed to overfascination with Fenway's Green Monster) for a team that, after all, had to play half of its games out on the wide-open road.

Such athletic considerations aside, the park's vast, rectangular two-deck grandstand, which intersected the short foul lines just beyond the edge of the infield dirt, placed most of the horseshoe-shaped ballpark's 55,000 seats in positions abutting the outfield. Unlike his Dodger counterpart, Giants' owner Stoneham could not complain that seating capacity of *his* home ballpark was too small. By far the largest venue in the National League, and the third largest (exceeded only by Yankee Stadium and Cleveland's Municipal Stadium) in all of major-league baseball, the Polo Grounds had more than 55,000 seats. Size alone, however, did not translate into a formula for financial success by the mid-1950s. The Polo Grounds offered a superabundance of cheap general-admission seats (35,000, the most in baseball) and a severe shortage of the box and reserved seats that could be sold at premium prices. Despite its huge capacity, the Polo Grounds had, in fact, fewer box seats than all but two other, much smaller, ballparks in the National League and, the smallest percentage of such desirable and expensive tickets of any facility in the majors.[39] This put a crimp in Giant ticket prospects just at the time when—as Walter O'Malley, for one, constantly reiterated—an increasingly affluent public was growing more demanding about what it expected out of a day at the ballpark, when the population dispersal made the advance sale of tickets more important than ever, and when the more casual act of witnessing a game could be more easily accomplished by flicking on the television set at home.

The Polo Grounds location was even more problematic. In a city and at a time when more rigidly defined conceptions of racial turf were developing, the Polo Grounds happened to be in Harlem, and this alone, rightly or wrongly, rang a warning bell to many white fans to stay away.

In a baseball business environment in which the weaker of the two major-league teams in Boston, St. Louis, and Philadelphia had been forced to find new homes elsewhere, a similar move by the Giants would not have been unexpected. Before his sudden death in 1936, Charles Stoneham had seen his Giants surrender to the Yankees their claim to rule the New York baseball world. Horace, Charles's son and successor, was fated to preside over the further decline of the once-dominant franchise. In the 1940s, the Dodgers hurtled past the Giants on the field and at the box office, and emerged as the Yankees' prime rival. The turning had come just before the war in 1939. Before that season, although long since outpaced by the Yankees, the Giants had consistently drawn more fans than Brooklyn. Thereafter, the Dodgers held the edge in fan loyalties and attendance—and passion.[40]

As the Giants faded in the standings, increasingly eclipsed by the Dodgers' postwar surge, New York's relationship with the Giants lost its intensity, leaving the Giants without the safety net of loyalty on which the Dodgers could still count—up until the moment the team left town. In confirmation of that loosening hold on the city's psyche, "the New York Giants have disappeared" from baseball's collective memory, as one still-heartbroken fan recently discovered amid the Dodger and Yankee clutter of the Hall of Fame's gift shop.[41] By the 1950s, the once-dominant Giants had become the third team in baseball's only three-team city, and Horace Stoneham was saddled with "the blame for letting his franchise go to seed."[42]

However, up until early May 1957, there is little evidence that Horace Stoneham was seriously contemplating moving the Giants out of New York. In preceding years, Stoneham had apparently, if idly, thought—from time to time, and without any deadline in mind—

about transferring the franchise to Minneapolis, a city that was the home of the Giants' top farm club, and that had just built a new municipal stadium. But he had done nothing about it, and apparently had not given it serious consideration.[43] When asked about his plans for the Giants, Stoneham repeatedly said that the "future of the Giants is in New York."[44]

There were two reasons for Stoneham's evident equanimity in the face of the Giants' declining fortunes on the field and at the turnstiles. The first was that an obvious alternative to the Polo Grounds was readily at hand. Ever since 1951, Stoneham had been saying that, when the time came to abandon the Polo Grounds, the Giants would simply cross the Harlem River and, reversing the past relationship of the teams, settle in as tenants of the Yankees in their stadium.[45] From time to time, he had discussed such a move with the Yankee ownership in general terms, but without pressing the issue or talking numbers. Yankee Stadium offered more parking, a larger seating capacity for big games against the Dodgers and Braves, and 12,000 box seats to the Polo Grounds' 3,600. "I'll probably be talking to [Yankee co-owner Dan] Topping in a couple of weeks at which time we'll get into figures," Stoneham said in November 1955.[46] The Giants, Stoneham insisted, would not be moving to Minneapolis; they would continue to play "in the Polo Grounds, perhaps in Yankee Stadium at some time."[47] In retrospect, it is unfortunate that New York City, preoccupied with O'Malley's impossible agenda, failed to press actively to implement the eminently reasonable Yankee Stadium solution for the Giants' problems, especially since Mayor Wagner was himself "a Giant fan from boyhood."[48]

The second cause of Stoneham's apparent complacency was financial. New York remained a profitable place to conduct baseball business for the Giants. By 1956, the economics of New York Giants baseball had been revolutionized, thanks to the advent of television and the steadily increasing income it yielded.[49] In 1946, before the television era, live admissions—at the Polo Grounds and on the road—contributed almost 80 percent of the Giants' baseball-related income, broadcasting a scant 5 percent.[50] In 1950, broadcasting revenue exceeded road-game income, and the share of income contributed by the live gate fell to 70 percent, while the television–radio share was up to 15 percent. By 1956, broadcast income contributed more than 30 percent of the Giants' total team income. As a result, even while Polo Grounds attendance was declining, the Giants did not slip into the red. The team earned a profit even in dismal 1956, despite running up the highest expenses in the National League.[51] Stoneham could easily afford to pay himself baseball's highest executive salary of $70,000, carry his son on the team payroll, and continue his family's traditional practice of declaring dividends whenever possible.[52] In 1956, the Giants, thanks to their broadcasting revenues, managed to post the third highest income in the National League, despite recording the league's lowest home attendance.

Fortified by the escalating increases in television revenues, Stoneham could look on his team's business prospects with equanimity, even as attendance fell. From the summer of 1955 through the spring of 1957, Stoneham had watched from the sidelines as the Dodgers waged their aggressive public campaign to win a new Brooklyn ballpark, not following up on his early request to participate in the city's meetings with O'Malley in August 1955, which he had only learned about through reading the newspapers.[53] The Giants' owner's oft-stated position was that a decision about the Giants' future in New York did not depend on what O'Malley did or did not do, and it would be made independently.[54] But no one believed this (even assuming that Stoneham himself did)—least of all, O'Malley. A full 30 to 40 percent of the Giants' total home attendance was being derived from their Polo Grounds games with the Dodgers, as Stoneham knew well, and he conceded that a move by Brooklyn would hurt Giants attendance.[55] The pundits agreed, asserting that the Dodgers were literally keeping the New York Giants alive.[56] Implicitly accepting this, Stoneham had stood by and let the debate over the Dodgers' future determine the fate of *his* team.

As the Dodgers edged closer to a move out of Brooklyn, Stoneham's composure crumbled. Once the Dodgers announced their acquisition of the Los Angeles territory from the Cubs in February 1957, Stoneham had to face the fact that the Dodgers were really going to be leaving town—and soon. If the eleven or so Polo Grounds games with the Dodgers would no longer attract a swarm of *Brooklyn* fans to the enemy's territory, the Giants' attendance might drop to below half a million.[57] There was no way the Giants could compensate for that lost patronage if the Dodgers left town. It was a backhanded tribute to the ancient glories of the team that its other rivalry, with the Chicago Cubs, had flowered and died decades earlier. The Giants, Stoneham believed, needed Brooklyn—or, more accurately, Brooklyn's *fans*—to survive.[58]

In making his pitch to Stoneham to join the Dodgers in a move to California, O'Malley did more than play on Stoneham's concerns about the Giants' future in a Dodger-less New York. He also provided a vision of the vast riches that awaited the Giants on the West Coast if they had the courage to make the move. O'Malley's key ally in this endeavor was Matthew Fox, president of a pioneering pay television company called Skiatron TV.

For all the wealth it had produced, there had been two things about the system of free commercial television, as it had evolved in New York during the first decade of its life, which had nettled the Dodger and Giant owners. The first was the practice of televising home games. As a matter of marketing theory, it would have been far preferable to televise road games, not home games. This would be using the medium to increase exposure, but it would steer enhanced interest through local turnstiles. However, television policy had been forged in the late 1940s, when primitive technology and high expense had precluded the televising of road games back to New York. Even into the middle of the 1950s, the expense barrier limited the number of road broadcasts, although by 1956 the Yankees and Dodgers were televising a selected number of away games. But to maintain the high number of programs that had to be furnished in exchange for the type of income to which the clubs had grown accustomed, the teams had to make their entire home schedules available for broadcast.

Stoneham and O'Malley at times refused to blame home-game telecasts as the primary cause for the attendance decline that had set in after 1950.[59] But the two owners believed, quite reasonably, that their television policies cut into the live gate for certain attractions, especially big night games. From time to time, they, together with Yankee management, canvassed the possibility of agreeing to black out home night games. Nothing came of it. The owners feared antitrust complications if they jointly agreed to a television policy that restricted the number of telecasts—a problem the National Football League had encountered—to the politically sensitive New York market.[60] Those legal questions aside, the owners found that it was impossible to come up with a compensating number of road games to beam back to New York without conflicting with someone else's home game being played at the same time. The fear was that unless such conflicts between home-screen and live attractions were eliminated, fans not inclined to make a night of it at a game[61] would simply flip the dial at home instead of trekking out to the ballpark to follow their preferred team's progress. Selective black-outs in a three-team city would be hard to manage.

There was also an even more fundamental disquiet about nothing less than the availability of ball games on "free" home television at all.

On this issue, the concern was not about finding a way to redirect fan interest out to the ballpark, but, instead, about maximizing the money that could be drawn out of the fan who stayed at home. That fan at home, contributing only indirectly, if generously, to the finances of the team by buying the "right" brand of cigarettes or beer, had haunted Walter O'Malley's bookkeeping ever since "that night we had 15,700 people in Ebbets Field and I asked a radio-wise man who was with me . . . how many sets were tuned in to that particular game and after some phone calling he came back and said, 'Walter, there are about 2,440,000 sets watching this game.'" "That," O'Malley said later, "made me convert right away"[62] to the idea of the need for a mechanism to make that fan pay directly for watching a telecast at home through a system of pay television, and the tithe it could levy on the distant but devoted fan.

In that innocent, prehistoric moment in the evolution of pay-television economics, the expected, almost effortless rewards were staggering. O'Malley foresaw nothing less than an immediate doubling of broadcast revenues—and that was just to start. Based on a one dollar fee for the privilege of tuning into each game, Stoneham's calculations were even more expansively sanguine. With 500,000 sets receiving any one particular game, gross receipts would amount to $500,000, and the ball club would claim one quarter—$125,000—of that, in accordance with receipts division formulas being discussed.[63] That *per-game* yield would add up to more than $10 million in the course of a season—a monumental figure, and one that Stoneham evidently took seriously. Indeed, Stoneham expected to realize that pay-TV bonanza from home-game telecasts alone, even with the inevitable toll they would exact from the live gate, which paled by comparison with the size of this novel revenue source.[64]

Fox was the messenger who had delivered the good news about pay television to Walter O'Malley and now was poised, at O'Malley's direction, to take it to Stoneham as well. Fox and O'Malley had met in February and March of 1957, and Fox flatly claimed that the technology of pay TV had, in fact, come of age. The message was so encouraging that he and O'Malley reached a tentative agreement in April 1957, assigning Skiatron pay-television rights to Dodger games, and the prospect of such an agreement with the Giants was then put to Stoneham.[65] In mid-May 1957, Horace Stoneham entered into a multimillion-dollar contract with Skiatron to telecast, on a closed-circuit system, the next year's Giant games if in San Francisco, and after the 1959 expiration of the Giants' current TV contract if the team was still in New York.[66]

According to Fox, pay-television presentation of Giant and Dodger games—and the edging of those games off the "free" home box—could begin as early as the 1958 baseball season. But, as Fox, Stoneham, and O'Malley each knew, this could not be done in Brooklyn or New York. Fox promised that the technology was ready, but the economics and politics of television broadcasting prevented any such imminent installation of such a system in the city, as did the teams' existing "free television" broadcasting contracts.[67]

In New York, adoption of a pay system would have to await the expiration of the commercial broadcasting agreements then in force. But even once those contracts expired—not before the 1959 season for each club[68]—the prospects for the substitution of a pay system for the existing free one were clouded. Furthermore, the City Council of the capital of the television world was alert to the welter of (exaggerated) rumors about the imminent coming of pay television, wholly apart from the Dodgers–Giants–Skiatron plans, and had already voted to bar the awarding of pay-television franchises within the five boroughs. Reversing that stance would take a fight. Whether or not Skiatron was ready, it was certain that New York was not going to welcome it with open arms.

As it turned out, Skiatron was not ready, and what it proposed could not be done in Los Angeles or in San Francisco either—not at that time, and not by Skiatron. To install even a quick-and-dirty cable system, Skiatron needed reserves of capital it did not have.[69] As the Securities and Exchange Commission (SEC) would later determine, "the issued and outstanding patents of [Skiatron] are not essential to the operations of either its over-the-air or its wire system," and Skiatron "had no source of income or credit sufficient to enable it to finance the establishment and construction of a subscription television system and to secure program material for its proposed system."[70] Within two years of Fox's talks with Stoneham, Skiatron was bankrupt and under investigation by the Securities and Exchange Commission, which in 1960 suspended registration of Skiatron stock for "misleading statements and omissions of material facts" in its SEC filings.[71]

But that reality hadn't hit when, abetted by the siren song of pay television, O'Malley gained Stoneham's interest in pursuing a San Francisco solution to his existing questions about the future of the Polo Grounds. O'Malley followed up his advantage immediately, bringing together Stoneham and Mayor George Christopher in New York within a few days of his return from Los Angeles.[72] In the interim, the Dodger owner dispatched his own engineer, Emil Praeger, to San Francisco to survey stadium sites.[73] On May 10, 1957, over a seafood lunch at New York's Hotel Lexington, with Stoneham and O'Malley, followed up with dinner in Stoneham's private eyrie at the Polo Grounds, Mayor Christopher laid out the general terms under which the Giants could play in the stadium San Francisco would build for them on the tidelands between Hunters Point and Candlestick Point. As O'Malley recalled, "I sat him down with Stoneham. . . . Neither Stoneham nor Christopher was clear about what kind of agreement was necessary so I took an envelope out of my pocket, and on the back of it I wrote out the terms for what became Candlestick Park."[74] The next day, the San Francisco press, unconstrained by a gag order imposed on the principals by Baseball Commissioner Ford Frick, proclaimed, "N.Y. Giants 'Sure' for S.F. in 1958."[75]

With Stoneham and the Giants on board, O'Malley moved swiftly to secure his fellow owners' approval of a franchise shift to California. His plans were now given an assist by major-league baseball's own political agenda. Renewed congressional hearings into organized baseball's business practices, and the continued court-sanctioned immunity from the antitrust laws, were scheduled to convene in Washington on June 10, 1957. The National League rescheduled an upcoming meeting from July 8 in St. Louis to May 28 in Chicago. In the first round of hearings in 1951, baseball's failure to expand to the West Coast had provoked pointed questioning. No apparent progress had been made in the interim, and baseball's expansion program, if any, was again on the agenda. The May 28 meeting provided an opportunity to toss Congress a preemptive bone that might ward off the one thing baseball feared most—congressional action to strip baseball of its antitrust immunity, the rock upon which baseball had built its monopolistic church.

As National League owners met at Chicago's Blackstone Hotel, evangelist Billy Graham was preaching in Madison Square Garden to a packed gathering of 17,500—greater than most Dodger or Giant crowds in recent years—that "the reason there is so much misery in New York is that there are so many who are spiritually dead."[76] There would be more misery in New York very soon. In 1920, an earlier "smoke-filled-room" gathering at the Blackstone had resulted in Warren Harding's nomination for president. This time, it was Los Angeles and San Francisco that won the nomination—for big-league status. O'Malley and Stoneham received unanimous approval to shift their franchises to LA and San Francisco, respectively, in 1958.[77]

The lure of vast pay-television receipts from these two cities in tandem, money that would be apportioned to visiting teams (as with gate receipts, but unlike free-television revenues), was too sweet to turn down. Team owners hoped for one, perhaps two, new Milwaukees—a city that was producing fully one-fourth of the league's total attendance and earning an average of $85,000 for the seven other teams in the league out of their visitors' share of that fabulous gate. Besides, staking out the two California cities meant stealing a march on an American League whose traditional financial superiority was eroding as a result of its desperate and poorly calculated moves into Baltimore and Kansas City. Grabbing Los Angeles offered the National League the prospect of domination over the American League, a decisive checkmate in the great game of expansion politics.

Organized baseball kissed off Brooklyn and New York just as unceremoniously as Boston had done four years earlier. The fraternity of team owners had no intention of denying the enterprising Stoneham and O'Malley a privilege that more than a few among them wanted to hold in reserve for themselves. And the Brooklyn–New York rivalry, stimulating for the city, had not been all that good for the league as a whole. The outlander teams had never shared in the windfall produced by that inbred competition, which accounted for a disproportionate share of Brooklyn and New York attendance. And for teams embroiled in negotiations of their own for improved playing or parking facilities, such as Cincinnati, which promptly capitalized on it, the fate of an abandoned Brooklyn and New York would encourage the others. In time, of course, the Yankees too would also bring this strategy to bear on New York, which, having loved and lost, had vowed neither to love nor to lose once again.

After the vote, O'Malley and Stoneham were publicly noncommittal about their future plans. "All I can say now is that this action opens the door for exploration of further possibilities," O'Malley deadpanned, notwithstanding all the assiduous spadework for a move that he had undertaken in recent months. Stoneham made a similar statement. But no one was fooled, and, perhaps for the first time, New Yorkers awoke to the fact that the teams might really be lost.[78] The willfully belated prognosis for the Dodgers' and Giants' future was grim. "Backed against the wall as they are because of declining attendance, which is a result of obsolete facilities and metropolitan New York's saturation with television baseball, the Dodger and Giant presidents unquestionably are receptive to making a change."[79] "New York," Tommy Holmes wrote in the *Herald Tribune*, "may have learned too late that the supposedly magic name isn't enough to compete with the desire and will of other city governments to promote enterprises for the pleasure and entertainment of their citizens." According to the *Daily News*, "New York City's do-nothing politicians and National League club owners Walter O'Malley and Horace Stoneham share the blame for the crumbling of big league baseball in Gotham." And Dan Daniel in the *World-Telegram* observed, "Yesterday's wildest dream is today's reality."[80]

After May 28, 1957, the game was up in Brooklyn and New York. O'Malley and Stoneham proceeded to finalize their negotiations with Los Angeles and San Francisco, respectively. As the life of the Brooklyn franchise ebbed, the Dodgers stumbled on the field as well. On Saturday, June 8, the team, making an "impressive move that didn't require taking a single step out of Flatbush,"[81] capped a five-game winning streak with a victory over the Redlegs at Ebbets Field, to take first place in the National League. It was the last time that Brooklyn's flag would ever fly at the head of the club standings. The next day, the aging Dodgers lost a doubleheader to Cincinnati and fell back into second, then dropped out of the pennant race altogether, en route to an eventual third-place finish behind Milwaukee and St. Louis. The more consistently mediocre Giants were in sixth place on May 28, which is where they ended their own dismal season.

On August 19, the Giants announced that they were leaving New York for the Golden Gate.[82] When Stoneham was asked how he felt about taking away the Giants from the children of New York, he would say, "I feel bad about the kids, but I haven't seen too many of their fathers lately." That Stoneham was ready to leave New York with such apparent ease surprised observers at the time. As one New York reporter wrote, "That Horace Stoneham would give up the ghost at the Polo Grounds at the mere crook of Walter O'Malley's finger seems inconceivable. Forsaking the traditions and background built by John McGraw and the rest of the Giant greats is coming easier than we would have thought for Stoneham. The past won't go west with Stoneham, only the shell of a once great franchise."[83]

Indeed, the Giants—more than the Dodgers—would find that the team's heritage and traditions would not travel well. The greatest casualty of Stoneham's calculus was Willie Mays. The great center fielder was a beloved figure on the New York sports scene. The images of his hat flying off his head while running the bases *and* of his laying stickball in the streets of Harlem were both indelibly burned into the city's collective memory. For New York's Giant fans, not even the loss of the team could dim the affection that was felt for him. "The team is out of my system now," Murray Kempton wrote a few years later. "I am only a Willie Mays fan."[84] San Francisco was different for Mays, on and off the diamond. He ran into racial discrimination when looking for a house, and the city's proud but provincial fans regarded him as something of an interloper. "Mays was the symbol of New York," his biographer Charles Einstein said, "being thrust down San Francisco's throat."[85] Mays would hear boos for the first time, and he would never receive the heartfelt devotion accorded "real" *San Francisco* Giants such as Orlando Cepeda or Willie McCovey—not to mention the ordeal he would endure batting in cold and foggy Candlestick Park, the oft-cursed "temple of the winds" that became the team's new home.

On the afternoon of September 29, 1957, only 11,600 fans, including John McGraw's widow, rattled around the massive, largely empty
grandstand as the Giants played their last game at the Polo Grounds.
They lost 9–1 and just like that, the Giants of New York—the Giants
of McGraw, of Terry, of Bobby Thomson and of Willie Mays, the
Giants too of Murray Kempton, Delmore Schwartz, Paul Auster, and
Roger Angell—were gone.

UNLIKE STONEHAM, Walter O'Malley deferred any official announcement about a move until after the 1957 season had ended if only to
keep the pressure on the LA City Council, which had to approve the
Chavez Ravine contract with the Dodgers.[86] Not that it mattered by
then, but in the middle of August, it was finally disclosed that the
Brooklyn Sports Center Authority would not be able to finance the
costs of the project—which those in the know had recognized for
months, and which had, indeed, precipitated O'Malley's intensified
pursuit of Los Angeles. The revelation that the total cost of the Long
Island Railroad terminal-area improvement, including the stadium,
would run to $50 million, finally killed off *any* lingering illusions that
the Dodger stadium solution would take *that* particular form.[87]

A final attempt by New York officials to satisfy O'Malley's original
plan—that the land he needed should simply be condemned and sold
to him at a markdown—emerged out of the blue in September under
the imprimatur of Nelson Rockefeller, then seeking a popular cause
for his upcoming race for governor against incumbent Averell Harriman, whose Sports Center plan had crashed and burned.[88] O'Malley
barely feigned interest in the proposal; he had made up his mind
months earlier. A last-minute Rockefeller family initiative had a few
years earlier saved the United Nations for New York. But the alternative for the UN had been Philadelphia; for the Dodgers, it was Los

Angeles. "Circumstances beyond the control of civil leaders enabled the Dodgers to pick up a great deal of loot. It's not just for a 'handful of silver' they are leaving us. They have stumbled into a bonanza," *Daily News* columnist Jimmy Powers ruefully recognized.[89]

On September 24, 1957, the Dodgers played what would be their last game at Ebbets Field, losing to the Pirates before 6,700 die-hard fans, who exited the stands as the organist played, "Auld Lang Syne." One week after the season ended, the Los Angeles City Council approved the terms of an agreement with the Dodgers for the Chavez Ravine site. Although LA's chief negotiator tried to save face for the city by claiming, "O'Malley has had to yield on many points," the basic demands on which O'Malley had insisted in May stood unchanged. Los Angeles would provide the land and O'Malley would build, own, and operate the ballpark. Three thousand miles from downtown Brooklyn, O'Malley would have what he had always wanted: a new ballpark, on his terms.

Some wrangling continued in Los Angeles over a deal that quickly attracted its share of critics as being overly favorable to the Dodgers,[90] but too much can be made of the political and legal challenges that did delay the construction of O'Malley's dream ballpark by a year or so. What really mattered was that O'Malley had found in Los Angeles a supportive political and economic establishment that had been lacking in New York—where, he complained, power was too fragmented. In Los Angeles, there was unity.[91] Los Angeles city and county politicians rallied to the side of the Dodgers when the agreement with the team was challenged in a June 1958 referendum. The decisive margin of victory came from black and Hispanic precincts, a vote of gratitude for breaking the color line, but an ironic payback to the *Brooklyn* where Jackie Robinson had made history.[92] Thereafter, a unanimous decision by the California Supreme Court upheld the legality of the Chavez Ravine–Wrigley Field swap.[93]

On October 8, 1957, the Brooklyn National League Baseball Club, Inc., announced that it would open the 1958 season in Los Angeles. Dick Young's self-described "obit" for the Brooklyn Dodgers in the *Daily News* was headlined, "Lust for More $ Killed Brooks," and his "preliminary diagnosis indicates that the cause of death was an acute case of greed, followed by severe political complications." But Young was not entirely unsympathetic to the Dodger owner, who "was getting the works" from New York's officials, who "quibbled, mouthed sweet nothings and had to place the blame elsewhere" when plans for a new Dodger home in Brooklyn fell through.[94] By then, the exact etiology of the demise of the Brooklyn Dodgers was irrelevant as far as the team's owner was concerned. He was looking ahead, not back. "Get your wheelbarrow and shovel," O'Malley wired Mayor Poulson, "I'll meet you in Chavez Ravine."[95] But posterity has granted Dick Young the last word: "And now Walter O'Malley leaves Brooklyn, a rich man and a despised man."[96]

IT WAS A shocking turn of events, and as the 1958 season opened, it relegated the nation's largest city to the forlorn status of a one-team town, joining the depressing precedents set by such obviously declining cities as St. Louis, Boston, and Philadelphia. It was yet another signpost to the decreasing importance of urban American in the Eisenhower era of interstate highways, suburban tract houses, and an emerging Sunbelt. Chicago was left as the only remaining two-team city in baseball. Yet another blow to New York pride was in the offing. In 1961, American League expanded to ten teams, and the creation of the Angels allowed Los Angeles to beat out New York's bid for renewed representation in both leagues.[97] The uniquely triangular geometry of New York's great interborough baseball rivalries had ended forever.

◇

ALL THAT remained for Brooklynites, wherever they might be, would be a blame game that has continued now for more than four decades and shows no signs of abating. "Who lost the Dodgers?" is a question that has aroused emotions perhaps comparable to those stirred by the "Who lost China?" debate—except that they have proven to be far more enduring. In early 1997, forty years after the future of the Brooklyn Dodgers had been scuttled by the impasse over the terms for a lease of a new stadium in Brooklyn, the O'Malley family announced that it was selling the Dodgers, stating that "commitment to the community, to Los Angeles and to Southern California is the number one priority" in their choice of a buyer. The reaction from points east was harsh. A veteran New York sportswriter wrote, "I applaud (Peter) O'Malley's loyalty to his community. It's too bad his dad didn't have the same loyalty. Now it is too late. I don't care so much where the Dodgers go now. . . . I do know where Walter O'Malley should have gone."[98] "In the last circle of Dante's Inferno," another observer wrote, striking a similar note, "three humans dangle from Satan's Jaws: Judas Iscariot, Brutus and Cassius. If it were up to Brooklynites, another would be added—Walter O'Malley."[99]

Along with Hitler and Stalin, O'Malley regularly tops the lists of "the ten worst human beings of the 20th century" compiled by old Brooklyn fans;[100] he is still berated as "Judas O'Malley," who "demanded that the city build a new ballpark, or he would move the team out of Brooklyn," and "insisted the Dodgers were not making enough money," although, in fact, "no team in baseball was more profitable."[101] The psychic wounds he is said to have inflicted extend well beyond the realm of sport alone: "O'Malley," Jack Newfield wrote, "killed a generation's innocence."[102] Two decades after Walter O'Malley's death, the tide of abuse remained so strong that Dodger announcer Vin Scully, who had followed the team west, uncharacteristically interrupted his call of a game to chastise East Coast baseball writers who were blackballing his old boss from the Baseball Hall of Fame.

Along with these passions, the policy issues raised by the Dodgers' abandonment of Brooklyn live on, as debate continues to swirl over local government's public purse and a sports team's pursuit of private profit. At the time, the circumstances under which 150 years (dating back to 1883) of accumulated National League baseball in New York City had come to such a sad end hardly resonated at all in political terms. Just over a month after O'Malley's announcement of the Dodgers' move, New York's voters handed a smashing victory to incumbent Mayor Robert Wagner, who rolled up a citywide majority of almost one million votes (more than double his victory margin in 1953's three-candidate contest), and taking 75 percent of the ballots in Brooklyn itself.[103]

Although the loss of the city's National League clubs was simply a nonissue in that particular campaign,[104] it has loomed large in more recent controversies over government assistance to the sports business. That debate, is, indeed, frequently informed (or, rather, misinformed) by folk memory about the events that brought an abrupt end to so many decades of National League baseball in New York. The Ken Burns televisions series on baseball claimed that O'Malley had demanded that "unless New York City built him a brand new stadium . . . he would have no choice but to take his team elsewhere."[105] "I guarantee you we learn from the mistakes of the past," New York Mayor Rudy Giuliani vowed, supporting municipal assistance for building a new home for the Yankees, on the grounds that New York had lost the Dodgers to California because the city had refused a request by O'Malley to build a stadium for the team.[106] Although this is not quite accurate about the Dodgers—who were willing to build

their own stadium if the city underwrote the acquisition of the necessary land—the cautionary point was valid: that the city ignored the
demands of a sports team seeking a new ballpark at its, and its citizens',
peril. It was certainly a lesson that the people of Brooklyn, including
a young Yankee fan named Rudy Giuliani, had learned with a
vengeance.

IN TRUTH, the circumstances under which the Dodgers left Brooklyn
were sufficiently complex to engender a legacy with many interpretations and emotional ramifications. Without question, the Dodgers'
move provides a convenient benchmark for a changing sport in a
changing America, meriting an entirely appropriate notice in general
histories of the postwar era.[107] As he began turning to Los Angeles for
a solution to his stadium problem, O'Malley was enlisting in, and
encouraging, a more general and fundamental point of passage in
national life—from East Coast to West, from city to suburb, from Rust
Belt to Sunbelt. "How sharply Ebbets Field, situated amid apartment
houses and shopping streets, near the Brooklyn Public Library, the
Botanic Garden, and Prospect Park, differed from the comfortable but
antiseptic Chavez Ravine stadium, floating in a sea of parking lots, that
O'Malley built for the Los Angeles Dodgers," one historian (clearly no
friend of the shift) has recently written.[108] O'Malley was leading the
Dodgers, and baseball, along a well-trod path that many others would
follow. Within a few years of the Dodgers' move, California would
become the most populous state (knocking the Empire State from a
perch it had occupied since 1820),[109] the television industry would
abandon New York for Los Angeles, the University of California at
Berkeley would displace Harvard as the nation's highest-rated university, and trend-spotters would be looking to the Golden State in the
ceaseless quest for the cutting edge.[110]

There is also no question that the move of one of baseball's great-est franchises to Los Angeles, and another to San Francisco, allowed major-league baseball to penetrate the new California territory under the best possible circumstances. The shift of the Dodgers and Giants to California had realigned the map of baseball into reasonable prox-imity with that of a demographically changing nation, making the sport's long-deferred expansion to the West Coast much more likely of success by providing potentially standoffish fans with proven, well-established teams to support. And it gave the National League a leg up on the American League by staking out a priority claim to the two most lucrative, previously unserved baseball markets. In the first ten years after 1958, the Dodgers and Giants would appear in five World Series.

The American League approach of expanding to California with a newly created team resulted in a far slower path to success. That expansion franchise, the Anaheim (formerly the Los Angeles, later the California) Angels, would not win, or even appear in, a World Series until 2002, more than four decades after its founding, and the team's lack of tradition and broad popular appeal contributed to that World Series's record-low television ratings, notwithstanding the Angels' dra-matic come-from-behind seven-game victory.[111] A dispassionate ana-lyst of the sport's geopolitics might well conclude that the Dodgers' and Giants' joint move to California was, in the familiar phrase, "in the best interests of baseball."

Although major-league baseball was bound to expand to the West Coast eventually, that "inevitable" outcome was the product of a par-ticular set of contingent circumstances that, in line with the sport's previous business practices, did not reflect any master plan. As of the spring of 1957, major-league baseball, after more than a decade of on-again, off-again thinking about such expansion, was no closer to doing something about it than it had ever been. Perhaps in time Brooklyn would have lost its team (to Queens, if nowhere else). But the when

and the how of that change were the work of one man, Walter O'Malley. The blame—as well as any credit—rightly belongs to him.

The fact that responsibility for implementing such a far-reaching
change was left to one individual's initiative was entirely consistent
with baseball's prior practice. Whether it was accommodating schedules to newly legalized Sunday ball games, developing the farm-
system model for procuring new talent in defiance of existing baseball
rules, or engaging in an every-team-for-itself scramble after the new
revenues made available by radio and then television, major-league
baseball never demonstrated the type of centralized, coordinated
planning pioneered by professional football and later adopted by
hockey and basketball. Instead, baseball's responses to such challenges and opportunities were characteristically haphazard, with key
decisions delegated by default to individual teams and their owners.
Expansion to the West Coast was just the latest in a long, and often
messy, tradition.

THE DODGERS' first year in Los Angeles turned out to be a disaster—
at least on the field, as the team finished in seventh place, the worst
showing since 1944—confirming O'Malley's bet that it was better to
make the move sooner rather than later to maximize his aging team's
value in negotiations for a new West Coast home. But Los Angeles
Dodgers baseball proved a box-office smash from the start, attracting
a club-record 1,845,000 fans to the team's massive temporary home at
the Coliseum, 40,000 more than the top mark in Brooklyn. The 1959
season was even better, in both respects. The Dodgers broke the 2 million attendance barrier and accomplished in their second year in Los
Angeles what it had taken more than half a century to do in Brooklyn—win a World Championship. By 1962, the Dodgers were
ensconced in their new O'Malley-built and -owned stadium in Chavez

Ravine, and although they again lost a pennant play-off to the Giants, attendance soared to an all-time major-league record of 2,755,000—well over a million higher than the attendance for the (yet again) World Champion Yankees.

The best was still to come for the Los Angeles Dodgers. In 1963, the Dodgers faced the Yankees in a World Series for the first time since 1956. The result was an unprecedented triumph for the Dodgers and for the National League—a four-game rout of the Bronx Bombers, the first time that anyone had been able to do that to the perennial powerhouse that had recorded six World Series sweeps of its own. The victories were recorded by Sandy Koufax, Don Drysdale, and Johnny Podres—all onetime Brooklyn Dodgers. It was sweet revenge indeed for all the heartache that the Yankees had inflicted on the Ebbets Field faithful in so many Octobers past, but the closest the Dodgers came to Brooklyn this time around was, of course, the Bronx.

Walter O'Malley had been measuring *his* Dodgers against the heretofore unassailable Yankees ever since the team's Brooklyn heyday, years when the stark contrast between cramped Ebbets Field and majestic Yankee Stadium underlined how far he had yet to go to compete on even terms. In Los Angeles, the gap between the two organizations closed. The Dodgers' beautiful new stadium in Chavez Ravine supplanted Yankee Stadium as the sport's most acclaimed venue, however much East Coast sportswriters might carp about fans who arrived late, left early, and clutched transistor radios to their ears in order to follow what was happening on the field. While still in Brooklyn, O'Malley had retooled the Dodger organization along the hierarchical lines pioneered by Jacob Ruppert and Ed Barrow, and he continued to run his transplanted franchise with an unsentimental efficiency that would have done Yankee management proud.[112] Within a few years of the move to the West Coast, the Dodgers became the team to beat—and to hate. "Nobody likes the Dodgers," it was said of the once-beloved Bums, and the team's increasingly influential owner was hailed, and feared, as the "boss of baseball."[113]

No one could know it at the time, but it was the Yankees who were about to take a long fall from the commanding heights of the sport they had dominated for so long. By 1966, the Dodgers would be playing in their third World Series in four seasons, while the Yankees would be finishing in last place for the first time since 1912. The Yankees had finally been brought low, at least for the moment, and the Dodgers were riding high. But thirty years after Bill Terry's dismissive put-down, Brooklyn was finally and truly no longer in the league.

PART FOUR

DAMN YANKEES, AFTER ALL

Interlude

———

AFTER EBBETS FIELD

AS THE DODGERS and Giants—and with them, the National
League—prepared to abandon New York in the summer of
1957, all seemed to be going well with the Yankees, New York's
remaining team. After all, the Bronx Bombers were rolling
toward their eighth American League pennant in nine years.
"Yankee Secrets?" asked *Sports Illustrated* that July. The magazine's lead article covered all the bases in giving "the answers to
five questions about baseball's greatest team."[1] *SI* detailed how
the Yankees managed to identify and acquire the best players,
explained that there was magic in their fabled pinstripes, that
they had skillfully, but not unethically or illegally, tapped a rich
source of young talent in the woeful Kansas City Athletics,[2] that
their ownership gave free rein—as long as they won—to the
team's baseball men to conduct the team's baseball business, on
and off the field. In answer to the final question, "Will they go on
forever?" *SI* asserted that "the Yankees have had the best team
in baseball for a long time—so long, in fact, that it is extremely
difficult to imagine the day when they will not." And true
enough, as the badly beaten third-place Dodgers and sixth-place
Giants packed up and left town, the Yanks ended the 1957 season with the American League pennant, finishing eight games in
front of the newly resurgent Chicago White Sox. The next year,

the Yanks repeated, extending their margin of victory over the Chisox to ten games.

After a hiccup in 1959, when the Yanks finished a weak third, fifteen games behind the White Sox, and won only seventy-nine games—their lowest total since 1925—the New Yorkers quickly rebounded. Abetted by White Sox owner Bill Veeck's killing off Chicago's future by trading away the team's most talented youngsters (including catchers Earl Battey and Johnny Romano, first basemen Norm Cash and Don Mincher, and outfielder Johnny Callison), the Yankees ran off with five pennants in a row beginning in 1960. The Yankee mystique would live on, well into the new decade. In the mid-1960s, a college student riding a Greyhound bus out of St. Louis en route to California struck up a conversation with a grizzled midwesterner whose first comment, when told that his fellow passenger came from New York, was a respectfully awestruck, "So you've seen the Yankees play ball."[3] And the baseball-disdaining boxing fan, A. J. Liebling, waiting in San Francisco for the rain-delayed 1962 World Series to end so that a middleweight championship fight could get underway at Candlestick Park, and bored by the endless post-mortems of the defeated Giants' fans, could write, "The Yankees are the least popular of all ball clubs because they win, which leaves nothing to 'if' about."[4]

But cracks were increasingly evident in the once-seamless façade of the Yankee dynasty. The Bronx Bombers were upended by the Milwaukee Braves in the 1957 World Series— the Yankees' second series defeat in three years, something that hadn't happened since 1921–23. And, indeed, the 1957 defeat marked an ebbing of the Yankee tide. Although the Yanks came back to beat the Braves in 1958, rallying from a deficit of three games to one, and continued to dominate the American League over the next half decade, their previous margin of superiority over National League rivals dwindled away. Facing a shaken-up National League, which threw a different challenger against them in their six fall appearances between 1958 and 1964 (only the Phillies and Cubs missed out), the erstwhile perennial World Champions suffered World Series defeats in 1960 to the Pirates, in 1963 to the Los Angeles Dodgers in a four-game sweep (sweet revenge), and in 1964 to the Cardinals, newly competitive after almost fifteen years in the doldrums. Yankee victories in 1958, in 1961 over Cincinnati, and in 1962 over the transplanted Giants did no more than offset those losses.

The 1960 loss to the Pirates was especially galling to pinstripe pride. In the first six games of the World Series, the Yanks outscored the Pirates forty-six runs to seventeen, winning three games by lopsided 10–0, 12–0, and 16–3 margins. Notwithstanding the disparity in cumulative firepower, the Yankees found themselves going into the bottom of the ninth of Game 7 with the series deadlocked three games to three, and the score tied at nine runs, before Pittsburgh's Bill Mazeroski hit his game- and series-winning home run to give the Pirates their first World Championship since 1925. Perhaps it was fitting that this most improbable upending of Yankee fortunes unfolded in the home-town of United States Steel. That an era was ending was dramatically underscored five days later, with the abrupt termination of Casey Stengel's managerial services. The seventy-year-old Casey, who had managed the Yankees to ten pennants (and seven World Championships) in twelve years at the helm, was abruptly deemed "too old" by Yankee management. The shock waves resonated throughout the baseball world—and beyond. Challenging Vice President Richard Nixon, who was touting his front-line service as his primary credential for the presidency, Democratic candidate John Kennedy wickedly observed, "The worst news for the Republicans this week was that Casey Stengel has been fired. It must show that perhaps experience does not count."[5] A month later, underscoring the point, Kennedy was in the White House and Stengel's front-office patron, General Manager George Weiss, had been ejected from the Yankee executive suite.

By the early 1960s, the business side of Yankee baseball was also in a slump, at least relatively speaking. The postwar "subway series" era had already taken its toll on the game's box-office appeal. Between 1947 and 1952, National League attendance fell by almost 40 percent; its modest recovery thereafter was almost entirely attributable to the Braves' move to Milwaukee in 1953 from Boston. In the American League, 11,150,000 paying spectators had slumped by 30 percent in the decade after 1947. The Yankee Stadium crowds, which numbered 2,200,000 in 1947, shrank to 1,497,000 by 1957, the last year they shared the city with the Giants and the Dodgers.

In 1958, even with the Dodgers and Giants gone from New York, the Yankee box office failed to benefit from their newfound monopoly. The previous year, two Dodger fans had written the mayor, saying, "We just can't imagine Brooklyn without [the Dodgers]. . . . We think the Yankees are wonderful and are probably the best team, but we just can't be Yankee fans. We get so mad when people say they are Yankee fans."[6] One month into the season, the question being asked of local baseball fans, was, "Where did they go?" as the Yankees were clearly failing to attract those who had watched the departed National Leaguers. Indeed, Yankee attendance was lagging well behind the previous season's.[7] That early trend held up, and at year's end Yankee Stadium attendance was down by 75,000 from 1957, dropping to

1,423,000, the lowest total since the war and almost one million below the team's attendance record set ten years earlier. Thereafter, attendance would pick up, at least slightly, but there could be no mistaking a persistent slackening of intensity in New York's baseball life. On October 1, 1961, when Roger Maris hit his sixty-first home run, there would be more than 40,000 empty seats in Yankee Stadium—almost double the 23,154 fans who did show up on that historic Sunday afternoon. And the price paid for the record-breaking ball—$5,000—was hardly evidence of a bull market in baseball.

Yet another incident tells much about this forlorn state of baseball affairs. On September 28, 1960, in Boston's Fenway Park, Ted Williams played his last ball game—hitting, as all the world knows, a home run in his final major-league at-bat. Williams had announced beforehand that he would be retiring, and John Updike was on hand to capture the moment for his classic account, "Hub Fans Bid Kid Adieu," but the sad—and, in retrospect, unbelievable—fact is that there were only about 10,000 Hub fans at Fenway that memorable afternoon.[8] As the sixties began, baseball was losing its once-all-embracing hold on the sports public, even in its traditional bastions.

Abruptly bereft of the Dodgers and Giants, a suddenly baseball-starved New York media quickly discovered a new passion—professional football. An already well-developed ability to set a national agenda for sports enthusiasms was enhanced by the rise of New York–based network television and the growth of New York–based magazine sports coverage, exemplified by the fledgling *Sports Illustrated*. The embrace of this newfound interest was mightily encouraged by the fact that the National Football League's New York Giants happened to be fielding a particularly stirring team. Little more than a year after the departure of the Dodgers and the baseball Giants, the football Giants (as they had always been called till then) squared off against the Baltimore Colts in what was immediately dubbed "the greatest football game ever played." Pro football was a compelling product, and it was sold strongly and bought widely.

Green Bay Packers football star "Golden Boy" Paul Hornung soon emerged as the first celebrity "playboy athlete," with greater appeal in a more sophisticated culture than any baseball player, while baseball's party animals such as Mickey Mantle remained trapped in the personas of "aw shucks" overaged Little Leaguers. Hornung was endorsing Scotch; Mantle, Wheaties. In baseball's bubble-gum-card world, public disclosure of a nightclub fracas could be—as it was for Billy Martin after the Copacabana incident in May 1957—a hanging offense. Not until the publication of *Ball Four* in the early 1970s was the veil lifted on baseball's extracurricular shenanigans, but Jim Bouton's revelations smacked more of the high school locker room than the post–sexual-revolution urban adult world that the NFL explicitly cashed in on, in the form of Broadway Joe Namath, whose public image made explicit the bedroom exploits that had still been implicit in the Hornung cult just a few years earlier.[9]

The NFL Giants and pro football, in general, filled the void that had so suddenly opened in the city's sporting affections. The New York press had a new faith to propagate. And they quickly did. By November 1959, Giants linebacker Sam Huff was appearing on the cover of *Time* magazine, which billed pro football as "A Man's Game." The next year, Huff would star in a CBS television documentary, "The Violent World of Sam Huff." Simultaneously, the "man's game" was outflanking baseball on the distaff side of the gender divide, with Giants quarterback Charlie Conerly's wife contributing weekly features during the football season to the Sunday *New York Times*. Week after week, Giant season ticket holders packed Yankee Stadium, while less fortunate (but equally impassioned) fans drove to motels in Connecticut just beyond the range of the NFL-imposed blackout on Giant home games. The NFL was riding so high that it even imposed a blackout of its championship game on hometown fans—without any measurable erosion in fan support.

If anything, lack of ready access only increased interest and made season ticket holders a privileged caste of sports-fan nobility. In their six (after 1961, seven) fall home contests, the Giants attracted about one-third as many fans to Yankee Stadium as their landlords did in more than ten times that number of games in the summer. Two weeks before the Yankees had ended their triumphant 1961 season with Roger Maris's home-run heroics in front of fewer than 24,000 fans, the football Giants had opened their season at Yankee Stadium before a crowd of 58,000.

The paradox was that this turnabout in America's sporting enthusiasms was occurring even as major-league baseball was making itself more and more available to the sporting public. Until recently, much of the country had been physically shut off from the sport by the geographies of time and space, which had confined it to daylight hours and the northeast quarter of the nation. In truth, traditional big-league baseball had hardly been a spectator sport at all. For most of its fans, most of the time, it was vicariously experienced through newspaper stories and box scores and World Series newsreels, not direct contact. Starting in the 1950s, just as major-league baseball was becoming more readily accessible, with increasing numbers of night games, expansion to the West Coast, and regular national television exposure, the sport's once-unchallenged hold on the popular imagination began to slip away. On the accelerating treadmill of public taste in mid-twentieth-century America, baseball was running faster, and farther, but as the fifties passed into the sixties, the national pastime was losing ground.

In the early 1960s, the New York Yankees stood at the unquestioned summit of baseball power: In the forty years since they first entered baseball's upper echelon, the Yankees had wrested baseball leadership from the Giants, held off the Cardinals' farm system, and decisively defeated the Dodgers on the field—before watching their beaten foes retreat 3,000 miles to the west. The ensuing decades would pose new tests for the team that had become the greatest franchise in all of professional sports.

◇

THE MOST pressing challenges the Yankees faced after 1960 arose not so much from its competitors on the field as from the changing institutional setting of the baseball business. The number of teams proliferated as the geographic reach of the sport continued to expand. The traditional economics of the game were revolutionized both by the growth of new revenue streams and the arrival of free agency for baseball's previously reserve-clause-shackled players. Tensions between owners and players, as well as those between small-market and large-market teams, cast constant shadows on the conduct of the sport's business. Even building a place to play required active engagement with the political process of the larger community.

The vastly increased economic dimensions of the game, in terms of both revenues and expenses, made management skills, or their absence, more critical than ever in determining a team's success. This was true whether success was measured by pennants or profits, as would be shown by the Yankees' own often rocky progress through the new landscape of the baseball business. How well the New Yorkers managed that task was of more than local interest. Given the Yankees' preeminent status in the sport's pantheon, their fortunes were not easily disentangled from that of baseball itself, as it fought to retain its status as "America's national game."

9

A DYNASTY STUMBLES

BETWEEN 1960 and 2000, the geographic, competitive, and economic landscape of major-league baseball was utterly transformed. In 1960, major-league baseball, just as it had in 1903, consisted of sixteen teams playing in two leagues. Only the Dodgers and the Giants were located on the Pacific Coast, and those California-based teams were, along with Kansas City, the only ones west of the Mississippi. No team was located south of Washington, D.C. Forty years later, there were thirty teams in the two major leagues, including eleven teams representing the trans-Mississippi west (six along the Pacific). The major leagues had expanded into Canada with two teams and moved into the states of the Old Confederacy with three.

Consistent with baseball's traditionally haphazard business methods, the realignment had hardly been carried out smoothly. In the process, that symbolic franchise for a national pastime, Washington, D.C., had been abandoned altogether, and the teams representing Kansas City and Milwaukee were replacements for clubs that had decamped to Oakland and Atlanta. For that matter, the team currently representing Seattle is the successor to a franchise that had moved to Milwaukee after a single waterlogged season in 1969. And Montreal and Minnesota only narrowly, and in Montreal's case perhaps only temporarily, avoided elimination altogether in 2002. Fewer than half the teams presently making up the standings of the clubs were doing business at the same location in 1960.

In that time span, baseball's physical environment had changed as drastically as its geography. The only ballparks from the early 1960s still in use forty years later were Boston's Fenway Park, Chicago's Wrigley Field, Dodger Stadium in Los Angeles, and New York's Shea and Yankee Stadiums. Since 1964, Cincinnati, St. Louis, Philadelphia, Pittsburgh, Chicago (White Sox), California (Anaheim), Kansas City, Baltimore, Cleveland, and Houston had provided new homes for their ball teams—and within a few years, even those "new" homes would be superseded by still newer construction in Philadelphia, Pittsburgh, and Houston, and new ballparks also rose in San Francisco, Milwaukee, and Detroit. Indeed, a whole cycle in stadium construction had come and was in the process of being gone in the interim. The symmetrical, artificially turfed, multiuse stadiums (never "fields" or "ballparks") of the 1960s, which had housed the Mets, the Cards, the Pirates, and the Phillies—not to mention the domes built for the Astros, the Twins, and the Mariners—had suddenly become obsolete in the wake of the 1992 opening of the Baltimore Orioles' defiantly retro Camden Yards ballpark, complete with natural turf, idiosyncratic dimensions, and inner-city ambiance. In short order, its clones would sweep across the baseball world, in places as steeped on old-time big-league baseball tradition as Cleveland and Pittsburgh, as well as in those utterly lacking in it, such as Texas, Colorado, and Seattle. The construction boom was accompanied by an outpouring of lavish public financial support for these increasingly expensive projects. The exclamations of outrage over the idea of any public financial support for a new stadium for the Dodgers in downtown Brooklyn, or the $25 million that New York City spent on Shea Stadium, seemed irremediably passé in an era when $200 million in public monies would be readily spent on Baltimore's

Camden Yards ballpark, not to mention all the other new, heavily sub-sidized ballparks that rose across the baseball landscape in the 1990s.[1]

The competitive landscape of the game had been correspondingly transformed as well. The two major leagues survived, but each had been subdivided—first into two, and then, beginning in 1994, into three divisions. In 1960, the World Series remained the singular climax to baseball's long, unforgiving season, a unique contest between two teams with the best records in their respective leagues over the six-month-long schedule. It was always played in the first week of Octo-ber. Forty years later, it had become almost anticlimactic, the last stage in a multiweek set of playoffs, which included (after 1994) teams that had failed even to win their own divisions as "wild card" teams with the best runner-up records—a second chance seized by the Florida Mar-lins in 1997 and the Anaheim Angels in 2002 to become World Cham-pions (the latter by defeating the San Francisco Giants in the first all-wild-card series).

Looking beyond the structural and the geographical, the sheer eco-nomic scale of the sport had undergone an equal, if not indeed greater, transformation over those four decades. In the early 1960s, major-league baseball remained the small-scale enterprise it had always been. Examining professional sports in a broader context, a prominent sports economist pointed out a few years later, "The total revenue of all teams in the four major team sports—baseball, basketball, football and hockey—is less than half the revenue of such mundane endeavors as the manufacture of cardboard boxes or the canning of fruits and veg-etables," and even the most successful ball team's revenues were no more than "those of a department store or large supermarket."[2] But a massive change was already under way by then. Big-league baseball would at long last become big business, and it would also learn to play by the ordinary rules governing such enterprises.

Two developments were critical to this process. The first was the explosive growth in revenue streams, both through greater attendance (at higher ticket prices) at the ballpark and, more particularly, through the vastly increased income available through the sale of television (both broadcast and cable) rights. Major-league attendance more than tripled—from 21,280,000 in 1964 to 72,748,970 in 2000. Average attendance per game was up from about 16,000 in 1960 to almost twice that forty years later. In 1964, only one team (the Dodgers) had drawn more than two million fans, and six teams had drawn fewer than one million. In 2000, ten teams attracted crowds of more than three million, and only one (Montreal) had drawn fewer than one million. Total revenues had increased dramatically as well—from $70–80 million in 1964 to almost $3 billion by the end of the century, and to $3.5 billion in 2001.[3] The increasingly important contribution of broadcast (including radio, television, and cable) revenues to baseball's income stream had increased from slightly under $20 million in 1964 to well over $1 billion in 2001.[4]

Team values soared. Walter O'Malley had acquired Branch Rickey's one-quarter interest in the Dodgers for what he regarded as a collusively inflated price of $1,050,000 in 1950; his son Peter sold the team in 1998 for $311 million.[5] In 1966, the sale price of the Cleveland Indians was $8 million; in 1999, it was $323 million. Gene Autry had acquired the expansion franchise for the Los Angeles Angels in 1960 for $2 million; it was sold in a two-stage transaction in 1996 and 1998 for $267 million. Even the relative laggards in this franchise-value boom prospered. The sale price of the Oakland Athletics increased from $3,800,000 in 1960 to $85 million in 1995, and that for the Kansas City Royals from $5,350,000 in 1968 to $96 million in 2000.[6] Not surprisingly, the Yankees set the pace. Sold for $14 million in 1964, the New York team was valued at more than $300 million by the early 1990s, and at $730 million ten years later, even as the sport teetered on the verge of a potentially crippling strike in the summer of 2002.[7]

These increases were especially impressive given the second key development in the sport's economic picture—the demise in 1975 of the reserve clause and the creation of a more or less free labor market in players, with attendant sharp upward movement in salary expense. In the sport's by-then-traditional fashion of lurching into new business terrain with an absence of planning or preparation, this revolutionary change did not come about through either the decades-long legal battle that had been waged against organized baseball's monopoly power under the antitrust laws, or negotiation at the collective bargaining table. Instead, it resulted from an arbitrator's interpretation of language in baseball's standard player contract that could easily have gone the other way. This decision in favor of the players unleashed a total transformation of the sport's salary structure, with the expense side revealing a seismic shift in the sport's finances. Salary expense went from less than 20 percent of team revenues to more than 60 percent. Team player payrolls, which had totaled some $9 million in 1964 (averaging about $18,000 per player), had increased more than 150 times by 2000—to $1.6 billion, an average of $2,500,000 per player. By 1992, the $100,000 gold-standard salary, which had defined the game's elite from DiMaggio in the late forties to Mays in the mid-sixties—was lower than the contractually mandated minimum for the rawest recruit.

Baseball entered the new millennium with its business environment radically transformed from that of forty years earlier. Free agency had overturned the sport's traditional economic model, under which the Yankees had thrived for so long. The moves of the Dodgers and the Giants turned the future of Yankee baseball in New York into a political issue that required novel skills to resolve. Yet, by 2003, a century after their move to New York City from Baltimore, the Yankees had withstood such new competitive and business pressures to hold onto a remarkably fixed position in that turbulent world. The Yankees were still playing in the Bronx ballpark that had been their home since 1923. Yankee Stadium, which in 1963 had been the newest ballpark in baseball's pre-expansion cities, had become, by 2002, the third oldest. On the ballfield, the pinstriped home uniforms remained unchanged, as did the traditional traveling grays—neither adorned with player names, only numbers. Announcer Bob Sheppard, whose "slow, dignified speech has such cadence you think every pitching change is the Gettysburg Address," continued to introduce the lineups over the public-address system as he had for half a century, since April 17, 1951.[8] Most important, the Yankees were playing—as they had in 1964, and for so many years before that—top-flight winning baseball, with three straight World Championships to their credit from 1998 through 2000, a close seven-game World Series loss in 2001, and a division championship in 2002. The New York Yankees, once the sport's great insurrectionists, had become its foremost custodians of tradition.

ON AUGUST 13, 1964, the Yankees were caught up in a tight battle for their fifth consecutive pennant under rookie manager (and vintage legend) Yogi Berra, but the big baseball news of the day was the announcement that the Columbia Broadcasting System (CBS) was buying the Yankees. The team that had for so long been perceived as the baseball equivalent of U. S. Steel, the embodiment of a cold, relentless, corporate fixation on the sport's bottom line—the win–loss standings of the clubs—was now itself to be, in the most literal sense, an entry on a corporate balance sheet. Beginning with Colonels Ruppert and Huston, Yankee management had taken a sport and run it like a business, with lucrative results, on and off the field. With the tables now turned, and a business inserting itself into a sport, the Yankees would be a test case for the success or failure of CBS's unprecedented initiative. Sadly for the team's fans, however, the Yankees faltered under CBS's tutelage. The team would not regain its stride until more entrepreneurial, single-minded leadership regained control after a decade of disappointment.

Dan Topping and Del Webb, along with Larry MacPhail, had purchased the Yankees from the Ruppert estate in January 1945 for a reported $2.8 million, amid the uncertainties of wartime and with the team caught in a mini-slump in which it finished no better than third for the three years between 1944 and 1946. In 1947, Topping and Webb bought out MacPhail's interest for an additional $2 million, underscoring what a bargain the 1945 deal had been. With Topping serving as club president, George Weiss (who had directed Yankee farm operations under Ed Barrow) became general manager in 1948 and brought Casey Stengel on board as field manager. With that front-office team in place, the Yankees won nine pennants over the next eleven years, and then added four more after Weiss and Stengel had been let go following the 1960 season.

By 1964, the recently all-powerful team was aging and the last-place Mets were drawing bigger crowds to their brand-new Shea Stadium in Queens. When CBS came calling, Topping and Webb were ready to cash out. For purposes of the sale, the Yankees were valued at $14 million; CBS paid $11.2 million for 80 percent of the team, effective November 1964, with an option to acquire within five years the 10 percent interest that Topping and Webb each retained.[9] CBS bought out Webb within a few months, and Topping two years later. By September 1966, CBS was the full owner of the team, and Mike Burke, the CBS executive who had originally brought the idea of the acquisition to the network, succeeded Topping as Yankee president.[10]

The sale to CBS triggered an avalanche of alarmed, often hostile comments. *New York Times* sports columnist Arthur Daley wrote, "The dollar sign is beginning to obscure the standings of the teams."[11] According to NBC anchorman Chet Huntley, it provided "just one more reason to hate the Yankees." For sportswriter Shirley Povich of the *Washington Post,* the CBS purchase signified a quantum step in the emerging unholy alliance between sports and television. "CBS," he wrote, paraphrasing Kahlil Gibran, "first invited into baseball's house as a paying guest, has indeed become successively the host, then master."[12] This was a theme that reverberated around the world, in places that generally managed to ignore developments in the quintessential American pastime. The *Times* of London commented that the sale "could pave the way for revolutionary changes in the promotion and commercial exploitation of baseball."[13] As far afield as Moscow, the official Soviet newspaper *Izvestia* (after placing the news in context for its readers by explaining that the Yankees were "as popular in the U.S.A. as, say, the Spartak soccer players of Moscow are here") declared that the sale "was further proof that some types of sports are becoming adjuncts of commercial television."[14]

Within the sport's innermost sanctum, where the antitrust exemption was guarded as the holy of holies, the sale spurred fears about the impact of the acquisition on that key legal shield. The deal gave "CBS, alone among the networks, the position of an insider in organized baseball's negotiations for broadcast right," a broadcasting trade journal pointed out.[15] But a careful strategy was mapped out to secure the continued viability of that critical legal immunity, notwithstanding this unprecedented intrusion of that most interstate of commerces—television and broadcasting—into the ownership structure of the sport.[16] Organized baseball's counsel duly obtained assurances from CBS that it would not jeopardize that exemption by asserting it as a defense to any action by the Justice Department to block the sale on antitrust grounds. CBS President Frank Stanton and Dan Topping defended the sale in testimony before the Senate Antitrust Subcommittee and, in the end, the sale was not challenged.[17]

Nor, as it turned out, were the fears realized among the Yankees' competitors that the team's acquisition by one of the giants of American business presaged a period of renewed, even heightened dominance for the perennial champion. To the contrary, CBS's nine-year stint as the Yankees' owner saw the team humbled as it had not been since the dead-ball era. Even as CBS closed its deal with Topping and Webb that fall, storm signals were flying, presaging a bumpy future. It was not so much that the Yanks had just lost the World Series to the Cardinals in seven games (their second straight series defeat, something that had never happened). It was also that the series would come to be seen, most notably in David Halberstam's definitive *October 1964*, as less a clash of teams, or even leagues, than of baseball cultures. The tradition-hobbled Yankees had come up short against the aggressive National League, which was, finally, parlaying a greater readiness to employ black talent into a formula for consistent baseball success. Mantle was hurting more and more; Jim Bouton was one season away from the sore arm that would cut short (at age twenty-six) his promising pitching career; Yogi Berra had proven no leader of pinstriped men; and the pennant-winning Yankees found themselves on the short end of an intercity popularity contest with the last-place Mets, who had attracted 400,000 more fans in that first season in their new city-built stadium.

These were genuine problems, but the way CBS's new unit went about dealing with them only made matters worse. Immediately after the World Series defeat, manager Berra was fired (a decision made late in the season when it looked like the Yanks would lose the pennant), replaced by winning Cardinal manager Johnny Keane (ready, in turn, to jump his championship team, which had similarly lost confidence in his skills during the season, before the epic collapse of the Phillies opened the way for St. Louis in the last days of the campaign).[18] These upsetting moves were then compounded by the still-mysterious firing of longtime announcer Mel Allen, truly the Yankees' number-one fan, whose entire existence was bound up with the team. Allen had been *the* Voice of the Yankees since 1939, his "How about thats" and "Ballantine Blasts" reassuring the team's fans that the Yankees were in command, his logorrheic smugness driving Yankee haters to infuriated distraction—yet another reason why Yankee fans held him in such high regard. Whether Allen's dismissal was Topping's last act (according to veteran announcer Lindsey Nelson, Topping had once said, "The last thing I'm going to do as President of the Yankees is to fire Mel Allen") or CBS's first (baseball was about to enter into its first truly national television contract, and an announcer so bound up with the Yankees would not be the best entree to such a wider audience) remains unclear, but as the news leaked out—no formal announcement was made—a once-indispensable ingredient of the Yankee mystique, its "class" (which is precisely what William Paley believed he was purchasing) was further devalued.[19]

The 1965 season would entirely upset any expectation by the "Tiffany network" that it was taking on a turnkey operation. The Yanks collapsed to sixth place, their poorest showing in forty years. Worse was to come, and quickly. In 1966, the recently eagerly courted Johnny Keane was fired as manager after the Yanks started the season by losing sixteen of the first twenty games, and Ralph Houk returned to the dugout in a desperate attempt to stave off disaster. This was to no avail, as the Yankees dropped to the bottom of the standings, finishing in last place for the first time since . . . 1912. Adding to the pain was the fact that the almost equally hapless *ninth-place* Mets managed to attract over 800,000 more spectators to witness their own flailings. The image of the charming loser, which the Mets had so skillfully nurtured, had never been the Yankees' style, and it didn't suit them, or their dynasty-bred fans, now.

The null point was reached on the rain-soaked afternoon of September 23, 1966, a few days after CBS completed its buyout of Topping's and Webb's remaining shares, when a grand total of *413* fans turned out for that day's game.[20] Up in the announcer's booth, Red Barber seized on the unprecedented paucity of "fannies in the seats," as a later Yankee owner would say. "I don't know what the paid attendance is today," Barber told his audience, "but whatever it is, it is the smallest crowd in the history of Yankee Stadium . . . and this smallest crowd is the story of the game." Barber's repeated requests to have the TV cameras pan across the rows of empty seats were rebuffed by his director, apparently acting on management orders. Barber prided himself on being a fact-based reporter, but the Yankee brass was not amused. A few days later, Barber scheduled a breakfast meeting with the recently appointed team president, Mike Burke, to discuss what he thought would be a routine renewal of his contract, only to be told that he was through.[21] Barber had been announcing major-league baseball since 1934, but he was only fifty-eight years old, and he confidently expected to be working for another major-league team the next season, express-ing interest in staying in New York and joining the Mets broadcasting team.[22] It was not to be. Although Barber would eventually find a new audience in the last decade of his life with his Friday-morning appear-ances with Bob Edwards on public radio, he would never call a ball game again.[23]

The dustup with Barber aside, Burke made an auspicious debut as Yankee president as the dismal 1966 season limped to an end. Tall and athletic, the fifty-year-old Burke cut a dashing figure as he wowed the press in his first sessions with them. Larry Merchant, no pushover for fluff or spin, gushed (no other word will do) over the "tall and terribly

fit" Burke's "looks of a Madison Avenue patrician" and "graceful physical manner,"—a man who spoke "in the soft voice of one who knows
that he will be listened to." Perhaps the iconoclastic Merchant was
writing with tongue somewhat in cheek, but not so for the invariably
staid Arthur Daley of the *New York Times*, who enthused for day after
day over the "dapper and debonair, handsome and impeccably tai-
lored" Burke, who chased "his listeners to their dictionaries by casual
use of the word 'pejorative.'"[24] And in truth, Burke may well have been
the most extraordinary man ever to sit in a ball club's owner's box; his
life was, as Daley said, "right out of the true-adventure magazines."

Press coverage at the time outlined a truly brilliant career. Burke
had been a prep school third baseman, but his real sport was football.
A star halfback at the University of Pennsylvania in the late 1930s,
Burke carved out a heroic record as an agent of the Office of Strategic
Services during the war, operating behind enemy lines in Italy and
France and becoming a drinking buddy of Ernest Hemingway along
the way. Awarded a Navy Cross and the Silver Star for his exploits, he
then served as technical adviser and writer on a film version of his
wartime adventures, the Fritz Lang film *Cloak and Dagger,* starring no
less a figure than Gary Cooper as his on-screen alter ego. From Holly-
wood, it had been off to Italy as a movie producer, a glamorous
fashion-model second wife in tow, before returning to government service in 1951 as an aide to the U.S. High Commissioner for Germany.
Next stop was a top position back home with the Ringling Brothers
Circus, which was followed by a return to Europe as director of European network programs for CBS, and finally an appointment in New
York as the network's vice president in charge of development. In that
capacity, he had overseen CBS's Yankee operations during the final
years of Topping's tenure as president.[25]

It was quite a record, but what made it even more remarkable was
that Burke's resume actually understated its subject's achievements.

For Burke's postwar career as the producer of a "couple of terrible Italian movies," as he described it, and special assistant to the High Commissioner for Germany were actually covers for his real job—as a top Europe-based operative of the fledgling Central Intelligence Agency, one of the "very best men" who came out of the wartime OSS, to staff the CIA as it came to grips with the Soviet enemy. About this part of his record, Burke chose to keep silent at the time,[26] thereby relegating to obscurity, for decades to come, one of the most fascinating episodes in a life story that teemed with them—his front-line involvement in one of the great, if most closely guarded, dramas of the early Cold War, the Anglo-American attempt to overthrow the Communist government of Albania, an adventure that was the one great exception to the accolade that "he was a success in everything he has undertaken."

When he eventually got around to telling a version of the story in his 1984 memoir, Burke, true to the code of the shadow warrior, related what he described as a "sanitized" account—one so vague about the details of places and persons that a reader would have trouble understanding what had been going on.[27] But the basic story has emerged from a number of other accounts.

Establishing a cover as the Italian representative of an outfit named "Imperial Films" (a fictitious entity consisting of a letterhead and a mailbox in New York), Burke organized a series of landings in Albania by air and sea in an attempt to foment an anti-Communist uprising in a country that had been geographically isolated from the Soviet Union by Yugoslavia's break with Stalin. Some sixty airdrops were made as part of the lavishly funded "Operation Valuable," but the infiltrators were almost effortlessly rounded up by Albanian security forces. Many of those involved came to believe that the scheme was doomed from the start, because the British liaison for the operation was none other than KGB master spy Kim Philby.[28] For his part, Burke reached the conclusion that "the operation would not have succeeded regardless of Philby."[29] In retrospect, Burke wrote, "It was impossible for me to reconcile the Philby I knew and liked with the Philby I did not know and recoiled from."[30] But, undeterred by failure in Albania, Burke returned to the front lines of the Cold War in Germany, parachuting agents into the Soviet Union itself in a nerve-racking game of cat and mouse with Soviet air defenses.[31] By 1954, Burke had had enough of the secret war and left the CIA, but not before, according to one account, a final argument with his superior officer ended with Burke's head being doused with a pitcher of water, "to cool him off."[32] With that, Burke was off to the world of entertainment, which had now taken him from the circus's big top to the House that Ruth Built in the Bronx.

In a fairer world perhaps, someone with Mike Burke's intelligence, abilities, and record of courageous service to his country would have been able to turn around the Yankees. Burke tried hard, and he hired as general manager an experienced baseball man—Lee MacPhail (son of Larry, former Cincinnati and Brooklyn general manager and one-time part-owner of the Yankees), who had built the once-lowly Orioles into the league's dominant team—but without much success. With nowhere to go but up from their last-place finish in 1966, the Yankees rose—but only to second-to-last in 1967. Thereafter, they made somewhat greater progress, with fifth-place finishes in 1968 and 1969 (although the latter was in the newly created six-team Eastern Division of the American League, as the league expanded to twelve teams and split into two divisions). Through it all, Ralph "the Major" Houk soldiered on as field manager, but the stars of yore fell by the wayside. Roger Maris was traded to the Cardinals after the 1966 season; future Hall of Famer, pitcher Whitey Ford, retired in 1967; and Mickey Mantle followed the next year. In happier times, the Yankees had been accustomed to filling any gap in their lineup with a late-season acquisition from a tail-ender. In August 1967, roles were reversed, with the

pennant-contending Red Sox picking up catcher Elston Howard from
the Yankees. His New York teammates continued to struggle, while
Howard played a small, but crucial, role in Boston's "impossible
dream" season.[33]

By 1969, first baseman Joe Pepitone and pitchers Mel Stottlemyre
and Al Downing were the only regulars from the 1964 pennant winners still wearing the pinstripes, and Pepitone and Downing would be
gone the next year. In 1970, the Yankees made a big leap toward
respectability, shooting up to second place in the East by winning
ninety-three games—which, however, left them fifteen games behind
division champ Baltimore. Thereafter, the upward march stalled, as
the team fell back to fourth place in 1971 and 1972, with the number
of wins dropping to eighty-two and then seventy-nine. With that, the
Yankees' CBS (and, as it turned out, rather to his surprise, Mike
Burke), era came to an abrupt end.

No CBS–Yankee juggernaut had materialized, either on the field
or at the box office. As it turned out, and first appearances to the contrary, a good measure of the problems that the Yankees encountered,
and then were unable to surmount, were bound up with the one-sided
nature of the Yankee relationship to its CBS parent. Bigger, in this
case, was not better.

The broadcasting giant had acquired the team as part of a "broad
policy of business diversification," CBS Chairman William Paley
explained.[34] The Yankees were but one of a number of enterprises—
including publisher Holt, Rinehart & Winston; educational toy maker
Creative Playthings; and piano manufacturer Steinway & Sons—that
CBS bought in pursuit of that policy. The goal was to strengthen the
financial position of the company's core business, not to deploy broadcasting profits on behalf of the acquired units. The Yankees would have
to look to their own operations for the revenues needed to compete on
the field. The CBS philosophy was encapsulated by Paley when he

reflected on what he had learned from his experience with the Yankees: "It costs just as much to run a losing team as a winning one and the income is far less."[35] This simply reversed baseball's time-tested economic equation between dollars and success: Winning was inevitably *more* expensive than losing. Similar failures by CBS to master the dynamics of other newly acquired businesses would lead to problems with those other units of the diversified corporation. Speaking of CBS's unsuccessful management of Steinway, a network executive said, "We were totally out of our element in the music business," a conclusion that could also have been applied to the baseball business.[36]

As a cog in a much greater machine, the Yankees existed to serve the larger interests of the CBS empire. Viewed from CBS headquarters at "Black Rock" in Manhattan, the Yankee team was a blip, barely a rounding error, on the corporate books. This was apparent in a number of ways, all revealing that the "big league deal is minor to CBS."[37] The Yankee purchase price amounted to less than two weeks of the network's nighttime programming expense; it was less than 2 percent of CBS's revenues; the team's annual revenues of about $6 million were entirely insignificant in the context of the corporation's $565 million. The entire purchase could have been financed just from the network's profits from its investment in the hit musical *My Fair Lady*.[38] Given these disparities of scale, it flattered the Yankees to write, as the *Sporting News* did, that "the giant of the broadcasting industry" was acquiring "the goliath of major league baseball."[39] The ball club and its new owner were simply not playing in the same financial league.

It was not surprising, therefore, that when Mike Burke became Yankee president, Paley had told him, "If you're in real trouble let me know. But I expect you to run this thing in your own way."[40] As far as CBS was concerned, Burke and the Yankees were on their own. Corporate ownership proved exactly the wrong way to run a winning baseball team, with the Yankees deprived of the single-minded focus that had been the team's defining characteristic—from the dugout up through the front office. The Yankees were now an ancillary, and rather insignificant, part of a much, much greater enterprise, one that had "more important" things on its mind than winning baseball games.

The fiercely competitive spirit that had carried the Yankees to victory dissipated. In his account of the epic pennant race of 1949, David Halberstam argued that, at some elemental level, the Yankees simply wanted to win more than the marvelously talented Red Sox did.[41] Joe DiMaggio once explained that he always played all-out because there might be a fan in the stands who had never seen him play before. And he was able to infuse his entire Yankee team with that tenacity of purpose, that determination to perform always at his best, in a way that Boston's Ted Williams—for all his undeniable great skills at the bat, courage, pride, and strength of character—was unable to do among *his* mates. Yankee General Manager George Weiss was hated—both by his players and by his competitors—but he had kept the winning machinery whirring with unmatched efficiency. The Topping–Webb decision to replace Weiss and Stengel so unceremoniously in 1960 emanated from that same relentless (even cold-blooded) commitment to doing what appeared necessary to keep the team on top by bringing in new blood sooner rather than later.

CBS was too grand for such "trivial" things, and Mike Burke—some would say to his credit—proved too "adult." "Running a ball club," he found, "was not the world's most demanding occupation. . . . The unhurried pace of the game itself seduces its administrators into a leisurely business tempo, often mistaken for work." Burke's unrequited energies spilled over into a host of nonbaseball pursuits—the Urban League, the National Book Committee, the University of Pennsylvania, charity work, the Auxiliary Mounted Police, a nationwide lecture series, even the "Big Love Affair" (Burke's capitals) of his life.

"Tending the Yankees," he would conclude, "was not work. Rather, it was a long, lilting holiday."[42] It was certainly reasonable for Burke to think that baseball was "a boy's game . . . and should be kept in proper perspective to the living of life," but one might equally reasonably suppose that such was not the best frame of mind to bring to the task of running a winning baseball team.[43]

To be sure, there were more mundane, down-to-earth reasons for the Yankees' downfall after 1964. Burke himself later blamed it on the "bare cupboard" of talent that CBS inherited and on the institution of the first free-agent draft in 1965, which prevented the Yankees from cornering the market on young talent through their greater purchasing power.[44] But more to the point, perhaps, was that the Yankees' tried-and-true method of picking over the rosters of weaker teams for key talent that would ripen in the Bronx had run its course. In the 1950s, George Weiss had been able to land pitchers Don Larsen and Bob Turley from Baltimore as part of an eighteen-player trade that sent a squad of marginal talent to the Orioles in return. And the Kansas City Athletics had notoriously been ready to engage in a series of one-sided deals that had brought to the Bronx a stream of key contributors to Yankee championships (including Roger Maris, Bobby Shantz, Clete Boyer, Ryne Duren, Hector Lopez, and Ralph Terry). At the opposite end of the baseball life cycle, the Yanks regularly made late-season deals for veterans such as Johnny Mize in 1949 (purchased for $50,000 from the Giants), Johnny Hopp in 1950 (for $40,000 paid to the Pirates), Johnny Sain (obtained from the Braves), and Enos Slaughter (acquired twice—in 1954 from the Cardinals and in 1956 from Kansas City), who, as their careers wound down, added value to the Yankees greater than their limited, but still potent, skills could elsewhere.[45] By the mid-1960s, however, the Orioles were building their own contending team, and the A's were headed west to Oakland, where Charlie Finley would do the same. Baseball's weaker franchises were simply not as weak or impoverished as they had been, nor as desperate to fill out talent-thin rosters with Yankee discards or threadbare coffers with Yankee dollars. After the acquisition of Roger Maris in December 1959—George Weiss's last great coup as general manager—no really beneficial trade would be made until, in CBS's last year as the team's owner, the Yanks acquired pitcher Sparky Lyle from the Red Sox and third baseman Gregg Nettles from Cleveland. In time, the Yankees would find a way to more or less resurrect their traditional methods of assembling winning teams, but that would not come until after CBS, and Burke, had left the scene.

The Yankees' struggles on the field were made even more bitter by the fact that, at the same time, their unquestionably great past was being written out of the sport's history. In the decade after 1964, the Yankees found themselves all but shut out of an innovative type of baseball writing that was just beginning to appear. This was writing that reached beyond the box score and "inside baseball" fare of the daily sports page; was targeted at an adult, rather than juvenile, audience; and was intended for reading long after the clash of arms (and bats) of any particular game or season had faded into memory. Perhaps because they were reacting against what was often derided as the "what Mickey Mantle ate for breakfast" mode of baseball writing, the pioneers of this emerging genre gave the Yanks short shrift—their darlings being the Red Sox, the Dodgers, even the Mets—the unYankees, as it were.

A harbinger was John Updike's 1960 *New Yorker* article, "Hub Fans Bid Kid Adieu," recounting Ted Williams's last game at Fenway Park. A decade later, Brooklyn's *Boys of Summer* found a bestselling chronicler in Roger Kahn; the *New Yorker*'s Roger Angell bade "Farewell, My Giants!"[46] and embraced the Mets (with a special dollop of affection for the Red Sox); and Lawrence Ritter found space in his account of *The Glory of Their Times: The Story of the Early Days of Baseball and the Men Who Played It* for the recollections of only one player (out of twenty-two interviewed) with a significant career on the Yankees—the team that had, after all, dominated much of those "early years." If anything, pinstriped tradition came off as more of a liability than an asset in a time of social change. The Yanks matched up against the Mets, Jimmy Cannon wrote in 1964, as Rudy Vallee did to the Beatles.[47]

Such neglect proved to be more considerate of Yankee sensibilities than the attention that the Yankees did in time receive. The one book about the Yankees that did find a place in this pantheon turned out to be former pitcher Jim Bouton's locker-room and bar-stool tales about his hard-drinking, sex-obsessed Yankee teammates. *Ball Four*'s tales out of school duly outraged the baseball establishment. But it proved just a warm-up for the ultimate demolition job on the Yankee Myth: Richard Ben Cramer's 400-page-plus (and companion public television documentary) unrelenting assault on the Yankee Clipper himself as a miserly, mobbed-up, misanthropic, thoroughly miserable sort of human being. It was a long way from the days, not so distant in time, when Hemingway's old fisherman had counseled, "Have faith in the Yankees, my son," and dreamed of taking "the great DiMaggio" fishing.

THE ON-FIELD and box-office record of the team under CBS and Burke's stewardship was a failure, but their tenure in the Yankee front office would have one enduring legacy—a renovated Yankee Stadium, which would keep the team in its Bronx home for another quarter century and counting. In so doing, Burke achieved for the Yankees what Walter O'Malley had spurned and Horace Stoneham had never seriously pursued—municipal financial support, on terms the city could live with, legally and fiscally, to ensure the team's continued presence in New York. It was not easy, or inexpensive, but Burke, with a crucial assist from Mayor John Lindsay, managed to do it.[48]

On the day he met the press for the first time as Yankee president, Burke had said, "The Yankee Stadium is baseball. We're going to do everything possible to make it so again."[49] After taking command, Burke found the stadium to be "in disrepair and deteriorating," urgently in need of a crash face-lift.[50] And as he spoke, the storm clouds that had inundated the historic home grounds of the Dodgers and Giants a decade earlier were gathering over the Yankees' palatial but aging stadium. The knives, sharpened by the team's last-place showing and declining attendance, were out for the old ballpark, echoing Ebbets Field's fate in the public relations war a decade earlier. "A major factor" in the team's decline, a *New York Times* analyst pronounced, "has been the gradual obsolescence of the Stadium structure, and the lack of parking around it," while the stadium's Ruthian dimensions posed problems for the team on the field as well.[51] The vast expanse of center field (more than 460 feet to the bleachers) required an outstanding fielder for that position, and the distance (450 feet) to the fence in left center posed an intimidating challenge to right-handed batters. Burke, while avowing his reverence for the stadium, would not rule out moving to a new ballpark or sharing Shea Stadium with the Mets.[52]

In achieving his goal, Burke had a number of arrows in his quiver. First, of course, was the fact that the Dodgers and Giants had abandoned the city. Regardless of how the blame for their departures was allocated, there could be no question that local politicians had failed to retain the teams that had meant so much, to so many, for so long. Second, the city had, of course, gone into the stadium business with the construction of Shea Stadium as a home for the expansion-team Mets—the city-owned Flushing Meadows facility that Robert Moses had proposed as the solution for the Dodgers' decision to abandon Ebbets Field. The price tag for the city amounted to some $25.5 million,[53] up from Robert Moses's $10.5 million 1957 estimate, to be sure,[54] but still relatively modest, and roughly what Los Angeles's Dodger Stadium, which had opened two years earlier, had cost to build.[55] The result was a pleasant, comfortable, and conveniently located plain-vanilla, multipurpose, obstructed-seat–free specimen of the wave of all-too-similar ballparks that would redesign the physical setting for the sport over the next few years.

Third, in the parlance of the time, the socially conscious Burke "gave a damn," admired Mayor John Lindsay for keeping the city calm by walking the streets of Harlem, and had the Yankees sponsor a variety of community-outreach efforts. The plan to rejuvenate the stadium could be presented as part and parcel of a grander blueprint to "save" a troubled neighborhood, and with it the city itself.[56] This was a sure-fire way to appeal to Mayor Lindsay, who most certainly also "gave a damn." Unlike Walter O'Malley's overly ambitious, abortive proposal for a Dodger stadium in the heart of downtown Brooklyn, renovation of Yankee Stadium would not require renewal of an entire neighborhood—a modest scope that would prove both a benefit and a limitation. Finally, there was the fact that the politically embattled mayor had quite visibly whooped it up in the Mets locker room after their improbable 1969 World Series victory, an image widely (and reasonably) credited with helping Lindsay prevail in his own difficult race for reelection that fall.[57] Doing something for the Yankees would balance the mayor's baseball political ticket.

And so in 1970, the Yankees came calling on City Hall for *their* share of the city's resources.[58] By then, an aggressive New Jersey Sports Authority was courting both the Yankees and its pro football tenant, the New York Giants, to move across the Hudson. Headed by Sonny Werblin, the former owner of the New York Jets, who had

signed Joe Namath to a then-record contract and put the American
Football League on course to achieve parity with the National Football League, the New Jersey agency would not be ignored: Burke's
plan—to have the city purchase and renovate Yankee Stadium,[59] lease
it back to the team, and build additional parking facilities—would survive the Giants' decision to abandon the Bronx for the New Jersey
Meadowlands and end up making a far greater claim on the city's treasury than the Mets had. But, in paradoxical fashion, even as the city's
finances skidded toward insolvency, the readiness to overspend only
accelerated, and what was true for welfare and municipal salaries
proved to be the case for stadium construction. As the South Bronx
neighborhood around the stadium continued to deteriorate, keeping
the Yankees in place assumed an ever-greater urgency as a symbol that
all was not lost. Lindsay overrode opposition from his top aides and
agreed to Burke's demand that the city should match what it had done
for the Mets. In March 1971, Lindsay announced that the city would
buy—through condemnation proceedings if necessary—and modern-
ize the stadium.[60] In July, the state authorized the city to act, and the
project went forward, despite the New York Giants' announcement
the next month that it would move to New Jersey.[61] In 1956, the football team's shift from the Polo Grounds to Yankee Stadium had
signaled that the days of the former were numbered. The same fate
would not befall the stadium, although it had now similarly been
spurned.

Lindsay blasted the Giants management as "selfish, callous and
ungrateful," and Burke reaffirmed the Yankees' pledge to stay put if
the stadium was renovated. A thirty-year lease was negotiated with the
Yankees, and the renovation plan was formally approved by the city in
March 1972—whatever the cost, a fateful but prescient commitment.[62] On October 1, 1973, a groundbreaking ceremony was held for
the renovation work. Mayor Lindsay presented home plate to Mrs.

Babe Ruth and first base to Mrs. Lou Gehrig.[63] As the project proceeded, the city's undertaking turned into a blank check, as costs spiraled steadily upward—from an initial commitment of $24 million (in
March 1971), to $27.9 million (April 1973), $39.8 million (November
1973), then to $55 million (December 1973), $66.4 million (October
1975), $75 million (December 1975), and finally to $97.4 million, not
including an additional $16 million for improved highway access, as
calculated when the refurbished stadium reopened on April 15, 1976,
before a sellout crowd who enjoyed a Yankee win over the Minnesota
Twins.[64] Such cost escalations were sadly familiar: The New Orleans
Superdome, for instance, proved *nine times* more expensive to build
than projected.[65] Not that everyone was asleep at the switch. Two years
after the refurbished Yankee Stadium opened, the alert eleven-year-
old son of a New York deputy mayor asked his father why, during the
off-season, the stadium was adorned with several illuminated signs,
paid for by the city. The lights were turned off—and the city saved all
of $10 a day.[66]

Whether or not such an investment of public funds was "worth it"
could easily be questioned—and was—and there has been no answer
to the convincing demonstrations by economists that such subsidies
for sports facilities do not yield the public economic benefits that have
been repeatedly promised as their justification.[67] But the age of the
purely private ballpark was gone. This much had been proven by the
debacle of the Dodgers' quest for a new home in Brooklyn—and the
substantial public assistance required to realize Walter O'Malley's
vision of a privately owned ballpark in Los Angeles. After all, the
money spent on Yankee Stadium, however poorly managed the project
no doubt was, amounted to a fairly small expense in a city that was
spending more than $10 billion each year.[68] True, as the city collapsed
into bankruptcy while the stadium work proceeded, the city did not
actually have the money to spend on the project, but one can be con-

fident that the city was spending more, and getting less in return, on a host of other endeavors that ran through similar amounts of money. As historian Fred Siegel writes, one such project had "very little to show for its efforts except the copy machines and telephone banks that helped keep [its political patrons] in office."[69] The Yankee Stadium renovation certainly benefited *its* cadre of well-connected insiders—contractors, insurance brokers, parking concessionaires, bankers, law firms, construction unions[70]—but at the end of the day, a refurbished Yankee Stadium emerged as a tangible and enduring end product.

Not that Yankee Stadium was quite what it had been in the glory days of the past. It had been updated and "modernized," losing much of its traditional character and sheer superhuman scale in the process.[71] The seating capacity was reduced to 55,000 (from nearly 70,000); the dimensions of the playing field were more symmetrical and less intimidating (center field was now 417 feet deep, down from more than 460); the great façade overhanging the upper decks of the outfield grandstands was eliminated (an ersatz replica was placed atop a large new scoreboard, which replaced much of the bleacher seating); and, perhaps the saddest change of all, the tombstonelike outfield monuments to Yankee greats were removed from the playing field in deepest center and placed in an enclosure behind the outfield fence. Some sight lines had been improved, columns and posts had been eliminated, modern conveniences had been added, but a good deal of the historic stadium's shrinelike quality was lost in the process. On the other hand, the first glimpse of the stadium from a subway car rising out of the ground as it approached the 161st Street Station never lost its capacity to thrill.

By reconstructing Yankee Stadium, New York officialdom had accomplished its main objective. The project kept the Yankees in the Bronx, demonstrated that officials were not about to write off a decaying area of the city, gave the sport's most historic venue a new lease on life, and saved the Yankees and their fans (at least for another generation) from both the boring symmetry of the stadia of the 1970s and the palpably contrived, overly planned "idiosyncrasy" of the 1990s. The stadium didn't transform the surrounding neighborhood,[72] but it became an easier and safer place to get to, whether by subway or automobile. The essence of one of New York's, and America's, great sporting experiences was preserved. In a very imperfect world, it was not such a bad bargain.

It was a bitter pill, no doubt, for those who remembered the failure of the Brooklyn Dodgers to succeed in *their* quest for a new home in *their* borough two decades earlier. In the intervening years, however, much had changed—and the projects were not entirely comparable. The Dodgers had been premature and overreaching in their ambitions, at a time when the city was still going through the motions, at least, of being fiscally responsible in satisfying basic needs and services. When the Yankees made their bid, the "urban crisis" had been discovered and named; cities had gotten into the business of ballpark building, not only in New York but around the country; a demonstration that a stadium could not be financed and operated on a self-sustaining basis was no longer fatal for a city that was prepared to step in and carry the project at an acknowledged loss. In the end, the Yankees had scored yet another victory over the Brooklyn Dodgers.

WHILE THE plans for the renovated stadium slowly took shape, the Yankees continued to struggle in their decaying, if recently repainted, home. By 1972, CBS was ready to abandon the baseball business, which had disappointed its expectations, both on and off the field. After six money-losing seasons out of eight, William Paley had had enough.[73] On January 3, 1973, the Yankees' CBS era came to an end with the sale of the team to a syndicate dominated by a little-known Cleveland shipbuilder and sportsman, George Michael Steinbrenner 3d.[74] The price was $10 million—about $3 million less than what CBS had paid to acquire the team nine years earlier. It had been an inglorious venture all around, and it ended with a feat worthy of the *Guinness Book of Records*—a baseball franchise sold for less than the purchase price. Perhaps only a Fortune 500 company could have done it—and issue a press release claiming that it had really come out ahead on the deal.[75]

Corporate ownership of the Yankees had failed as a model for baseball team management. Building a winning team required expenditures in funds and energy that easily seemed excessive in terms of any cost-benefit analysis, and the "returns" on such investments not only were often intangible but also devilishly difficult to predict with any degree of accuracy. CBS's media-company successors in baseball ownership—Fox with the Los Angeles Dodgers and Disney with the Anaheim Angels in the 1990s—had a hard time doing much better than CBS had. Disney's Angels did win the 2002 World Series, but that was only after the team had been on the auction block for some time, with no ready takers, and the only likely result of that surprising victory was a higher asking price, with no ongoing benefit in store for either the team or its corporate owner. The Yankees' own post–CBS future would be determined by their new principal owner's very different, and very uncorporate, ownership style.

It turned out that George Steinbrenner possessed the indispensable ingredient for success in the baseball business—he wanted to win and would accept nothing less as his (and the Yankees') due. It was a sharp break with the team's recent past. The urbane and sophisticated Mike Burke had been a man with the time and imagination to contemplate the beauty of "watching the shadows move out toward the pitcher's mound."[76] Bill Paley had tired of a game in which losing cost as much as winning. Steinbrenner didn't concern himself with the beauty of shadows, and he knew that winning would cost a lot more than losing. In his single-minded devotion to being on top, Steinbrenner was a throwback to the franchise's hard-edged pre–CBS ethos. Jacob Ruppert, whose idea of a perfect day at the ballpark was seeing "the Yankees score eight runs in the first inning and slowly pull away," had a worthy successor in George Steinbrenner, who was never comfortable with a lead in a pennant race unless, he said, "it's 10 games in front and pulling away."[77] Or, as a Yankee player and later manager put it, "He's the kind of owner who likes a 163-game lead with 162 games left."[78] Indeed, Steinbrenner's reputation for single-minded commitment to winning would transcend the sport of baseball itself. It was to the Yankee owner that the United States Olympic Committee turned for recommendations about training and organizational practices after a disappointing performance by American athletes at the 1988 Winter Games. Steinbrenner's report had a stark message—that the primary goal of the USOC should be winning medals—and it charted the course that would see the United States medal yield increase from six medals in Calgary to thirty-four at Salt Lake City twelve years later.[79]

In the beginning, however, Steinbrenner modestly claimed that he would defer to Mike Burke, and he downplayed the significance of the sale. "We plan absentee ownership as far as running the Yankees is concerned," he explained. "We're not going to pretend that we're something we aren't. I'll stick to building ships."[80] With club president and fellow general partner Burke standing beside him, Steinbrenner added, "I won't be active in day to day operations of the club at all."[81] Echoing Burke's own remarks when he had taken over the Yankee helm in 1966, Steinbrenner said, "The Yankees are baseball. They're as American as apple pie. There are still great things about the past that are worth going back to and grabbing into the present. I think that's so with the Yankees."[82]

It did not take long, however, for Steinbrenner's actions to belie his self-denying ordinance, as Mike Burke was the first to learn. Even the sharp contrast in appearance between the modishly long-haired Burke and the close-cropped Steinbrenner foretold friction ahead. At their initial press conference, Steinbrenner trumpeted what he described as the bargain price paid for the team, thereby gracelessly embarrassing (as Burke saw it) CBS in general and Paley in particular.[83] Their relationship went downhill from there. Within weeks, the urbane and charismatic Burke, who had expected to continue as the team's president, found himself pushed aside by the initially deferential Steinbrenner. The self-described "absentee" owner quickly brought in experienced executive Gabe Paul to run the Yankees' baseball operations. By April, Burke was on the sidelines, a "limited" rather than a "general" partner who was carried on the Yankee payroll for a while as a "consultant"—the kind that never is consulted.[84] Control of New York's premier sports franchise passed out of the city for the first time in its history. To Red Smith, they were now the "Cleveland Yankees."[85]

Burke had enjoyed an excellent press and had carved out something of a cult of celebrity among the team's fans.[86] Red Barber, nursing his wounds over his dismissal by Burke, was emphatically one of the deposed Burke's relatively few nonadmirers. "A friend at CBS," Barber had written a few years earlier, "told me not to turn my back on Mike Burke—that he had the fastest knife on or off the CBS television screen."[87] Not fast enough, as it turned out. When Burke was asked, shortly after his own ouster by Steinbrenner, how he was feeling, he is said to have replied, "I'll feel a lot better as soon as I get this knife removed from my back."[88] However fair or unfair Barber's assessment, George Steinbrenner now joined Albanian dictator Enver Hoxha and Soviet mole Kim Philby on the very short list of men who had gotten the better of Mike Burke.

George Steinbrenner hailed from a notably provincial background for an owner of the New York Yankees. The son of the owner of a Cleveland shipping company, Steinbrenner was born in 1930 and entered the family business after running track (and singing in the glee club) at Williams College, service in the U.S. Air Force, and several years as a football coaching assistant at a Columbus, Ohio, high school and at Northwestern and Purdue. His father, Harry, was a demanding, even "cruel," perfectionist, a keenly attentive spectator of George's athletic efforts, who instilled in him an all-consuming will to win from an early age, along with a robust self-reliance. George would later say of his father that "anything I ever accomplish I owe to him." In time, Steinbrenner would succeed his father and rescue the family business from a forced sale. He converted the firm's five ore carriers into control of the much larger American Ship Building Company, which tripled its sales to more than $100 million under his leadership and became, by the early 1970s, the leading grain carrier on the Great Lakes.[89]

For the young Steinbrenner, growing up in Cleveland, "when the Yankees came to town, it was like Barnum and Bailey coming to town. . . . Watching them warm up was as exciting as watching the game. Being in Cleveland you couldn't root for them, but you would boo them in awe."[90] Although by the time he took control of the Yankees, Steinbrenner had established a foothold in New York as an investor in a number of Broadway shows and an interest in a limousine company, his midwestern base marked a sharp break in the traditional ownership lineage of the Yankees. The team's previous owners were much more rooted in the textures of New York life—whether Tammany Hall's Frank Farrell and Bill Devery, brewer Jacob Ruppert, "epitome of the millionaire sportsman"[91] (or "playboy and wastrel"),[92] Stork Club habitué Dan Topping, or media mogul Bill Paley. Steinbrenner—and the city from which he hailed—didn't fit into this metropolitan lineup. Cleveland might as well have been on the other side of the moon as far as New Yorkers were concerned. Baseball fans recalled that the heavily favored Indians had been ignominiously swept four straight by the

Giants in the 1954 World Series. To New Yorkers at large, Cleveland was "the mistake by the lake," the epitome of the grimy, declining Rust Belt city, so cursed that even its river had caught fire a few years earlier.[93]

Nor was the new owner's previous foray into the world of professional sports likely to impress anyone in the big city. In the early 1960s, he had taken the semipro basketball Cleveland Pipers into the newly formed professional American Basketball League, a venture that quickly failed, leaving Steinbrenner with a debt of $125,000, which he scrupulously paid off. Also to his credit—and a break with one of the Yankees' more unfortunate traditions of years past—he had hired the first black coach (John McLendon) in any major-league sport, although McLendon did not, in a preview of what lay ahead for New York sports fans, make it through his first season behind the Piper bench.[94]

A close friend once said that two things were important to Steinbrenner—"winning and power"[95]—and control of the Yankees provided a fast track to both. The transplanted owner was hardly cowed by his new surroundings, as his dealings with Burke showed. Almost from the start, Steinbrenner involved himself in the day-to-day baseball affairs of the team in an unusually intrusive, and easily caricatured, fashion. On Opening Day at Yankee Stadium, Steinbrenner surveyed his charges as they stood hatless during the playing of the national anthem, compiled a list of those whose hair he considered too long, and passed it on to manager Ralph Houk. When an outfielder committed a routine error, Steinbrenner told his general manager, "I will not have that man on my team," and he was soon banished. Houk was bombarded with notes: "Call George Steinbrenner immediately"; one season with the new owner proved all that Houk could or would take.

Steinbrenner's missteps became legendary. When the team acquired pitcher Pat Dobson in a trade, Steinbrenner explained, "We needed a left-handed pitcher and we got one," which would have been more persuasive had not Dobson been right-handed. Some were laughed off less easily. After the 1973 season, Steinbrenner rushed to announce the signing of Oakland manager Dick Williams as his new manager, but he had to beat an embarrassing retreat, since Williams (who had just led the A's to their second straight World Series win) was still under contract and Oakland owner Charlie Finley declined to release him.[96] It was a pattern of behavior that would characterize the way Steinbrenner ran the team over the decades to come, an over-the-top hands-on style that would be caricatured on the TV series *Seinfeld*, and result in the word *Steinbrennerish* being used as shorthand for managerial meddling.[97]

A far more serious distraction arose early in Steinbrenner's tenure when the Yankee owner was charged with multiple counts of illegal campaign contributions and obstruction of justice in connection with American Ship Building's contributions to the 1972 Nixon reelection campaign.[98] The Yankee owner pleaded guilty and paid a $15,000 fine, the highest imposed on any corporate official caught up in the scandal. Steinbrenner would claim that the contributions had been extorted by Nixon campaign officials as the price of doing business with the government, a necessary customer for American Ship Building's products. In 1989, he received a presidential pardon, but more jaundiced observers questioned his self-exculpatory account. Although Baseball Commissioner Bowie Kuhn duly suspended the Yankee owner from active involvement in team operations for two years, in one respect Steinbrenner had lucked out—had the scandal surfaced before his purchase of the team, it is doubtful that he would have been approved as a team owner.

If Steinbrenner was lucky in this, so too were the team and its fans. Beyond the bombast and sheer foolishness, which were all too frequently in evidence, there *was* method in his madness. Faced with the new challenges and opportunities presented by the sudden demise of baseball's traditional system of labor relations at Christmastime 1975, Steinbrenner first restored the team's competitiveness after the mediocrity of the CBS years and later led it to its greatest successes since the heyday of Mickey Mantle. Money, which Steinbrenner freely spent, played its role in compiling that record, but, as always, money was not enough. For much of the time, Steinbrenner was, indeed, more often berated for wasteful, nonproductive spending than credited (or demonized) with buying championships by spending well. Under Steinbrenner, as with his successful predecessors in the owner's box at Yankee Stadium, it was the way in which the Yankee organization was managed, not simply the scale of its expenditures, that provided the key to victory.

10

FREEING THE SERFS

YANKEE history is replete with important dates, but December 23, 1975, belongs at the top of any list of the turning points in the team's affairs, although that day's events had nothing directly to do with the Yankees. That December day the decision of an arbitrator dealt a fatal blow to the cornerstone of baseball's labor relations by striking down the "reserve clause," the shorthand term for the mutually reinforcing, interlocking system of contractual provisions and major-league rules that had theretofore bound player to ball club in perpetuity.

The ruling opened the way to the selling of a player's services to the highest bidder and a sharp escalation in baseball salaries. It also touched off an ongoing debate about the impact of player free agency on competitive balance in a sport in which teams entered the talent marketplace with widely disparate economic resources. A revived Yankee team had begun to take shape with the acquisition of Lou Piniella and Chris Chambliss after the 1973 season, but it was the advent of free agency that put the Yankees back on top. That the Yankees took immediate advantage of the new opportunity for acquiring star players to power their way to four World Series appearances in the first six years after that decision provoked immediate concerns about the apparent ability of free-spending organizations to dominate the sport. Their subsequent missteps belied any simple equation between money and success, but the reemergence of the Yankees as baseball's greatest team in the late 1990s rekindled the debate, and indeed provoked apocalyptic warnings that the free spending of Yankee dollars placed in jeopardy the very future of the sport as a viable enterprise.

In the long sweep of baseball history, however, Yankee success was not, of course, a novel phenomenon. The Yankees' mastery of the new rules of the talent market replicated their earlier decades-long ability to dominate the sport's old economic order. As an economist had explained some years before the advent of free agency, money inevitably had an effect on the talent marketplace, whether or not players were subject to the reserve clause, with the difference being simply that, "in a market subject to the reserve rule, part of the price for the player's services is paid to the team that sells his contract, and part of the value is kept by the team that holds his contract; in the free market the player gets his full value."[1] Nor, as demonstrated by the experiences of the Yankees' free-spending and unsuccessful rivals, both past (the Boston Red Sox in the 1930s and 1940s) and present (the Red Sox in 2002), has money alone ever been enough. The ways in which that money is spent have been, and remain, the decisive factor in the equation of winning major-league baseball—as the Yankees' own record of failure (as well as success) over the past quarter-century demonstrates. No one, not even the Yankees, is immune to that simple but often frustrating truth.

BASEBALL'S traditional mode of labor relations had taken center stage in one of the more unusual commentaries on CBS's purchase of the Yankees. On August 16, 1964, *Izvestia* weighed in on the transaction, drawing an ideologically predictable—but not for that reason inaccurate—moral. "And so the Yankees have been sold" the Soviet Union's official newspaper reported, explaining that these were "not the Yankees who traditionally are accustomed to buying everything, from Rembrandt canvases to living puppets. No, the Yankees who traditionally are the objects of purchase and sale." *Izvestia* then offered its understanding of the place of the players—the "Yankees" themselves—in the sport's economic structure:

> *In the spirit of the best commercial traditions, the living merchandise of the New York Yankees were not even asked about anything. . . . They do not like to mention in America that sports are dominated by business. It is naive to repeat that the Volga flows into the Caspian Sea and that horses eat oats. The sensational sale of the New York Yankees is further proof that some types of sports are becoming adjuncts of commercial television. Television companies pay hundreds of thousands and millions of dollars for the right to broadcast baseball. . . . But they receive still larger sums of money from the firms whose goods they advertise. . . . At the foot of the pyramid of dollars, running, sweating, shining with strength and skill and often maiming one another, are the New York Yankees, the Detroit Tigers, the Cleveland Indians, the Minnesota Twins and other athletes who are bought and sold by businessmen.*[2]

The unusual attention being paid in the Soviet Union to an American sports story was widely noted here, under headlines such as "The Party Line on Deal."[3] The American press had trouble keeping a straight face in noting *Izvestia*'s approach to the sale, with tongue-in-cheek stories about "Soviet sympathy" for "Yankee serfs" such as Mickey Mantle and Roger Maris, poking fun at the Soviets' claim that "the sale of the New York Yankees is a typical capitalistic plot designed to exploit the working people—in this case, Yogi Berra and Company."[4] But, in fact, *Izvestia* had zeroed in on an aspect of the transaction, and of the fundamental structure of the sport, that the American media and sporting public ignored as being too axiomatic for comment, but that was, in fact, more vulnerable than was apparent at the time. For even as the Soviet paper thundered, a time bomb was ticking away at the very core of the one-sided contractual relationship between owners and players that *Izvestia* decried, and that the American press took for granted. With steelworkers' union official Marvin Miller's election in March 1966 as the first executive director of the Major League Baseball Players Association (MLBPA), that bomb was primed to explode.[5]

Not for nothing would Red Barber later couple Marvin Miller with Babe Ruth as "one of the two men who changed baseball the most,"[6] and he was not alone in that opinion. Until Miller came on the baseball labor scene, the Players Association, formed in 1954, had been a toothless "company union" (if, indeed, it was even that) concerned with such peripheral matters as spring training expense money and the supply of an adequate number of towels in the clubhouse. While the Players Association wrestled with such momentous issues, the players were the beneficiaries of a pension plan that, in key respects, was inferior to that available to a steelworker, and the minimum major-league salary had barely nudged from $5,000 to $6,000, which actually was a decrease when inflation was taken into account.[7] Miller wasted no time in pointing out these deficiencies to his new charges, but from the outset, he was after bigger game—nothing less than the reserve clause itself.

The classic strategy for prying open the reserve clause's restraints on player mobility and freedom to contract had been through legal challenges to baseball's judicially crafted exemption from the antitrust laws. Miller's early tenure at the Players Association was marked by one further effort to pursue that line of attack. In 1969, outfielder Curt Flood was traded by the St. Louis Cardinals to the Philadelphia

Phillies. Flood refused to report to Philadelphia, consulted with Miller, and obtained the financial backing of the Players Association for a lawsuit he filed in early 1970 against Baseball Commissioner Bowie Kuhn. The suit attacked the reserve system—which granted the Phillies, to whom his contract had been assigned, the exclusive claim on his services—as an illegal combination in restraint of trade under the antitrust laws.[8] The stage was thus set for the federal courts to reconsider its five-decade-old ruling that baseball was not subject to those laws.

There were grounds to believe that Flood had a decent chance of overturning baseball's increasingly anomalous immunity from the law. True, baseball had been lucky in its previous encounters with the Supreme Court. The plaintiff in the *Federal Baseball* case had, after all, not been an aggrieved player but a less sympathetic baseball team, which had in fact incorporated a "reserve clause," granting club owners the option to extend a player's contract from year to year, in its own agreements.[9] The assertion that the plaintiff was "shocked, shocked" by such personnel practices was undercut by the fact that its legal attack had been mounted only after it found itself shut out of that "illegal" monopoly. The Supreme Court's subsequent encounter with organized baseball, the 1953 case of *Toolson v. New York Yankees,* had been filed by a more sympathetic plaintiff—a minor leaguer in the Yankee organization whose path to the major leagues allegedly was blocked by the team's vast farm system—but it arose in the immediate aftermath of Congress's exhaustive investigation into baseball's player-procurement and contract practices.[10] In those 1951 hearings, chaired by New York Congressman Emanuel Celler of the House Judiciary Committee, organized baseball had circled the wagons in defense of the antitrust exemption and the reserve clause. Those who testified in support of baseball's traditional way of doing business included Baseball Commissioner Ford Frick, league presidents, team owners (Phil

Wrigley of the Cubs),[11] minor-league officials, star ballplayers, past and present (Ty Cobb, Lou Boudreau, Pee Wee Reese), and sportswriters. Most prominent among the latter were J. G. Taylor Spink of the *Sporting News* and Red Smith. Smith was a reluctant witness, characterizing himself as a "bystander" who had nothing to contribute to the investigation beyond the opinions that were readily available to anyone possessing a nickel. But after asking why Congress wasn't devoting its time to more important matters (the Korean War was raging at the time), Smith aligned himself with the sport's establishment, testifying that the reserve clause was necessary and that ballplayers were "pretty well treated." He brushed off the complaints of the "few men" who objected, saying, "I wonder if they have an inferiority complex—or if they were just inferior."[12] In the end, Congress had huffed and puffed, but no legislative action was taken to bring baseball within the ambit of antitrust law, and the court was content to respect the status quo and leave any remedial action to Congress.

By the time Flood brought suit, *Federal Baseball* and *Toolson* had hardly gained stature as legal monuments, and baseball's antitrust exemption had grown ever more peculiar, as other professional sports were being held subject to the antitrust laws. When the National Football League had come asking for a similar legal umbrella, the Supreme Court had unblushingly said that *Toolson* "was a narrow application of the rule of *stare decisis,* applicable to no other industry or professional sport.[13] By 1970, against the ever-accumulating evidence that baseball was a business plainly engaged in interstate commerce—including expansion to the West Coast, CBS's purchase of the Yankees, the increasing revenues generated by national television contracts—it was reasonable to doubt that the courts could remain faithful to the fifty-year-old determination of Justice Holmes.

The Flood case went to trial in the late spring of 1970. It had some Court TV–worthy moments: baseball humorist Joe Garagiola's ham-

handed jests meeting with a stern judicial rebuff; Flood's lawyer evis-
cerating one of baseball's economist experts on cross-examination, culminating in the admission that the reserve system had not produced a
satisfactory level of competition on the playing field; and a parade of
baseball greats (including Jackie Robinson, Hank Greenberg, and Bill
Veeck) testifying for Flood. But Flood himself found the proceedings
tedious, and, by his own account, spent his time "boozing and bed-
ding" while waiting for the trial court's decision to come down.[14]

In the end, the Flood case proved more of a legal dead end than
the harbinger of a new birth of baseball freedom. It was no surprise to
either players or owners when District Judge Irving Ben Cooper
upheld the antitrust exemption and the Court of Appeals swiftly
affirmed. These courts, predictably enough, considered themselves
bound by Supreme Court precedent, even if, as one eminent appeals
judge had recently written, "We freely acknowledge our belief that
Federal Baseball was not one of Mr. Justice Holmes's happiest days."[15]
In June 1972, the Supreme Court went along too, rebuffing Flood's
claim in an opinion by Justice Harry Blackmun, which began with a
rhapsodic tribute to what he called "the Game," including a roll call of
baseball greats, from Ty Cobb to Lefty Grove, and quotations from
baseball poetry of such doubtful legal relevance that two of the justices
(including Byron "Whizzer" White, the only sports star among them)
who joined in the result expressly dissociated themselves from that
portion of the Court's opinion.[16] Echoing the ruling in the *Toolson*
case, the Court once again sidestepped Justice Robert Jackson's dictum—that "We are not final because we are infallible, but we are infallible because we are final"—and deferred to congressional action (or,
in this case, inaction) as the "final" arbiter of baseball's antitrust status.
And so Flood had lost and the antitrust exemption appeared safe. But
within four years, the reserve system—the impregnable target of the
Baltimore Federal League club, then of George Toolson, and finally of

Curt Flood—which had governed owner–player relations from the inception of the organized game, would be shattered beyond repair.

The decisive assault on the reserve clause was launched far from the bright lights, august surroundings, and media scrutiny of the public courtrooms in which the sport's legal battles had been waged in the past. Before Miller's appointment as Players Association chief, the players and their representatives had previously steered away from any challenge to the "reserve clause," but Miller had it in his sights from the start. When he took the helm of the Players Association, Miller later remembered, "If someone had asked me what the reserve rule meant . . . I would have replied, 'It means that a player cannot choose to leave the club that first signs him.'"[17] It was not a bad answer, and was more or less what Baseball Commissioner Ford Frick had told Congress in 1951—that the "popular understanding" that the reserve clause was "a provision in the player contract which gives to the club in organized baseball which first signs a player a continuing and exclusive right to his services" was "essentially correct."[18]

As Frick had then pointed out in his testimony, and as Miller quickly learned, the reserve clause (or reserve system, or reserve rule—take your pick) was rather more complicated than that, as was suggested by the varied nomenclature, and it consisted of a "labyrinth of interrelated rules"[19] and contract provisions that had evolved over time and were the outcome of an often-contentious history.[20] Cutting through the complexities, and the history, Miller rapidly focused on paragraph 10a of the Uniform Player Contract, in effect in its then-current form since 1947, as the crux of the reserve system—and as the point at which the fundamental underpinnings of baseball's entire economic structure was most vulnerable to attack.

That paragraph—the successor to a long series of similar efforts by baseball's ruling powers to restrict a player's ability to sell his services on the open market—provided that, in the event a player and his team failed to reach agreement on a contract for the ensuing season, "The club shall have the right by written notice to the player . . . to renew this contract for the period of 1 year on the same terms," provided that the amount of compensation, to be set by the club, "shall be an amount payable at a rate not less than 75 percent of the rate stipulated for the preceding year."[21] The right *"to renew . . . on the same terms"* was the critical language. Team management contended that "when a Club renews a Player's contract for the renewal year, the contract in force during that year contains the 'right on renewal' clause as one of its terms, entitling the Club to renew the contract in successive years."[22] Miller disagreed. He immediately concluded that, far from providing for such a perpetual claim on a player's services, "the plain meaning of this section of the contract, as I read it, gave a club a one-year option on a player's services after his contract expired," and "nothing more."[23]

One of Miller's early successes as Players Association chief had been to secure the right of players to arbitrate grievances before a panel of three arbitrators (one named by the owners, one by the players, and the third—who would cast the decisive vote—to be a jointly selected "neutral").[24] The parties would later wrangle about the extent of the arbitrators' authority over contract disputes as they impacted the reserve system, but that agreement to arbitrate provided a forum within which Miller could challenge, as he had envisaged when he had first read paragraph 10a, the reserve clause as a matter of contract interpretation, stripped of the extraneous—and heretofore unassailable—legal baggage of the sport's antitrust exemption. Before the 1971 season started, Miller made his annual tour of baseball spring training camps and told the players he believed that a player could become a free agent by playing for one year under a renewed contract.[25] All that was necessary to put Miller's theory to the test was someone who would do just that.

The first test of the arbitration route as a means of cracking open the reserve system came when Oakland A's pitcher Jim "Catfish" Hunter filed a grievance against team owner Charlie Finley after the 1974 season, claiming breach of contract after Finley failed to make certain payments required under its terms.[26] The neutral arbitrator, Peter Seitz, found in favor of Hunter, terminated the pitcher's contract with Oakland, and declared him a free agent. Hunter signed a $3.7 million five-year contract with the Yankees—more than a third of the purchase price for the Yankee team two years earlier.[27]

That the A's were thereby providing reinforcements for the New Yorkers (albeit unwillingly this time around) was hardly a new development. The Yankee teams of the 1950s had been bolstered by such key acquisitions as Roger Maris from the Philadelphia and Kansas City predecessors of the Oakland team. Taken in isolation, the Hunter acquisition could be seen as nothing more than an updated version of the process that had funneled talent to New York for decades. Hunter had won because of a specific breach of his particular contract. The arbitrator's decision did not promulgate a new doctrine of general application—although it did presage a commitment to focus on specific contract language, and ruled that a player was a free agent based on a contractual right to "terminate" a contract in the event of breach, independent of the baseball rules that might otherwise dictate a player's status.[28] But the *next* arbitration case would change the rules of the player personnel game irrevocably.

In 1974, pitcher Andy Messersmith signed a one-year contract with the Los Angeles Dodgers. After winning twenty games, Messersmith and the team were unable to agree on terms for 1975; the Dodgers renewed his contract for 1975, exercising its right to do so under the 1974 contract's renewal provision. If Messersmith didn't sign a new contract, he would be in position to initiate an arbitration, once the season ended, to obtain a ruling that he was then a free agent, since the Dodgers were entitled—according to Miller's interpretation of the renewal right—to only a one-year extension of the contract of an unsigned player. As Messersmith and the Dodgers tried to negotiate new contract terms during the course of the season, Miller secured Montreal Expo pitcher Dave McNally, who was also playing without a signed contract that season, for what he called "insurance," in the event the Dodger pitcher agreed to terms with his club, which would moot any potential grievance over the length of the renewal period. As it turned out, however, Messersmith and the Dodgers didn't agree on a new contract. In October 1975, the Players Association filed grievances on behalf of both pitchers, alleging that each had completed the "renewal year" under their prior contracts, which had thereby expired as of the end of the 1975 season, and that each then "became free to negotiate with any of the 24 clubs with respect to his services for 1976."[29]

When the grievance was filed, the owners expected to prevail by showing that the contractual renewal right did carry over from one year to the next, in perpetuity. Their most telling evidence came, in fact, from the prior interpretation of the contract language by both friends and foes of the reserve system, including the players themselves and their representatives. As one judge later concluded, up until the filing of the Messersmith–McNally grievances, "No player had slipped, or even intimated that he could slip, the bindings of the reserve system by merely playing out a one year option."[30]

To the contrary, the uniform weight of authority agreed that, "by accepting the 'reserve clause'—and all players in organized baseball must 'accept' it—a player binds himself not to sign a contract with, or to play for, any club other than the club which originally employs him or its assignee," a prominent federal judge had written in 1949 in a case brought by blackballed Mexican League contract jumper Danny Gardella.[31] In the course of his antitrust hearings in 1951, Congressman Emanuel Celler, major-league baseball's quondam adversary, had said that the reserve system provided ball clubs with successive renewal rights after each season, "so, in effect, it is self-perpetuating for an indefinite tenure."[32] This interpretation was buttressed by that of an even more commanding legal eminence, no less than a future member of the United States Supreme Court, John Paul Stevens, who had, as a young antitrust lawyer in 1951, served as counsel to the Celler Committee. That committee's report flatly stated, "Since the club's right to renew the contract on the same terms is itself one of the terms of the contract, the renewal clause *obviously* gives the club a perpetual option on the player's services."[33]

More recently, in the Flood case itself, which Miller had supported and the Players Association had financed, Curt Flood's complaint had alleged that, "by a series of rules and practices . . . Organized Baseball has a lifetime grip on any player who wishes to play professional baseball," and that the "reserve system is an unreasonable restraint of trade" precisely because "the club's 'option' to renew the contract for an additional year after its termination . . . is, in effect, a contract for perpetual service."[34] At the Flood trial, Dodger great Jackie Robinson, testifying for Flood, stated that the reserve clause "means to me that a player is tied to a ball club for life," and Marvin Miller's own trial testimony was that under the terms of the Uniform Player Contract, once a player "has signed his first contract, as long as the club never lets its option renewal lapse, he may never play for any other club." "Into perpetuity," Miller elaborated, "as long as the club is interested in exercising this option, the player has no say whatsoever in terms of what conditions he plays under, always bearing in mind he has the one alternative: he may decide to find a different way to make a living."[35]

Given the interpretation of the reserve system offered by Flood himself, it had been *undisputed* that, as the trial judge had stated the facts in an opinion denying Flood's request for a preliminary injunction, "The Uniform Player Contract provides in part that if in the year of expiration of the contract a player and a club do not reach agreement on a new contract by a certain date, the club may unilaterally renew the existing contract," and that "such renewal contract would itself contain this renewal clause," the result being that "the club with which a ballplayer initially signs thus has a right to his services for as long as it wishes to renew his contract, subject only to his right to retire from baseball."[36] At the conclusion of the trial, the court's interpretation of paragraph 10a was unchanged: "Any contract so renewed would itself contain the renewal clause."[37]

In pleading his appeal to the Supreme Court, Flood had argued similarly, painting the darkest possible picture of the monopolistic effect of the reserve system as "the scheme which binds every American professional baseball player to one team, or its assignee, for life."[38] Justice Thurgood Marshall's dissent from the majority's ruling against Flood agreed that "the essence of [the reserve] system is that a player is bound to the club with which he first signs a contract for the rest of his playing days."[39]

Unfortunately for the owners, when the arbitration commenced in November 1975, arbitrator Peter Seitz, the neutral chairman, approached the dispute just as Miller had wanted it framed a decade earlier—as "a matter of contract construction,"[40] isolated from the historical context so heavily relied upon by the owners. Seitz even dismissed as irrelevant the Players Association's own express contention in the Flood case that "the renewal contract" subjects "the player to a state of perpetual bondage to the single club so long as it wishes to renew his contract."[41] The club owners had thought they could respond persuasively to Marvin Miller's reading of paragraph 10a with the famous dictum of Justice Holmes that "the life of the law has not been logic; it has been experience." But, the baseball owners found that their appeal to history was failing, in large part because they had been, if anything, too successful in shaping that history. Marvin

Miller's first reaction to the Uniform Player Contract had been that "it had obviously been drafted by the owners' lawyers—no document that had been *negotiated* could ever have been so one-sided."[42] A judge who later refused to set aside the arbitration ruling noted, "The rights of the parties are not controlled by what may have been the unilateral practice of owners from 1878 to the signing of the 1968 Basic Agreement" with the players' union.[43] In the winter of 1975, arbitrator Seitz evidently was ready similarly to discount the legacy of that one-sided past.

In the end, the owners struck out on three pitches. After three days of closed-door hearings, 842 pages of sworn testimony, and ninety-seven exhibits, arbitrator Peter Seitz issued his ruling on December 23, 1975.[44] First, he decided that the dispute was within his jurisdiction, that there was "nothing in [the] Basic Agreement or in any other document evidencing the agreements of the parties, to exclude a dispute as to the interpretation or application of Section 10(a) of the Uniform Players Contract or the Major League Rules dealing with the Reserve System from the reach of the broad grievance and arbitration provisions in" the Basic Agreement. Strike one.

Proceeding to the merits, Seitz didn't mince words: "The grievances of Messersmith and McNally are sustained." He ruled:

> *There is no contractual bond between these players and the Los Angeles and Montreal clubs respectively. Absent such a contract, their clubs had no right or power, under the Basic Agreement, the Uniform Player Contract, or the Major League Rules to reserve their services for their exclusive use for any period beyond the "renewal year" in the contracts which these players had heretofore signed with their clubs.*

Seitz concluded, "There is nothing in section 10(a) which, explicitly, expresses agreement that the Players Contract can be renewed for any period beyond the first renewal year,"[45] and that court rulings in cases involving professional basketball players in which "in respect of the renewal clause in basketball which does not differ materially or significantly from Section 10(a) in the baseball Players Contract, the Courts construed the renewal clause as providing for an extension of the term of the contract only for the 'renewal year' without any option to exercise additional and successive renewals."[46] As to whether baseball rules concerning the teams' mutual agreement (apart from player contract provisions) to respect the reservation "rights" of other clubs, the arbitrator dismissed their significance, finding that these rules depended on the existence of a contractual relationship between team and player, a relationship that, he ruled, did not extend beyond the renewal year and hence were of no greater force and effect.[47] Strike two.

Undeterred, the owners went to federal court, challenging the arbitration as outside the proper scope of the arbitrator's jurisdiction and arguing that the "arbitration panel was without authority to alter the agreed-upon operation of the reserve system." But the scope of judicial review of an arbitrator's decision is very limited. In all but the most extraordinary circumstances, arbitrators are given the last word, and in this instance the courts duly concluded—although one appeals court judge considered it a "very close case"—that "the arbitration panel had jurisdiction to resolve the dispute, that its award drew its essence from the collective bargaining agreement," and "We cannot say that those provisions are not susceptible of the construction given them by the panel."[48] Organized baseball's appeal failed; the arbitrator's ruling stood. Messersmith and McNally—and, by extension, any player who played out his renewal year—were free agents. Strike three.

Arbitrator Seitz's ruling overturned the existing reserve system but did not establish a replacement for it. That would be the subject of bargaining between owners and players, and the process would be anything but amicable. Free agency had come about through an ex cathedra pronouncement, not a meeting of the minds of the interested parties—owners and players. The owners had held the whip hand for so long that they disdained repeated suggestions that they settle the dispute over the reserve clause through negotiation. Now they were stuck with a decision that abruptly reversed the power relations between baseball management and labor and that put the owners at the mercy of their long-impotent adversary. The owners might lash out in anger and fire arbitrator Seitz as they did immediately (exercising their right to do so under the collective bargaining agreement), but that was hardly a viable strategy for dealing with the long-term consequences of the sudden demise of the reserve system.

Much like other controversies decided by what the losing side believed was arbitrary judicial fiat—abortion rights, school prayer, busing—the Seitz free-agency ruling was not accepted as legitimate by the owners. One judge, who nevertheless felt compelled to uphold the ruling in light of the broad discretion conferred on arbitrators and the very limited judicial review of their decisions (especially in labor cases), concluded that the owners *were* justified in their claim that disputes about the reserve clause were not intended to be the subject of arbitration, but he found that they had failed to express such intention with sufficient clarity to allow the court to override the arbitrator.[49] Right or wrong, this viewpoint was strongly embraced by the owners, who were doubtlessly inflamed by the conviction that they had been "had" by Miller. Their court appeals failed, and they would have to live with the Seitz ruling, but they have fought it ever since, by fair means and foul—mostly foul, if subsequent arbitral and judicial rulings are any indication.

A contentious bitterness would pervade the dealings between the parties thereafter, yielding a record of labor turmoil without parallel in any other segment of American business over the past quarter-century.

Salaries escalated in the aftermath of the free-agency ruling. Messersmith himself, who had been paid $90,000 in 1974, signed a multiyear contract with Atlanta for $1.75 million in the spring of 1976.[50] Total big-league payrolls rose from $32 million in 1976 to $284 million a decade later. The owners responded with desperate measures to restrain further increases. As an arbitrator would dryly find, "coincident" with meetings among owners and general managers after the 1985 season, bidding on free agents coming on the market ceased. The players filed grievances, arbitrations were held, and baseball management suffered further stinging legal defeats, as arbitration awards in 1987 and 1988 determined that the owners were guilty of collusion.[51]

At the bargaining table, the same battle was waged in the open. As the term of each collective bargaining agreement expired, players and owners proved unable to negotiate a new contract without undergoing a work stoppage. A lockout of spring training camps in 1976 was followed by a strike in the summer of 1981, another strike in August 1985, a lockout in the spring of 1990, and finally the calamitous 1994 strike, which shut down the season in midcourse, resulted in the cancellation of the World Series, and only ended the next spring with a judicial ruling that barred the owners from imposing their own unilateral contract package and starting the season with replacement players. The particulars of the disputes in each instance have varied (the parameters of a free-agency system in 1976, free-agent compensation in 1981, salary and pension freezes in 1985, limits on salary arbitration in 1990, owner proposals for a salary cap and revenue sharing in 1994), but the constant theme of the struggle has been that most elemental thread in labor–management relations: the desire by owners to find some means of controlling payroll costs in the absence of the reserve system's blanket restraint on a player's ability to sell his services on the free market, and the players' determination to resist such limitations.

Following the calamitous 1994–95 strike, a new agreement was negotiated in August 1996 and reluctantly approved by the owners only in November 1996. It provided for increased revenue sharing and an unprecedented "luxury tax" on the highest payrolls, devices to transfer at least some resources from the haves to the have-nots and to inhibit escalating salaries by penalizing the freest spenders, but it fell far short of the owners' desires for a firm limitation on payroll levels, a salary cap comparable to those in other professional sports.

Neither side regarded it as anything but an interim truce in a war that would be renewed as each side contended for radically different visions of the future economic structure of the sport.[52] The 1996 agreement expired at the end of the 2001 season. As bargaining for a new contract proceeded fitfully during spring training 2002, there was scant indication that the fundamental divide between owners and players (who, indeed were reported to be threatening a boycott of the All-Star Game, "to stick it to [Baseball Commissioner] Bud [Selig]") would be resolved on anything other than an interim basis, and even that might be out of reach.[53] A new agreement was eventually drawn up in August 2002, on the eve of the strike deadline set by the players, but it consisted of little more than patchwork grafts onto already existing luxury taxes and revenue sharing, not a fundamental restructuring of the sport's finances. It was merely a temporary armistice between two sides unable to agree on enduring principles to govern baseball's economic structure.

With the coming of free agency, the sense of entitlement that characterized baseball's self-conception passed at a stroke from owners to players, who had held the short straw for so long. Management and labor in other sports shared a common burden of subordinating (at least to some extent) their own particular agendas to the joint effort required to make their sports major presences on the American sporting scene. Sharing of revenues among teams, profit sharing with players, salary caps to equalize personnel expenditures—all played roles in presenting a "package" that would be attractive to would-be buyers (of advertising) and viewers (the fans). The baseball owners had grown so dependent on the antitrust exemption that they were simply unable to anticipate a day when that shield would be pierced, and they failed to negotiate a formula that would keep salaries under control when they had the chance.

Baseball had been "the national pastime" for so long that such a cooperative mind-set was entirely alien to the interested parties. Control now passed to the players, and the owners' pleas for moderation fell on deaf ears—as well they might, given their own previous lack of moderation. The owners had rebuffed all suggestions to negotiate a voluntary modification of the reserve system, as the arbitrator himself had urged before issuing his fatal ruling. "I pointed out to the parties," Seitz wrote at the time, "that the fortuitous coincidence of the Panel's duty to decide these grievances and the fact that they were currently engaged in bargaining for a new contract, afforded them a unique opportunity to resolve their reserve system disputes as well as those involved in these grievances," but, "whatever the reasons may have been, the parties, to the present, have not been successful in achieving the objectives I had in mind."[54] Indeed, even what appears to have been Seitz's unmistakable suggestion that he was about to decapitate the reserve system proved insufficient to move the owners—their heads neatly laid out on the chopping block—to compromise.[55]

A quarter-century later, it was late in the day indeed for owners to don the mantle of disinterested statesmanship and claim to be acting for the good of the game. The players, kept down for so long, weren't buying, now that *they* were on top. The Yankees—resistant to proposals for revenue sharing or team payroll limits that would inhibit their ability to obtain the talent they wanted at the price they were willing to pay—emerged as the players' free-spending and stalwart friend and ally in the contemporary baseball labor market.[56] *Izvestia,* had it still existed, would have been pleased.

Owners joined forces to contend with players across the bargaining table, but they then had to compete with each other on the playing field. The key to success in such competition was what it had always been—access to player talent. The rules of how to obtain and how to keep that talent—not to mention the price that had to be paid—had utterly changed, but that fundamental fact of baseball life remained. For the Yankees, along with everyone else, success would be measured by how well that traditional objective could be achieved in the revolutionary era of free agency that the Messersmith–McNally case had brought into being, so suddenly and so completely.

11

PLAYING UNDER NEW RULES

UNDER George Steinbrenner, the Yankees moved quickly to take advantage of the player market's new rules. The signing of Oakland pitcher Catfish Hunter in December 1974 was just the beginning. When free agency was institutionalized as a result of the Messersmith–McNally arbitration case, the Yankees were ready to compete in the newly open market by paying top dollar for top talent. Hunter pitched the 1976 Yankees to the American League pennant, but the team came up short in the World Series that year, losing in four straight games to the Reds. Steinbrenner moved aggressively to bring the team up to the next level, snaring slugger Reggie Jackson in a furious bidding war. Jackson became the self-described "straw that stirred the drink," and the team thrived amid unusually intense clubhouse rivalries as it won the World Series in 1977—the Yankees' first since 1962—led by Jackson's record-setting five home runs, including three in the decisive sixth game. The Yankees were back—but Steinbrenner didn't rest. The Yanks signed free agent relief pitcher Rich "Goose" Gossage in the off-season, priming the team to stay on top, even if it meant displacing 1977's bullpen ace, Sparky Lyle. Although Lyle had just won the Cy Young Award as the league's outstanding pitcher in that championship season, Gossage was seven years his junior and would provide years of outstanding service, leading the league twice in saves, while Lyle, traded away in 1978, played out his career with limited effectiveness in Texas, Philadelphia, and Chicago. It was the type of move—making a change too early rather than too late—that had long been the key to keeping a winning team winning. It had been the trademark of Branch Rickey's team-rebuilding philosophy, and there was certainly no better model to emulate. Steinbrenner had more money to work with than Rickey, but a similarly ruthless (and similarly effective) baseball intelligence was at work in both cases, given the different business contexts within which each executive operated.

Although the unprecedented sums he was throwing around to secure newly available talent in the free-agent marketplace bespoke an immediate adaptation to an utterly transformed contractual universe, Steinbrenner's methods were also a throwback to past Yankee player-procurement practices. This time, however, the deals were made directly with the players, not with the owners who had controlled their contracts. Steinbrenner's acquisitions of players in the free-agent market—most especially Catfish Hunter, Reggie Jackson, and Rich Gossage—were the updated equivalents of the blockbuster trades of yore, such as the purchase of Babe Ruth and the platoon of Red Sox who soon followed, the one-sided trade that brought pitchers Don Larsen and Bob Turley from Baltimore, and the Roger Maris deal with Kansas City. The result may have been just as unpalatable to the Yankees' foes, but Steinbrenner could hardly be faulted for playing (and playing so well) by the updated rules of what union head Marvin Miller would call "the whole different ball game" that free agency had wrought.

The turnaround in the Yankees' fortunes under Steinbrenner's ownership extended well beyond the diamond. In the battle for New York baseball's hearts, minds, and dollars, the resurgent Yankees shot past the Mets, who had attracted more fans than the Yanks in every season since the opening of Shea Stadium in 1964. In 1976, the refurbished Yankee Stadium reopened, and Yankee attendance increased by almost 800,000 over the previous year, surpassing the two million mark for the first time since 1950. That same year, Met attendance dropped by 250,000, falling below 1,500,000 for the first time since the team's second season. Between 1975 and 1976, the Yankee share of the total New York baseball market went from 42 to 58 percent—to this day, the greatest single-season swing in attendance between New York's two teams. And the Yankees would hold on to the attendance leadership for seven years thereafter. Steinbrenner's investment was appreciating at a rapid rate: The value of the team was placed at about $25 million by 1978, more than double the purchase price just five years earlier.[1] Twenty years later, the team's value would be placed at $425 million, with Steinbrenner holding a 60 percent stake.[2]

But even by the time the Yanks fought their way into the 1981 World Series, the madness was beginning to overwhelm the Steinbrenner method, abetted by the tragic death of catcher Thurman Munson in a private plane crash in August 1979. In 1980, the Yanks would go on to win their division but lose the pennant play-off to Kansas City in a three-game sweep; they would win the ad hoc American League play-offs fashioned to determine a pennant winner in strike-shortened 1981 before losing to Los Angeles in that year's World Series, after winning the first two games.

By then, the front-office dysfunction that would soon consign the team to the baseball wilderness for the next decade had clearly set in. During the series itself, Steinbrenner blasted his players for mental errors, vowed to eliminate such laxness in the future, and reported that he had gotten into a fight with two Dodger fans after the Dodgers had won the fifth game to take the lead. A key relationship, with outfielder Dave Winfield—who had been signed to a record ten-year, $20 million contract the previous year as the designated successor to an aging Reggie Jackson—was poisoned when Winfield batted a microscopic .045 in the World Series (one hit in twenty-two at-bats) and drew from the Yankee boss the scornful moniker "Mr. May," in derisive contrast to

Jackson's "Mr. October." When Steinbrenner publicly apologized for the team's poor play, the entire team was incensed. After 1981, fifteen years would pass before the Yankees again appeared in a World Series, longer even than the drought of the 1960s and 1970s. Before long, the team's record of success in the first years of the free-agency era (four league pennants and two World Championships between 1976 and 1981) would be the stuff of ancient history, with no connection to the team's dismal misfortunes in the 1980s.

Whatever woes befell the team after 1981, there was no question that the buck stopped at the principal owner's desk. A business associate would say, "Nothing is as limited as being a limited partner of George Steinbrenner." As general partner, Steinbrenner had invested $168,000 of the $4 million in cash (the other $6 million was borrowed) raised by his group to purchase the Yankees from CBS, and by 1979 he had increased his stake to 55 percent by buying out limited partners.[3] He had taken charge from day one, and the Yankees' George 3d had no one to blame but himself for a degree of front-office turmoil unseen in New York since the Giants' triumvirate of Stoneham, McGraw, and McQuade had waged civil war in the 1920s. That had been a three-man job, but Steinbrenner seemed intent on a solo performance to outdo their joint ability to destroy a championship team.

The collapse of the Yankees in the 1980s proved, once again, that baseball success could *not* be bought, whether by the Yankees or anyone else. As Steinbrenner's increasingly pathological relationship with the on-again, off-again field manager Billy Martin played out over the years, the Yankees fell apart. A call was even made that Steinbrenner be, in effect, expropriated, and that "New York City ought to take over the Yankees"—but perhaps only a sociologist could believe that a city that had recently mismanaged its own affairs into bankruptcy and was unable to deliver basic services to its citizens would be able to turn around the fortunes of a ball club.[4] Whatever one might think of that particular nostrum, there was no question that the method that once had tempered the madness was yielding ever-more-diminishing returns. Steinbrenner's quest for veteran free agents loaded down the club with the likes of Dave Winfield, Don Baylor, Steve Kemp, Ken Griffey, and Omar Moreno, highly expensive examples of the "older player well past the high noon of his career," who "were getting paid for what they did for other teams in other years." The 1984 Yanks had assembled an all-star lineup—but it was that of 1979, and the team appeared headed toward its worst win–loss record since 1913.[5] That fate was avoided in 1984, however, as the team, after stumbling to a 20–29 start, finished in fourth place at 87–75, but that sad day would indeed soon come to pass.

As the Yankees stumbled, they found themselves once again shuffled off the center of the New York baseball stage. By the mid-1980s, it was the Mets who were ascendant in the New York baseball universe, narrowly beaten by the Cardinals for the National League East title in 1985, winning 108 games and a memorable World Series over the Red Sox in 1986, suffering a close defeat to the Dodgers in the 1988 playoffs. Led by pitcher Doc Gooden and outfielder Darryl Strawberry, the Mets appeared to have an unlimited future ahead of them.

In a flash, or so it seemed, the baseball excitement was at Shea, not Yankee, Stadium, and Met attendance topped that for the Yankees nine years running (starting in 1984); broke the three-million-fan mark twice (in 1987 and 1988), which the Yankees had never done even with Reggie in his glory years; and provoked George Steinbrenner to raise loud questions about the future of the Bronx ballpark as the Yankees' home. But by 1991, Gooden and Strawberry had self-destructed, the Mets' surge was spent, and Shea Stadium crowds were down by almost 50 percent from their peak just four years earlier. Not that the Yankees were taking up the slack. In 1992, as the Yankees finished in fourth place (twenty games off the pace) with a 76–86 record, they attracted only 1,748,000 fans to the Bronx—fewer fans than the Mets did with an even worse record, and their own lowest attendance total (aside from strike-shortened 1981) since 1975.

In 1992, the Yankees finished below the .500 mark for the fourth straight season, a record of hapless consistency that had not been achieved even in the otherwise-dismal CBS years—the first time that had happened, in fact, since 1915. The nadir had been reached with a last-place finish in 1990, a record of 67–95, and a winning percentage of .414, the lowest mark since the 1913 team's .377 in their first year at the Polo Grounds, their second year in pinstripes.

Failure on the field had been compounded—with interest—by a total meltdown in the front office. In March 1990, the *Daily News* reported that the long-simmering feud between Steinbrenner and Dave Winfield, which had spilled over into the charge and counter-charge of litigation the previous year, had led Steinbrenner to pay gambler Howard Spira $40,000 for allegedly derogatory information on the erstwhile star. The fallout was immediate, and tumultuous. Spira was indicted on March 23 for threatening to release information about his dealings with Steinbrenner; Winfield was traded in May. That summer, following an investigation by the Baseball Commissioner that revealed, among other things, that Spira had made nearly 500 phone calls to Steinbrenner or one of his top aides, Steinbrenner agreed to a lifetime ban from the sport. Announcement of the news was greeted with relief at Yankee Stadium, as jubilant fans chanted, "Good-bye, George." The team and its owner had hit bottom.[6]

To be sure, the utter collapse of the Yankees, and the disgraceful woes that befell the one-of-a-kind George Steinbrenner school of baseball management, brought to some observers a measure of reassurance about the future of the sport. Those who had worried a decade earlier that Steinbrenner's readiness to put together "the best team that money can buy" threatened to destroy competitive balance, found their fears misplaced. Indeed, Steinbrenner's Yankees were held up as *the* paradigm of how *not* to run a franchise. Steinbrenner, George Will wrote, was "an error machine" who had single-handedly ruined the Yankees with his "ten-thumbed touch," nothing less than "baseball's dumb-o-meter: study his decisions, do the opposite, and you will do well."[7] The Yankees under his leadership provided the prime example of how "the absence of baseball acumen in the front office can be a great leveler regardless of financial assets."[8] That such apparent mismanagement of baseball's premier franchise had resulted in a benefit for the game as a whole—that "the end of free agency did not bring on an era of *Sturm und Drang* and ruinous imbalance"[9]—was certainly an outcome that held no appeal for the Yankees or their once and future front-office leader. And it would soon change.

By August 11, 1994, when baseball was shut down by the eighth work stoppage since 1972, the club standings flashed the clear message that the first-place Yankees *had* come back from the accumulated disasters of that dreadful summer of 1990. And George Steinbrenner was back, too. The Yankee owner's "lifetime" expulsion from the sport had come to an unexpected end on July 24, 1992, when Baseball Commissioner Fay Vincent lifted the ban, effective with the 1993 season.[10] For much of Steinbrenner's period of exile, confusion had reigned in the Yankee front office, as Steinbrenner and Vincent clashed over who would replace Steinbrenner as the team's managing partner. Eventually, Steinbrenner's son-in-law Joe Molloy took command. The nucleus of a competitive team was assembled through trades (pitcher Jim Abbott and outfielder Paul O'Neill) and free-agent signings (third baseman Wade Boggs, pitcher Jimmy Key, and shortstop Spike Owen), as the Steinbrenner cash spigot remained in the "on" position, despite the owner's absence from the scene—and there were doubts aplenty about how "absent" he really was. Whatever the truth, the team that greeted Steinbrenner's much-ballyhooed return to the helm was much improved over the one that he had left three summers earlier.

In 1993, the Yankees moved up to second place in the American League East, winning eighty-eight games, for their best finish since 1986. Attendance surged by 650,000 to 2,416,000, topping that of the crosstown Mets for the first time in ten years. And the Yankees were just getting started in what would turn out to be the most dominant showing of any ball team since the great Yankee dynasty of the late 1940s to early 1960s. Pennant hopes in 1994 were thwarted by the strike in August, but amid widespread public disgust with both sides in the dispute—which only ended in the spring of 1995 after a judge's ruling in favor of the players—the 1995 team capitalized on the expansion of the post-season by grabbing a newly established "wild card" spot (for the nondivision winner with the best record) and coming just short of a chance for a pennant, losing to Seattle three games to two in an exciting first-round play-off series. It was Don Mattingly's last season, and "Donnie Baseball" would indeed go into the record books as the greatest Yankee player never to have appeared in a World Series.

The next season, the Yankees won it all, rallying from a 6–0 deficit to win the fourth game of the World Series against Atlanta, to even the series, and then took the next two contests for a four-games-to-two triumph. But the bad feelings left by the players' strike lingered, as 1996 attendance fell short of the pre-strike 1993 total by more than 150,000 and, indeed it would not be until 1999 that 1988's record 2,633,000 mark was surpassed.

On the diamond, the Yankees were doing their best to erase any lingering backlash from the turmoil that had wrecked what had been shaping up as a great 1994 season and had resulted in the first World Series cancellation since 1904 (when the domineering Giants had refused to follow the precedent set by Pittsburgh the previous year and play the champions of the upstart American League). Against the entire weight of their traditionally aloof image, the Yankees were fielding a team that "even a Brooklyn fan could enjoy," as George Vecsey admitted in what he said was a "hard column to write."[11] Steinbrenner and General Manager Bob Watson, he noted, "have produced lightning in a bottle with some future," and that would indeed prove to be true.

The Yanks were stopped by Cleveland in the 1997 play-offs, but Steinbrenner vowed, "We'll win it all next year. Mark that down."[12] And they did, more than making up for that defeat, winning 114 games in the 1998 regular season and overwhelming San Diego 4–0 in the World Series. Another four-game series sweep, this time over Atlanta, followed in 1999. When that series ended, the Yankees had won an unprecedented eleven straight World Series games.

On this record, there was glory enough for all—not excluding the principal owner. Many credited a new, more "mellow" Steinbrenner, who emerged from what he referred to as his "Elba" more patient and less bellicose, staying "within generally accepted standards of adult behavior"—eager to share his love for the novels of Thomas Hardy, less inclined to second-guess players and managers.[13] Perhaps so, but despite a healthy shift in his choice of breakfast from glazed doughnuts to freshly juiced carrots, celery, apples, and bananas, the "old Steinbrenner" was a more than fitful presence. He bullied Manager Buck Showalter into a precipitous departure from the team that had fallen just one game short of reaching the American League Championship Series in 1995. "George Steinbrenner," Dave Anderson wrote, "never leaves well enough alone."[14] (Two years later, General Manager Bob Watson would suffer a similar, unfair fate.) In the last weeks of the 1996 season, with the Yankees leading their division by a comfortable margin, having been in first place for 121 consecutive days, he had put new manager Joe Torre on the spot with a truculent and very public challenge: "Whether or not we make it is up to him."[15] A loud protest about umpiring in the 1995 play-off against Seattle drew a $50,000 fine[16]—but perhaps paid dividends (and more) the next season when the umpires disallowed a claim of interference by Baltimore on teenage fan Jeff Maier's notorious catch, which turned an apparent out into a Yankee home run.

Mellow or not, the "new" George Steinbrenner wanted to win just as much as the "old" one did, and he still knew how to go about it. He insisted that success meant nothing less than winning the World Series: "If you're a competitor you always thirst for those days. If . . . you're just putting some team out there, then you don't belong in New York."[17] And no one would ever accuse him of "just putting some team out there." As the Yankees went from triumph to triumph in the late 1990s, the team featured an array of talent—Derek Jeter, Mariano Rivera, Bernie Williams, Andy Petite—brought along as young prospects and then paid enough to stay in the fold; Steinbrenner "rescue jobs" Darryl Strawberry and Doc Gooden, which paid surprising and heartening dividends; and out-of-the-blue gambits, notably the signing of Orlando "El Duque" Hernandez after his desperate escape from Cuba. With Torre a mature and generally stoic presence in the dugout, the front office skillfully deploying the team's unmatched financial resources in the player market, and George Steinbrenner actively overseeing it all and instilling an unmatched will to win, the Yanks appeared to have struck a successful division of management responsibilities reminiscent of the formula that had first propelled them to the top in the Ruppert–Barrow–Huggins era. And, not coincidentally, the current edition of the Yankees was compiling a record to match.

In 2000, everything came together, at least for New Yorkers. The Yankees again finished first in the Eastern Division and then beat Oakland and Seattle in the play-offs, albeit not without a fight. But of greater interest—again, at least to New Yorkers—was that in an unprecedented convergence of baseball fortune, the Yanks would square off against the New York Mets in that season's World Series. After forty-four years, the "subway series" was back.

In the decades since the Mets had relaunched National League baseball in New York after the flight west by the Dodgers and Giants, the Mets had been good and they had been bad, as had the Yankees, but the two teams had never played in synch. The final three years of the Yankees' postwar dynasty had coincided with the Mets' pathetic birth pangs. When the Mets established themselves as serious World Series contenders between 1969 and 1973, the Yanks remained far out of contention in their own league. The Yankees' resurgence in the first years of the free-agent era coincided with some of the worst seasons in Mets history. The Mets' recovery in the mid-to-late 1980s found no echo in the Bronx, as the Yankees slid toward disaster. In 1985, each team finished second in its division, and won almost exactly the same number of games (ninety-eight for the Mets, ninety-seven for the Yanks), but the Mets were on the way up, the Yankees on the way down. As the Yankees forged themselves into *the* dominant team in baseball in the years after the 1994 strike, the Mets lagged behind. This had been the permanent yin and yang of New York's baseball experience since 1962.

Attendance patterns followed performance; the fight for the New York baseball dollar was waged for hearts and minds that, when converted to dollars, were more malleable than steadfast.[18] The Mets led the Yankees in attendance every year between 1964 and 1975; the Yankees then led from 1976 through 1983; the Mets reversed things narrowly in 1984 and then outdrew the Yankees every season until 1993, when leadership passed to the Yankees—with whom it has stayed ever since. Until the mid-1980s, it had been particularly brutal competition, as overall New York attendance remained fairly steady, and a gain for one resulted in a decline for the other in this zero-sum game for the

New York baseball dollar.[19] The intramural competition eased some-what after 1985, as total attendance increased—in 1988, it finally sur-passed the record (5,585,000) for major-league attendance in New York that had been set (by three teams, of course) way back in 1947—and both teams shared in the rebound in attendance in the late 1990s, following the 1994 strike. Through it all, the Yanks maintained an edge over their younger rivals in the New York baseball mind. Their atten-dance lows were never as low, and their highs were higher, compared with the Mets.[20] Loyalty to the Yankees appears to have been "stickier" in the bad times and more expansive in the good ones.

IN 1999, when for the first time each team reached the play-offs, total New York baseball attendance exceeded six million (3.2 million for the Yankees, 2.8 million for the Mets), but only the Yankees made it into the World Series, as the Mets were beaten by Atlanta in the National League Championship Series. But in 2000, the Mets—at last—joined the Yankees in the fall classic, and their combined attendance reached a record high of 6,027,000. The local media, after the near-miss of the previous year, were intoxicated. Finally, what had become in the decade after World War II a phenomenon that New Yorkers came to expect as a right, two New York teams would wage a face-off for the championship of the baseball world.

Of course, a subway series in 2000 was not, and could not be, quite what it had been in those earlier years. Even its Giuliani-era renais-sance could not conceal the fact that, as the eyes of the baseball world zeroed in on New York City, the place of the city in its region has changed. The city's population was down by about half a million from its mid-1950s levels, and it was a declining percentage of the popula-tion of the New York metropolitan area. Far more of the baseball fan base now lived in the suburbs, distant from any subway line or station.

Many of the Yankees who tormented their crosstown rivals five out of six times in those previous encounters lived on the Grand Concourse during the baseball season, but most, if not indeed all, of the Yankees of 2000 only encountered the Bronx on Game Day. It was no different for their National League foes. The days when the "Boys of Summer" actually lived in Brooklyn or Willie Mays played stickball in Harlem were memories without echoes for the Met ballplayers, who had a similarly strictly professional connection with their Queens home ground. As for the subways' own place in their eponymous series, the glory days of yore were the worst of times, as annual ridership plunged from 2 billion in 1947 to 1.3 billion in 1956, a level of ridership (in a vastly expanded universe of commuters) that has only recently been matched after decades of further decline. And the thousands of cars cramming the parking lots surrounding Yankee Stadium and Shea Stadium were the most eloquent witnesses of all to the diminished role of the subways in taking the fans out to the ball game. In both cases, it was a far cry from old Ebbets Field and its 400 parking spaces.

Then, too, by the turn of the millennium, the place of the World Series in the texture of urban life was utterly different. Gone were the afternoon games, with the fall shadows creeping remorsefully across Yankee Stadium's vast outfield, apt metaphor for the waning of the season itself. Gone was the incessant, pressure-packed rhythm of playing day after day, with no time off for "travel." Gone, too, was the World Series as an immediate, unforgiving climax to the regular campaign, a sudden-elimination contest bereft of the long-haul percentages that could get a team through a bad patch during the run for the pennant.

In its millennial year incarnation, the series followed a rather endless three weeks of "post-season" play-offs, which even provide a second chance for teams that fell short during the regular season—as it did in 2000 for the "wild card" Mets, and as it had in 1995 for the Yankees. The scheduling of the series had been domesticated and made safe for prime time. All games were played at night, even on the weekend. No matter that the rivals were separated by no more than the length of the Triborough Bridge, the games still were duly punctuated by days off for "travel."

Utterly gone was baseball's once-imperious insistence on its overriding importance, on its claim to impose itself on the rhythms of the workaday world, the afternoons when, as Roger Angell wrote when memories of those days were still fresh, "the sounds of baseball fell from every window and doorway in town,"[21] and schoolboys hid transistor radios under schoolbooks in the back rows of classrooms.

But as the Yankees stood off the underdog Mets in six games, one thing about the subway series had not changed all that much. For all the hoopla, and the special newspaper supplements it generated, all the sound bites about the "good old days" generated by the aging "boys of summer," the harsh reality was that, playing before a national audience for the first time in forty-plus years, the subway series revival laid an egg, drawing the lowest television ratings (12.4) in World Series history, almost 25 percent below that for the Braves–Yankees intersectional contest the previous year, while the season premiere of *Frasier* attracted one-third as many viewers as the third game of the series.[22] True, fault could be found with the Fox Network's coverage, but it is doubtful that one complaint—that "Fox continues its near-total amnesia about playing up the Subway Series angle," and didn't have enough sound bites with former Yankees, Dodgers, and Giants—had accurately identified whatever it was that hurt the ratings.[23] Way back in the spring of 1956, sportswriter Tom Meany had observed that "concentration of the baseball empire around New York is not good for the game. Play enough subway series and the only people interested will be the transit companies."[24] The long hiatus had clearly not done much to increase the appeal of a subway series to audiences west of the Hudson River.

◇

AS THE SPORTING landscape shifted so radically, and at times so suddenly, in the years after 1960, it had not been easy for the Yankees to perpetuate the dynasty that had once loomed imposingly over so much of baseball's history. The line from the era of Mantle, Maris, and Ford to that of Jeter, Giambi, and Petite did not run directly from success to success. There had been bumps aplenty in the road. For a time, the team had collapsed into mediocrity as the stepchild plaything of a vast conglomerate with more important things on its corporate mind than baseball. In the early 1990s, the Yankees were written off as a woefully mismanaged, terminally crippled franchise. By the end of that decade, the team was viewed as a money-fueled steamroller with an impregnable advantage over its hopeless competitors. What the recent history of the Yankees illustrates (if anything), however, is that money alone is not—and indeed has never been—the Holy Grail of winning baseball. Just as was true for the Giants under Stoneham, the Cardinals under Rickey, and the Dodgers under O'Malley, the way the Yankees have been managed, as a business and as a team, has determined whether it has won or lost, moved or stayed. If the triumphs, as well as the setbacks, of the last four decades of Yankee history teach any lesson, that is the most important one.

Epilogue

BASEBALL'S ENDURING PARADOX

I N 2001, the Yankees repeated as American League champions, but the Mets faltered and the Arizona Diamondbacks took their place as the National League's World Series representative. That fall's series was a classic, with the Yankees coming close to reversing their dubious achievement in the 1960 World Series, when they had outscored the Pirates fifty-five runs to twenty-seven but lost the series four games to three. On October 27, 2001, it was the Yankees who had been outscored (thirty-five runs to fourteen) going into the ninth inning of the seventh game—holding a 2–1 lead and with their unhittable relief ace Mariano Rivera on the mound. But Rivera, who had recorded twenty-three straight postseason saves, gave up two runs, and the Diamondbacks were World Champions, in only their fourth season in the major leagues.

With the contenders spanning the continent, not just the East River, the 2001 World Series rebounded to an average television rating of 15.6; the Diamondbacks' seventh-game win attracted a rating of 27, the highest for a series game since 1991, reaching 71 million viewers at some point in the broadcast.[1] In the aftermath of September 11, 2001, the Yankees became the improbable sentimental favorite of fans from around the country—even, it was said, in Boston. The team was the defiant symbol of a tragically vulnerable New York City as the nation went to war against terror. That the Diamondbacks rallied to win the World Series seemed almost unpatriotic. But warm feelings for the suddenly heroic, human-sized New York Yankees proved fleeting, at least within the high councils of the sport.

The return of the subway series in 2000 had already triggered questions about the economic future of the game reminiscent of those that had accompanied the intra-New York matchups of the 1950s. Then, the "subway-series decade" provoked the media to ask, "Can Baseball Survive?"[2] "Does Baseball Pay?"[3] and "Why Is Baseball in Trouble?"[4] This time, a barrage of similar questions came from within the command structure of major-league baseball itself, and it was hardly abated by the Yankees' loss to the unlikely Anaheim Angels in the first round of the 2002 play-offs, or the Mets' disastrous second-division finish that year.

In January 1999, Baseball Commissioner Bud Selig had convened a "blue ribbon panel" to conduct an inquiry into baseball's economic and competitive condition and future prospects. The panel included four "independent members" drawn from outside the world of baseball, and their eminence was simply astonishing. They were Richard Levin, president of Yale University; former Federal Reserve Chairman Paul Volcker; former Senate majority leader and international peacemaker George Mitchell; and prizewinning political commentator (and quondam author of best-selling baseball books) George Will. In the summer of 2000, they issued their report.[5]

Focusing on the five poststrike seasons of 1995 to 1999, in which the Yankees had won three World Series and appeared in the play-offs every year, the report concluded that "large and growing revenue disparities exist and are causing problems of chronic competitive imbalance," and that "these problems have become substantially worse

during the five complete seasons since the strike-shortened season of
1994, and seem likely to remain severe unless Major League Baseball
undertakes remedial actions commensurate to the problem." What
were labeled as the "anachronistic aspects of MLB's economic
arrangements"—notably, the unequal division of local revenues
between large- and small-market teams—were "having perverse
effects that pose a threat to the game's long-term vitality," as "widen-
ing payroll disparities" were giving rise to an "unacceptable level of . . .
competitive imbalance" in recent years. Only three clubs (the Yankees,
the Indians, and the Rockies) had been profitable over the five-year
period studied, and total major-league baseball losses exceeded $1 bil-
lion.[6] The future was grim:

> *The growing gap between the "have" and the "have not" clubs—*
> *which is to say the minority that have a realistic chance of suc-*
> *ceeding in postseason play and the majority of clubs that have*
> *poor prospects of reaching the postseason—is a serious and*
> *imminent threat to the popularity, health, stability and growth of*
> *the game.*[7]

These conclusions were documented in thirty-one tables and
twenty-seven charts, replete with careful statistical analyses of payroll
expenses, revenue sources and amounts, and wins and losses on the
playing field. And they were seconded in Baseball Commissioner Bud
Selig's testimony to Congress in December 2001, in which he said that
the problem of competitive imbalance had only worsened since the
release of the *Blue Ribbon Report,* that the play-offs continued "to be
dominated by high payroll clubs, and those payrolls continue to escalate," and that the "payroll and performance correlation is unmistakable and powerful." According to Selig, the financial condition of the
sport was grim: operating losses of almost $1.4 million over the previ-

ous seven years; only two teams (the Cleveland Indians and the New York Yankees) showing profits from operations over that period; a $519 million loss in 2001 alone. "Our economic problems are obvious," he testified.[8]

One couldn't help but feel, however, that the case had not been made quite as conclusively as the *Blue Ribbon Report* and the commissioner had asserted. It was not surprising that the players' union responded to Selig's testimony with open skepticism about baseball's alleged financial plight and disputed the calculation of the losses claimed by Selig.[9] Nor was it hard to find "nonpartisan" critics who doubted whether the bleak survey of the sport's economic scene, painted by the commissioner, actually accorded with the reality of a business whose revenues—according to Selig himself—had almost doubled, from $1.8 to $3.5 billion in five years, and who questioned the assumption that competitive imbalance was either a novel or especially pressing threat to the well-being of the sport.[10] Selig's attempt to buttress the credibility of his presentation by having the Ernst & Young partner in charge of baseball's audit accompany him to a post-testimony press conference fell flat at a time of eroding public confidence in the major accounting firms. "I'm responsible for a lot," Selig plaintively told reporters, "but don't make me responsible for Enron."[11] Nor was his case helped when, in the spring of 2002, *Forbes* published an analysis of the current economics of major-league baseball, calculating a $75 million profit for the sport, not the loss of $232 million claimed by the commissioner.[12] Not that this settled matters. A few months later, an appraiser appointed to resolve a dispute between the New York Mets' feuding owners placed a $391 million value on the team, well below *Forbes's* $482 million valuation.[13] One could only conclude that, as always, baseball economics was more of an art than a science.

Whatever the exact numbers, there was much reason to question a message of doom, premised on the inexorable dominance of large-market teams. The "facts on the ground" appeared to allow for a much more upbeat prognosis. In the late 1990s, attendance had recovered from an immediate poststrike downturn back up to prestrike levels. Fan interest rebounded, spurred by the home-run chases of Mark McGwire and Sammy Sosa (in 1998) and Barry Bonds (in 2001). The debut of new ballparks in San Francisco, Seattle, Detroit, and Houston drove attendance upward in those cities. The astonishing success of no-frills Seattle and Oakland and the resurgence of the sport's greatest brand name, the New York Yankees, were signs of strength, not weakness. Attendance in 1998 broke the 70 million barrier for the first time, as the majors expanded to thirty teams and stayed above that mark in subsequent seasons. As recently as 1982, total big-league attendance had been under 45 million, and it had only exceeded 50 million for the first time in 1987. Until 1993, only three clubs—the Dodgers (on seven occasions, the first in 1978), the Mets (in 1987 and 1988), and the Cardinals (in 1987)—had ever drawn more than three million fans in a single season. In prestrike 1993, seven teams attracted more than three million fans to their home games. In 1998, that level was reached by eight teams, and in 2000 by no fewer than ten (Cleveland, Baltimore, Yankees, Seattle, St. Louis, San Francisco, Colorado, Atlanta, Houston, and Los Angeles)—one-third of all teams.

Nor did the results of no more than a half-dozen seasons—out of the century or so of major-league baseball's experience—necessarily provide a blueprint for the future. As the *Blue Ribbon Report* conceded, as recently as 1992, an earlier study had concluded that no such threat to baseball's competitive balance then existed. One had to wonder whether the world had really changed that much in the few seasons since then. Indeed, just two years before he signed off on the *Blue Ribbon Report*, panel member George Will, as close a student of the sport as one could wish, had written, "So far, free agency in the context of surging but vastly disparate team revenues has not had the consequence predicted: It has not resulted in diminished competitive balance. Quite the contrary."[14] Will had, it is true, also noted that "money matters," and that, "in the long run, large and chronic differences in teams' resources will destroy in many cities what draws fans through the turnstiles—the hope that springs each spring."[15] Were just two more *years* of additional data sufficiently probative to upset the lesson of greater competitive balance that Will had drawn from the overall experience of the first *two decades* of free agency?

Franchises given up for dead in the past—including the San Francisco Giants, Seattle Mariners, Atlanta Braves, and Oakland A's—had not only survived, they had prospered. The Jacobs brothers had purchased the Cleveland Indians in 1986, and when Dick Jacobs died in 1992, his obituary recorded that the brothers' "previous success in business did not translate to the running of a major league baseball team," and that they had "failed to reverse the team's losing fortunes."[16] But the Indians would go on to post the American League's second-best record over the following decade—trailing only George Steinbrenner's Yankees, who had similarly been written off in the early 1990s. And other examples could also be cited of a team's ability to turn things around and become competitive, on the field and off, in ways that projecting apparently chronic woes into the future would not have predicted.

George Will had tempered some of his earlier concerns about long-term trends in baseball economics by recalling John Maynard Keynes's maxim, "In the long run, we are all dead."[17] Keynes was, of course, warning economic policymakers about the dangers of trusting that everything would be all right "in the long run." A similar caution would certainly be in order for those baseball policymakers who worried too much that they might *not* be.

Moreover, a certain wariness about structural changes that would overturn fundamental aspects of the conduct of the baseball business was surely prudent when it was considered how contingent some of the "unbalanced" competitive outcomes (on which the report relied so heavily) actually were. The cold print testifying to an apparently remorseless Yankee machine rolling over the opposition was at odds with a much more touch-and-go reality. After all, the Yanks were on the verge of being beaten decisively by Atlanta in the 1996 World Series before coming back from a 6–0 fifth-inning deficit in Game 4, after being down two games to one. And before they had even gotten that far, their path through the play-offs had been eased to an incalculable degree by the entirely fortuitous intervention of hooky-playing schoolboy Jeffrey Maier, whose quick hands turned a fly ball hit by Derek Jeter from a long out into a crucial home run against the Baltimore Orioles.

Then, too, although the *Blue Ribbon Report* duly acknowledged that competitive balance had hardly been the rule in much of the sport's past (as how could it have not?),[18] the panel's message of crisis was out of kilter with such a contextual view of the game's history and likely prospects. According to one calculation, the percentage of World Series participants from the largest markets had actually *declined* over the years—from about 80 percent in the decades before 1960 to 42 percent in the five years after the 1994 strike.[19] The metropolitan areas in the American League whose teams compiled the best cumulative win–loss percentages over the 1997–2001 seasons—New York, Cleveland, Seattle, Boston, and Oakland— ranked first, twelfth, tenth, sixth, and fifth in population, respectively. In the National League, the top five—Atlanta, San Francisco, New York, Houston, and Arizona[20]— similarly revealed no large-market stranglehold on recent competition; those teams represented metropolitan areas that ranked (in order) seventh, fourth, first, sixth, and tenth in population. Major-market teams in Los Angeles, Chicago, and Philadelphia posted results that were conspicuously mediocre (the Dodgers and White Sox, with winning percentages of slightly over .500) or worse (the Cubs and Phillies, well below that break-even mark). Before the Anaheim Angels' victory in 2002, the last large-market team, other than the Yankees, to win a World Series was Oakland in 1989. The only other large-market teams even to make it into the World Series in the last decade were the Giants in 2002, the Mets in 2000, and the Phillies in 1993.

Nor was the linkage between payroll and performance that the blue ribbon panel charted for the 1995–99 seasons much different from what had prevailed in earlier years, when the reserve clause reigned supreme. As Table 5.1 in the appendix illustrates, comparing the 1950 and 1999 seasons reveals that the correlation between winning and payroll expense could be even stronger in that earlier era.[21]

Indeed, when Congress, in the course of its 1951 inquiry into baseball's antitrust exemption, considered the impact of the reserve clause on competition, "It was forcefully argued that the unenviable status of the minor league player, the ossification of the major league territorial map, and the tendency of farm systems to enable the richest clubs to engross the player market, are all at least in part the result of the reserve clause."[22] Fifty years later, the blue ribbon panel was arguing the opposite: that it was the demise of the reserve clause that was permitting the richer clubs to "engross" the player market and dominate the game. These contradictory assessments would not, however, surprise an economist. In a pioneering analysis of the "baseball players' labor market," Simon Rottenberg of the University of Chicago had concluded in 1956 "that a market in which freedom is limited by the reserve rule . . . distributes players among teams about as a free market would," and that the reserve rule did not, despite common claims to the contrary, equalize the distribution of players among teams more than a market in which there is perfect freedom."[23] As between 1951 and 2000, only the target of the criticism for that consistent outcome had changed.

The *Blue Ribbon Report*'s call for greater revenue sharing and higher taxes to solve the perceived problem of competitive imbalance had an oddly familiar ring to it. Such measures had, after all, been incorporated into baseball's collective bargaining agreement in 1996, and expectations were that the World Champion Yankees were now facing a "difficult task" if they were to stay on top.[24] Indeed, the Yankees had provided $105 million over the previous six years as the leading contributor to baseball's revenue-sharing mechanism for assisting less-well-off clubs—and then saw a club such as the Kansas City Royals turn such payouts into profits (as one of five teams, according to the commissioner, to make money in 2001), forgoing investment in competitive personnel.[25] Despite these transfer payments, the Yankees had gone on to solidify their competitive dominance, and the aftermath of such measures, if the report was to be trusted, was a decline in competitive balance (sufficient, indeed, to threaten the future of the game). That the "remedy" prescribed by the report was to redouble such measures was the type of analysis that, applied to such skewed outcomes in government policy, could expect no sympathy from—to pick a name at random—George Will.

Baseball certainly has structural problems, many rooted in the fact that, alone among major professional sports, its basic economic structure took shape in a pretelevision age and has struggled to adapt to a changing economic environment after having already established itself as a major presence in America's sporting life. The result has hardly been a seamless fit, most notably with respect to the division of local revenues, which accrues to the benefit of the teams in larger markets—a legacy of the time before national broadcast contracts, when baseball teams were on their own in exploiting the then-new media of first radio and then television. Even critics of Selig's historical analysis and prospective remedies acknowledged that "the revenue gap is an authentic problem getting worse,"[26] especially in light of the escalating local cable and pay-television income derived by teams in the largest markets, notably New York. Baseball's all-too-often-lazy reliance on an antitrust exemption not available to other sports had long sheltered owners from any need to work out an enduring formula for salary restraint with the players—until the reserve clause was suddenly swept away. Then it was too late.

At this juncture, to summon up the bogeyman of the large-market teams as *the* great threat to the sport's future viability was to leap beyond current fact and slight the lessons of the past. Yankee fans, and not Yankee fans alone, might suspect a hidden agenda in the blue ribbon panel's alarums about large-market dominance. Looking behind such a generalization, one would find that it really boiled down to the success of one team—the Yankees, who were the *only* large-market team to enjoy consistent success in recent seasons. In fact, apart from the Yankees—who did indeed appear in the 1996, 1998, 1999, 2000, and 2001 World Series, winning all but the last one—the only large-market team to make the fall classic in those seasons was the New York Mets, with one appearance, in 2000.

The other contestants for baseball's championship in those post-strike years hailed from such smaller markets as Cleveland, Atlanta, Phoenix, Miami, and San Diego. The teams from the large markets other than New York—Los Angeles, Philadelphia, the San Francisco Bay area, Boston, and Chicago—were entirely shut out of the World Series after the strike, until 2002, when Anaheim and San Francisco squared off in the third all-California and first all–wild card series. Other teams (notably Los Angeles and Boston) had spent lavishly and achieved little in return. The Dodgers increased payroll from $37 million (1996) to $48 million (1997) to $60 million (1998), and then to $76 million (1999), and over that time, Dodger regular-season wins fell from ninety to eighty-eight to eighty-three to seventy-seven. The Orioles outspent everyone, including the Yankees, in 1998; and for their $77 million in salaries that year, they reaped just seventy-nine wins—thirty-five fewer than the Yankees racked up for their $73 million payout. Similar examples could be multiplied endlessly. Perhaps the *only* absolute that emerged from the seasons studied by the blue ribbon panel was that the team with the highest payroll expense *never* won the greatest number of games in any given year.

Casting a wider net, of the twenty-eight teams (four each year) qualifying for the National League play-offs between 1995 and 2001, only six came from large-market cities; in the American League, they numbered twelve (five, excluding the Yankees). It would not take an ardent Yankee fan to notice that the dread specter of large-market dominance summoned up by the panel essentially boiled down to the success of the Yankees alone. That was hardly a novel theme in the history of baseball, or one requiring especially urgent action *right now*. Instead, it was one that also smacked of a bad case of 20–20 hindsight, never the best of guides to the predictably unpredictable future.

Yankee success in recent years was hardly predestined. The team's championship record rather confounded the expectations of some of the most perceptive observers of the sport. In the fall of 1995, Frank Deford wrote off the Yankees as "Steinbrenner's Whim," an "irrelevance in pinstripes," which "have descended into a jejune mediocrity."[27] Two springs later, as the Yanks were poised to run off three consecutive World Series titles, Keith Olbermann, the epitome of the hip, omniscient sportscaster, labeled the Yankee owner "shortsighted Steinbrenner," who was "sacrificing the future for a dubious present" through a series of questionable trades.[28] Perhaps the Yankees juggernaut had not been as inexorable as the blue ribbon panel's rear-window perspective made it out to be.

If there was anything that *did* threaten the future viability of the sport, it was the prospect of yet another player strike, with the collective bargaining agreement reached in 1995 set to expire in 2001. Baseball had dodged that bullet before, most notably by staging a surprisingly quick recovery from the 1994–95 shutdown, but another work stoppage surely would put baseball's remarkably enduring hold on the sporting nation's heartstrings to its most severe test yet. Yet the panel's recommendations were certain to do just that. The effect of its key proposals—notably a substantial increase in the sharing and redistribution of local revenues and an expanded "competitive balance tax" on the highest payrolls, expressly designed to "constrain" them—would be to cap player salaries.[29] This was anathema to the players' union, and such an ownership bargaining posture was certain to provoke another work stoppage. That this would be an especially risky course of conduct was only underscored by the erosion in baseball's popularity in recent years, with less than half of adults expressing interest in the sport in the summer of 2002 as yet another strike loomed.[30]

As bargaining between owners and players proceeded fitfully over the summer of 2002, the sport appeared headed toward another disastrous midseason shutdown. Only at the last minute was an ominously inevitable strike averted by an agreement that merely tweaked the existing business structure of a sport that the commissioner and his advisers had portrayed as requiring fundamental change in order to survive.[31] Owners and players agreed on formulas for increased sharing of local revenues as well as taxes on the highest payrolls, which would transfer some additional monies to weaker clubs. The amounts involved, however, fell well short of bridging the gap between baseball's rich and poor. They did not fill the prescriptions offered by Commissioner Selig or the blue ribbon panel for the sport's allegedly ruinous competitive and economic ills.

The new labor agreement certainly did not deter the Yankees from their free-spending ways as the 2003 season approached, even while signs of pay restraint by other teams inspired player-union suspicions of collusion.[32] Evidently unconcerned about the prospect of luxury-tax transfer payments, the Yankees bid aggressively in the off-season free-agent market, sending their total payroll toward the $170 million mark. Japanese power hitter Hideki Matsui was signed to a three-year contract for $21 million, and the Yanks won a particularly bitter bidding war with—who else?—the Boston Red Sox for the services of defecting Cuban pitcher José Contreras. Although Boston General Manager Theo Epstein heatedly denied a New York newspaper report that he had angrily broken a window and door after the Sox were rebuffed in favor of New York's four-year, $32 million offer, the Boston team president's charge—"the evil empire extends its tentacles into Latin America"—left no doubt about the hard feelings involved. In Boston, the Yanks were seen as winning through brute financial force; the New York press played up the intangible pinstripe mystique as the key to Contreras's decision, quoting the pitcher as saying, "For me it's an honor to play for the Yankees."[33]

By presenting a program of reforms that, if insisted upon, would have triggered a work stoppage, perhaps the panel had taken its eye off the ball that really mattered. Yankee haters, as well as Yankee lovers, might well pause to consider how closely a precipitous initiative to "break up the Yankees" had come to breaking up baseball itself—during a season that, after all, ended with the Yankees and their $175 million payroll being soundly thrashed by the Angels, whose players were paid $100 million less.[34] Yankee success or failure could hardly be attributed solely to George Steinbrenner's open-handed pay practices. Satirists might write, "Yankees ensure 2003 pennant by signing every player in baseball,"[35] but the Yankees' owner necessarily took a more practical tack. Unhappy with the team's 2002 play-off defeat, Steinbrenner combined key free-agent signings with his characteristic attention to team motivation. He leveled pointed criticism at his top talent, challenging All-Star shortstop Derek Jeter ("How much better would he be if he didn't have all his other activities?") and manager Joe Torre and his coaches ("I want his whole staff to understand that they have got to do better this year") to perform at a higher level in the upcoming season. Claiming affinity with General George Patton, Steinbrenner brushed off criticism of his aggressive off-season moves. "What is wrong with winning?" he rhetorically asked at a midwinter news conference. "I don't think anything's wrong with winning. I don't like people who don't understand that."[36]

Whatever the future held for the Yankees as a competitive force, Bud Selig's case for the impending collapse of the economics of the sport had hardly been reinforced by the announcement, two weeks after the commissioner's December 2001 congressional appearance, of the sale of one of the money-losing franchises he had cited—the Boston Red Sox. The sale price (including the assumption of $40 million in liabilities) was a record $700 million, and it was consummated amid complaints by an unsuccessful bidder that the sale procedure had unfairly prevented him from making an even higher offer![37] The sale included a sports television network, but the valuation placed on the Red Sox was $410 million, well in excess of the previous top team-sale prices—$323 million for the Cleveland Indians and $311 million for the Los Angeles Dodgers.[38] True, the Bosox are one of the sport's premier franchises, but the placing of such an enormous bet that was, after all, entirely dependent on the continued viability of the major-league baseball enterprise as a whole, hardly buttressed Selig's cries of woe. And it was certainly intriguing, in terms of the credibility of such prophecies of doom, that the new ownership group included former Senator George Mitchell, one of the co-authors of the *Blue Ribbon Report*, which had starkly concluded that the sport's "economic structure [is] untenable in the long run."[39] It was tempting to consider reversing a time-tested challenge and ask whether newly hatched magnate Mitchell would now put his mouth where his money was.

In the end, a look back at baseball history could help provide some perspective about claims that the sport had entered into a new and unprecedented era in which the old rules no longer applied. There is something of a steady rhythm in the life of the business and sport of baseball. This should not surprise when we look at the wider world and see that the "new economy" had not repealed the business cycle and that the Dow was not irreversibly headed up toward 10,000 after all. Were today's ballplayers a bunch of money-grubbing mercenaries, pursuing personal financial bottom lines and lacking in the rugged competitive zeal of their predecessors? Maybe so, but almost half a century ago, Dodger star Duke Snider proclaimed, "I Play Baseball for Money—Not Fun," and Gay Talese described a flock of "Gray-Flannel-Suit Men at Bat," who "subscribe to the *Wall Street Journal* and would not think of tripping their mothers, even if Mom were rounding third on her way home with the winning run."[40] Not that players needed to be shorn of any Olympian stature even then for readers with good memories. In 1915, the *Sporting News* surveyed the aftermath of the Federal League baseball war under the headline, "Outlook Rosy for Prosperity in Game—Fans, However, Will Never Take Same Viewpoint—They Know the Player Is No Hero Now and Never Again Will He Be Placed on a Pedestal."[41]

That games were too long was a common complaint at the turn of the millennium. A relatively low-scoring 4–2 affair in the 2000 World Series required 3½ hours in playing time—*more than one hour longer* than the epic finale of the 1960 World Series, which had been won by the Pirates 10–9 and involved nine pitchers, virtually every roster player, and an interruption for an injury when Yankee shortstop was felled by a bad hop on a ground ball. Even the most nostalgia-crazed

New Yorker found that a subway series in 2000 led to bleary-eyed fatigue that had not attended the daytime schedule of the subway series of yore. But as long ago as the 1950s, commentators were complaining that "gaps in action annoy fans," bemoaning what seemed to be the excessively slow pace of play[42]—and perhaps they had a point: 2½-hour games must have dragged to fans weaned on the two-hour, and even hour-and-a-half, games that were common a generation earlier. In any event, a major-league baseball venture with Real Networks, Inc., announced on the eve of the 2002 season, to provide eighty-five-pitch, twenty-minute condensed online replays of complete games—thereby "adapting the deliberate pace of the national pastime to the short attention spans of the Internet"—was hardly a promising solution.[43]

Were the time-hallowed rituals of a day at the ballpark being swept aside amid the insistent contemporaneity of nonstop, ear-deafening rock music? Any older fan would easily agree with that, and the press was reporting that one of those rituals, keeping score, had become a "dying art."[44] But, if true, this was hardly news: In 1950, the *Sporting News*, keeper of the flame, found that "few fans actually keep score," and that only eight out of 100 fans then knew the rudiments of what was a far-from-thriving "art" even then.[45] The ultimate, though doubtlessly unwanted, effect of such elegies is to summon up thoughts of the rather similar lamentations that portentously discover *the* end of American "innocence" in—take your pick—the quiz-show scandals of the 1950s, the assassination of JFK, the turmoil of 1968, the aftermath of World War I, as well as the years that preceded that conflict—or who knows what else and how long ago.[46]

YESTERDAY, today, and tomorrow, major-league baseball has been, is, and likely will be what it had always been—the sporting world's last frontier of unbridled individualism on the field and off, a relic perhaps of a distant time, removed from the orchestrated machinations of professional football and basketball with their owners marching in lockstep to a master plan of marketers and broadcasters. The blue ribbon panel wanted baseball to become more like those other sports,[47] but there was much to be said for baseball's traditional ways, for the scope it gave to innovation and initiative by individual franchises' unwillingness to submit to the leveling-down process implicit in the quest for competitive balance—a quest that, as the National Football League was finding out, could easily lead to cooperative mediocrity. There was something appealing—and, yes, quintessentially *American*—about baseball's entrepreneurial freebooters, whether Charlie Finley, Ted Turner, or even George Steinbrenner, marching to the beat of their own inner drums and beholden to no one, or to the constraints of the past, ready to make five out of two plus two and change the face of the game, on and off the field.

Baseball has always demanded a massive commitment of civic energies, its ticket-buying base for an eighty-one-game home schedule necessarily reaching beyond the hard-core season-ticket purchasers who made up the cash customers for hockey, basketball, and football with their shorter schedules (and, in the case of hockey and basketball, far smaller arenas). But to mobilize these energies, baseball required a concomitant entrepreneurial spirit that could only be generated by those with the incentive and will to make a splash in the baseball arena. The Jacobs brothers in Cleveland, Bob Lurie in San Francisco, the Haas family in Oakland—all had stepped in and saved franchises headed for extinction. Along with such predecessors as Jacob Ruppert, Branch Rickey, and Walter O'Malley, they stepped up to the plate and swung away against the status quo. One doubts that they would have made the commitments in cash and energy required to build winning teams, according to their own lights, if their efforts to break free from the pack had been constrained by a "ministry of competition" run out of the commissioner's office, which subjected them to a "Mother, may I?" regulatory scheme, all to be administered "in the best interests of baseball"—a positively Orwellian phrase indeed.

Baseball can never expect to regain the once-dominating place it had held before the 1950s in the nation's sporting life. The fragmentation of interests and the proliferation of sporting (not to mention the full range of entertainment) attractions has ensured that. Television ratings for the World Series are generally only about one-third those for the Super Bowl, which has become the nation's preeminent sports event. Game 7 of the exciting 2001 World Series could muster no more than a rating of 27, about two-thirds that for a typical recent Super Bowl. The television ratings for the 2002 matchup between the Giants and the Angels were the lowest ever, with hitting great Barry Bonds unable to deliver the same kind of audience as baseball's perennial marquee attraction, the Yankees.[48] Even figure skating, which was hardly on the national radar screen until recent years, and indeed was not really a "sport" to many, could, on occasion, such as during the 2002 Winter Olympics, attract a television audience equal to that of the deciding game of a great World Series.[49]

The 2002 All-Star Game was labeled a "prime-time dud," garnering the lowest television rating since the game was switched to the evening in 1967; it was viewed by 10 million households, half the number watching twenty years earlier.[50] But perhaps fewer was better in that instance, given the debacle that resulted when a thrilling 7–7 game was declared a tie after the eleventh inning because the managers had run out of fresh pitchers. It was an especially untimely slap in the face to the fans in the stands and at home, who were doing their utmost to stick by their sport amid distressing reports of an impending player strike and widespread steroid use (which, much like the simultaneous uproar over fast-and-loose corporate accounting practices, potentially tainted the splurge in home-run hitting that had paralleled that now-suspect stock market boom).

Any fan could draw up his own list of complaints about a sport that often seemed intent on squandering its unique traditions and strengths. The designated hitter remained an abomination; the dismantling of the World Champion Florida Marlins had been shameful; contraction, even if objectively justifiable, was an inappropriate mechanism for bailing out a Minnesota team owner dissatisfied with the market price of his franchise; interleague play (which was hardly the economic panacea it was claimed to be) had obliterated one of baseball's distinctive traditions; and why couldn't World Series games be played in the daytime, at least on weekends, as God had surely intended? Above all, there was too much readiness on both sides of the labor–management divide to risk another strike, which would ratchet up baseball fans' disgust with the degree to which their noses were inescapably, and unpleasantly, rubbed into the business side of the game.

Yet through it all, baseball has tenaciously held on to a special standing in the American popular imagination, sometimes to the detriment of the perceived interests of its powers-that-be. Team owners had parlayed the sport's status into support for their position in legal battles in years past—witness Supreme Court Justice Harry Blackmun's tribute to the lore and legacy of the game in his opinion in the Curt Flood case, a case in which the trial judge too was very mindful of the fact that "baseball has been the national pastime for over one hundred years and enjoys a unique place in our American heritage."[51] It was perhaps only fair that such sentiments were now being mobilized to thwart organized baseball's own narrowly focused business decisions, such as the contraction plan announced in December 2001 to eliminate struggling franchises in Minnesota and Montreal. Indeed, a Minnesota court would enjoin baseball's unilateral abandonment of its Minnesota franchise, announced by Commissioner Selig in December 2001, on the grounds that Twins fans "would suffer irreparable harm if the Twins failed to play their 2002 home games at the Metrodome," in light of the "role of baseball as a tradition and as a national pastime, the history of the Twins in Minnesota for some 40 years, including two World Series championships, the role of Twins legends who have bettered the community by their volunteer work with children, and the availability of Twins games as affordable family entertainment," such that a "vital public trust" was involved, which "outweighs any private interest."[52]

Most important is the continuing vitality of the game—and of the sport. Down on the field, the essence of the game remained fair in a fundamentally changeless way. Free of the remorseless tyranny of a clock, no one ever caught its essence better than Oriole manager Earl Weaver, reflecting on his team's stunning defeat by the Mets in 1969: "You can't sit on a lead and run a few plays into the line and just kill the clock. You've got to throw the ball over the goddam plate and give the other man his chance. That's why baseball is the greatest game of all."[53] Baseball retained its unique place within the sports calendar, the one game that moved in harmony with the natural rhythm of the seasons, with its own "shoures sote" in the spring, passing, with games being played day after day for no less than half the year, through the height of summer, and climaxing in the fall, as the solar year itself was winding down.

Nor does any other sport so assiduously cultivate its history and make it a part of the continuing life of the game. "Baseball fans have an abiding interest in the history of the game," a California judge recently wrote, rejecting, on First Amendment grounds, an effort by a number of retired players to prevent major-league baseball from using their names and likenesses on websites, documentaries, and game programs. "The public has an enduring fascination in the records set by former players and in memorable moments from previous games. . . .

The records and statistics remain of interest to the public because they provide context that allows fans to better appreciate (or deprecate) today's performances. Thus, the history of professional baseball is integral to the full understanding and enjoyment of the current game and its players."[54] Controversies simmer on for decades—and can even be born anew well after the fact, as witness the flap, fifty years later, over whether Bobby Thomson stole the sign on the pitch he hit for the "shot heard round the world" in 1951.[55] Uplifting legends are celebrated, whatever their truth, as with the plan to erect a statue in Brooklyn commemorating white Southerner Pee Wee Reese's supportive embrace of Dodger teammate Jackie Robinson in response to racist taunting during Robinson's color-line-breaking debut season, although there is no contemporary account of the incident and the evidence that it happened is contradictory at best.[56] Debate goes on—and on and on, at least to the uninitiated—over such chestnuts as Babe Ruth's "called" home-run shot in the 1932 World Series, Fred Merkle's failure to touch second base in a crucial game in *1908*, and Shoeless Joe Jackson's expulsion from baseball and exclusion from the Hall of Fame. And, "somewhere in this favored land," you can still find twelve-year-olds who will exclaim, "Willie Mays!" if you make a basket catch while tossing the ball around the backyard.

Indeed, the history of the sport is so rich, and so compelling to the adult imagination, that it can provide reference points for life moments that have much darker markers for those fated to grow up in less fortunate countries—perhaps serving, for good or ill, as a narcotic against the ravages of the broader history of the last century. An American sportswriter has remembered how, as a college freshman, "My childhood ended on October 3, 1951," as he listened to a radio broadcast of Bobby Thomson's pennant-winning home run against the Dodgers.[57] The recent memoir of a French historian recounts, in similar language, that same rite of passage, but the context could not have been more different—that of a fifteen-year-old schoolgirl sitting in a Paris park on July 16, 1942, after witnessing the Vel d'Hiver roundup of Jews in her neighborhood: "It was on that bench that I left my childhood."[58]

Four decades ago, a veteran Boston sportswriter, Harold Kaese, responded to the sale of the Yankees to CBS by writing, "If ever a paradox were true, it is that big league baseball is strictly a business to those who make money off those who think it is strictly a sport."[59] Although the sport and business are still, as they have always been, inextricably linked, the greatest challenge facing baseball is to preserve some degree of separation between the two. It is, after all, the sport, not the business, that is the only reason for the existence of the institution of major-league baseball in the first place, the only reason there is any money to be made from it at all, by player and owner alike. The paradox endures.

APPENDIX

Prologue

TABLE 0.1. AMERICAN LEAGUE "AVERAGE"
SEASON STANDINGS, 1920–1960

Team	Wins	Losses
Yankees	94	60
Indians	82	72
Tigers	79	75
Red Sox	74	80
Senators	73	81
White Sox	72	82
A's	69	85
Browns / Orioles	62	92

Part One

TABLE 1.1. SUNDAY HOME DATES FOR NEW YORK TEAMS, 1920–1924

	Giants	Dodgers	Yankees
1920	13	19	12
1921	12	18	13
1922	13	18	12
1923	12	19	13
1924	13	17	11

Part Two

TABLE 2.1. 1921 NATIONAL LEAGUE SOURCES OF
REGULAR PLAYERS (BY TEAM)

Team	From Minors	From Majors	Reclaimed from Minors
Brooklyn	4	6	3
Boston	3	8	2
Chicago	4	8	2
Cincinnati	1	8	3
Pittsburgh	9	6	1
New York	5	9	0
St. Louis	4	8	3
Philadelphia	5	10	1
TOTALS	35	63	15
First Division	21	31	6
Second Division	14	32	9

TABLE 2.2. 1921 RECORDS OF "RECLAIMED" PLAYERS

Team	Batters	Pitchers
Boston	Powell .306	Fillingham 15–10, 3.45
Brooklyn	Schmandt .306	Smith 7–11, 3.90
Chicago	Maisel .310	York 5–9, 4.73
Cincinnati	Duncan .308 Bohne .285	Luque 17–19, 3.38
Philadelphia	Meusel .353	———
Pittsburgh		Adams 14–5, 2.64
St. Louis	Fournier .343 Clemons .320	Doak 15–6, 2.59 Pertica 14–10, 3.37
New York	———	———

TABLE 2.3. 1926 RECORDS OF "RECLAIMED" PLAYERS

Team	Batters	Pitchers
Boston	Burrus .270	———
Brooklyn	Jacobson .247	Petty 17–17, 2.84 McWeeny 11–13, 3.04 McGraw 9–13, 4.59 Vance 9–10, 3.89
Chicago	———	Root 18–17, 2.82 Blake 11–12, 3.60
Cincinnati	Hargrave .353	Luque 13–16, 3.43 J. May 13–9, 3.22 Lucas 8–5, 3.68
Philadelphia	Huber .245	Knight 3–12, 6.62
New York	———	———
Pittsburgh	———	———
St. Louis	———	———

TABLE 2.4. 1926 NATIONAL LEAGUE SOURCES OF
REGULAR PLAYERS (BY TEAM)

Team	From Minors	From Majors	Reclaimed from Minors
Brooklyn	5	5	5
Boston	9	8	0
Chicago	6	6	2
Cincinnati	5	5	4
Pittsburgh	10	5	0
New York	11	5	0
St. Louis	10	4	1
Philadelphia	6	9	2
TOTALS	62	47	14
First Division	31	19	7
Second Division	31	27	7

TABLE 2.5. ST. LOUIS ATTENDANCE, 1910–1945° (IN THOUSANDS)

Year	Cardinals	Browns	Totals
1910	**355**	249	604
1911	**447**	207	654
1912	**241**	214	455
1913	203	**250**	453
1914	**256**	244	500
1915	**252**	150	402
1916	224	**335**	559
1917	**288**	210	498
1918	110	**122**	332
1919	167	**349**	516
1920	326	**419**	745
1921	**384**	355	739
1922	536	**712**	1,248
1923	338	**430**	768
1924	272	**533**	805
1925	404	**462**	866
1926	**668**	283	951
1927	**749**	247	996
1928	**761**	339	1,100
1929	**399**	280	679
1930	**508**	152	660
1931	**608**	179	787
1932	**279**	112	391
1933	**256**	88	344
1934	**325**	115	440
1935	**506**	80	586
1936	**448**	93	541
1937	**430**	123	553
1938	**291**	130	421
1939	**400**	109	509
1940	**324**	239	563
1941	**633**	176	809

Year	Cardinals	Browns	Totals
1942	**553**	256	809
1943	**517**	214	731
1944	461	**508**	969
1945	**594**	482	1,076

°Attendance leader for year in bold type.

Part Three

TABLE 3.1. DODGERS AND GIANTS ATTENDANCE, 1946–1956 (IN THOUSANDS)

Year	Brooklyn	New York
1946	1796	1234
1947	1807	1599
1948	1398	1459
1949	1633	1218
1950	1185	1009
1951	1282	1059
1952	1088	984
1953	1163	811
1954	1020	1155
1955	1033	824
1956	1213	629

TABLE 3.2. DODGERS–BRAVES ATTENDANCE, 1952–1956°

Team	1952	1953	1954	1955	1956
Dodgers	1,088,704	1,163,419	1,020,531	1,033,589	1,213,562
Braves	281,278	1,826,397	2,131,388	2,005,836	2,046,331

°Braves in Boston in 1952, in Milwaukee in 1953–56.

TABLE 3.3. DODGERS–BRAVES FINANCES COMPARED, 1952–1956°

	1952		1953		1954		1955		1956	
	BKN	**BOS**	**BKN**	**MIL**	**BKN**	**MIL**	**BKN**	**MIL**	**BKN**	**MIL**
Home Game	1,398	312	1,524	2,218	1,464	2,476	1,549	2,556	1,790	2,603
Road Game	309	150	331	215	444	280	444	251	430	342
TV–Radio	580	316	539	141	609	136	787	135	888	125
Concession	215	43	245	425	240	548	245	510	284	542
Other	87	111	106	73	57	68	106	106	150	84
World Series°°	243	—	261	—	—	—	368	—	334	—
Total Income	**2,833**	933	**3,009**	3,074	2,816	3,510	**3,501**	3,560	3,880	3,697
Expenses	1,859	1,174	2,232	2,339	2,040	2,326	2,216	2,384	2,384	2,506
Net Pretax Income	974	(241)	777	734	776	1,183	1,284	1,176	1,496	1,190
Farm Income (Loss)	(301)	(217)	(420)	(57)	(321)	(223)	(459)	179)	376)	(207)
Net Pretax Income	673	(459)	356	734	455	959	824	997	1,120	983
After-Tax Income	446	(459)	290	637	209	457	427	409	487	362

°Numbers in 000s of dollars.
°°World Series income, including club's share of receipts and estimated concession income. Based on *Baseball Hearings: 1957*, pp. 354–56, 2046–47; *Sporting News Baseball Guide* (1953–1957 editions).

TABLE 3.4. MAJOR LEAGUE BALLPARKS IN 1952°

City	Park	Year Built	Capacity	Gross $ at Capacity
Boston	Fenway Park (AL)	1912	34,831	54,122
	Braves Field (NL)	1915	37,746	53,481
Brooklyn	Ebbets Field (NL)	1913	31,902	54,069
Chicago	Comiskey Park (AL)	1910	48,556	70,112
	Wrigley Field (NL)	1914	38,710	62,678
Cincinnati	Crosley Field (NL)	1912	29,939	47,657
Cleveland	Municipal Stadium (AL)	1932	73,811	116,023
Detroit	Briggs Stadium (AL)	1912	54,151	80,988
New York	Yankee Stadium (AL)	1922	67,163	113,285
	Polo Grounds (NL)	1911	53,131	80,046
Philadelphia	Shibe Park (AL & NL)	1909	33,222	54,842
Pittsburgh	Forbes Field (NL)	1909	33,730	61,513
St. Louis	Sportsman's Park (AL & NL)	1902	30,808	53,801
Washington	Griffith Stadium (AL)	1911	29,920	38,903

°Compiled from *Sporting News*, April 16, 1952.

TABLE 3.5. NATIONAL LEAGUE TEAM INCOME
FROM ALL SOURCES (IN THOUSANDS)

Team	1950	1953–1955
Brooklyn	$2612	$3100 ($2898)°
New York	2012	2768 (2711)°°
Cincinnati	1122	1388
Chicago	1964	1621
Philadelphia	2035	1703
Pittsburgh	2167	1295
St. Louis	2076	1994
Bos/Mil.	1705 (Boston)	3381 (Milwaukee)

°1953–1955 average (computed in parentheses without 1953 and 1955 World Series, including concession, income).
°°1953–1955 average (computed in parentheses without 1954 World Series income).

TABLE 3.6. TRENDS IN TEAM INCOME: BROOKLYN AND NEW YORK

Sources of Income as Percentages of
Total Regular Season Operating Income (Excluding World Series)

New York Giants	1946	1950	1952	1953	1954	1955	1956
Total Income ($000s)	1703	1753	2135	1974	2605	2477	2235
Home Receipts %	68	59	59	55	58	51	45
Road Receipts %	13	14	10	12	13	13	13
Broadcast %	5	14	18	21	19	26	33

Brooklyn Dodgers	1946	1950	1952	1953	1954	1955	1956
Total Income ($000s)	2483	2331	2503	2642	2759	3027	3396
Home Receipts %	72	59	56	58	53	51	53
Road Receipts %	14	16	12	13	16	15	13
Broadcast %	6	14	23	20	22	26	26

National League (6 other teams)	1946	1950	1952	1953	1954	1955	1956
Total Income ($000s)	7932	10160	7620	9723	11015	11452	13495
Home Receipts %	66	65	64	66	65	65	65
Road Receipts %	15	13	12	10	16	12	12
Broadcast %	3	10	13	9	10	10	10

TABLE 3.7. PERCENTAGE OF GIANTS
ATTENDANCE FROM DODGER DATES

1941	1947	1948	1951	1954	1955	1956
39	25	25	33	34	41	37

Part Four

TABLE 4.1. YANKEES AND METS—WINS AND ATTENDANCE, 1962–2002
(Year's Leader in Bold)

Year	Yankees Wins	Mets Wins	Yankees Attendance°	Mets Attendance°
1962	**96**	40	**1,493**	922
1963	**104**	51	**1,308**	1,080
1964	**99**	53	1,305	**1,732**
1965	**77**	50	1,213	**1,768**
1966	**70**	66	1,214	**1,932**
1967	**72**	61	1,259	**1,565**
1968	**83**	73	1,185	**1,781**
1969	80	**100**	1,067	**2,175**
1970	**93**	83	1,136	**2,697**
1971	82	**83**	1,070	**2,266**
1972	79	**83**	966	**2,134**
1973	80	**82**	1,262	**1,912**
1974	**89**	71	1,273	**1,722**
1975	**83**	82	1,288	**1,730**
1976	**97**	86	**2,012**	1,468
1977	**100**	64	**2,103**	1,066
1978	**100**	66	**2,335**	1,007
1979	**89**	63	**2,537**	788
1980	**103**	67	**2,627**	1,192
1981	**59**	41	**1,614**	704
1982	**79**	65	**2,041**	1,323
1983	**91**	68	**2,257**	1,112
1984	87	**90**	1,821	**1,842**
1985	97	**98**	2,214	**2,761**
1986	90	**108**	2,268	**2,767**
1987	89	**92**	2,427	**3,034**
1988	85	**100**	2,633	**3,055**
1989	74	**87**	2,170	**2,918**
1990	67	**91**	2,006	**2,732**

Year	Yankees Wins	Mets Wins	Yankees Attendance	Mets Attendance
1991	71	**77**	1,863	**2,284**
1992	**76**	72	1,748	**1,779**
1993	**88**	59	**2,416**	1,873
1994	**70**	55	**1,675**	1,151
1995	**79**	69	**1,705**	1,273
1996	**92**	71	**2,250**	1,588
1997	**96**	88	**2,580**	1,766
1998	**114**	88	**2,949**	2,287
1999	**98**	97	**3,292**	2,725
2000	87	**94**	**3,227**	2,800
2001	**95**	82	**3,264**	2,658
2002	**103**	75	**3,461**	2,804

°Attendance in thousands.

Epilogue

TABLE 5.1. PAYROLL/WIN RANK ORDERS, 1950 AND 1999

1950			1999		
Team	**Payroll**	**Wins**	**Team**	**Payroll**	**Wins**
NY AL	1	1	NY AL	1	3
Boston AL	2	3	Texas	2	8
Detroit	3	2	Atlanta	3	1
Cleveland	4	4	Baltimore	4	14
St. Louis NL	5	9	Los Angeles	5	16
Boston NL	6	8	Boston	6	9
Philadelphia NL	7	5	Cleveland	7	4
NY NL	8	7	NY NL	8	6
Brooklyn	9	6	Arizona	9	2
Chicago NL	10	12	Houston	10	4
Philadelphia AL	11	16	Colorado	11	22
Pittsburgh	12	15	Chicago NL	12	27
Chicago AL	13	14	Anaheim	13	23
Cincinnati	14	11	Toronto	14	12
Washington	15	11	Seattle	15	13
St. Louis AL	16	10	San Diego	16	20
			St. Louis	17	18
			San Francisco	18	11
			Milwaukee	19	20
			Cincinnati	20	6
			Tampa Bay	21	24
			Detroit	22	24
			Philadelphia	23	16
			Oakland	24	10
			Chicago AL	25	18
			Pittsburgh	26	14
			Montreal	27	26
			Kansas City	28	28
			Florida	29	28
			Minnesota	30	30

Spearman Rank–Correlation Coefficient: 1950: .80206 (p = .0002)
1999: .66021 (p < .0001)

NOTES

PROLOGUE

1. *Sporting Life,* March 29, 1902.
2. *Sporting Life,* June 16, 1900.
3. American League President Ban Johnson, quoted in *Sporting Life,* December 20, 1902.
4. *Sporting Life,* April 12, 1902.
5. Foreword by Warren Giles, in Lee Allen, *The National League Story* (New York: Hill & Wang, 1961), p. vii.
6. See *Sporting Life,* December 20, 1902; *Sporting News,* December 13, 20, 1902, and January 10, 17, 1903. For the terms of the Cincinnati Peace Compact, see *Sporting Life,* January 17, 1903, and U.S. House of Representatives, *Hearings before the Subcommittee on the Study of Monopoly Power of the Committee of the Judiciary, Part 6: Organized Baseball,* 82d Cong., 1st sess., 1952, 519–21.
7. *Sporting Life,* December 20, 1902.
8. From 1903 through 1919, the Yankees' cumulative winning percentage was .484, better only than perennial also-rans Washington and St. Louis. *New York Times,* April 11, 1920.
9. Jonathan Hughes, *The Vital Few: The Entrepreneur and American Economic Progress* (New York: Oxford University Press, expanded ed., 1980), p. 3.

CHAPTER 1: THE RISE OF THE YANKEES

1. The attendance record didn't last long; it was eclipsed by the crowd of 62,430 two days later, which was in turn surpassed by the 62,817 on hand when the World Series returned to Yankee Stadium for the fifth game.
2. Damon Runyon in the *New York American,* October 11, 1923.
3. *New York Times,* October 11, 1923.
4. *New York Tribune,* October 11, 1923.
5. Charles Alexander, *Our Game: An American Baseball History* (New York: Henry Holt and Company, 1991), p. 191.

6. U.S. House of Representatives, *Report of the Subcommittee on the Study of Monopoly Power of the Committee of the Judiciary: Organized Baseball* (82d Cong., 2d sess., 1952, 111. This report will be cited hereafter as *Organized Baseball Report*.

7. *Organized Baseball Report*, p. 40.

8. *Organized Baseball Report*, p. 40. Legal action proved an ineffective barrier to contract jumping. The National League Phillies secured an injunction from the Pennsylvania Supreme Court to enjoin Lajoie from violating his reserve clause and signing with the American League Athletics. In response, the Athletics transferred his contract to Cleveland. When Cleveland played in Philadelphia, Lajoie stayed away to avoid Pennsylvania process, and the courts of Ohio refused to give effect to the Pennsylvania injunction. Ibid., p. 41.

9. Estimated 1902 attendance was 2,200,457 in the American League, compared with 1,681,212 in the National League. Attendance figures in U.S. House of Representatives, *Hearings before the Subcommittee on the Study of Monopoly Power of the Committee of the Judiciary, Part 6: Organized Baseball*, 82d Cong., 1st sess., 1952, pp. 1617–18. The hearings, held in July, August, and October 1951, were chaired by Brooklyn Congressman Emanuel Celler and elicited testimony and documents that are of incomparable value for the study of baseball's business history and organization. The transcript of these hearings will be cited hereafter as *Baseball Hearings: 1951*.

10. *Organized Baseball Report*, p. 41. Attendance in St. Louis in 1902 was about double (272,000, up from 139,000) the 1901 total in Milwaukee. *Baseball Hearings: 1951*, p. 1618.

11. Blanche Sindall (Mrs. John) McGraw and Arthur Mann (ed.), *The Real McGraw* (New York: David McKay, 1953), p. 152.

12. Ibid., p. 152.

13. Frederick G. Lieb, *The Baltimore Orioles* (New York: G. P. Putnam's Sons, 1955), pp. 82–84; McGraw, *The Real McGraw*, pp. 114–15.

14. Lieb, *Baltimore Orioles*, pp. 83–88.

15. Ibid., pp. 88–89.

16. Baltimore, with a population of 508,000 in 1900, was then America's sixth largest city. The only larger cities not only would hang on to their baseball franchises but also would be represented in both major leagues after the American League established itself.

17. Black population percentages in 1900 for these three cities: Washington (31 percent), Baltimore (16 percent), and Louisville (19 percent). Of the cities remaining in the National League after downsizing, St. Louis had the largest black population percentage, a significantly lower 6 percent. U.S. Department of Commerce, *Statistical Abstract of the United States* (1920), pp. 50–53.

18. "Report of the Major League Steering Committee, August 27, 1946," in *Baseball Hearings: 1951*, pp. 474–88. Most of the report is devoted to player–owner contract issues; the section on what was termed the "Race Question" appears on pp. 487–88. Although the report was published in 1952 as part of the Celler

Committee hearings transcript, its discussion of baseball integration did not attract attention until the appearance of Jules Tygiel, *Baseball's Great Experiment: Jackie Robinson and His Legacy* (New York: Oxford University Press, 1983), pp. 82–86.

19. Whether the signing of Jackie Robinson had the impact on black attendance that is often asserted is questioned in Henry D. Fetter, "Robinson in 1947: Measuring an Uncertain Impact," in Joseph Dorinson and Joram Warmund, *Jackie Robinson: Race, Sports and the American Dream* (Armonk, N.Y.: M. E. Sharpe, Inc., 1998), pp. 183–92.

20. Lieb, *Baltimore Orioles,* pp. 109–10.

21. The model was adopted a century later by major-league soccer in the United States.

22. Peter Levine, *A. G. Spalding and the Rise of Baseball* (New York: Oxford University Press, 1985), pp. 66–70.

23. Alexander, *Our Game,* pp. 79–81; Levine, *A. G. Spalding,* pp. 66–69; *Organized Baseball Report,* pp. 40–41.

24. McGraw, *The Real McGraw,* pp. 166–67; Lieb, *Baltimore Orioles,* pp. 116–17.

25. Lieb, *Baltimore Orioles,* pp. 116–17.

26. For the text of the agreement between the two leagues, see *Baseball Hearings: 1951,* pp. 519–21; see also *New York Times,* January 11, 1903.

27. *New York Times,* March 13, 1903.

28. Michael Gershman, *Diamonds: The Evolution of the Ballpark* (Boston and New York: Houghton Mifflin, 1993), pp. 76–77.

29. *New York Times,* January 14, 1939.

30. Quoted in *New York Times,* January 14, 1939.

31. *The Sporting News Dope Book 1957* (St. Louis: Charles C. Spink & Sons, 1957), p. 120.

32. Estimate derived from financial data in McGraw, *The Real McGraw,* p. 152; 1901 attendance figures reported in *Baseball Hearings: 1951,* pp. 1617–18.

33. All financial figures can be no better than fairly rough estimates for this period. Various estimates for baseball's receipts can be derived from the financial information and estimates found in *Baseball Hearings: 1951,* pp. 1616–19, 1322–23. A 1909 analysis of "The National Game in Dollars and Cents" calculated major-league income at about $3,500,000 (but relying on attendance estimates that are almost surely overstated). *New York Times,* May 2, 1909. The one season for which a comparison can be made between contemporary estimates and paid attendance as reported by the major leagues—1910—suggests that the pre-1910 estimates (the only figures available) are high by 10 to 15 percent. See tables in *Baseball Hearings: 1951,* pp. 1617–18.

34. *New York Times,* October 2, 1903.

35. *New York Times,* October 9, 1915.

36. Baltimore had been represented in the National League from 1892 to 1899 and the American League in 1901–2; Kansas City in the National League in 1886 and the American Association in 1888–89; Indianapolis in the American

Association in 1884 and the National League in 1886; and Buffalo in the National League from 1879 to 1885, as well as the Player's League in 1890. See Exhibit 7-A, "Major Leagues and Major League Cities," in *Baseball Hearings: 1951*, pp. 153–54.

37. On the Federal League "war," see *Organized Baseball Report*, pp. 50–57.

38. *New York Times*, April 19, 1925 (Charles Ebbets obituary on Dodgers sale); *New York Times*, June 5, 1929 (Harry Frazee obituary on Red Sox sale).

39. *Sporting News*, December 30, 1915.

40. A. J. Liebling, "The Man Who Changed the Rules" and "A Look at the Record," in *The Press* (New York: Ballantine Books, 1975); W. A. Swanberg, *Citizen Hearst* (New York: Bantam Books, 1963).

41. See *New York Times*, January 26, 1900.

42. U.S. Department of Commerce, *Historical Statistics of the United States: Colonial Times to 1970* (Washington, D.C., 1975), p. 401; A. G. Spalding, *America's National Game* (New York, 1911).

43. *Historical Statistics*, p. 320.

44. On Sullivan, see Andy Logan, *Against the Evidence: The Becker–Rosenthal Affair* (New York: McCall Publishing, 1970), esp. pp. 53–62.

45. Harold Seymour, *Baseball: The Golden Age* (New York: Oxford University Press, 1971), p. 54.

46. Edwin G. Burrows and Mike Wallace, *Gotham: A History of New York City to 1898* (New York: Oxford University Press, 1999), p. 1192.

47. At the time of the purchase of the Yankees, only Ruppert held the rank—honorific as it may have been—of colonel. Huston was still a captain, based on his Spanish-American War service, and he only became a colonel when he reenlisted during World War I. Tom Meany, *The Yankee Story* (New York: E. P. Dutton, 1960), p. 15.

48. Meany, *The Yankee Story*, p. 13.

49. On Huston, see obituary in *New York Times*, March 30, 1938; on Ruppert, obituary in *New York Times*, January 14, 1939, and his entry in John Garraty and Mark C. Carnes, eds., *American National Biography*, vol. 2 (New York: Oxford University Press, 1999). On the elder Jacob Ruppert, see *The National Cyclopedia of American Biography*, vol. 29 (New York: James T. White & Co., 1941), pp. 488–89.

50. On Ebbets, see *New York Times*, April 19, 1925, and January 21, 1912. On John T. Brush and his family, see *New York Times*, November 27, 1912 (Brush obituary) and March 27, 1938 (obituary of Harry Hempstead, Brush son-in-law and successor). Ebbets had started out as Brooklyn's assistant secretary in the 1880s and Brush had parlayed ownership in an Indianapolis clothing store into ownership of the Indianapolis club that same decade.

51. On the sale price of the Yankees, see *New York Times*, January 27, 1945. At the time of Ruppert's death, his obituary estimated the value of the Yankees at $7 million, so the valuation of his estate at $100 million may have been similarly inflated, although the wartime vicissitudes of baseball may have contributed to any reduction in value from 1939.

52. *Sporting News*, January 6, 1916.

53. Testimony of August Herrmann in Record on Appeal in *Federal Baseball Club of Baltimore, Inc. v. National League of Professional Baseball Clubs, et al.*, 259 U.S. 200 (1922), p. 398.

54. *New York Times*, February 24, 1915. The pinstriped uniform had been adopted in 1912, when "the fad for the pinstripe in baseball toggery, introduced by the Cubs a few years ago, . . . reached the Hilltop." *New York Times*, February 27, 1912. It was not chosen, as legend (and the authoritative *Dictionary of American Biography*, in its entry on Ruppert) has it, with the desire to "slim down" Babe Ruth's ample profile. He would not be a Yankee, of course, until 1920.

55. In fact, the Red Sox were undefeated in World Series play. No World Series had been played in 1904, the year they won their second American League pennant.

56. *New York Times*, June 5, 1929; Don Dunn, *The Making of No, No, Nanette* (Secaucus, N.J.: Citadel Press, 1972), p. 21. On *Madame Sherry*, which opened on August 30, 1910, see Gerald Bordman, *American Musical Theater: A Chronicle* (New York: Oxford University Press, 1986), pp. 258–59.

57. *Sporting News*, January 31, 1918.

58. Frederick G. Lieb, *The Boston Red Sox* (New York: G. P. Putnam's Sons, 1947), p. 91.

59. Lieb, *Boston Red Sox*, pp. 116, 154.

60. As reported in Lieb, *Boston Red Sox*, p. 155.

61. *New York Times*, November 2, 1916; February 10, 11, 1920; June 5, 1929. See the admirably balanced effort to account for Frazee's tenure in Glenn Stout and Richard Jackson, *Red Sox Century* (Boston: Houghton Mifflin, 2000), p. 117, but it breaks down the sale price as being half in cash, half in notes.

62. *New York Times*, February 10, 1920.

63. For the economics of the New York theater in the first decades of the twentieth century, see Jack Poggi, *Theater in America: The Impact of Economic Forces* (Ithaca, N.Y.: Cornell University Press, 1968), pp. 46–77, on which the calculations in this paragraph are based.

64. *Baseball Hearings: 1951*, p. 1620.

65. *Sporting News*, January 17, 1918.

66. *The Sporting News Dope Book 1957*, p. 116.

67. *New York Times*, April 20, 1920.

68. Eugene C. Murdock, *Ban Johnson: Czar of Baseball* (Westport, Conn.: Greenwood Press, 1982), p. 166.

69. Murdock, *Ban Johnson*, p. 166; Seymour, *Baseball: The Golden Age*, pp. 249–52.

70. Murdock, *Ban Johnson*, p. 167; J. G. Taylor Spink, *Judge Landis and Twenty-Five Years of Baseball* (New York: Thomas Y. Crowell, 1947) pp. 49–50; *American League Baseball Club of New York v. Johnson*, 109 N.Y. Misc. 138 (Supreme Court, October 1919).

71. *Baseball Hearings: 1951*, p 1618.

72. *Sporting News*, December 20, 1917.

73. *New York Times,* February 11, 1920.

74. For the terms of the settlement, see Record on Appeal in *Federal League Baseball Club of Baltimore, etc.,* at pp. 564–67.

75. For the verdict and judgment in the trial court, see *New York Times,* April 14, 1919, and *Organized Baseball Report,* pp. 56–57.

76. *New York Times,* February 10, 11, 1920; Stout and Jackson, *Red Sox Century,* p. 149.

77. Ruth's twenty-nine home runs in 1919 had broken Gavvy Cravath's mark of twenty-four, set in 1915. The next season, Cravath had hit only eleven home runs. Cravath had been second to Ruth in 1919, with twelve home runs.

78. *Sporting News,* December 5, 1919.

79. *New York Times,* April 14, 1919.

80. On the turmoil in "organized baseball" at the time, see Spink, *Judge Landis,* pp. 41–56; Seymour, *Baseball: The Golden Age,* pp. 259–74; *Organized Baseball Report,* pp. 58–59.

81. Robert W. Creamer, *Babe: The Legend Comes to Life* (New York: Simon and Schuster, 1974) pp. 207–9.

82. Creamer, *Babe,* p. 207.

83. Simon Rottenberg, "The Baseball Players' Labor Market," *Journal of Political Economy,* 64 (June 1956), p. 256.

84. Ethan Mordden, *Make Believe: The Broadway Musical in the 1920s* (New York: Oxford University Press, 1997), p. 75.

85. *New York Times,* April 11, 1920.

86. Stout and Jackson, *Red Sox Century,* pp. 146–47.

87. Peter Golenbock, *Fenway: The Players and the Fans Remember* (New York: G. P. Putnam's Sons, 1992), p. 64; see also Dan Shaughnessy, *The Curse of the Bambino* (New York: E. P. Dutton, 1990).

88. It is notable by its absence from the classic inquest into the team's travails: Al Hirshberg, *What's the Matter with the Red Sox?* (New York: Dodd, Mead, 1973).

89. On Barrow, see entry in *American National Biography,* op. cit., pp. 244–46 (by Lee Lowenfish); Meany, *The Yankee Story,* pp. 53–68.

90. Huston ceded full ownership of the team to Ruppert after the 1922 season, leaving with a golden parachute estimated at $1.2 million as the return on his initial $240,000 investment ten years earlier.

91. *New York Times,* January 14, 1939.

92. Alfred D. Chandler, Jr., *The Visible Hand: The Managerial Revolution in American Business* (Cambridge: Belknap Press of Harvard University Press, 1977), pp. 6–8.

CHAPTER 2: THE FALL OF THE GIANTS

1. *New York Tribune,* January 15, 1919.

2. Frank Graham, *The New York Giants* (New York: G. P. Putnam's Sons, 1952), pp. 8–9.

3. Harry Golden, *For Two Cents Plain* (Cleveland: The World Publishing Company, 1959), p. 228.

4. See, for example, Mac Davis, *Lore and Legends of Baseball* (New York: Lantern Press, 1963), pp. 32–33; Geoffrey C. Ward and Ken Burns, *Baseball: An Illustrated History* (New York: Alfred A. Knopf, 1994), p. 96; and most recently, the catalogue of the Baseball Hall of Fame's traveling exhibit of memorabilia: John Odell, ed., *Baseball in America* (Washington, D.C.: *National Geographic*, 2002), pp. 131–32. For various versions of Norworth's recollection of the song's origins, see *New York Herald Tribune,* September 2, 1959, *Sporting News,* April 16, 1958, September 9, 1959. Perhaps the story about Norworth's lack of familiarity with the game *is* too good to be true. Norworth's other classic song was "Shine On, Harvest Moon" (also written in 1908, his "career year" as a songwriter!). As his obituary noted, an oft-told story about the origins of that song—that female co-star Nora Bayles (who would become his second wife) heard the song, demanded to sing it, and was told that "she could have it only if she took him too"—was a press agent's invention. *New York Herald Tribune,* September 2, 1959.

5. Seymour, *Baseball: The Golden Age,* p. 149.

6. See, for example, *Sporting News,* November 2, 1922.

7. *Sporting News,* September 24, 1908.

8. On McGraw, see Charles C. Alexander, *John McGraw* (New York: Viking Penguin, 1988); John J. McGraw, *My Thirty Years in Baseball* (New York, Boni and Liveright, 1923); Joseph Durso, *The Days of Mr. McGraw* (Englewood Cliffs, N.J.: Prentice-Hall, 1969).

9. McGraw, *My Thirty Years in Baseball,* p. 3.

10. Durso, *Days of Mr. McGraw,* p. 126.

11. Durso, *Days of Mr. McGraw,* p. 175.

12. Graham, *The New York Giants,* pp. 106–7.

13. *New York Times,* April 7, 1955.

14. *New York Tribune,* January 15, 1919.

15. Graham, *New York Giants,* p. 108. A claim against McQuade and McGraw for a finder's fee by a retired New York police captain was settled with a payment from Stoneham. Ibid.

16. Roger Angell, *Five Seasons: A Baseball Companion* (New York: Popular Library, 1978), p. 266.

17. Louis Guenther, "Pirates of Promotion," *World's Work,* November 1918.

18. Details on the sale, and subsequent stock transfers, in *McQuade v. Stoneham,* 230 App. Div. 57 (1930), reversed in 263 N.Y. 323 (1934).

19. As described by counsel for McQuade at the trial of McQuade's case against Stoneham and McGraw in *New York Times,* December 23, 1931.

20. *New York Tribune,* January 15, 1919.

21. *Sporting News,* April 10, 1919. For Pepper's account of the case, see George Wharton Pepper, *Philadelphia Lawyer* (Philadelphia: J. B. Lippincott, 1944), pp. 356–60.

22. Pepper, *Philadelphia Lawyer,* p. 357.

23. The trial judge's ruling in *New York Times*, April 12, 1919.

24. *New York Times*, April 14, 1919.

25. Ibid.

26. *National League of Professional Baseball Clubs, et al. v. Federal Baseball Club of Baltimore, Inc.*, 269 Fed. 681 (App. D.C. 1921).

27. *Federal Baseball Club of Baltimore, Inc. v. National League of Professional Baseball Clubs, et al.*, 259 U.S. 200 (1922). The legal issues raised by the case are addressed by law professor G. Edward White in *Creating the National Pastime: Baseball Transforms Itself 1903–1953* (Princeton, N.J.: Princeton University Press, 1996), pp. 69–83.

28. Graham, *New York Giants*, p. 120.

29. McGraw, *My Thirty Years in Baseball*, p. 2.

30. *Baseball Hearings: 1951*, p. 1636 (Table: "Margin of Profit on Gross Operating Income, Major League Clubs, 1920–1950"). Some perspective on the actual scale of the amounts involved comes from noting that this works out to no more than about $130,000 per club.

31. National League Financial Reports of 1910 and 1920, submitted to Congress in 1951 and printed in *Baseball Hearings: 1951*, pp. 1321–27.

32. See *New York Times*, April 19, 1998, for one example among many.

33. Indeed, the crucial role played by the coming of Sunday baseball in the eviction decision was recognized at the time (*New York Tribune*, May 15, 1920), in memoir (McGraw, *The Real McGraw*, pp. 277–78), and in subsequent scholarship, notably Steven A. Riess, *Touching Base: Professional Baseball and American Culture in the Progressive Era* (Westport, Conn.: Greenwood Press, 1980), pp. 106–7, but all to no avail as far as the collective memory of the "baseball mind" is concerned.

34. *New York Times*, April 7, 1955.

35. *New York Times*, April 8 and 21, 1919.

36. *New York Times*, April 9, 23, and 30, 1919.

37. *New York Times*, April 16 and May 3, 1919.

38. *New York Tribune*, May 5, 1919.

39. *New York Times*, April 7, 1955.

40. *New York Tribune*, May 5, 1919.

41. *New York Times*, May 2, 1920.

42. *New York Times*, May 15, 1920; *New York Tribune*, May 15, 1920.

43. *Sporting News*, May 20, 1920.

44. *New York Tribune*, May 15, 1920.

45. Sid Mercer, quoted in McGraw, *The Real McGraw*, pp. 277–78. On the Giants, see Seymour, *Baseball: The Golden Age*, p. 37.

46. *New York Tribune*, May 15, 1920.

47. Ibid.

48. Spink, *Judge Landis*, p. 50.

49. *American League Baseball Club of New York v. Johnson*, 109 N.Y. Misc. 138 (Supreme Court, October 1919).

50. Seymour, *Baseball: The Golden Age,* pp. 270–71; Murdock, *Ban Johnson,* pp. 175–76; Spink, *Judge Landis,* pp. 51–52.
51. Murdock, *Ban Johnson,* pp. 175–76; Seymour, *Baseball: The Golden Age,* p. 270.
52. *New York Times,* May 15, 1920 ("Stoneham Discusses Move").
53. Seymour, *Baseball: The Golden Age,* pp. 270–72; *New York Times,* October 21, 1920; Murdock, *Ban Johnson,* pp. 176–77; Spink, *Judge Landis,* pp. 66–67.
54. See discussion of these various conspiracy theories in Murdock, *Ban Johnson,* pp. 175–76.
55. *New York Times,* May 22, 1920.
56. *New York Times,* August 25, 1920.
57. *New York Times,* September 14, 1920.
58. Seymour, *Baseball: The Golden Age,* p. 54.
59. *New York Times,* February 6, 1921.
60. Ibid.
61. *New York Times,* September 14, 1920; February 6, 1921; May 17, 1921.
62. *New York Times,* May 22, 1920.
63. *Sporting News,* January 18, 1923.
64. A summary of the allocation of Sunday dates among the New York teams over the next few seasons appears in Table 1.1 in the appendix.
65. Quoted in *New York Times,* April 19, 1998.
66. On Yankee Stadium's opening, see *New York Times,* April 19, 1923.
67. *New York Tribune,* April 19, 1923.
68. Meany, *The Yankee Story,* p. 57.
69. *New York Tribune,* October 13, 1923, seconded by the *Sporting News,* October 18, 1923.
70. Quoted in *New York Times,* January 14, 1939.
71. *Baseball Hearings: 1951,* p. 1600.
72. Gershman, *Diamonds,* p. 104.
73. *New York Tribune,* March 18, 1919.
74. In their final three years at the Polo Grounds, the Yankees attracted 1,289,000 (1920), 1,230,000 (1921), and 1,026,000 (1922) fans to the Giants' 929,000, 973,000, and 945,000 in those seasons.
75. A team's proportional share of attendance would, of course, be one-eighth in the eight-team American and National Leagues that existed until expansion to ten teams in 1961 and 1962, respectively.
76. *Baseball Hearings: 1951,* pp. 1619–20.
77. Such was the case in the 1930s, when the New Deal was waging war against the "economic royalists" and the IRS reported the largest salaries being paid by corporations, including those to star ballplayers. Comparison between those "hard" numbers and press accounts revealed a substantial inflation factor in previously reported figures. See *Sporting News,* January 16, 1936. Fuzziness about the "real" economics of the sport remains true today, even in an era of heightened exposure and scrutiny, as witness *Forbes* magazine's deconstruc-

tion of the profit-and-loss calculations presented by Baseball Commissioner Bud Selig to Congress in December 2001 (*Forbes,* April 15, 2002).

78. Team-by-team profit-and-loss figures (1920–1950), as reported in *Baseball Hearings: 1951,* pp. 1599–1600.
79. Details in *McQuade v. Stoneham,* 230 App. Div. 57, 60 (1930).
80. *Baseball Hearings: 1951,* pp. 1599–1600.
81. See Arthur Garfield Hays, *City Lawyer: Autobiography of a Law Practice* (New York: Simon and Schuster, 1942), pp. 108–11.
82. On gambling and game fixing before the Black Sox scandal, see Seymour, *Baseball: The Golden Age,* pp. 288–93.
83. *New York Times,* January 7, 1936.
84. *New York Times,* January 12, 1924; January 7, 1936.
85. Swanberg, *Citizen Hearst,* pp. 437–38.
86. See coverage of the trial in *New York Times,* January 14, 1925, *et seq.*
87. Hays, *City Lawyer,* pp. 111–12.
88. *In re Fuller, et al.,* 9 F.2d 553 (2d Cir. 1925).
89. *New York Times,* March 21, 1927, p. 21.
90. *New York Times,* December 15, 1931.
91. *McQuade v. Stoneham,* 230 App. Div. 57 (May 29, 1930).
92. Reports on the trial in *New York Times,* December 15, 16, 17, 18, 19, 22, 1931; January 13, 1932.
93. For the trial decision, see *McQuade v. Stoneham,* 142 Misc. 842 (January 12, 1932).
94. *McQuade v. Stoneham,* 263 N.Y. 323, 331–332 (1934).
95. On McQuade and the Seabury investigation, see *New York Times,* December 1, 9, 10, 1930; and Herbert Mitgang, *The Man Who Rode the Tiger: The Life and Times of Judge Samuel Seabury* (Philadelphia and New York: J. B. Lippincott, 1963), pp. 189–90; on McQuade's pension suit, see *New York Times,* April 7, 1955.

INTERLUDE: NEW YORK TO ST. LOUIS

1. See Ernest Hemingway, "The Three-Day Blow," in *The Fifth Column and the First Forty-Nine Stories* (New York: Charles Scribner's Sons, 1938), pp. 215–16.

CHAPTER 3: THE PROBLEM

1. *New York Times,* November 13, 1931; see also *Washington Post,* November 13, 1931; *Chicago Tribune,* November 13, 1931.
2. *Sporting News,* November 19, 1931. Martin's response left the voluble Landis at a loss for words: "Why, that'll do fine, Judge," Martin, whose salary was $4,500, told the $65,000-a-year commissioner, "if we can trade salaries too."
3. On Martin's career, see *Sporting News,* November 19, 1931.

4. *Sporting News,* November 19, 1931.
5. Roster of winter 1928 farm teams in "Minutes of Joint Meeting of American and National Leagues," in Mann, *Branch Rickey,* pp. 152–53.
6. Frederick G. Lieb, *The St. Louis Cardinals* (New York: G. P. Putnam's Sons, 1994), pp. 84–85.
7. Citations in "A Wholesaler in Peanuts," *Sporting News,* October 4, 1928, and Lieb, *The St. Louis Cardinals,* p. 61.
8. The basic sources for the Rickey story remain Lieb, *The St. Louis Cardinals;* Arthur Mann, *Branch Rickey: American in Action;* J. Roy Stockton, *The Gashouse Gang* (New York: A. S. Barnes, 1945); and the entry in *Current Biography* (1945), as well as the two best available substitutes for the autobiography that Rickey, regrettably, never wrote—his lengthy testimony at the 1951 baseball antitrust hearings in *Baseball Hearings: 1951,* pp. 977–1049, and Robert Rice's profile in *The New Yorker,* May 27 and June 3, 1950.
9. Rickey testimony in *Baseball Hearings: 1951,* p. 988; also "Branch Rickey" in *Current Biography* (1945), p. 498.
10. James Neal Primm, *Lion of the Valley: St. Louis, Missouri* (Boulder, Colo.: Pruett Publishing Company, 1981), pp. 345–49, 418–19; Kenneth T. Jackson, *Crabgrass Frontier: The Suburbanization of the United States* (New York: Oxford University Press, 1985), p. 140; Carlos F. Hurd, "St. Louis: Boundary Bound," in Robert S. Allen, ed., *Our Fair City* (New York: Vanguard Press, 1947), pp. 235–55; Jon C. Teaford, *Cities of the Heartland: The Rise and Fall of the Industrial Midwest* (Bloomington and Indianapolis: Indiana University Press, 1993), pp. 63, 102–3.
11. Population calculations in *Baseball Hearings: 1951,* p. 1594.
12. *Baseball Hearings: 1951,* p. 1591 ("Mean Percent of League Attendance").
13. *Baseball Hearings: 1951,* pp. 1596–97 ("Attendance Strength—Major League Clubs 1910–1950"). The committee measured "attendance strength" as "a sliding three year mean of the difference between the club's actual percent of league attendance and the expected share of league attendance for the average major league club of the same playing ability."
14. *Sporting News,* September 26, 1918.
15. Breadon, quoted in *Sporting News,* January 7, 1948; on the Browns' abortive 1941 plans, see Charles Alexander, *Our Game: An American Baseball History* (New York: Henry Holt, 1991), p. 195. The plan was derailed by Pearl Harbor, and it is doubtful that transportation and scheduling considerations could have accommodated such a move at that time, in any event. Ibid., 239.
16. *Sporting News,* January 7, 1948.
17. For Cardinals/Browns attendance figures, see Table 2.5 in the appendix.
18. On the disposition of the Browns pursuant to the Federal League "peace agreement," see Transcript of Record on Appeal in *National League of Professional Baseball Clubs, et al. vs. Federal Baseball Club of Baltimore, Inc.* (U.S. Supreme Court), pp. 337, 341.
19. The case had been filed on March 29, 1916. It was called for trial in June 1917.

The plaintiffs then withdrew the complaint and reinstated it in September 1917 in the District Court of the District of Columbia. The trial was held in April 1919.

20. Mann, *Branch Rickey,* pp. 87–91.
21. Ibid., p. 89.
22. Ibid.
23. Ibid., p. 91.
24. Road attendance calculated from National League "Report of receipts from 5 percent assessment on gate receipts," in *Baseball Hearings: 1951,* p. 1323. Estimated Cardinal road attendance of 265,000 in 1910, based on that league report, was 200,000 lower than that drawn by the road-attendance–leading Cubs and 55,000 below second-worst Boston.
25. Rickey testimony in *Baseball Hearings: 1951,* p. 988.
26. Ibid., pp. 987–88.
27. Robert Rice, *New Yorker,* June 3, 1950, "Thoughts on Baseball—II."
28. *Baseball Hearings: 1951,* p. 988.
29. Mann, *Branch Rickey,* p. 106.
30. Ibid.
31. Rickey testimony in *Baseball Hearings: 1951,* p. 982.
32. For the creation of the National Commission, see *Organized Baseball Report,* pp. 42–43.
33. On the development of the reserve clause, see *Organized Baseball Report,* pp. 111–12.
34. Text of National Agreement in *Baseball Hearings: 1951,* pp. 521–25.
35. *Baseball Hearings: 1951,* p. 981.
36. *Organized Baseball Report,* p. 45.
37. Leslie O'Connor testimony in *Baseball Hearings: 1951,* p. 657; *Organized Baseball Report,* p. 45.
38. O'Connor testimony in *Baseball Hearings: 1951,* p. 657; *Organized Baseball Report,* p. 46.
39. Mann, *Branch Rickey,* pp. 102–4; Rickey testimony in *Baseball Hearings: 1951,* p. 988.
40. The bidding would, of course, inure to the benefit of the minor-league club, not the player involved, given the reserve provisions that bound the player to the team.

CHAPTER 4: THE OPPORTUNITY

1. The chronology of the Perry case is derived from the June 12, 1918, decision of the National Commission, reported in the *Sporting News,* June 20, 1918.
2. Although it has been written—even in the newspaper dispatches that reported the conclusion of the controversy in 1918—that the $500 had been paid, the text of the commission proceedings makes it clear that the money had not changed hands.

3. J. G. Taylor Spink, *Judge Landis and Twenty-Five Years of Baseball* (New York: Thomas Y. Crowell, 1947), pp. 41–42.
4. Harold Seymour, *Baseball: The Golden Age* (New York: Oxford University Press, 1971), p. 262.
5. Herrmann quoted in *Sporting News,* June 27, 1918.
6. *Sporting News,* June 27, 1918.
7. J. Roy Stockton, "Singing Sam, the Selling Man," *Saturday Evening Post,* February 22, 1947. On Breadon, see obituaries in *New York Times,* May 11, 1949, and *Sporting News,* May 18, 25, 1949.
8. J. G. Taylor Spink in *Sporting News,* May 25, 1949.
9. Ibid.
10. Ibid., May 18, 1949.
11. Ibid., March 27, 1924.
12. "King of the Weeds," *Sporting News,* January 6, 1927.
13. The politics of Sunday baseball in New York provided a force for balance here. Interestingly, the pennant-winning Dodgers played before the smallest aggregate road crowds—and for the same reason that the Giants showed so well on the road. The Giants played all of their Sunday intracity contests with the Dodgers in Brooklyn—four lucrative home dates for the Dodgers (93,000 total)—in order to make their home park available for the tenant Yankees to play at home on Sunday. The only way to preserve equality of the use of the Polo Grounds, and to provide a maximum number of Sunday dates in New York for the convenience of those teams that could not play at home on Sundays, was to play all New York–Brooklyn games in Brooklyn. On those four dates, the Yankees hosted the A's twice, Boston once, and Washington once.

CHAPTER 5: THE AMBIGUOUS PAYOFF

1. This trade would be made in 1926.
2. For the procurement sources of 1921 National League regulars, see Table 2.1 in the appendix. Tables 2.1–2.4 are derived from the applicable annual editions of *Who's Who in Baseball* (New York: Baseball Magazine Co.).
3. See Table 2.2 in the appendix for the 1921 records of such "reclaimed" players.
4. The only "reclaimed" men who were on the championship roster were pitchers Syl Johnson (0–3 in very limited action), Allen Sothoron (3–3), Duster Mails (0–1), and deep reserve catcher Bill Warwick (9 games). Note: Mails, not Warwick, was in the series.
5. *Sporting News,* January 26, 1927.
6. See Table 2.3 in the appendix for records of "reclaimed" players in 1926.
7. For a team-by-team tabulation of player procurement sources based on 1926 rosters, see Table 2.4 in the appendix.
8. On the disposition of Hornsby's Cardinal stock, see *Sporting News,* January 13, February 3, and April 14, 1927.

9. Mann, *Branch Rickey,* pp. 150–51 The Cardinals, tenants in Sportsman's Park, did not have a similar investment in St. Louis itself.

10. Southworth had played right field in 1926. Holm played in 1927; he was released after the 1929 season, having not played regularly since 1928. George Harper had been given his chance in 1928—he had been obtained from the Giants shortly after the 1928 season started and then was traded to Boston for 1929. Orsatti had played there in 1929, supplanted by Watkins in 1930.

11. On Commissioner Landis's dealings with Rickey and the Cardinal farm system, see Spink, *Judge Landis and Twenty-Five Years of Baseball,* pp. 232–43.

12. *Current Biography (1944),* p. 434.

13. See American League Balance Sheet for 1940 in *Baseball Hearings: 1951.*

14. See Leonard Koppett, "Baseball's Competitive Imbalance Is a Longstanding Problem," *New York Times,* May 20, 2001.

INTERLUDE: ST. LOUIS TO BROOKLYN

1. Murray Kempton, *America Comes of Middle Age* (Boston: Little, Brown, 1963), p. 379.

CHAPTER 6: THE CASE AGAINST BROOKLYN

1. On Emmett Kelly's hiring, see *Sporting News,* February 6, 1957, and *New York Times,* January 29 and April 14, 1957.

2. Three (Lou Gehrig's farewell speech, Joe DiMaggio's fifty-six-game hitting streak, and Jackie Robinson's breaking the color line) made the top ten (out of a total of thirty choices) in the voting by fans, as announced during the 2002 World Series. To the consternation of many, at least those of a certain age, Bobby Thomson's 1951 play-off–winning home run did not make it—perhaps because he was not included (unlike Robinson and Gehrig) in the promotional advertisement aired during the season by the contest's sponsor, MasterCard. See "Major League Baseball Memorable Moments," at mlb.com.

3. John Durant, *The Dodgers* (New York: Hastings House, 1948), p. 49.

4. For the National League team's cumulative win–loss totals for 1947–56, see *Sporting News,* February 6, 1957.

5. *Death House Letters of Ethel and Julius Rosenberg* (New York: Jero Publishing Company, Inc., 1953), pp. 67, 109; James G. Ryan, *Earl Browder: The Failure of American Communism* (Urbana: University of Illinois Press, 1997), p. 145.

6. *New York Times,* April 10, 1953; Burt Solomon, *The Baseball Timeline* (New York: Avon Books, 1997), p. 532. Fans and the press continued to refer to the team as the "Reds"; they officially reverted to their traditional name in 1959.

7. *Sporting News,* April 17, 1957.

8. *New York Times,* January 20, 1957; *New York Herald Tribune,* January 20, 1957.

9. *Sports Illustrated,* April 15, 1957.

10. *Daily News,* October 9, 1957.

11. See comments collected in Jules Tygiel, *Baseball's Great Experiment: Jackie Robinson and His Legacy* (New York: Oxford University Press, 1983), pp. 52–53.

12. Roger Kahn, *The Boys of Summer* (New York: Harper & Row, 1972), p. 426.

13. See Table 3.1, Dodgers and Giants Attendance, 1946–1956, in the appendix.

14. Game-by-game attendance figures and receipts in *New York Times,* September 29 to October 5, 1955. Walter O'Malley's analysis in U.S. House of Representatives, *Hearings before the Antitrust Subcommittee of the Committee on the Judiciary, Organized Professional Team Sports,* 85th Cong., 2d sess., 1957, p. 1859. The 1957 hearings were chaired, as in 1951, by Brooklyn Congressman Emanuel Celler. (This source is cited hereafter as *Baseball Hearings: 1957.*) The differential was still greater for the last two games (1952 and 1956) played in Brooklyn, since after four games had been played, the teams alone shared in the bulk of the receipts—the prayers' pool was limited to the receipts from the first four contests.

15. *Baseball Hearings: 1957,* p. 1858.

16. *Time,* April 28, 1958, p. 59.

17. *Baseball Hearings: 1957.* O'Malley testimony on p. 1883.

18. Quoted in Harvey Frommer, *New York City Baseball: The Last Golden Age 1947–57* (New York: Macmillan, 1980), p. 3.

19. Quoted in Frommer, *New York City Baseball,* p. 3. See also Melvin Durslag, "A Visit with Walter O'Malley," *Saturday Evening Post,* May 14, 1960.

20. *Sports Illustrated,* April 15, 1957.

21. *Sporting News,* April 26, 1923; *New York Tribune,* October 13, 1923.

22. "Baseball and Parking Space," *Sporting News,* October 18, 1923, p. 4.

23. John Lardner, "Would It Still Be Brooklyn?" in *New York Times,* February 26, 1956.

24. Tommy Holmes, "The Chin Music at the Capital," *Brooklyn Eagle,* October 19, 1951 (in *Baseball Hearings: 1951,* p. 1494).

25. *Sporting News,* August 31, 1955.

26. Arthur Daley, "Like Pitchin' in a Phone Booth," *New York Times Magazine,* September 1, 1957, pp. 13–16.

27. *Sports Illustrated,* April 15, 1957.

28. Ibid. As for the Giant's Polo Grounds, "ushers are numerous, and expect tip for any service."

29. See, e.g., *New York Times,* August 21, 1955.

30. Arthur Daley, "The Deserted Village," *New York Times,* September 27, 1956.

31. *New York Times* September 27, 1956.

32. *New York Times,* August 18, 1955.

33. See Table 3.4 in the appendix, comparing seating capacities and revenues, derived from "Table of Seating Capacities and Price Ranges for Major League Clubs" *Sporting News,* April 16, 1952, reprinted in *Baseball Hearings: 1951,* p. 1640.

34. *Sporting News,* April 16, 1952.

35. Mark Mulvey, "Slow Death by Committee in Boston," *Sports Illustrated,* June 12, 1967.

36. *Sporting News,* April 29, 1953.

37. *Plus ça change, plus c'est la même chose.* In the summer of 2002, the new owners of the Red Sox were reported to be considering renovating Fenway Park and abandoning the previous ownership's plans to replace what it had termed the "obsolete" ballpark with a new, largely public-financed stadium. *Boston Globe,* July 1, 2002.

38. *Saturday Evening Post,* May 28, 1932.

39. "The Frick–McKinney Report of the National League of Professional Baseball Clubs," in *Baseball Hearings: 1951,* pp. 88–91.

40. See Bill Veeck with Ed Linn, *Veeck as in Wreck* (New York: Ballantine Books, 1976), pp. 290–302.

41. The Milwaukee team was moved to St. Louis for the 1902 season, and Baltimore shifted to New York City in order to compete head-to-head with the Giants just before peace was declared between the leagues in 1903.

42. *Sporting News,* March 7, 1956.

Chapter 7: Stadium Games

1. Kahn, *The Boys of Summer,* p. 427.

2. My account of O'Malley's family background and career is based on O'Malley's 1957 congressional testimony in *Baseball Hearings: 1957,* 1850–85: *Current Biography Yearbook,* 1954, pp. 494–95; *Time,* April 28, 1958; Kahn, *The Boys of Summer;* Ed Linn, "The Dodgers Boss Rocks the Boat," *Sports,* July 1957; Durslag, "A Visit with Walter O'Malley," p.104; Jack Mann, "The King of the Jungle," *Sports Illustrated,* April 18, 1966; Gerald Holland, "A Visit with the Artful Dodger," *Saturday Evening Post,* July 13, 1968; *Los Angeles Times,* August 10, 1979; *Who's Who in America* (various editions).

3. Mann, "The King of the Jungle," p. 122.

4. Ira Berkow, *Red: A Biography of Red Smith* (New York: Times Books, 1986), p. 92.

5. Norman Podhoretz, *Making It* (New York: Random House, 1967), p. 3.

6. On the Brooklyn Museum, see Norval White and Elliot Willensky, eds. *AIA Guide to New York City* (New York: Collier Books, 1978), p. 442. For the Murphy quote, see Red Smith, "Oldest Established Drifter," *New York Herald Tribune,* February 7, 1956.

7. *Baseball Hearings: 1957,* p. 1866.

8. Notable among such is Doris Kearns Goodwin, who lived out her Dodgers fandom from Long Island's Rockville Centre.

9. Red Barber interview on National Public Radio, April 4, 1990.

10. Jim Bishop, *FDR's Last Year,* (New York: Morrow, 1974), p. 156.

11. *Baseball Hearings: 1957,* p. 1853.
12. On the origins of Ebbets Field, see Michael Gershman, *Diamonds: The Evolution of the Ballpark* (Boston and New York: Houghton Mifflin, 1993), pp. 110–13; *New York Times,* April 6, 1913; *New York Times,* August 19, 1955.
13. Hugo Ullitz, *Atlas of the Borough of Brooklyn, City of New York,* vol. 2 (E. Belcher Hyde, 1904, corrected to 1912), plate 26.
14. For the 1920 strike, see *New York Times,* September 4, 1920 ("Little things like transit strikes can't keep the Brooklyn fans from seeing the Robins play."); September 6, 1920 ("Some 20,000 Brooklyn fans defying a transit strike to see the Braves slaughtered again by the league leading Robins").
15. New York City lacked any kind of zoning law until 1916. When enacted in that year, it was the first such regulation in the United States.
16. Robert Moses to Walter O'Malley, August 15, 1995 ("Every conference we have attended over several years, including the last one at the *News . . .*"), in Robert F. Wagner, Jr., Papers, New York City Municipal Archives (hereafter RFWP–NYCMA).
17. *Baseball Hearings:* 1957, p. 1853.
18. Ibid., pp. 1853–54.
19. *New York Times,* August 18, 1955.
20. *Baseball Hearings: 1957,* p. 1860.
21. *New York Times,* August 18, 1955.
22. Interim Report of Brooklyn Sports Center Authority, November 15, 1956, in RFWP–NYCMA (assessed land value $9.831 million, total improved value $17.12 million); Memorandum from George McLaughlin to Mayor Robert F. Wagner, Jr., June 13, 1957 in RFWP–NYCMA (land and relocation costs to the city to obtain stadium site estimated at $10 million, with additional costs to the city for neighborhood improvements of $10 million); *New York Times,* August 7, 1957 (engineering report estimates cost of land at $9 million).
23. Moses to O'Malley, August 15, 1955, in RFWP–NYCMA.
24. Neil Sullivan, *The Dodgers Move West* (New York: Oxford University Press, 1987), p. 56.
25. Cashmore to Wagner, June 19, 1956 (enclosing June 13 Clarke–Rapuano Report), RFWP–NYCMA.
26. George McLaughlin to Wagner, June 13, 1957, RFWP–NYCMA.
27. Robert Moses to Deputy Mayor John Theobald, April 22, 1957, RFWP–NYCMA.
28. *New York Times,* August 7, 1957.
29. O'Malley testimony in *Baseball Hearings: 1957,* p. 1860.
30. Sullivan, *The Dodgers Move West,* p. 55.
31. *New York Times,* September 16, 1955.
32. *New York Times,* August 29, 1956.
33. On the origins of the Title I program, see Robert M. Fogelson, *Downtown: Its Rise and Fall, 1880–1950* (New Haven: Yale University Press, 2001), pp.

376–80; for its operation in New York City generally, see Jeanne R. Lowe, *Cities in a Race with Time* (New York: Random House, 1967), pp. 70 ff.

34. For a brief summary of Moses's career, see Jameson W. Doig, "Regional Conflict in the New York Metropolis: The Legend of Robert Moses and the Power of the Port Authority," *Urban Studies* (Vol. 27, No. 2, 1990), pp. 203–4.

35. Moses to O'Malley, August 15, 1955, in RFWP–NYCMA.

36. Moses to O'Malley, August 15, 1955, in RFWP–NYCMA.

37. *New York Times,* August 17, 1955.

38. *New York Times,* August 17, 1955.

39. See Table 3.2 in the appendix for comparative Dodgers–Braves attendance figures.

40. Kahn, *The Boys of Summer,* p. 428.

41. Linn, "The Dodger Boss Rocks the Boat."

42. Durslag, "A Visit with Walter O'Malley," p. 104; see also O'Malley comments in 1953 in Kahn, *The Boys of Summer,* p. 428, and Linn, "The Dodger Boss Rocks the Boat."

43. Durslag, "A Visit with Walter O'Malley," p. 104.

44. *Baseball Hearings: 1957,* pp. 354–56, 2046–47. The figures are also presented in a convenient comparative table in *Sporting News,* July 3, 1957. Brooklyn's pretax net income in 1956 was $1,120,000; in 1955, it had been $824,000. Even in the non–World Series year of 1954, it was $455,000. Indeed, looking only at the numbers for the major-league club, and stripping out the losses incurred for minor-league operations, the results were even more impressive—with pretax income of $1,500,000, $1,284,000, and $776,000 in 1956, 1955, and 1954, respectively.

45. *Baseball Hearings: 1951,* pp. 1608–9; *Baseball Hearings: 1957,* pp. 354–56, 2046–47.

46. Cincinnati, which had been ignored by the postwar boom, also showed an advance, and the Braves earned more in Milwaukee than in Boston. For comparative team income data, see Tables 3.5 and 3.6 in the appendix.

47. World Series income has been excluded in Table 3.6 (see appendix) to provide a truer comparison among the teams, only one of which, of course, could appear in the World Series in any one year.

48. See Table 3.3 in the appendix.

49. For the years 1952–56, Dodger net farm-club expenses totaled $1,900,000, twice those of the Braves (*Sporting News,* July 3, 1957).

50. Average attendance at the Jersey City games was slightly higher than that for the games played in Brooklyn.

51. *New York Times,* August 18, 1955.

52. *Baseball Hearings: 1957,* p. 1866.

53. *New York Times,* August 18, 1955.

54. *New York Herald Tribune,* August 18, 1955; *New York Times,* August 18, 1955.

55. *New York Times,* August 23, 1955.

56. *New York Times,* August 20, 1955.
57. Chris McNickle, *To Be Mayor of New York* (New York: Columbia University Press, 1993), pp. 116–17.
58. *New York Times,* August 18, 1955.
59. *New York Times,* August 19, 1955.
60. *New York Times,* August 20, 1955.
61. *New York Times,* August 20, 1955.
62. O'Malley, quoted in *New York Herald Tribune,* August 20, 1956; Moses to Cashmore, August 26, 1955 in RFWP–NYCMA.
63. *New York Times,* August 20, 1955.
64. *New York Times,* August 26, 1955.
65. *New York Times,* August 19, 1955.
66. Letters in RFWP–NYCMA, August 1955.
67. On the role of the borough presidents, see Wallace S. Sayre and Herbert Kaufman, *Governing New York City: Politics in the Metropolis* (New York: W. W. Norton, 1960).
68. Lowe, *Cities in a Race with Time,* p. 80.
69. *New York Times,* February 6, 1956.
70. *New York Times,* April 9, 1956.
71. *New York Times,* February 22, 24, 29, 1956.
72. *New York Times,* March 20, 22, 1956.
73. Mayor Wagner, press release, February 6, 1956 in RFWP–NYCMA.
74. *New York Times,* March 2, 1956.
75. For the text of the law, see Chapter 951 of the 1956 Laws of the State of New York, "An act to amend the public authorities law, in relation to the creation of Brooklyn sports center authority, with power," etc.
76. A natural choice had been Bernard Gimbel, chairman of New York City's Convention and Visitors Bureau, who had been a lobbyist for the authority law. Gimbel, a close Moses ally on planning matters, played the offer cautiously before a telephone call from O'Malley settled his mind about it. O'Malley, he reported to Moses, "is only interested in having the Authority build a ballpark to his requirements." Bernard Gimbel to Moses, July 16, 1956. Gimbel declined to serve, and the three eventual appointees were selected from a list provided by the Dodgers owner. Peter Campbell Brown to Wagner, June 27, 1956, RFWP–NYCMA; O'Malley to Brown, July 5, 1956, RFWP–NYCMA.
77. The three designees were Chester Allen, president of the Kings County Trust Company—the last "purely" Brooklyn bank—and of the Brooklyn Chamber of Commerce; Robert Blum, chairman of Abraham and Straus, the great Brooklyn-based department store, and also a leading borough philanthropist; Charles Mylod, named as chairman of the Brooklyn Sports Center Authority. Mylod was a leading Brooklyn realtor, the one board member who lived in Brooklyn—and the closest personally to O'Malley, who had been godfather to one of his sons. They made up, O'Malley later said, a well-balanced team of

"two Democrats and one Republican . . . a Catholic, a Protestant and a Jew," a classic political ticket in the ethnic world of New York. *Baseball Hearings: 1957*, p. 1856.

78. Brooklyn Sports Center Authority, Interim Report, November 15, 1956, in RFWP–NYCMA.

79. The final version of the city-financed study, known as the Clarke–Rapuano Study, was delivered to Cashmore, who turned it over to the Sports Center Authority in late November (*New York Times*, November 28, 1956). It contained the same recommendations as the preliminary version, which had been completed and released in July. Neil Sullivan's account does not distinguish between the Clarke–Rapuano Study and the board's own interim report and errs in stating that the authority was proceeding on the basis of the Clarke–Rapuano Study, which it had actually rejected (Sullivan, *The Dodgers Move West*, p. 78).

80. Moses to Wagner, December 7, 1956, RFWP–NYCMA.

81. *New York Times*, December 28 and 29, 1956.

82. Michael J. Madigan to Charles Mylod, January 31, 1957, RFWP–NYCMA.

83. Ibid.

84. Madigan to Mylod, January 31, 1957, in RFWP–NYCMA. Subsequent separate calculations confirmed this estimate. See Memo by James Felt (Chairman of City Planning Commission) re Mtg w/Madigan and Kubley May 31, 1957, RFWP–NYCMA (financing a "specialty of this nature would, in all probability, be regarded as highly speculative" and would require net rental of $2.1 million to service debt on a $15 million project). Moses's calculations, based on a twenty-five-year, $10 million issue, with a 1.4 coverage factor, and including annual maintenance expense, required a $1.1 million annual rent (Robert Moses to John Theobald, April 22, 1957, RFWP–NYCMA).

85. *Baseball Hearings: 1957*, pp. 1867, 1859–60.

86. Mylod to Madigan, January 31, 1957.

87. Sullivan, *The Dodgers Move West*, p. 72.

88. Robert Caro, *The Power Broker*, (New York: Alfred A. Knopf, 1974), p. 1018; Sullivan, *The Dodgers Move West*, pp. 49–50; Michael Shapiro, *The Last Good Season: Brooklyn, the Dodgers, and Their Final Pennant Race Together* (New York: Doubleday, 2003); *Baseball Hearings: 1957*, pp. 1862, 1867.

89. Perhaps most notably, Moses's proposed Lower Manhattan Expressway, slicing through what would become "SoHo," was never built, and even a small group of mothers, pushing baby carriages, was able to stop Moses's bulldozers from turning a Central Park playground into a parking lot in 1956. See Caro, *The Power Broker*, pp. 984–1004; Robert A. M. Stern, Thomas Mellins, and David Fishman, *New York 1960: Architecture and Urbanism between the Second World War and the Bicentennial* (New York: Monacelli Press, Inc., 1995), pp. 259–63. On the limits of Moses's power generally, see Leonard Wallock, "The Myth of the Master Builder," *Journal of Urban History* (August 1991), pp.

339–62, and Doig, "Regional Conflict in the New York Metropolis," pp. 201–32.

90. Joel Schwartz, *The New York Approach* (Columbus: Ohio State University Press, 1993), p. 297.

91. As evidenced by Congressman Celler's sharp questioning of Walter O'Malley at his antitrust subcommittee hearings in June 1957, and Stark's own testimony at those hearings. *Baseball Hearings: 1957*, pp. 1811–22, 1854–55.

92. At least on Robert Moses's paper. See Moses's calculations of Flushing Meadows expenses and revenues, Moses to Theobald, April 22, 1957, in RFWP–NYCMA. This was an illusion. When the city finally built the stadium to house the Mets on the site six years later, it did not work out that way. But at least on paper, a political case could be made for it that could not be duplicated for the downtown Brooklyn plan, and this was important to get the project started.

93. Moses to Theobald, April 22, 1957, in RFWP–NYCMA. Even the eventual $20 million cost of the completed Shea Stadium, twice Moses's 1957 projection, was less than half of the costs entailed by the downtown Brooklyn site. On Shea Stadium construction expense, see *New York Times*, April 17, 1964.

94. Minutes of Meeting of Sports Center Committee of the Board of Estimate, March 12, 1957, RFWP–NYCMA.

95. *Baseball Hearings: 1957*, pp. 1862–63.

96. Durslag, "A Visit with Walter O'Malley," p. 104.

97. Minutes of Meeting of Sports Center Committee of the Board of Estimate (3/12/57) in RFWP-NYCMA.

98. *New York Times*, September 14, 1957.

99. *Baseball Hearings: 1957*, p. 1872.

100. Sullivan, *The Dodgers Move West*, pp. 107–8.

101. Ibid., pp. 120, 44.

102. *Baseball Hearings: 1957*, p. 1864.

CHAPTER 8: FROM EAST TO WEST

1. *Los Angeles Times*, August 10, 1979 (O'Malley obituary).

2. *Los Angeles Times*, October 12, 1956.

3. Ibid.

4. *Baseball Hearings: 1957*, p. 1865.

5. *Baseball Hearings: 1957*, p. 1861.

6. *Los Angeles Times*, March 6, 1957 (reporting January visit).

7. See "Public Housing and the Brooklyn Dodgers," *Frontier* (June 1957). For a photographic essay on the "hidden village," see Don Normark, *Chavez Ravine, 1949: A Los Angeles Story* (Chronicle Books, 1999).

8. *Chicago Tribune*, February 22, 1957.

9. Wrigley testimony in *Baseball Hearings: 1951*, p. 725.

10. Wrigley testimony in *Baseball Hearings: 1951,* pp. 742–43.

11. *Los Angeles Times,* February 22, 1957.

12. *Chicago Tribune,* February 22, 1957. Rowland called it Wrigley's "second sacrifice" in the cause of expansion, noting that he had waived territorial rights to Milwaukee in voting for the transfer of the Braves from Boston.

13. Ibid.

14. *New York Herald Tribune,* February 22, 1957.

15. Poulson at Los Angeles City Council meeting, quoted in *Los Angeles Times,* September 18, 1957.

16. O'Malley testimony in *Baseball Hearings: 1957,* p. 1860.

17. "All that was asked of the Mayor was that he keep his hands off the hard-line Police Department and work with the City Council and the bureaucracy to keep the streets well-maintained and clean" (Bill Boyarsky, "Los Angeles Remains a City in Search of a Plan," *Los Angeles Times,* May 10, 1981).

18. Most likely, Poulson, bitter about his defeat in a bid for a third term in 1961— which he blamed on perceptions that he had been taken advantage of by O'Malley—found it comforting to argue that, whatever the costs to the city of the deal he had ultimately struck with O'Malley, it was less expensive than kowtowing to an alleged Dodger demand that the city finance construction of a stadium. For Poulson's claim: see Norris Poulson, "The Untold Story of Chavez Ravine," *Los Angeles* (April 1962), which blames "baseball enemies" for contributing to his defeat; and Sullivan, *The Dodgers Move West,* pp. 97–98. Poulson's account further contains a number of chronological errors that vitiate its reliability. Skepticism about Poulson's "Untold Story" version of events was expressed by *Los Angeles Times* sports columnist Jim Murray in "Norrie's Nest," *Los Angeles Times,* April 9, 1962.

19. See *Time,* April 28, 1958. The best source on the somewhat elusive Vero Beach talks is the series of statements by the principal Los Angeles officials involved in the Dodger move (Metropolitan News section, *Los Angeles Times,* August 25, 1963). This report appeared while the Dodgers were involved in a dispute with the county assessor over property taxes on their recently completed stadium. See, especially, the statements by Assessor Phillip E. Watson, City Attorney Roger Arnebergh, County Supervisor Kenneth Hahn, and Assistant County Chief Administrative Officer John H. Leach.

20. The draft release stated that, once the stadium was built by the city and/or county, "a carefully-prepared lease and management agreement could be legally worked out with Mr. O'Malley's attorneys." Text of proposed press release, dated May 2, 1957, in *Baseball Hearings: 1957,* pp. 1912–14.

21. The finalized release, bearing O'Malley's handwritten note ("This supersedes proposed press release that I vetoed in toto. . . . Approved WFO'M") reflected O'Malley's insistence on preserving the private option. The county counsel's opinion concerning public funding was now merely "exploratory." That legal opinion had not, as the original release said, set out "all of the legal aspects and . . . the various legal methods open to the County," but "should not be con-

strued as outlining the only possible legal manner of bringing major-league baseball to Los Angeles." The reference to a legal memorandum prepared by the city attorney, "outlining several different methods of legally providing major league baseball for Los Angeles," was cut; and a cautionary mention of government control of any facility so that "public money has not been improperly expended for private gain" was cut. Press release dated, May 6, 1957, in *Baseball Hearings: 1957,* p. 1915.

22. Memorandum dated May 3, 1957, in *Baseball Hearings: 1957,* p. 1852.
23. Although O'Malley would attempt to disclaim responsibility for the memorandum, testifying a month later that it was a proposal from the city, bearing the initials of LA City Attorney Roger Arnebergh, which he did not accept, its wording ("it was indicated that the City and County should be prepared to make an offer") makes it clear that it represented O'Malley's outline of what he would be willing to accept from Los Angeles. The Los Angeles city attorney would later confirm that the memorandum "sets forth what Mr. O'Malley had felt it would be necessary for the city and county to do in order to obtain any major league baseball team for Los Angeles." "Arnebergh Explains His '57 Memorandum," in *Los Angeles Times,* August 25, 1963.
24. When later challenged in the courts as an illegal gift of government property, the exchange was upheld by the California Supreme Court as providing sufficient consideration for the transaction. *City of Los Angeles v. Superior Court,* 51 Cal. 2d 423 (1959).
25. On these issues, see the testimony of Baseball Commissioner Ford Frick, in *Baseball Hearings: 1951,* pp. 85–87.
26. Giles memo in *Baseball Hearings: 1957,* p. 1412. The memorandum stated, "My estimate is each club would have to draw about 125,000 more people in LA and Frisco than New York and Brooklyn to break even on travel." This would mean an increase in total attendance for the two teams to 2.5 million from the 1.7 million they drew in 1957.
27. *New York Times,* August 20, 1955.
28. See Kahn, *The Boys of Summer,* pp. 395–96.
29. Had Robinson not retired, he would, of course, have been following in the footsteps of Sal Maglie and Leo Durocher, who had managed to swap uniforms and allegiances between the rival teams.
30. *Los Angeles Times,* March 22, 1957.
31. *New York Herald Tribune,* October 4, 1951.
32. Ibid.
33. Ibid.
34. *Baseball Hearings: 1951,* p. 1601.
35. Ibid., pp. 1608–9.
36. *New York Times,* October 4, 1951; Don DeLillo, *Underworld* (New York: Scribner, 1997).
37. *New York Times,* October 3 and 4, 1951.
38. The opportunity cost in lost admissions was significant. Giants attendance

averaged 6,000 fans for the afternoon contests in 1954–56 and fell off to an average of 4,500 in the last two pennant-less years of that period—down to 3,400 in 1956 alone. This was more than *10,000* lower than average night-game attendance over that span.

39. The Polo Grounds had only 3,814 box seats, compared to Brooklyn's 5,562, Wrigley Field's 14,163—or Yankee Stadium's 17,836 (*Sporting News,* April 16, 1952).

40. The Giants did top the Dodgers in attendance in three subsequent, scattered campaigns—1944, 1948, and 1954.

41. Vic Ziegel, *Daily News,* August 10, 2000.

42. Arthur Daley in *New York Times,* June 4, 1957.

43. *New York Herald Tribune,* May 11, 1957.

44. *Sporting News,* February 8, 1956; July 6, 1955.

45. *New York Times,* November 26, 1955, p. 15.

46. *New York Times,* November 26, 1955.

47. *Sporting News,* February 8, 1956; for Stoneham's earlier comments, see *Sporting News,* July 6, 1955.

48. Arthur Daley, "The Passing Baseball Scene," *New York Times,* June 4, 1957.

49. See Table 3.6 in the appendix.

50. "Baseball-related income" excludes income derived from renting out the Polo Grounds for prizefights, football, and the like. This will be the measure of income in the discussion here.

51. *Baseball Hearings: 1957,* p. 2046 (Revised Profit and Loss Statements for NL 1956).

52. *Baseball Hearings: 1957,* pp. 356, 1929–30, 2047. Between 1920 and 1950, the Giants had paid out almost $3 million in dividends, over $1 million more than any other team in baseball, and were the only "major market" team to have no retained earnings for the period. *Baseball Hearings: 1951,* p. 1601.

53. Stoneham telegram to Wagner, August 18, 1955.

54. *New York Times,* August 20, 1955.

55. *New York Times,* February 23, 1957.

56. Arthur Daley in *New York Times,* February 9, 1956; John Lardner in *New York Times Magazine,* February 26, 1956.

57. See Table 3.7 in the appendix.

58. *New York Times,* February 23, 1957.

59. Stoneham testimony in *Baseball Hearings: 1957,* p. 1946.

60. *New York Times,* August 25, 1955, p. 26.

61. *New York Times,* September 18, 1955.

62. O'Malley testimony in *Baseball Hearings: 1957,* p. 1874.

63. Stoneham testimony at 1953; even at a more conservative fee of fifty cents per game, which Stoneham believed more realistic, the revenue would far eclipse that from free television.

64. Stoneham testimony in *Baseball Hearings: 1957,* p. 1954.

65. *Baseball Hearings: 1957,* pp. 1868, 1951.

66. Stoneham testimony in *Baseball Hearings: 1957*, pp. 1951, 1954. For a discussion of the Giants' contract with Skiatron, see *In the Matter of Skiatron Electronics and Television Corporation,* 40 S.E.C. 236 (1960).

67. Stoneham testimony in *Baseball Hearings: 1957*, pp. 1951–53.

68. Ibid. The contracts did provide, however, that a team could move operations to another city, without liability, canceling the agreement.

69. *Baseball Hearings: 1957*, pp. 1957–58.

70. *In the Matter of Skiatron Electronics and Television Corporation.*

71. Ibid.

72. *New York Herald Tribune,* May 12, 1957.

73. *San Francisco Chronicle,* May 9, 1957.

74. Holland, "A Visit with the Artful Dodger," p. 57.

75. *San Francisco Chronicle,* May 11, 1957.

76. Graham quoted in *San Francisco Chronicle,* May 29, 1957.

77. Minutes of meeting in *Baseball Hearings: 1957*, pp. 1404–6. Also see *New York Times,* May 28 and 29, 1957.

78. As reflected in Doris Kearns Goodwin, *Wait Till Next Year: A Memoir* (New York: Simon & Schuster, 1997), pp. 223–24.

79. *New York Times,* February 22 and 25, May 29, 1957.

80. See *San Francisco Chronicle,* May 30, 1957 ("Low, the Brooklyn Scribes; Politicians, Owners Blamed").

81. *New York Times,* June 9, 1957.

82. *New York Times,* July 18, 19, 20, 21, August 20, 1957; Stoneham testimony in *Baseball Hearings: 1957*, p. 1945.

83. Quoted in *San Francisco Chronicle,* May 29, 1957.

84. Kempton, *America Comes of Middle Age,* p. 379.

85. Quoted in David Plaut, *Chasing October: The Dodgers–Giants Pennant Race of 1962* (South Bend, Ind.: Diamond Communications, 1994), p. 133. After Soviet Premier Nikita Khrushchev's 1959 visit to San Francisco, columnist Frank Conniff wrote, "It's the damndest city I ever saw. They cheer Khrushchev and boo Willie Mays." Ibid., p. 133.

86. *Los Angeles Times,* September 18, 1957.

87. *New York Times,* August 7, 1957.

88. Cary Reich, *The Life of Nelson Rockefeller: Worlds to Conquer 1908–1958* (New York: Doubleday, 1996), pp. 690–92.

89. *Daily News,* October 9, 1957.

90. For details, see Sullivan, *The Dodgers Move West,* pp. 137–89; Cary S. Henderson, "Los Angeles and the Dodger War 1957–1962," *Southern California Quarterly* (fall 1980, pp. 261–89); *Los Angeles Times,* April 10, 1962.

91. O'Malley testimony in *Baseball Hearings: 1957*, pp. 1860, 1862.

92. See the analysis of the vote in *Los Angeles Newsletter* (No. 201, July 5, 1958), p. 2.

93. *City of Los Angeles v. Superior Court,* 51 Cal. 2d 423, 333 P. 2d 745 (1959).

94. Dick Young, "Lust for More $ Killed Brooks," *Daily News,* October 9, 1957.

95. *Los Angeles Times,* April 10, 1962.

96. *Daily News,* October 9, 1957.

97. New York had to wait another year before the creation of the Mets returned New York to the ranks of two-team cities.

98. Stanley Isaacs quoted in *Time,* January 20, 1997.

99. Andrew Zimbalist, "Not Suitable Families," *U.S. News and World Report,* January 20, 1997.

100. Jack Newfield, "O'Malleys Can't Dodger Their Shame," *Daily News,* January 29, 1990.

101. Peter Golenbock, *Bums: An Oral History of the Brooklyn Dodgers* (Chicago: Contemporary Books, 2000), pp. 472–73.

102. Newfield, "O'Malleys Can't Dodger Their Shame."

103. Election statistics in Kenneth Jackson, ed., *The Encyclopedia of New York City,* (New Haven and London: Yale University Press, 1995), p. 740.

104. McNickle, *To Be Mayor of New York.* Less fortunate, ironically enough, was Los Angeles Mayor Norris Poulson, whose reward for capturing a big-league team for his city was defeat at the polls when he came up for reelection in 1961, although the controversy over the city's financial arrangements with the Dodgers and the clearing of Chavez Ravine were not decisive to that defeat. (The thrust of victorious candidate Sam Yorty's campaign was opposition to the separation of trash for collection.) Poulson, however, was sufficiently defensive about the move that, when it came time for him to relate his version of events, the story he told had only a passing acquaintance with the actual record. He portrayed himself in the unlikely role of Horatio at the gates of the city treasury, fending off O'Malley's unbridled greed and striking a deal that, he misleadingly insisted, fell far short of what the Dodgers had demanded. Raphael J. Sonenshein, *Politics in Black and White: Race and Power in Los Angeles* (Princeton, N.J.: Princeton University Press, 1993), p. 38. Like McNickle with respect to New York, Sonenshein makes no mention of the Dodgers move as a political issue. For Poulson's version of events, see "The Untold Story of Chavez Ravine," *Los Angeles* (April 1962), and local sports columnist Jim Murray's critique of that account in "Norrie's Nest," *Los Angeles Times,* April 9, 1962.

105. Geoffrey C. Ward and Ken Burns, *Baseball: An Illustrated History* (New York: Alfred A. Knopf, 1994), p. 347.

106. *New York Times,* December 14, 1995.

107. See, for example, James T. Patterson, *Grand Expectations: The United States 1945–1974* (New York: Oxford University Press, 1996), pp. 315–16.

108. Joshua Freeman, *Working-Class New York: Life and Labor Since World War II* (New York: The New Press, 2000), p. 175.

109. According to California officials, this occurred in December 1962; the Census Bureau placed it in July 1964. See *New York Times,* December 18, 1962, September 1, 1964.

110. On the shift in the television industry, see Laurence Bergreen, *Look Now, Pay Later: The Rise of Network Broadcasting* (New York: Doubleday, 1980). On

the rise of the University of California (Berkeley) to preeminence, see Clark Kerr, *The Gold and the Blue: A Personal Memoir of the University of California 1949–1967, Volume One: Academic Triumphs* (Berkeley: University of California Press, 2001), pp. 56–70. For contemporary perceptions of California, generally, see *Life*, October 19, 1962; *Look*, September 25, 1962; "New Rush to Golden California," *National Geographic*, June 1954; "California, the Golden Magnet," *National Geographic*, May 1966.

111. *Los Angeles Times*, October 29, 2002. The national ratings were 25 percent lower than those for the previous year's World Series between Arizona and the Yankees.

112. Linn, "The Dodger Boss Rocks the Boat"; Durslag, "A Visit with Walter O'Malley."

113. Jim Brosnan, "Nobody Likes the Dodgers," *Sports Illustrated* (August 14, 1961); Bill Veeck with Ed Linn, "Walter O'Malley: Boss of Baseball," *Look*, July 3, 1962.

INTERLUDE: AFTER EBBETS FIELD

1. Roy Terrell, "Yankee Secrets?" *Sports Illustrated*, July 22, 1957.
2. For a more jaundiced assessment of the Yankee–Kansas City relationship, see Arthur Mann, "How to Buy a Ball Club for Peanuts," *Saturday Evening Post*, April 9, 1955.
3. I am grateful to Jeremy Williams for sharing this story with me.
4. A. J. Liebling, "The Men in the Agbadas," in *A Neutral Corner: Boxing Essays* (New York: Fireside, Simon & Schuster, 1992), p. 201.
5. *The Speeches of Senator John F. Kennedy: Presidential Campaign of 1960* (Washington, D.C.: U.S. Government Printing Office, 1961), p. 667.
6. Letter in Robert F. Wagner, Jr., Papers, New York City Municipal Archives (RFWP–NYCMA).
7. "Where Did They Go?" *New York Times*, May 16, 1958.
8. John Updike, "Hub Fans Bid Kid Adieu," *The New Yorker*, October 22, 1960.
9. Compare Dick Schaap, *Paul Hornung: Pro Football Golden Boy* (New York: Macfadden-Bartell Corp., 1962), and Joe Willie Namath with Dick Schaap, *I Can't Wait Until Tomorrow . . . 'Cause I Get Better Looking Every Day* (New York: Random House, 1969).

CHAPTER 9: A DYNASTY STUMBLES

1. See Mark S. Rosentraub, *Major League Losers: The Real Cost of Sports and Who's Paying for It* (New York: Basic Books, 1999), pp. 18–19.
2. Roger G. Noll, "Major League Team Sports," in Walter Adams, ed., *The Structure of American Industry*, 5th ed. (New York: Macmillan, 1977), p. 365.
3. The 1964 revenue estimate is extrapolated from 1956 data in *Baseball Hearings: 1957*, pp. 2046, 2048, taking into account attendance increases, with

adjustments upward for increase in consumer price level; the 1964 broadcast revenue income comes from Table 1 (Revenue from Baseball Broadcast Rights) in Roger G. Noll, ed., *Government and the Sports Business* (Washington, D.C.: Brookings Institution, 1974), p. 287; 1999 data come from *Report of Independent Members of Commissioner's Blue Ribbon Panel on Baseball Economics,* July 2000, p. 15; 2001 data are from "2001 team-by-team revenues and expenses forecast," at www.usatoday.com/sports/baseball/stories/2001-12-05.

4. For 1964, see Table 1 (Revenue from Baseball Broadcast Rights) in Noll, ed., *Government and the Sports Business,* p. 287; for 2001, see *Sporting News Baseball Guide (2000),* p. 165, *Sporting News Baseball Guide (2001),* p. 165, and "2001 team-by-team revenues and expenses forecast," at www.usatoday.com/sports/baseball/stories/2001-12-05.

5. *New York Times,* October 25, 1950; *Los Angeles Times,* August 28, 2002; Jack Mann, "The King of the Jungle," *Sports Illustrated,* April 18, 1966, pp. 115–34.

6. James Quirk and Rodney D. Fort, *Pay Dirt: The Business of Professional Team Sports* (Princeton, N.J.: Princeton University Press, 1997), Table 2.7 (Average Annual Rates of Increase in Franchise Prices, Baseball), pp. 52–53; *Los Angeles Times,* August 28, 2002.

7. On the 1964 sale, see *New York Times,* August 15, 1964; on the team's value in the early 1990s, see Jill Lieber, "Will the Boss Behave Himself?" *Sports Illustrated,* March 1, 1993; on the 2002 valuation, see *Los Angeles Times,* August 28, 2002.

8. Stephen Barnett, "'Voice of God' Presides over Yankees," *USA Today,* October 25, 2000, at www.usatoday.com/sports/baseball/comment/sbco115.htm.

9. *New York Times,* August 14, 1964. The return on Topping and Webb's original investment was even greater than a comparison of their purchase and sale prices indicated. In 1953, they had sold Yankee Stadium, along with a ballpark in Kansas City that had housed a Yankee farm team, for $6.5 million. *New York Times,* March 3, 1971. For details of the transaction, see Arthur Mann, "How to Buy a Ball Club for Peanuts," *Saturday Evening Post,* April 9, 1955.

10. *New York Times,* August 14, 1964, September 20, 1966; Michael Burke, *Outrageous Good Fortune* (Boston: Little, Brown, 1984), pp. 236–38. As recounted by Burke, Webb and Topping came off badly in the negotiations for their minority interests. Webb, who needed cash right away, accepted $1 million for his 10 percent interest, which had a proportionate value of $1.4 million under the original acquisition agreement; that then set the price to be paid to Topping as far as CBS was concerned when it came time to buy out Topping.

11. *New York Times,* August 16, 1964.

12. *Sporting News,* August 29, 1964.

13. *The Times* (London), August 15, 1964.

14. *Izvestia,* August 16, 1964, reprinted and translated in *The Current Digest of the Soviet Press,* September 9, 1964, p. 27. For more on *Izvestia*'s commentary on the Yankee sale, see chapt. 10, note 2, below.

15. *Broadcasting,* August 17, 1964.

16. Lionel S. Sobel, *Professional Sports and the Law* (New York: Law-Arts Publishers, 1977), pp. 80–82.

17. Stanton's and Topping's testimony in *Professional Sports Antitrust Bill—1965 Hearings,* pp. 6–36.

18. Keane's departure followed the ouster of his front-office ally, Cardinals General Manager Bing Devine, in early August (with Keane slated for firing after the season), apparently at the instigation of "special consultant" Branch Rickey, in what was to be the Mahatma's final—but hardly finest—appearance as a major player in the sport's history. See *Sporting News,* August 29, 1964.

19. On Allen's firing, see Jack Mann, *The Decline and Fall of the New York Yankees* (New York: Simon & Schuster, 1967), pp. 205–8; Lindsey Nelson, *Hello Everybody, I'm Lindsey Nelson* (New York: William Morrow, 1985), pp. 350–53; Curt Smith, *Voices of the Game: The First Full Scale Overview of Baseball Broadcasting, 1921 to the Present* (South Bend, Ind.: Diamond Communications, 1987), pp. 263–64; Red Barber, *The Broadcasters* (New York: Dial Press, 1970), pp. 204–7. Allen himself attributed his ouster to belt-tightening by longtime sponsor Ballantine Beer, but he was promptly replaced in the team's four-man broadcasting unit by ex-catcher and budding celebrity Joe Garagiola, so there was little to be gained in economic terms by the beer company, which only held a one-third sponsorship. See *New York Times,* June 17, 1996 (Mel Allen obituary). On Paley's motivations, see Sally Bedell Smith, *In All His Glory: The Life of William S. Paley* (New York: Simon & Schuster, 1990), p. 440.

20. The number was the subject of some banter. "That 413 never happened," right fielder Roger Maris said. "There's no way there were that many people." New York *World Journal Tribune,* September 23, 1966. There were explanations ("rationalizations," as Tom Tresh put it) for the low turnout—the team was in last place, the game was an unscheduled makeup after two rain-outs, the weather forecast was bleak, and, sure enough, attendance rebounded the next day—all the way up to *1,040. New York Post,* September 23, 24, 1966.

21. Barber, *The Broadcasters,* pp. 215–18; *New York Post,* September 27, 1966. The official reason for his termination was a decision to reduce the number of broadcasters from four to three. *New York Post,* September 27, 1966. Remaining in the Yankee broadcast booth was a trio of ex-players—Joe Garagiola, Phil Rizzuto, and Jerry Coleman. Their ethos was different from Red's. "I'm a house man," Garagiola said. "That's what they're paying me to be." *New York Post,* September 27, 1966.

22. *New York Post,* September 27, 1966.

23. Bob Edwards, *Fridays with Red: A Radio Friendship* (New York: Pocket Books, 1995), pp. 162–65.

24. *New York Post,* September 22, 1966; *New York Times,* September 22, 23, 28, 1966. The *Times*'s erudite sportswriter Leonard Koppett was also taken by Burke's "setting an extraordinary high standard for literacy among top baseball

executives." *New York Times,* September 21, 1966. Writing his memoirs two decades later, Burke wryly recalled how he had wowed the press by using such a "fifty-cent word in a baseball interview." Burke, *Outrageous Good Fortune,* p. 244.

25. *New York Times,* September 20, 1966.

26. As Burke later wrote, "One thing I did not reveal was my CIA service in the early fifties. I rang up Dick Helms, then the director of the Central Intelligence Agency and a longtime friend, and asked his advice. Though it was not a point of great importance, he thought I should finesse it if I could without any embarrassment." Burke, *Outrageous Good Fortune,* p. 245. Even after Burke's CIA experience was disclosed (both by him and by others), it would still be overlooked in accounts of his life, as it was in his obituary in the *New York Times,* February 7, 1987.

27. Burke, *Outrageous Good Fortune,* pp. 139–54.

28. The most detailed account of the Albanian operation is in Nicholas Bethell, *Betrayed* (New York: Times Books, 1984). See also Robin Winks, *Cloak & Gown: Scholars in the Secret War 1939–1961* (New York: William Morrow, 1987), pp. 396–400; Burton Hersh, *The Old Boys: The American Elite and the Origins of the CIA* (New York: Scribner, 1992), pp. 266–74; Evan Thomas, *The Very Best Men* (New York: Simon & Schuster, 1995), pp. 33–39; Thomas Powers, *The Man Who Kept the Secrets: Richard Helms and the CIA* (New York: Alfred A. Knopf, 1979), pp. 44–45.

29. Burke quoted in David C. Martin, *Wilderness of Mirrors* (New York: Harper & Row, 1980), p. 55.

30. Burke, *Outrageous Good Fortune,* p. 153.

31. Ibid., pp. 159–62.

32. Thomas, *The Very Best Men,* p. 127.

33. Burke, *Outrageous Good Fortune,* pp. 267–68.

34. William S. Paley, *As It Happened: A Memoir* (Garden City, N.Y.: Doubleday, 1979), p. 337. CBS President Stanton's account of the acquisition and of CBS's diversification strategy is in *Professional Sports Antitrust Bill—1965 Hearings,* pp. 7–8.

35. Paley, *As It Happened,* p. 338.

36. See D. W. Fostle, *The Steinway Saga: An American Dynasty* (New York: Scribner, 1993), p. 509.

37. *New York Times,* August 15, 1964.

38. *New York Times,* August 15, 1964; *Broadcasting,* August 17, 1964.

39. *Sporting News,* August 29, 1964.

40. Burke, *Outrageous Good Fortune,* p. 238.

41. David Halberstam, *Summer of '49* (New York: Morrow, 1989).

42. Burke, *Outrageous Good Fortune,* pp. 284, 323.

43. Ibid., p. 245.

44. Ibid., p. 265.

45. See *Sporting News,* September 12, 1951, for an admiring account of the Yankees' skill in making such acquisitions, and the benefit derived therefrom on the playing field.

46. Roger Angell, "Farewell, My Giants!" *Holiday,* May 1958.

47. Quoted in *Sporting News,* August 29, 1964.

48. This was the one achievement—out of many in a long and varied life—that was the lead in Burke's obituary. *New York Times,* February 7, 1987.

49. New York *World Journal Tribune,* September 20, 1966.

50. Burke, *Outrageous Good Fortune,* pp. 266–67.

51. *New York Times,* September 20, 1966.

52. New York *World Journal Tribune,* September 20, 1966.

53. *New York Times,* April 17, 1964.

54. Robert Moses to Deputy Mayor John Theobald, April 22, 1957 in RFWP–NYCMA; Robert Moses, "Robert Moses on the Battle of Brooklyn," *Sports Illustrated,* July 11, 1957.

55. *Los Angeles Times,* April 10, 1962, estimated the cost of Dodger Stadium (and related improvements) at $24.1 million, not including the cost of acquiring the site the team had acquired in the controversial swap for its Wrigley Field property in south-central Los Angeles.

56. Burke, *Outrageous Good Fortune,* pp. 253–58, 306.

57. Chris McNickle, *To Be Mayor of New York* (New York: Columbia University Press, 1993), pp. 233–34; Vincent J. Cannato, *The Ungovernable City: John Lindsay and His Struggle to Save New York* (New York: Basic Books, 2001), p. 436.

58. Burke, *Outrageous Good Fortune,* pp. 301–10.

59. Following a series of transactions in the 1950s, the stadium itself was owned by Rice University and the land was the property of the Knights of Columbus. *New York Times,* March 3, 1971, and Mann, "How to Buy a Ball Club for Peanuts."

60. *New York Times,* March 3, 1971.

61. *New York Times,* July 7, and August 27, 1971.

62. *New York Times,* August 27, 28, 1971; March 24, 1972.

63. *New York Times,* October 2, 1973.

64. *New York Times,* March 3, 1971; April 6, November 8, and December 5, 1973; October 11 and December 1, 1975; April 16, 1976.

65. Ken Auletta, *The Streets Were Paved with Gold* (New York: Random House, 1979), p. 143.

66. *New York Times,* December 8, 1978.

67. Rosentraub, *Major League Losers: The Real Cost of Sports and Who's Paying For It*; Quirk and Fort, *Pay Dirt: The Business of Professional Team Sports,* pp. 125–178; Benjamin A. Okner, "Subsidies of Stadiums and Arenas," in Noll, ed., *Government and the Sports Business,* pp. 325–47.

68. Charles R. Morris, *The Cost of Good Intentions: New York City and the Liberal Experiment* (New York: W.W. Norton, 1980), pp. 128, 218–22.

69. Fred Siegel, *The Future Once Happened Here* (New York: Free Press, 1997), p. 236.

70. See the rundown in Nicholas Pileggi, "Was the Stadium Worth It?" *New York*, April 19, 1976, pp. 36–37.

71. For an account of Yankee Stadium's rebuilding, see Michael Gershman, *Diamonds: The Evolution of the Ballpark* (Boston and New York: Houghton Mifflin, 1993), pp. 203–11.

72. Auletta, *The Streets Were Paved with Gold,* p. 143.

73. Paley, *As It Happened,* p. 338.

74. *New York Times,* January 4, 1973.

75. *New York Times,* January 4, 1973; see Michael Burke, *Outrageous Good Fortune,* p. 315; Paley, *As It Happened,* p. 338.

76. Neil Amdur, "Yankees' Man of Independence," *New York Times,* January 4, 1973.

77. *New York Times,* August 29, 1996.

78. Quoted in Tony Kornheiser, "That Damn Yankee," *New York Times Magazine,* April 9, 1978.

79. Randy Harvey, "Behind in the Count, Yanks Hit a Home Run," *Los Angeles Times,* February 24, 2002; Randy Harvey, "By George, U.S. to Show Its Medal Now," *Los Angeles Times,* February 9, 2002.

80. *New York Times,* January 4, 1973.

81. Ibid.

82. Ibid.

83. Burke, *Outrageous Good Fortune,* pp. 315–16.

84. On Burke's ouster, see Dick Schaap, *Steinbrenner* (New York: G. P. Putnam's Sons, 1982), pp. 108–15; Ed Linn, *Steinbrenner's Yankees* (New York: Holt, Rinehart & Winston, 1982), pp. 57–61; Burke's account is in *Outrageous Good Fortune,* pp. 315–25.

85. Burke, *Outrageous Good Fortune,* p. 325.

86. Amdur, "Yankees' Man of Independence."

87. Barber, *The Broadcasters,* pp. 210–18.

88. Schaap, *Steinbrenner,* p. 116.

89. On Steinbrenner's background, see Kornheiser, "That Damn Yankee"; *Current Biography (1979),* pp. 367–70; Murray Chass, "New Owner Held Yanks in Awe," *New York Times,* January 4, 1973. On Harry Steinbrenner as a "cruel perfectionist," see Chris Smith, "Winning Isn't Everything," *New York,* November 11, 1996.

90. *New York Times,* January 4, 1973.

91. *New York Times,* May 20, 1974.

92. *Izvestia,* August 16, 1964.

93. See R.W. Apple, "Oh, to Be in Cleveland, Now that Pride Is There," *New York Times,* October 22, 1995.

94. On Steinbrenner and the Cleveland Pipers, see *Current Biography (1979),* p. 368; Quirk and Fort, *Pay Dirt: The Business of Professional Team Sports,* p. 323.

95. Kornheiser, "That Damn Yankee."

96. See Schaap, *Steinbrenner*, pp. 117–20.
97. *New York Times*, March 5, 2002, p. B-8 ("A perfunctory, passive donor he [George Soros] isn't; a meddling Steinbrennerish donor he is").
98. Stanley Kutler, *The Wars of Watergate: The Last Crisis of Richard Nixon* (New York: W. W. Norton, 1990), pp. 434–35.

CHAPTER 10: FREEING THE SERFS

1. Simon Rottenberg, "The Baseball Players' Labor Market," *Journal of Political Economy*, 64 (June 1956), p. 256.
2. *Izvestia*, August 16, 1964, p. 27. The fact that the lead CBS executive involved was a former top officer in the CIA could, of course, have provided additional fodder for Soviet commentary on the sale, but apparently that escaped Moscow's notice!
3. *New York Herald Tribune*, August 16, 1964.
4. *New York Times*, August 16, 1964; *New York Herald Tribune*, August 16, 1964.
5. Marvin Miller, *A Whole Different Ball Game: The Sport and Business of Baseball* (New York: Birch Lane Press, 1991), pp. 33–38.
6. Barber quoted in Miller, *A Whole Different Ball Game*, back cover.
7. See Gerald W. Scully, *The Business of Major League Baseball* (Chicago: University of Chicago Press, 1989), p. 34, and Miller, *A Whole Different Ball Game*, pp. 4, 41.
8. *Flood v. Kuhn*, 407 U.S. 258, 264–266, 92 S. Ct. 2099 (1972); Miller, *A Whole Different Ball Game*, pp. 174–87.
9. Record on Appeal in *National League of Professional Baseball Clubs et al. v. Federal Baseball Club of Baltimore, Inc.*, 259 U.S. 200 (422), pp. 120, 173–75. Federal League contracts did, however, provide that a player was entitled to a release after ten years of service.
10. *Toolson v. New York Yankees*, 346 U.S. 356, 74 S. Ct. 78 (1953).
11. *Baseball Hearings: 1951*, pp. 730–32.
12. Smith testimony in *Baseball Hearings: 1951*, pp. 832 ff. Smith later changed his mind, denounced the "obnoxious reserve system that bound employees for life," and regretted his 1951 testimony. See Ira Berkow, *Red: A Biography of Red Smith* (New York: Times Books, 1986), pp. 157–58, 203–5; Red Smith, "Capitol Hill Rumblings," *New York Times*, July 6, 1981.
13. See *Flood v. Kuhn*, 309 F. Supp. 793, 802 (S.D.N.Y. 1970).
14. Curt Flood with Richard Carter, *The Way It Is* (New York: Trident Press, 1971), p. 207. Excerpts from the trial record are contained in the *Appendix to Flood's Petition for Certiorari to the Supreme Court*.
15. *Salerno v. American League*, 429 F. 2d 1003 (2d. Cir., 1970).
16. *Flood v. Kuhn*, 407 U.S. 258, 92 S. Ct. 2099 (1972).
17. Miller, *A Whole Different Ball Game*, pp. 41–42.
18. *Organized Baseball Report*, p. 111; Frick testimony in *Baseball Hearings: 1951*, p. 123.

19. Miller, *A Whole Different Ball Game*, p. 42.
20. For a historical sketch of the development of the reserve system, see *Organized Baseball Report*, pp. 111–18. A classic account is Lee Lowenfish and Tony Lupien, *The Imperfect Diamond* (New York: Stein and Day, 1980).
21. Uniform Player Contract, reprinted in *Baseball Hearings: 1951*, p. 1248; see *Organized Baseball Report*, p. 113, fn. 66. *In re the Twelve Clubs Comprising National League, etc. [hereafter Professional Baseball Clubs]*, 66 Labor Arbitration, pp. 101, 104–105 (December 23, 1975).
22. *Professional Baseball Clubs*, 66 Labor Arbitration, p. 112.
23. Miller, *A Whole Different Ball Game*, p. 41.
24. *Kansas City Royals v. Major League Baseball Players*, 532 F. 2d 615, 623–624 (8th Cir. 1976).
25. *Kansas City Royals v. Major League Baseball Players*, 532 F. 2d, p. 626.
26. Miller, *A Whole Different Ball Game*, pp. 228–36.
27. Kenneth M. Jennings, *Balls and Strikes: The Money Game in Professional Baseball* (New York: Praeger, 1990), pp. 187–88.
28. As noted in the subsequent ruling in the Messersmith–McNally case. See *Professional Baseball Clubs*, 66 Labor Arbitration, p. 109 fn. 19.
29. *Professional Baseball Clubs*, 66 Labor Arbitration, pp. 101–2, 110–11; Miller, *A Whole Different Ball Game*, pp. 238–44.
30. *Kansas City Royals v. Major League Baseball Players*, 532 F. 2d 615, 633 (8th Cir. 1976) (Gibson, C.J., concurring).
31. *Gardella v. Chandler*, 172 F. 2d 402, 409–410 (2d Cir., 1949).
32. *Baseball Hearings: 1951*, p. 730.
33. *Organized Baseball Report*, p. 113 (italics added).
34. Flood Complaint para. 15–18 in *Appendix to Flood's Petition for Certiorari*, p. 10–11.
35. Robinson testimony in *Appendix to Flood's Petition*, p. 172; Miller testimony, pp. 161–62.
36. *Flood v. Kuhn*, 309 F. Supp. 793, 796 (S.D.N.Y., 1970). Flood had "agreed to be confined in this application [for a preliminary injunction] to the facts that are admitted on both sides and not in controversy." 309 F. Supp., p. 795 n. 3.
37. *Flood v. Kuhn*, 316 F. Supp. 271, p. 274 n. 4 (S.D.N.Y., 1970).
38. Supreme Court Brief for Petitioner Flood (filed December 17, 1971), p. 4.
39. *Flood v. Kuhn*, 407 U.S. 258, 289, 92 S. Ct. 2099, 2115 (Marshall, J., dissenting).
40. *Professional Baseball Clubs*, 66 Labor Arbitration, p. 111.
41. *Professional Baseball Clubs*, 66 Labor Arbitration, p. 107 fn. 18.
42. Miller, *A Whole Different Ball Game*, p. 41.
43. *Kansas City Royals v. Major League Baseball Players Association*, 409 F. Supp. 233, 245 (W.D. Missouri 1976).
44. *Professional Baseball Clubs*, 66 Labor Arbitration, p. 101.
45. *Professional Baseball Clubs*, 66 Labor Arbitration, pp. 110, 113, 118.
46. *Professional Baseball Clubs*, 66 Labor Arbitration, p. 114.

47. *Professional Baseball Clubs,* 66 Labor Arbitration, pp. 114–17.
48. *Kansas City Royals v. Major League Baseball Players Association,* 532 F. 2d 615 (8th Cir., 1976).
49. *Kansas City Royals v. Major League Baseball Players,* 532 F. 2d 615, 633 (8th Cir., 1976) (Gibson, C.J., concurring).
50. Miller, *A Whole Different Ball Game,* p. 253.
51. On the collusion cases, see *Sporting News Baseball Guide 1988,* pp. 15–16, and *Sporting News Baseball Guide 1989,* pp. 18–20.
52. *New York Times,* November 27, 1996; *Sporting News Baseball Guide 1997,* pp. 150, 153.
53. "MLB, MLBPA differ on revenue sharing proposal," mlb.com, March 6, 2002; Murray Chass, "Selig Has Become Target of Some Players' Anger," *New York Times,* March 5, 2002.
54. *Professional Baseball Clubs,* 66 Labor Arbitration, p. 118.
55. Murray Chass, "Insiders Recall Birth of Free Agency 10 Years Ago," *New York Times,* December 22, 1985.
56. Chass, "Selig Has Become Target of Some Players' Anger."

CHAPTER 11: PLAYING UNDER NEW RULES

1. Kornheiser, "That Damn Yankee."
2. *New York Times,* March 13, 2002; Anthony Bianco, "The Money Machine," *Business Week,* September 28, 1998.
3. Bianco, "The Money Machine"; *Current Biography (1979),* p. 369.
4. Herbert Gans, "Stop Letting George Do It," *New York Times,* June 4, 1984.
5. Dave Anderson, "Yankees: Not Since 1913," *New York Times,* June 3, 1984.
6. *Sporting News Baseball Guide 1991,* pp. 12–13.
7. George Will, "George Steinbrenner: An Acquired Taste," *Newsweek,* August 6, 1990, reprinted in George Will, *Bunts: Curt Flood, Camden Yards, Pete Rose and Other Reflections on Baseball* (New York: Scribner, 1998), p. 139.
8. George Will, *Men at Work: The Craft of Baseball* (New York: Macmillan, 1990), p. 311.
9. Ibid.
10. Jill Lieber, "Will the Boss Behave Himself?" *Sports Illustrated,* March 1, 1993.
11. *New York Times,* September 27, 1996.
12. "Nice Moves: 10 Keys to '98," *Sports Illustrated,* October 28, 1998.
13. Bruce Weber, "Mellow Boss Lets Bats Do the Talking," *New York Times,* October 1, 1996; Chris Smith, "Winning Isn't Everything," *New York,* November 11, 1996; Lieber, "Will the Boss Behave Himself?"
14. Dave Anderson, "On Leaving Well Enough Alone," *New York Times,* October 13, 1995.
15. *New York Times,* August 29, 1996.
16. *New York Times,* October 11, 1995.

17. *New York Times,* September 28, 1966.
18. See Table 4.1, comparing Yankees and Mets Records and Attendance Figures 1962–2002, in the appendix.
19. For the years 1962–1984, the correlation coefficient between Yankees and Mets attendance is a strongly negative –.70.
20. See Table 4.1, comparing Yankees and Mets attendance, in the appendix.
21. Roger Angell, *The Summer Game* (New York: Popular Library, 1972), p. 96.
22. "Series lowest-rated ever," *Daily Variety,* October 30, 2000; "Game 3 ratings down 26 percent from '00 Series," ESPN.com, October 26, 2000. Even the four-game sweeps in 1998 and 1999 garnered higher audiences, with ratings of 14.1 and 16.0, respectively, compared with 12.4 in 2000.
23. Richard Sandomir, "TV Sports," *New York Times,* October 27, 2000.
24. "Tom Meany's Baseball Picks for '56," *Collier's,* March 30, 1956.

Epilogue: Baseball's Enduring Paradox

1. "Fox Also a Series Winner," CNN.com, November 5, 2001.
2. *Look,* June 11, 1957.
3. *Business Week,* October 5, 1957.
4. *U.S. News & World Report,* September 7, 1959.
5. *Report of the Independent Members of the Commissioner's Blue Ribbon Panel on Baseball Economics, July 2000* (hereafter, *Blue Ribbon Report*).
6. *Blue Ribbon Report,* pp. 46–47.
7. *Blue Ribbon Report,* pp. 1–4, 11.
8. On Selig's testimony, see *New York Times,* December 7, 2001; MLB press release, "Major League Baseball Competitive Balance Worsens," mlb.com, December 6, 2001.
9. Ross Newhan, "Selig, Fehr in a War of Words," *Los Angeles Times,* December 7, 2001; "Latest Developments Get Fehr Going," mlb.com, December 6, 2001.
10. Leonard Koppett, "The Business of America's National Pastime Is Unpatriotic Obfuscation," *New York Times,* March 10, 2002; Leonard Koppett, "Baseball's Competitive Imbalance Is a Longstanding Problem," *New York Times,* May 20, 2001; Ross Newhan, "Off the Field, It's a Numbers Game," *Los Angeles Times,* December 6, 2001.
11. *New York Times,* December 7, 2001.
12. *Forbes,* April 15, 2002.
13. *New York Times,* July 12, 2002.
14. George Will, *Bunts: Curt Flood, Camden Yards, Pete Rose and Other Reflections on Baseball* (New York: Scribner, 1998), p. 328.
15. Will, *Bunts,* p. 329.
16. *New York Times,* September 19, 1992.
17. Will, *Bunts,* p. 329.
18. *Blue Ribbon Report,* p. 5.

19. Koppett, "Baseball's Competitive Imbalance Is a Longstanding Problem."
20. The years 1998–2001 for Arizona, which began play in 1998.
21. For Table 5.1 in the appendix, 1950 payrolls are from *Baseball Hearings: 1951*, p. 1610; 1999 data are from *Blue Ribbon Report*, p. 77.
22. *Organized Baseball Report*, p. 229.
23. Simon Rottenberg, "The Baseball Players' Labor Market," *Journal of Political Economy*, 64 (June 1956), pp. 247–48, 255.
24. Jack Curry, "Yanks May Alter Plans after the Rules Change," *New York Times*, November 27, 1996.
25. Murray Chass, "Selig Has Become Target of Some Players' Anger," *New York Times*, March 5, 2002.
26. Koppett, "Baseball's Competitive Imbalance Is a Longstanding Problem."
27. Frank Deford, "Irrelevance in Pinstripes," *New York Times*, October 24, 1995.
28. Keith Olbermann, "Shortsighted Steinbrenner," *Sports Illustrated*, April 13, 1998.
29. *Blue Ribbon Report*, p. 8.
30. *New York Times*, July 26, 2002.
31. For the terms of the 2002 agreement, see *Los Angeles Times*, August 31, 2002.
32. Tyler Kepner, "Cold Free-Agent Market Has the Union Suspicious," *New York Times*, January 30, 2003.
33. *New York Times*, December 25, 2002; *Boston Globe*, December 25, 2002.
34. Team payroll expenses for 2002 in *New York Times*, November 13, 2002.
35. "Yankees Ensure 2003 Pennant by Signing Every Player in Baseball," *The Onion*, February 5, 2003. I am indebted to Dave Kowal for this reference.
36. Mal Florence, "Nobody Beats Him in Blame Game," *Los Angeles Times*, December 30, 2002; Tyler Kepner, "Defiant Steinbrenner Still Swinging, With His Checkbook," *New York Times*, January 8, 2003.
37. "Red Sox to Be Sold to Henry Group," mlb.com, December 20, 2001; "Red Sox Owners Recommit Support to Henry Group," mlb.com, January 13, 2002.
38. *New York Times*, July 12, 2002.
39. *Blue Ribbon Report*, p. 5.
40. Duke Snider and Roger Kahn, "I Play Baseball for Money—Not Fun," Collier's, May 25, 1956; Gay Talese, "Gray-Flannel-Suit Men at Bat," *New York Times Magazine*, March 30, 1958. As if to prove the point, Snider had just appeared in *Collier's* endorsing "Murine for tired eyes." *Collier's*, April 13, 1956.
41. *Sporting News*, December 30, 1915. The paper continued, "The baseball war served to show conclusively that a ballplayer is common clay, sometimes more common than less."
42. *Sporting News*, February 8, 1956; *New York Times*, August 5, 1957.
43. "MLB.com debuts new subscription service," mlb.com, March 5, 2002; *Los Angeles Times*, March 6, 2002.
44. *Wall Street Journal*, July 10, 2001.
45. *Sporting News*, March 15, 1950.

46. See, variously, *The Quiz Show Scandal* (transcript at www.pbs.org/wgbh/amex/quizshow); Eliot Asinof, *1919: America's Loss of Innocence* (New York: D. I. Fine, 1990); Jon Margolis, *The Last Innocent Year: America in 1964—The Beginning of the "Sixties"* (New York: William Morrow, 1999); Henry F. May, *The End of American Innocence: A Study of the First Years of Our Own Time, 1912–1917* (New York: Knopf, 1959); Jules Witcover, *The Year the Dream Died: Revisiting 1968 in America* (New York: Warner Books, 1997); Charles Kaiser, *1968 in America: Music, Politics, Chaos, Counterculture, and the Shaping of a Generation* (New York: Weidenfeld & Nicolson, 1988).

47. *Blue Ribbon Report*, p. 6.

48. "Fox Also a Series Winner," CNN.com, November 5, 2001; *Los Angeles Times*, October 29, 2002.

49. The Nielsen rating for the 2002 women's freestyle skating final was 26.8 for the evening, peaking at 32.5 (53 percent of households watching television at that time) in the last half hour. *New York Times*, February 23, 2002. Indeed, when things were *really* hot on the ice, as with the Nancy Kerrigan–Tonya Harding showdown in 1994, the figure-skating ratings (48.5) could exceed those for any Super Bowl since 1983. See *1997 World Almanac and Book of Facts*, p. 296. The 2000 World Series averaged a Nielsen rating of 12.4 (with a 21 share of the audience). *Daily Variety*, October 30, 2000.

50. *Los Angeles Times*, July 11, 2002.

51. *Flood v. Kuhn*, 309 F. Supp. 793, 797 (S.D.N.Y. 1970).

52. See *Metropolitan Sports Facilities Commission v. Minnesota Twins Partnership*, Minnesota Court of Appeals Case No. C2-01-2010 (January 22, 2002), available at www.msfc.com/ycommissionnews_detail.cfm?releaseID=49.

53. Quoted in Roger Angell, *The Summer Game* (New York: Popular Library, 1972), p. 247.

54. *Gionfriddo v. Major League Baseball*, 114 Cal. Rptr. 2d 307, 315 (Cal. App. 1 Dist. 2001).

55. See Joshua Harris Prager, "Giants' 1951 Comeback, the Sport's Greatest, Wasn't All It Seemed," *Wall Street Journal*, January 31, 2001, and Corey Kilgannon, "Love of Game Led to Story of Intrigue," *New York Times*, February 12, 2001. For a statistically driven dissent, see Stan Jacoby, "The Numbers Say It Ain't So, Bobby," *New York Times*, March 4, 2001.

56. On the plans for erecting the statue in Brooklyn to show the "Brothers Arm-in-Arm" and "commemorate a special moment in the history of baseball and in American race relations," see Jack Newfield, "Brothers Arm-in-Arm," *New York Post*, August 29, 1999, and "Dodger Duo Gets Their Due," *New York Post*, September 9, 1999. As Robinson's family-authorized biographer points out, "Exactly where and when this moment came is uncertain." He presents several different versions in Arnold Rampersad, *Jackie Robinson* (New York: Alfred A. Knopf, 1997), pp. 182–83. As Rampersad notes, the first account of any such incident did not appear until a ghostwritten article by Robinson in August 1949. That version provides neither a place nor a date for the event and

does not have Reese placing his arm around Robinson's shoulder. Jackie Robinson as told to Ed Reid, "Robinson's Team Stands by Him," *Washington Post,* August 28, 1949 (reprinted from the *Brooklyn Eagle*). There was no mention of any such gesture by Reese in Robinson's 1948 autobiography: Jackie Robinson as told to Wendell Smith, *Jackie Robinson: My Own Story* (New York: Greenberg Publisher, 1948). Later accounts place the incident in Cincinnati or in Boston, in 1947 or 1948, while Robinson was playing first base or second base or running the bases, during a game or during practice before a game, in response to taunting by opposing players or by racist fans, which was directed at Robinson or at Reese. See, variously, Carl T. Rowan with Jackie Robinson, *Wait Till Next Year* (New York: Random House, 1960) pp. 227–28; Arthur Mann, "The Truth About the Jackie Robinson Case," *Saturday Evening Post,* May 13, 20, 1950; Bill Roeder, *Jackie Robinson* (New York: A.S. Barnes, 1950), p. 138; *Los Angeles Times,* August 15, 1999 (quoting Dodger executive Buzzie Bavasi); *Los Angeles Times,* August 19, 1999 (quoting Roger Kahn); *New York Times,* August 15, 1999 (quoting Duke Snider); *New York Times,* August 19, 1999 (quoting Rachel Robinson). Reese himself underplayed any single dramatic gesture, simply recalling, "There were times when I went over to talk to him on the field thinking that people would see this and figure we were friends and this might help Jack." Reese quoted in Roger Kahn, *The Boys of Summer* (New York: Harper & Row, 1972), p. 325.

57. Dick Schaap, *Flashing Before My Eyes* (New York: William Morrow, 2001), p. 32.

58. Annie Kriegel, quoted in Julian Jackson, *France: The Dark Years 1940–1944* (New York: Oxford University Press, 2001), p. 367.

59. Quoted in *Sporting News,* August 29, 1964.

INDEX

ABOUT THE AUTHOR

HENRY D. FETTER, a graduate of Harvard Law School, holds degrees in history from Harvard College and the University of California, Berkeley. He has written on law, baseball, and history for the *Journal of Sport History, The Public Interest,* and the *Times Literary Supplement,* among other publications. He attended his first baseball game at Ebbets Field on Memorial Day 1955 and eventually followed the Dodgers west to Los Angeles, where he lives with his wife and has practiced law for more than twenty years.